The Criminal Law Library

# MISUSE OF DRUGS

**The Criminal Law Library**

**Editor-in-Chief:**
Rt. Hon. Lord Elwyn-Jones, PC, CH

**General Editor:**
Gavin McFarlane, LLM(Sheffield), PhD(Lond),
*Barrister and Harmsworth Scholar of the Middle Temple*

The Criminal Law Library—No. 2

# MISUSE OF DRUGS

PATRICK BUCKNELL, MA(Cantab),
*Of the Inner Temple, Barrister*

and

HAMID GHODSE, MD, PhD, FRCPsych, DPM,
*Consultant Psychiatrist,*
*St George's and St Thomas's Hospitals, London,*
*Secretary of the Society for the Study of Addiction*
*to Alcohol and other Drugs*

WATERLOW PUBLISHERS LIMITED

*First Edition 1986*
© P. Bucknell and H. Ghodse 1986

Waterlow Publishers Limited
Oyez House
27 Crimscott Street
London SE1 5TS
A member of the British Printing & Communication Corporation PLC

ISBN 0 08 039203 2

**British Library Cataloguing in Publication Data**
Bucknell, Patrick
   Misuse of drugs.—(The Criminal law library; no. 2)
   1. Drug abuse—Law and legislation—Great Britain
   I. Title   II. Ghodse, Hamid   III. Series
   344.104′4463     KD3460

Printed in Great Britain by
A. Wheaton & Co Ltd, Exeter, Devon

# Preface to the Series

BY THE RT. HON. LORD ELWYN-JONES, PC, CH

After half a century in the law, I find that one of the most striking changes has been the enormous increase in criminal work coming before the Courts. There has been a lamentable increase in the number of crimes, both major and minor, which have been committed, particularly in recent years, and the volume of both trial and appellate work, at all judicial levels, has increased greatly.

English criminal law, which is an uncodified mixture of common law and statute law, has in my time increased both in quantity and complexity. Although most crimes are now defined by Act of Parliament, many are still offences at common law.

The law is a living law which has had to be adjusted to the changes in our society. A great deal of law reform has been generated by the Law Commissions and the Law Revision Committee. Parliament and Ministers have produced a flow of Acts of Parliament and Statutory Instruments to meet the demands for revision and reform. Criminals, for their part, have been adept in exploiting commercial, industrial and technical change. Fraud is no longer a fairly simple matter of falsifying entries in manuscript ledgers. Computer systems may be tampered with so that accounts can be milked on an international scale. When I was called to the Bar in Grays Inn in 1935 it took four days to cross the Atlantic by the fastest liner from Southampton to New York. Today a determined drug dealer or fraudsman can have visited four continents in that time. New criminal offences have had to be made, in piecemeal fashion, to catch up with offenders of all ages. New procedures have had to be introduced in the Courts to cope with the ever-increasing backlog of work. Conflicting lines of authority abound, perhaps inevitably when the sheer volume of case law being produced is so immense.

The law's penal provisions have also been greatly changed. Courts are exhorted to regard imprisonment as a last resort method of dealing with offenders. A considerable array of alternatives to imprisonment have been introduced into our penal system.

It is perhaps surprising that against this background criminal law has not received the same concentrated attention from specialised textbooks as many other major branches of the law. There are series of practitioners' texts for example in common law, conveyancing, local government and shipping law, but until now there has not been available a series of specialised books for the practitioner analysing in depth the major topics of criminal law on an individual basis. It is I think timely that such a comprehensive and accessible series should now be published and it is good that Waterlow Publishers are to fill this lacuna with their Criminal Law Library.

*Elwyn-Jones*

# Foreword

BY GRIFFITH EDWARDS

*Professor of Addiction Behaviour, Institute of Psychiatry, University of London*

We must all have experienced that familiar and recurrent feeling that there really *must* be an authoritative book on such-and-such a subject, if only we could track it down. The need may be for something so arcane as the standard work on antique barometers or a requirement so ordinary as a guide book to that patch of Europe we hope to visit next summer. The librarian is usually able to help or a friend gives us the clue, and once more we gratefully discover exactly the book to meet our demands.

I have often thought that someone must have published a text which dealt in authoritative and comprehensive fashion with the whole complex issue of controlled drugs and the law, and which not only covered these matters from the legal angle but which also gave the necessary medical background. Up to now though I have been unable to find that text in any library, and although friends and colleagues in both the Law and Medicine agreed that there was an aching need for a volume of this kind, they assured me that it remained unwritten.

Now comes this joint publication by a practising barrister and a psychiatrist specialising in the drugs field. When they showed me their typescript, I personally had that grateful and much relieved feeling that the book for which I had been searching for so long was at last to hand. And I am sure that many other people who have sensed this gap in the library shelves are going to have exactly the same response. It is a work of distinction and authority and at the same time a handbook which will be of great practical utility to all members of the legal profession and to doctors who are called on to give evidence in court. It ranks immediately as an essential library text and is also a volume which many of us will have to own.

The authors are to be congratulated and thanked for so admirably filling a long-felt need. Their partnership has produced a book which will deservedly win recognition as the standard authority on drugs and the law.

*Griffith Edwards*

# Preface

The supply of drugs for non-therapeutic purposes to illicit drug users is a major growth industry of our time. The problem of abuse of drugs, so far as Western society is concerned, first developed on a large scale in the United States of America between the wars. Since 1949 the same problem has developed in almost all the countries of Europe and it has not been excluded from Eastern Europe by the Iron Curtain. It is well known that Hong Kong has a daunting number of heroin users, but it is not often realised that problems of heroin misuse have developed in Burma and Thailand, whilst abuse of opium, cannabis and psychotropic drugs is increasing in Egypt. Cannabis use in Nigeria has spread into secondary schools and universities. In Jamaica cannabis use has spread from the rural working class and Rastafarians to middle-class youth. In South America the abuse of cocaine is on the increase.

Some drugs are more harmful than others. Some drugs are more popular than others. There seems to be a growth in the United Kingdom of people who use more than one drug or who are prepared to fall back on a second choice. Lawyers and probation officers find themselves operating in a field where a certain technical and medical knowledge is assumed but seldom available. Part I of this work sets out to make this technical knowledge readily available to laymen. Such knowledge is particularly necessary when it comes to dealing with the sentencing of convicted addicts. A list of clinics and agencies where addicts can be treated and looked after is given in Appendix XIV.

Increased abuse of drugs is reflected in the increased number of drug offences which are being prosecuted in our courts and by the rapid growth of case-law on the subject. It is apparent that the Courts are sometimes making decisions without being aware of previous decisions on the same subject. One object of the present work is to make available within the covers of one book the statutes and statutory instruments concerned with the importation, manufacture, supply and abuse of drugs together with the decisions which the Courts have made on the meaning of the legislation. In addition the Single Convention of Narcotic Drugs and the Convention on Psychotropic Substances, which form the basis of our international obligations, are included in Appendices XI and XII.

The authors acknowledge the assistance they have derived in writing Chapter 1 from "Drugs and Social Policy: the Establishment of Drug Control in Britain 1900–1930" by Virginia Berridge, *British Journal of Addiction*, Vol. 79, March 1984.

We have endeavoured to state the law as at 31 October 1985.

# Contents

**Chapter 3—DRUGS OF DEPENDENCE**

## Chapter 4—TREATMENT OF DRUG DEPENDENCE

## PART II—CUSTOMS AND EXCISE ACTS

## Chapter 5—OFFENCES RELATING TO IMPORTATION AND EXPORTATION OF CONTROLLED DRUGS

## Chapter 6—EVIDENTIAL AND PROCEDURAL PROVISIONS

# Table of Cases

Prosecutions by the Crown are listed under the name of the defendant.

# Table of Statutes

# Table of Statutory Instruments

# Conversion Table

| Grams | Ounces | Pounds |
|-------|--------|--------|
| 1 | 0.0353 | |
| 5 | 0.1764 | |
| 10 | 0.3527 | |
| 20 | 0.7055 | |
| 30 | 1.0582 | |
| 40 | 1.4109 | |
| 50 | 1.7637 | |
| 100 | 3.5274 | 0.2205 |
| 200 | 7.0547 | 0.4409 |
| 250 | 8.8184 | 0.5512 |
| 300 | 10.5821 | 0.6614 |
| 400 | 14.1094 | 0.8818 |
| 500 | 17.6368 | 1.1023 |
| 600 | 21.1642 | 1.3228 |
| 700 | 24.6915 | 1.5432 |
| 750 | 26.4552 | 1.6535 |
| 800 | 28.2189 | 1.7639 |
| 900 | 31.7462 | 1.9841 |
| 1000 | 35.2736 | 2.2046 |

CHAPTER 1

# The Development of International Control and of United Kingdom Legislation

## THE POSITION BEFORE THE GREAT WAR

*Opiates*

**1.01** Until 1868 opium was freely available in the United Kingdom. Opium and laudanum (a solution of opium in alcohol) were bought for self-medication from grocers and other shopkeepers. Interlinked medical use and "recreational" use was common. The greatest danger that was perceived at the time was of opium poisoning.

The first measure of control over the sale of opium was won by pharmacists as a means of defining and demonstrating their expert status. This was section 17 of the Pharmacy Act 1868, which ended the open sale of most popular poisons and placed them under various degrees of pharmaceutical control. Opium, provided it was sold and labelled as a poison by a pharmacist, was freely available. In addition sales of patent medicines containing opium, such as chlorodyne, were not restricted.

In the meanwhile a new danger developed from the enthusiastic adoption by the medical profession of hypodermic injection of morphine. Morphine, the chief alkaloid in opium, was first isolated by a German pharmacist in 1803. The hypodermic needle came into use in the 1850s. It was thought that by injecting the most powerful pain-killer known to man directly into the bloodstream the dangers of addiction could be avoided. Morphine was freely used in the treatment of casualties in the American Civil War and soon after it became clear that many of them had become dependent on the drug.

In 1874 a London chemist, C. R. Alder Wright, described how, by boiling morphine with acetic anhydride, he had produced diacetylmorphine, now known as diamorphine. It was popularised in the 1890s by a German scientist, Heinrich Dreser, as "heroin" (powerful or heroic). Its use was advocated as a non-addictive treatment for coughs and chest and lung ailments. The Bayer Company advertised heroin widely together with aspirin and other products. However, it soon became apparent that heroin was just as addictive as other narcotic drugs.

*Cocaine*

Coca leaves are traditionally chewed by Indians in the Andes as a stimulant, easing the discomfort of hard labour. They achieved a measure

1

**THE COCOAINE FIEND.**

Those addicted to drug-taking soon become victims to the most extraordinary illusions.

["*Poy*," *in the London* "*Evening News.*"

*Cartoon, 19 Dec 1918 (British Library)*

of popularity in the United Kingdom in the 1870s as a means of increasing powers of endurance in such pastimes as mountain climbing. Cocaine was isolated from coca by Albert Niemann in 1860 and a period of enthusiasm for the drug ensued. In 1884 Sigmund Freud advocated the use of cocaine to treat morphia addiction. It was used as a local anaesthetic and as the active ingredient in numerous "coca wines". However as the harmful effects of the drug became apparent, disenchantment developed. In the Sherlock Holmes stories the hero injected himself with cocaine when he needed to concentrate—this practice was later discouraged by Dr. Watson!

*Cannabis*

In India, the Middle East and North Africa the products of the hemp plant have long played a similar role to that played by alcohol in Europe. Although cannabis was used in some patent medicines in the nineteenth century, it did not attain any measure of popularity as a recreational drug in the United Kingdom until the 1950s—and even then its popularity was due to influences from the West rather than from the East. The effects of the drug were the subject of enquiry in India[1] but it is likely that the following description of the effect of the drug in Egypt taken from the *Wide World* magazine[2] would have received general acceptance:

> "The effects of this most insidious form of intoxication are at once more pernicious and more deadly than those of alcohol. From the first stages of delectation, the victim soon passes into a state of permanent imbecility; his wits are sapped with his strength, and the term Hashash is synonomous in the vernacular with the word lunatic."

Subsequent legislation tightened up the controls on the sale of opiates and on their use in medicines and included cocaine in the system of control. The Poisons and Pharmacy Act 1908 moved morphine, cocaine, opium and derivatives containing more than 1 per cent morphine into Part I of the Poison Schedule (the part of the schedule containing such poisons as arsenic and cyanide). This restricted sale to persons known to the pharmacist and they had to sign the poisons book.

## Moral disapproval develops

**1.02** Whilst opium was freely available no clear distinction was apparent between use of the drug as a painkiller and use as a source of pleasure. The *Confessions* of De Quincy were greeted with raised eyebrows but the real strength of the habit was not revealed until supplies began to be cut off by tightening legislative controls.

Events on the other side of the world, however, led to the foundation in England of the Society for the Suppression of the Opium Trade in 1874. The British East India Company processed opium in former Dutch factories in Bengal. The bulk of the produce was exported to China at a very great profit. The damage that the opium habit could do was apparent to the Chinese authorities, who attempted to suppress the trade. Their confiscation of opium chests at Canton led to the Opium War of 1841, and the seizure of Hong Kong. The story is well told by Maurice Collis in his book *Foreign Mud*. Many people, and especially Quakers,

---

1 Hemp Drugs Commission Report, 1894.
2 M. Scie, "The Hasheesh Smugglers' Museum", *Wide World*, 1898, p. 85.

*An Opium Den in the East End of London—Wood engraving by A. Doms after Gustave Doré, 1872 (Wellcome Institute Library, London)*

were ashamed of the British connection with this traffic. In the course of their campaign they succeeded in convincing the British public that the opium habit was evil. Addicts to narcotic drugs came to be seen as persons whose moral fibre had been destroyed by addiction. They were perceived as being perverted, shiftless and unable to hold down regular jobs.

**Medical Attitudes**

**1.03**   The medical profession also began to study addiction. One of the first treatises was *Morbid Craving for Morphia* by E. Levinstein, published in 1877 in Germany with an English edition in 1878. Addiction came to be seen by the medical profession as a direct result of the pharmacological properties of the drug. In this they were reinforced by the physical symptoms of withdrawal suffered by addicts when they were deprived of supplies of their drug.

The Society for the Study and Care of Inebriety (now called the Society for the Study of Addiction to Alcohol and other Drugs) was founded in 1884. Originally membership was confined to members of the medical profession but it was concerned from the beginning with the craving for drugs as well as drink. Alcoholism and drug addiction were studied as a disease—the drug was regarded as an infecting agent.

## MOVES TOWARD INTERNATIONAL CONTROL

**1.04**   A number of international conferences took place commencing with the Shanghai Opium Commission of Control meeting in 1909, followed by a series of conferences at the Hague. The first conference at the Hague resulted in the Hague Opium Convention of 1912 whereby each of the thirty-four signatory nations undertook to tighten control on opiates and cocaine (the Hague Convention). It was also decided that a study of the abuse of Indian hemp (or cannabis) was required.

The Second Opium Conference was held in Geneva in 1924. Middle Eastern countries at that time were far more concerned with the problems caused by hashish (cannabis resin) than those caused by opium. As a result of Egyptian insistence cannabis and cannabis resin were added to the list of drugs subject to international control (the Geneva Convention).

Although the Hague Convention only called for the various drugs to be confined to legitimate medical purposes, the United States Government set out on a course which ended in a total ban on the use of heroin in the United States of America.

**Wartime Control 1916–1920**

**1.05**   Britain was a signatory to the Hague Convention but at first little was done to give effect to it in the United Kingdom. No government department wished to take on the responsibility. The medical profession and the pharmacists wished to maintain their professional control.

The first world war changed things. Public concern grew about the smuggling of opium to the United States on British ships and about the growth of recreational use of cocaine by British troops. The Home Office, represented by Sir Malcolm Delavigne, at last took the decisive initiative in 1916. The first step was an order by the Army Council forbidding the supply of cocaine and other drugs to any member of the forces except by a doctor on prescription. This was followed in July 1916 by Regulation 40B under the Defence of the Realm Act 1914, which made it an offence for anyone except doctors, dentists, veterinary surgeons and pharmacists to possess cocaine or opium.

### The League of Nations and the Dangerous Drugs Act 1920

**1.06**   The Versailles peace settlement gave the League of Nations general supervision over international narcotics agreements. Article 295 of the Treaty ensured the universal application of the Hague Convention.

Delavigne succeeded in keeping the coming Dangerous Drugs Bill under the control of the Home Office rather than that of the newly established Ministry of Health. This became the Dangerous Drugs Act 1920 which added morphine, heroin and medicinal opium to the list of controlled drugs.

The Dangerous Drugs Act 1920 made it unlawful to import or export raw opium except under licence. Where the importation of raw opium was forbidden by any other country, the licence to export from the United Kingdom was to contain conditions to prevent exportation of opium to that country. The Act also forbade the importation or exportation of prepared opium, morphine, cocaine, heroin and their salts etc. The Act further empowered the government to bring other drugs under control by Order in Council. Section 5 made it an offence to manufacture or deal in prepared opium, to possess it, to allow premises to be used for manufacture, dealing or smoking and made it an offence to smoke opium or to possess opium pipes or other materials for use in connection with the smoking of opium. Section 7 empowered a Secretary of State to make regulations prohibiting the manufacture, sale or distribution of drugs specified in section 8 (morphine, heroin, cocaine and medicinal opium), to regulate the issue by medical practitioners of prescriptions for such drugs and requiring manufacturers and distributors to keep records. Powers of inspection and arrest were provided. The maximum penalty was £200 or six months imprisonment for a first offence and £500 or two years' imprisonment for subsequent offences under the Act and a fine of £100 or three times the value of the goods for importing or exporting drugs under the Customs Consolidation Act 1876.

The penalties for offences against the Dangerous Drugs Act were increased to a maximum of £1000 or 10 years' imprisonment by the

Dangerous Drugs and Poisons (Amendment) Act 1923 but prosecution or indictment could only be instituted by or with the consent of the Attorney-General or the Director of Public Prosecutions. The 1923 Act also made it an offence in Great Britain to aid, abet or procure the commission of an offence outside Great Britain in contravention of a corresponding law in force in that place.

As a result of the United Kingdom Government signing the Geneva Convention in 1925 it became necessary to add Indian hemp and resins obtained from Indian hemp to the drugs controlled by the Act of 1920. This was done by means of the Dangerous Drugs Act 1925. The Finance Act 1935 increased the penalty for importing or exporting drugs to a maximum of two years' imprisonment. The various pre-war Acts were consolidated in the Dangerous Drugs Act 1951.

It is obvious that the making of an activity criminal that was previously legal, especially when the ultimate customers might be physically and mentally unable to give up their consumption, will create problems of enforcement. The 1920 Act, especially after the 1923 increase in penalties, created the beginnings of a black market in drugs and posed the question of how far doctors were entitled to prescribe controlled drugs to persons who required them to maintain their level of addiction and avoid withdrawal symptoms. Then, as now, there were doctors who were themselves addicts and doctors who were prepared to prescribe generous quantities to a mainly addicted clientèle.

## The Rolleston Committee

**1.07** In September 1924 the Minister of Health appointed the Departmental Committee on Morphine and Heroin Addiction under the chairmanship of Sir Humphrey Rolleston, President of the Royal College of Physicians. The purpose of the Committee was:

> "To consider and advise as to the circumstances, if any, in which the supply of morphine and heroin (including preparations containing morphine and heroin) to persons suffering from addiction to those drugs, may be regarded as medically advisable and as to the precautions which it is desirable that medical practitioners administering or prescribing morphine or heroin should adopt for the avoidance of abuse, and to suggest any administrative measures that seem expedient for securing observance of such precautions."

The Committee in its Report[3] defined an addict as:

> "A person who, not requiring the continued use of a drug for the relief of symptoms of organic disease, has acquired, as a result of repeated

3 Ministry of Health, *Report of the Departmental Committee on Morphine and Heroin Addiction*, H.M.S.O., 1926.

administration, an overpowering desire for its continuance and in whom withdrawal leads to symptoms of mental or physical distress or disorder."[4]

It found—and it is unlikely that such a finding would be made in the very different circumstances of today—that:

> "There was a general agreement that in most well-established cases the condition must be regarded as a manifestation of disease and not as a mere form of vicious indulgence. In other words, the drug is taken in such cases not for the purpose of obtaining positive pleasure, but in order to relieve a morbid and overpowering craving."

The Committee also stated, and here, in spite of all the efforts of dedicated doctors, clergy and others who have tried to help addicts, the situation has not changed, that:

> "Evidence we have received from most of the witnesses forbids any sanguine estimate as to the proportion of permanent cures which may be looked for from any method of treatment, however thorough. Relapse, sooner or later, appears to be the rule, and permanent cure the exception."

The Committee concluded that it was legitimate to use heroin and morphine for the relief of pain due to organic disease such as inoperable cancer even if it might lead to addiction. It also concluded that it was legitimate to use such drugs for the treatment of addicts by the gradual reduction method as part of a plan of treatment. Finally, and more controversially, it concluded that it was legitimate to prescribe such drugs for persons who would otherwise develop such serious symptoms that they could not be treated in private practice and for those who were capable of living a normal and useful life so long as they took a certain quantity, usually small.

These liberal and humane conclusions have underlain our legislation ever since, although it has been necessary to restrict the power of medical practitioners to prescribe heroin, cocaine and dipipanone to addicts. It is to be hoped that, whatever hysteria may be whipped up over our present epidemic of abuse, they will continue to do so.

The Committee was against the prosecution of doctors who over-prescribed. It recommended the setting up of professional tribunals composed primarily of doctors to decide whether or not a doctor's right to prescribe controlled drugs should be withdrawn. This recommendation was put into effect in 1971. The Home Secretary now wields such a power under sections 12 to 14 of the Misuse of Drugs Act 1971 acting on the recommendations of professional tribunals (see Chapter 22 *post*).

The idea of compulsory notification of addicts to the Home Office by doctors was dropped because the British Medical Association argued

4 It is interesting to compare this definition with that contained in the Misuse of Drugs (Notification of and Supply to Addicts) Regulations 1973 (S.I. no. 799)—see para. 22.02 *post*.

that it would constitute a breach of professional confidence. Such a system was, however, introduced in 1968 and is now prescribed by the Misuse of Drugs (Notification of and Supply to Addicts) Regulations 1973 (S.I. no. 799) (see Chapter 22 *post*).

## The Single Convention on Narcotic Drugs 1961

**1.08** International control of dangerous drugs was revised and consolidated in the Single Convention on Narcotic Drugs 1961 which, as amended by the 1972 Protocol, is the foundation of the current system of control.[5] The Convention was ratified by the United Kingdom on 2 September 1964.

The Convention lists controlled drugs in four schedules which may be amended by the Commission on Narcotic Drugs. Cannabis is still defined there as the "flowering or fruiting tops of the cannabis plant" (see discussion in para. 9.03 *post*). The drugs listed in Schedule I are subject to all measures of control—the list roughly corresponds to Class A of the Misuse of Drugs Act 1971 but it also includes cannabis and cannabis resin which are Class B drugs. The drugs listed in Schedule II are subject to slightly less control—the list is similar to Class B of the Act of 1971 but does not of course include cannabis and cannabis resin nor does it include amphetamines, which are covered by the Convention on Psychotropic Substances 1971. The drugs in Schedule IV are subject to extra controls.

Parties to the Convention undertake to give effect to the Convention within their own territories and to co-operate with other parties in executing its provisions. They are required:

(1) to limit exclusively to medical and scientific purposes production, export, import, distribution and possession of drugs (Article 4(C));

(2) to make annual estimates and statistical returns of quantities of drugs required, manufactured and utilised and of seizures (Articles 19 and 20);

(3) to put strict limitations on manufacture and importation of drugs and the production of opium, coca or cannabis (Articles 21, 21 bis, 22);

(4) to license and supervise the production and distribution of drugs (Articles 29 and 30);

(5) not to permit the export of drugs except in accordance with the laws of the recipient nation (Article 31);

(6) not to permit the possession of drugs except under legal authority (Article 33);

---

**5** The division of responsibilities between the various international bodies is explained at para. 1.18 *post*.

(7) to make arrangements for repressive action against illicit traffic both at national level and by co-operation with other parties and to co-operate by transmitting legal papers internationally for the purposes of prosecutions (Article 35).

Article 36 is the most important provision from the point of view of the Convention's specific requirements on English criminal law. Paragraph 1 requires parties to adopt suitable penal measures and measures for the treatment and rehabilitation of drug abusers. Paragraph 2(d)(iii) provides that foreign convictions for offences under the Convention shall be taken into account for the purposes of establishing recidivism. Sub-paragraph (iv) requires that nationals and foreigners in a territory, if they cannot be extradited, shall be prosecuted in that territory for offences committed in the territory of another party to the Convention. This last requirement is effected by section 20 of the Misuse of Drugs Act 1971 (para. 15–02 *post*). Paragraph 2(b) is concerned with extradition.

The Courts in England and Wales have not been given any special sentencing powers dealing with the treatment and rehabilitation of addicts.

The relevant provisions of the Convention are set out in Appendix XI.

### The 1971 Convention on Psychotropic Substances

**1.09**   This Convention extends international control to new types of psychoactive substances, such as amphetamines, barbiturates and LSD, which have proved harmful and the subject of abuse. The Convention is to be ratified by the United Kingdom shortly.

This Convention also lists controlled drugs in four schedules. By 1 January 1985 all the substances in Schedules 1 and 2 and most of the substances in Schedule 3 were included in Schedule 2 to the Misuse of Drugs Act 1971. The remaining substances scheduled in the Convention will need to be brought under domestic control before ratification.[6]

The relevant provisions of the Convention are set out in Appendix XII.


## RECOMMENDATIONS FOR CHANGE IN THE LAW

### The First Brain Committee Report

**1.10**   At the beginning of the 1960s heroin addiction in the United Kingdom began to increase and the bulk of the new addicts were recreational rather than therapeutic in origin. They were young and deviant. At the same time cannabis use was spreading to young people of native British stock.

6 See Appendix XV.

However an Interdepartmental Committee of the Ministry of Health chaired by Sir Russell Brain was able to report[7] in November 1960 that no change was required in the British approach to drug addiction because the situation had not changed appreciably in the years since the issue of the Rolleston Report. The Report was not issued until the spring of 1961, by which time the second conclusion was clearly revealed to be a mistaken one. Both official statistics and the congregation of addicts in and about Piccadilly Circus in London revealed that something was going wrong.

**The Second Brain Committee Report**

**1.11**   In July 1964 the Brain Committee was reconvened to consider whether their 1961 advice in relation to the prescribing of addictive drugs by doctors needed revision.

In July 1965 the Committee issued its second Report[8]. It described the sharp increase in the number of addicts—almost all of whom were young, non-therapeutic users. The report went on:

> "From the evidence before us we have been led to the conclusion that the major source of supply has been the activity of a very few doctors who have prescribed excessively for addicts. Thus we were informed that in 1962 one doctor alone prescribed almost 600,000 tablets of heroin (i.e. 6 kilograms) for addicts . . . . . . Supplies on such a scale can easily provide a surplus that will attract new recruits to the ranks of addicts . . . The evidence shows that not more than six doctors have prescribed these very large amounts of dangerous drugs."

The Committee believed that it would be possible to discourage the development of a black market by constructing a system whereby an addict could obtain a steady supply of his drugs without being able to get a quantity surplus to his essential requirement. In this the Committee accepted the then commonly held view that the absence of an organised black market in the United Kingdom was attributable to the fact that addicts had been able to obtain supplies of drugs legally.

The Report recommended:

(1) that the power of doctors to prescribe drugs should be limited by restricting the power to prescribe or administer heroin or cocaine to addicts to doctors specially licenced by the Secretary of State. Doctors' power to prescribe such drugs to the organically ill was to remain unrestricted. This recommendation is now effected by Regulation 4 of the Misuse of Drugs (Notification of and Supply to Addicts) Regulations

7 Ministry of Health and Department of Health for Scotland, *Drug Addiction: Report of the Interdepartmental Committee*, H.M.S.O., 1961.
8 Ministry of Health and Department of Health for Scotland, *Drug Addiction: The Second Report of the Interdepartmental Committee*, H.M.S.O., 1965.

1973 (S.I. no. 799) (set out in Appendix VI). Licences are normally issued only to doctors working in drug-dependence clinics;

(2) that there should be an obligation on doctors to report to the Home Office the particulars of persons coming to their notice as being addicted to controlled drugs. This recommendation is now effected by Regulation 3 of the Misuse of Drugs (Notification and Supply to Addicts) Regulations 1973 in respect of drugs specified in the schedule to the Regulations;

(3) that there should be a system for disciplining doctors who violated the rules without having to resort to the criminal courts. This system is provided for in the Misuse of Drugs Act 1971 (see Chapter 23 *post*).

### Amphetamine Abuse

**1.12**   Amphetamine was first synthesised in 1887 but it did not become generally available until the 1930s under the name "Benzedrine". It was found to be of some use in the treatment of asthma and of congestion. Benzedrine inhalers could be purchased from chemists without the need for a prescription. The effect of amphetamine is similar to that of cocaine.

Widespread abuse of amphetamines became the subject of concern in the 1950s and 1960s. This was the first time that drug abuse had been associated particularly with young people. It was adopted as part of their life-style by a section of the community whose behaviour was in other respects also perceived as undesirable. At much the same time it became apparent that some patients who had been prescribed amphetamines by their doctors for the treatment of obesity had become psychologically dependent on the drug. A dangerous development was the use of Methedrine for injection. This was the original meaning of "speed". Prolonged injection of amphetamine, like the illicit injection of all drugs, is associated with hepatitis, abscesses, collapsed blood vessels and even the loss of limbs.

Amphetamines were made controlled drugs by the Drugs (Prevention of Misuse) Act 1964. They remain the second most popular drugs of misuse—only cannabis produces a larger number of seizures.[9] Meanwhile the medical profession, alerted to the dangers of amphetamine, has endeavoured to reduce the number of prescriptions. In 1959 there were 5,600,000 National Health Service prescriptions of amphetamines; by 1982 these had fallen to 1,718,000.[10] Manufacture of some amphetamines in the United Kingdom has been discontinued but amphetamine sulphate is manufactured illicitly and large quantities are smuggled into the country.

9 *Statistics of Misuse of Drugs in the United Kingdom 1983,* Home Office 18/84.
10 Source: Department of Health and Social Security, 1983.

## CHANGES IN THE LAW-1964 TO 1967

**1.13** The Dangerous Drugs Act 1964 made it an offence to cultivate cannabis or to permit premises to be used for smoking or dealing in cannabis or cannabis resin. It also substituted a schedule containing most Class A and Class B drugs (but not amphetamines or methaqualone) for the drugs to which Part III of the Act of 1951 applied. The Drugs (Prevention of Misuse) Act 1964 applied a measure of control to amphetamines and to Class C drugs—chlorphetermine and pemoline. LSD was added in 1966. In this legislation the British Government was ahead of the international system of control. The Dangerous Drugs Acts 1951 and 1964 (but not the Drugs (Prevention of Misuse) Act 1964) were consolidated in the Dangerous Drugs Act 1965.

The Dangerous Drugs Act 1967 implemented the recommendations of the Second Brain Committee Report. The Home Secretary was given power to make regulations requiring medical practitioners to furnish particulars of patients who were addicts and to prohibit medical practitioners, unless specially authorised, from prescribing specified drugs to addicts. The Act also gave the Home Secretary powers over medical practitioners who contravene such regulations. Provision was made for a tribunal to advise the Home Secretary in respect of such practitioners. The Home Secretary was also empowered to make regulations concerning the safe custody of drugs. The maximum penalties for importing and exporting drugs were increased to ten years' imprisonment. Regulations were made in 1968 prohibiting practitioners from prescribing heroin or cocaine to addicts except for the treatment of organic disease or injury[11] and licences to use such drugs for addicts were issued in respect of treatment at drug dependence clinics. Regulations[12] were also made for the notification of addicts to the Home Office.


## THE PRESENT SCHEME

### Departmental Control

**1.14** The Home Office is primarily responsible for policy and for administering the legislation concerning the misuse of dangerous drugs, including the licensing of doctors to treat addicts and the disciplining of doctors who prescribe irresponsibly. The Home Office is also responsible for licensing and inspecting manufacturers and wholesalers and the issue of import and export licences. Provision of facilities for the treatment of addicts is the responsibility of the Department of Health and Social Security.

11 S.I. 1968/416.
12 S.I. 1968/136.

### The Advisory Council on the Misuse of Drugs

**1.15** This is a body appointed by the Home Secretary under section 1 of the Misuse of Drugs Act 1971. It is made up of members of the medical, dental, veterinary and pharmaceutical professions (see Schedule 1 to the Act set out in Appendix III) and of persons having wide and recent experience of social problems connected with the misuse of drugs. The objects of the Council are set out in section 1—they include keeping under review drugs which are, or are likely to be, misused and advising the government, whether they are consulted on the matter or not, on measures which ought to be taken for preventing the misuse of drugs. The Council may, and does, appoint expert committees to consider specific subjects. Their findings are published—for example they published *The Report of the Expert Group on the Effects of Cannabis Use* in 1982.[13]

The Advisory Council fulfils a vital function in keeping a fast-moving problem under review. The number of amendments and additions to the drugs listed in the Schedules to the Act and Regulations bears witness to its activity. These do not necessarily tally with the controls or classifications under the Conventions.

### Imports and Exports

**1.16** These are controlled by the Customs and Excise who are responsible for ensuring that controlled drugs are not imported or exported except as authorised under the Regulations or under a licence issued by the Home Office. They exercise the same powers as apply to prohibited and uncustomed goods. This is achieved by section 3 of the Misuse of Drugs Act 1971, which prohibits the importation and exportation of controlled drugs. The only special provision relating to controlled drugs is that enhanced penalties are provided by Schedule 1 to the Customs and Excise Management Act 1979 (see para. 8.01 *post*).

### The Misuse of Drugs Act 1971

**1.17** This Act is the principle vehicle of control. It consolidates and builds on the previous legislation. Section 2 defines controlled drugs by reference to Schedule 2. That Schedule lists all drugs subject to control in three categories, Classes A, B and C, according to their perceived degree of dangerousness. Preparations of Class B drugs designed for injection are designated Class A drugs. Mode of trial of offenders and maximum punishments are determined by the category of drug to which the offence relates as specified in Schedule 4.

13 Home Office, 1982.

An important feature of the scheme of control is that the medical and allied professions retain all their powers to prescribe drugs for persons (or animals) suffering from illness or injury. The only restrictions are designed to prevent the abuse of controlled drugs. In particular only doctors specially licensed by the Home Secretary may prescribe cocaine, heroin or dipipanone to addicts (see Chapter 19).

Offences relating to production, cultivation, supply and possession are defined in sections 4, 5 and 6. Offences which may be committed by occupiers of premises are defined in section 8. There are no requirements for the consent of the Attorney-General or the Director of Public Prosecutions to be given to the institution of prosecutions.

Powers of arrest, detention and search are contained in Sections 23 and 24[14] and forfeiture of things relating to offences is provided for in Section 27. The Home Secretary has power under various sections[15] to make regulations to supplement the control imposed by the Act. In particular he has made regulations concerning notification and treatment of addicts[16] and safe custody of controlled drugs.[17] He has also made general regulations concerning the legitimate use of controlled drugs.[18] He can license activities which would otherwise be prohibited.

The Home Secretary has power under section 12 to prohibit doctors or pharmacists who have been convicted of criminal offences from prescribing or possessing controlled drugs or to limit their powers to prescribe them. He also has such powers under section 13 in respect of practitioners who prescribe irresponsibly or are in breach of the regulations. Directions under section 13 are subject to a procedure involving a reference to a professional tribunal (see Chapter 23).

An important provision is contained in section 28, the object of which is to make it clear that mens rea is an element in the commission of the principal offences under the Act. This is secured by making it a defence for a defendant to prove that he did not, and had no reason to, suspect the existence of some fact alleged by the prosecution which is an essential element of the offence. Sub-section (3)(a) contains a limitation on this defence—it is not a defence to prove only that the defendant did not know that the substance in question was the *particular* controlled drug alleged.

Section 20 makes it an offence to assist in the United Kingdom in the commission elsewhere of an offence punishable under a corresponding

---

14 S. 24 has been repealed and replaced by the Police and Criminal Evidence Act 1984.
15 Notably ss. 10, 22 and 31.
16 The Misuse of Drugs (Notification of and Supply to Addicts) Regulations 1973 (S.I. no. 799).
17 The Misuse of Drugs (Safe Custody) Regulations 1973 (S.I. no. 798).
18 The Misuse of Drugs Regulations 1973 (S.I. no. 797). All these Regulations are set out in Appendices IV–VI.

law. Section 36 defines a "corresponding law" as a law certified to be a law made for the purpose of enforcing the Single Convention on Narcotic Drugs of 1961 or any other convention concerned with dangerous drugs to which the United Kingdom is a signatory.

It is worth noting that no such status as "registered addict" has been created, although it is often claimed by defendants in court. The fact that the particulars of an addict have been notified to the Home Secretary by a general practitioner or a hospital confers no status on the addict. The most such an expression can mean is that the addict is attending for treatment at a drug dependence clinic.

### International Agencies

**1.18**    *The United Nations* has taken over the responsibility of the League of Nations for ultimate control and supervision of international efforts to confine the use of drugs to proper medical purposes. It operates through the Secretary-General and the Economic and Social Council.

*The Commission on Narcotic Drugs* assists and advises the Economic and Social Council. It is the central policy-making body of the United Nations for dealing with all aspects of drug abuse control. The Commission prepares draft conventions and advises on changes in the scope of control of the various drugs. It meets annually. It is allotted various functions under the provisions of the two Conventions.

*The Division of Narcotic Drugs* at Vienna is part of the United Nations Secretariat under the direct authority of the Secretary-General. It is concerned with drug control laws, administration and law enforcement. It is the central repository for professional and technical expertise in drug control. It evaluates information on drug related matters and produces reports to the Secretary-General, the Council and the Commission.

*The International Narcotics Control Board* at Vienna superseded the Permanent Central Opium Board which had been established under the Geneva Conventions. It is an independent body reporting to the Council through the Commission. Its functions are laid down in the Conventions. Its major responsibility is to endeavour to limit the cultivation, manufacture and use of drugs to medical and scientific purposes. It is concerned with statistics and forecasts and receives estimates and reports from all parties to the Conventions. The annual report constitutes a review of the world situation.

*The United Nations Fund for Drug Abuse Control* is a trust fund to which parties (and charities) contribute on a voluntary basis. It supplements the other United Nations bodies. It was founded in 1971 in order to strengthen the technical and financial resources for the fight against drug abuse. In particular it has helped governments to implement programmes to limit the cultivation of the opium poppy through rural development and substitution of other crops.

*The World Health Organisation* is, *inter alia*, concerned with making recommendations for such matters as the advertising and labelling of pharmaceutical products. The Convention impose on the Organisation responsibility to assess the dependence liability and therapeutic usefulness of substances and to recommend changes in control and the placing of substances in the various schedules to the Conventions. Recommendations are made to the Commission.

The complex system of international control is explained in *Guidelines for the Control of Narcotic and Psychotropic Substances* published by the World Health Organisation and obtainable in the U.K. from H.M.S.O.

PART I

*THE DRUGS*

# CHAPTER 2

# The Nature of Drug Addiction

## Definitions

**2.01** It is very difficult to define the essential character of drug addiction, nowadays more correctly referred to as drug dependence. Perhaps it is necessary to explain that the term "drug" means any substance (licit/illicit, medically-prescribed or not, even a food substance) that when taken into the body may modify one or more of its functions. This is clearly a very broad definition, permitting a very broad-based approach to the study of drug dependence. The problem of defining drug dependence is immediately comprehensible in view of the wide range of drug-taking behaviour that has to be encompassed by the definition—e.g. the Eastern opium smoker, the alcoholic, the middle-aged housewife taking daily tranquillisers, the American free-basing cocaine, the adolescent solvent-sniffer, etc.

The choice of the term "drug-dependence" rather than "drug addiction" is made because in 1964 the World Health Organisation (WHO), on the recommendation of an expert committee, stopped trying to distinguish between drug addiction and drug habituation, which until then had been regarded as separate entities, and adopted the term "drug dependence" instead. It is defined as: "A state, psychic and sometimes also physical, resulting from the interaction between a living organism and a drug, characterised by behavioural and other responses that always include a compulsion to take the drug on a continuous or periodic basis in order to experience its psychic effects, and sometimes to avoid the discomfort of its absence. Tolerance may or may not be present. A person may be dependent on more than one drug". When, in this book, the terms "drug addiction" or "drug addict" are used, they should be understood to be synonymous with "drug dependence" and "drug dependent individual".

The above definition encompasses the two important components of drug dependence—psychological dependence and physical (or physiological dependence).[1]

## PSYCHOLOGICAL DEPENDENCE

**2.02** Psychological dependence is the condition in which a drug produces

1 World Health Organisation Expert Committee on Addiction-Producing Drugs, WHO Technical Report Series No. 273, Geneva: WHO, 1964.

a feeling of satisfaction and a psychic drive that requires periodic or continuous administration of the drug to provide pleasure or to avoid discomfort. It is the need and the desire for the drug, which may become an overwhelming craving or compulsion. The nature of psychological dependence is difficult to understand for anyone who has not experienced it and who may underestimate its importance in continued drug taking.

## PHYSICAL/PHYSIOLOGICAL DEPENDENCE

**2.03**  Physical/physiological dependence is an adaptive state manifested by intense physical disturbances when the administration of the drug is suspended. These disturbances, known as the withdrawal or abstinence syndrome, are a specific array of symptoms and signs characteristic of each drug type and are immediately relieved by further drug administration. Only some drugs of dependence cause physical dependence, so that an abstinence syndrome does not always occur on drug withdrawal. For example there is no withdrawal syndrome with LSD.

For the sake of completeness it should also be noted that there are drugs, which are used therapeutically, that cause physical dependence, and hence an abstinence syndrome when they are withdrawn. However, because they very rarely cause psychological dependence, there is no compulsion to continue drug use and these drugs are not the subject of control.

### Tolerance

**2.04**  Tolerance is a state of reduced responsiveness to the effects of a drug caused by its previous administration. It is as if the body "gets used" to the drug and in order to maintain its effect, the dose has to be increased. Many (but not all) of the common drugs of dependence induce tolerance and therefore those who are dependent upon them and taking them repeatedly, can consume without intoxication far larger doses than could be tolerated by someone without prior exposure. Indeed, drug-dependent individuals may actually need large doses of their drug merely to prevent the development of the abstinence syndrome.

### Cross-Tolerance

**2.05**  Tolerance is not completely drug-specific: if an individual has become tolerant to the effects of heroin, for example, he can take large doses of similar drugs, such as morphine, pethidine or dipipanone—in other words, large doses of other opiates. If his heroin were withdrawn, the resultant abstinence syndrome could also be relieved by other opiates in appropriate dosage. This phenomenon is known as cross-tolerance. It exists between drugs of the same class or type.

**Types of Dependence**

**2.06** So far in this chapter we have used the term "drug dependence" to include all kinds of drug dependence. In fact, the nature of the dependence depends on which drug is being taken. Some drugs may cause marked physical dependence so that the abstinence syndrome is severe; others cause less physical dependence but profound psychological dependence. The extent to which tolerance develops also varies with different classes of drugs. It is therefore essential to specify the particular type of drug dependence under discussion, and 8 types have been described by the World Health Organisation:-

(1) *Alcohol-barbiturate type*, e.g. ethanol alcohol (not controlled), barbiturates (Class B) and certain other drugs with sedative effects such as chloral hydrate (not controlled), chlordiazepoxide (not controlled), diazepam (not controlled), meprobamate (not controlled), methaqualone (Class B).

(2) *Amphetamine type*, e.g. amphetamine, dexamphetamine, methamphetamine, methylphenidate, and phenmetrazine (all Class B).

(3) *Cannabis type*—preparations of *Cannabis sativa L,* such as marijuana, ganja and hashish (Class B).

(4) *Cocaine type*—cocaine and coca leaves (Class A).

(5) *Hallucinogen type*, e.g. lysergide (LSD), mescaline and psilocybin (Class A).

(6) *Khat type*—preparations of *Catha edulis* (not controlled).

(7) *Opiate (morphine) type*, e.g. opiates such as morphine (Class A), heroin (Class A), codeine (Class B; injectable-Class A), and synthetics with morphine-like effects such as methadone (Class A) and pethidine (Class A).

(8) *Volatile solvent (inhalants) type*, e.g. toluene, acetone and carbon tetrachloride (not controlled).

This list is not exhaustive and dependence on other drugs is also recognised, e.g. minor analgesics (such as aspirin) and laxatives. A person may be dependent on more than one drug, or may be dependent on one and take others according to whim or availability or cost.

## DIAGNOSIS

**2.07** By now it should be apparent that there is no single diagnostic test that can be applied to identify "a drug addict". The diagnosis is made on the basis of the history of drug-taking, physical and psychological examination and laboratory tests. An accurate history of drug-taking may be difficult to obtain because some drug dependents may attempt to conceal the extent of their drug-taking, while others may exaggerate it in the hope of obtaining a larger prescription of the drug that they want.

Physical examination may reveal how the drug is administered (intravenous injections, intramuscular injections, sniffing etc), and its effect on the body. Psychological examination demonstrates the effects of the drug on the individual's mental state—for example, some stimulants cause hallucinations. Laboratory tests of urine and/or blood can reveal the presence of certain drugs, which if present repeatedly are good evidence of regular consumption and perhaps of dependence.

### Urine Tests

**2.08** The laboratory plays an important role in the diagnosis and management of drug dependence, mostly because the individuals concerned are not always truthful about their drug consumption and an independent, objective source of information is essential. Analysis of the urine for drugs provides some of this information. Clearly, a single urine specimen cannot provide all the answers; at best, it may provide some information about drugs taken within the previous 24 hours (approximately). Repeated urine tests help to build up a more complete picture of drug-taking over a period of time.

Before carrying out a urine test, it is essential to be absolutely sure that the urine specimen being tested has actually come from the patient who is being assessed. Substitution of specimens is not unknown. Negative urine results, in other words, the absence of drugs, may be as informative, or even more informative, than positive results. For example, the repeated absence of opiates from the urine of an individual claiming to be dependent, and seeking a prescription, gives more precise information than the presence of opiates which could mean either that the individual is dependent or that he is an occasional user.

The ability of the laboratory to detect abused drugs in random specimens of urine is generally limited by time and money rather than by lack of suitable methods.

*Methods*

Chromatography is a method for separating chemical substances that depends on differences between their rates of transfer from a moving stream of liquid or gas to a stationary material, which is usually a finely divided solid or a film of liquid on the surface of such a solid. With thin-layer chromatography the finely divided solid stationary material is spread as a thin layer on a sheet of glass. In high-performance liquid chromatography the stationary material is packed into a steel tube and a moving stream of liquid is pumped through at high pressure, whilst in gas chromatography a moving stream of gas is forced through at high pressure.

Immunoassay is a method for detecting and measuring chemical substances that depends on the interaction between the substance being measured and an antibody to that substance. The antibody is produced in an animal as a result of being injected with the chemical substance of interest or a derivative of it, and is isolated from the blood.

Mass spectrometry, by accurate analysis of molecular weight, can determine molecular structure and hence identify specific drugs.

Sophisticated equipment is needed to carry out these tests and as it is expensive to instal and to run, it is available only in specialised centres that provide a drug screening service with a high level of expertise for surrounding hospitals, thus achieving economy of scale. All hospitals have access to a drug-screening service.

Two screening methods commonly used are thin-layer chromatography (TLC) and enzyme immunoassay such as EMIT. These methods generally detect barbiturates, morphine, methadone and amphetamines. Confirmation of positive results is by specific gas-liquid chromatography (GLC) or high performance liquid chromatography (HPLC). In addition, specific immunoassay methods are available for some drugs and their metabolites (break-down products). The most sensitive and specific method available in some specialised laboratories is gas-liquid chromatography linked to a mass-spectrometer (GCMS).

*Interpretation of Results*
The interpretation of the results depends upon the sensitivity and specificity of the analytical method used. Most laboratories use screening procedures for the common drugs that will just detect a single minimum therapeutic dose for about 24 hours after administration. There are, however, large variations in drug metabolism and excretion between individuals so that the drug may be detected for less than 24 hours in some patients, whilst in others it will persist for much longer.

A negative result of a drug screen by these methods, means that the urine specimen contains less than the lowest amount of drug detectable by the method. It does not mean the complete absence of the drug. On the other hand a positive result may signify a small dose taken recently or a much larger dose taken some days previously.

Positive results must also be interpreted in relation to the specificity of the method. Identification of a drug solely by screening methods is fraught with difficulties and confirmation by a more specific method is essential. However due to pressure of work many laboratories report results on the basis of screening procedures.

The following common drugs of abuse can be detected:
(1) *Central Nervous System Depressants*
    *Barbiturates*: (Class B)
       Detected by TLC and EMIT methods. Glutethimide (not con-

trolled) and Phenytoin (not controlled) can give positive results.
*Chlormethiazole* (Heminevrin):
Sedative drug commonly used for alcohol detoxification (not controlled). Detected by TLC screen.
*Benzodiazepines*: (not controlled at present)
Not detected by routine screen but can be detected by a separate TLC-method and by EMIT.

(2) *Central Nervous System Stimulants*
*Amphetamines, Methylamphetamines*: (*Class B*)
Detected by TLC and EMIT screen, but not specific. Ephedrine (not controlled) and similar drugs give positive results. Results must be confirmed by GLC.
*Ephedrine* (*not controlled*), *Methylphenidate* (*Class C*), *Diethylpropion* (*Class C*), *Fenfluramine* (*not controlled*):
Not detected by screening methods but can be detected by GLC.
*Cocaine*:
Not detected by routine screen. Benzoylecgonine, a metabolite of cocaine, can be detected by a specific EMIT method and by special TLC methods. It indicates that cocaine must have been ingested.

(3) *Narcotic Analgesics*
*Heroin* (*Class A*), *Morphine* (*Class A*), *Codeine* (*Class B*):
EMIT identifies all three drugs as morphine; the presence of "morphine" in the test result therefore means that either heroin, morphine or codeine, or any combination, could have been taken. TLC identifies heroin and morphine as morphine but can detect codeine separately. EMIT also gives a positive result with some synthetic narcotics.
*Dipipanone* (*Class A*):
Is commonly marketed as Diconal which also contains cyclizine. TLC screen detects the cyclizine, which is an anti-travel-sickness drug that may also be abused.
*Dihydrocodeine* (*DF 118*) (*Class B*):
Can be detected by TLC screen but must be confirmed by specific method.
*Methadone* (*Class A*):
The drug and metabolites can be detected by TLC and EMIT screen.

(4) *Hallucinogens*
*Lysergic acid diethylamide* (*LSD*) (*Class A*):
Cannot be detected in urine by normal methods.
*Phencyclidine*: (*Class B*):
Can be detected by specific EMIT method and GLC.

(5) *Cannabis* (*Class B*)

    Can be detected in urine by specific EMIT, TLC and radio-immunoassay. The methods are very sensitive and can detect the drug for some days after the last dose.

## CAUSES OF DRUG DEPENDENCE

**2.09** The causes of drug dependence are not known. More specifically it is not known why some people, but not others in the same situation, take or experiment with drugs, or why some, but not others, then continue to take them and become dependent upon them. It is however generally accepted that drug-related behaviour, including drug dependence, results from the interaction of three factors the drug, the individual and the environment. In other words, there is no single cause for drug dependence and indeed it seems unlikely that there could be in view of the vast range of dependence behaviour that exists world-wide.

    The availability of the drug is obviously a prerequisite for dependence, and although a few people become dependent on apparently extraordinary drugs, like laxatives, most drug dependence is concerned with only a few types of drugs; admittedly a large number of drugs are involved, but they are grouped into the eight classes listed by the World Health Organisation. The question arises, therefore, about how these types of drugs produce dependence. Although the avoidance of the unpleasant symptoms of the abstinence syndrome may be an important reason why a drug dependent individual continues taking a drug (if it is one that causes physical dependence), this is not the only reason. Many opiate addicts, for example, continue to seek illicit heroin while receiving sufficient supplies of methadone (another opiate), to prevent withdrawal symptoms. In the laboratory too, animals can exhibit drug-seeking behaviour. For example, animals taught to press a lever to obtain a drug will do so repeatedly, even if they are not physically dependent on the drug. Not all drugs induce this behaviour; those that do are said to have 'reinforcing' properties because they reinforce or increase the behaviour resulting in drug administration. Drugs shown to be powerful reinforcers in animals are opiates and cocaine, and to a lesser extent, some sedatives-hypnotics and alcohol. These drugs are the ones with a high dependence liability in man, but it is not known why they are reinforcers while other drugs of abuse and dependence (e.g. cannabis and LSD) are not. Nor is it known why drugs with such different chemical and pharmacological properties should share this ill-understood property of increasing drug-taking behaviour.

    As well as studying the drugs of dependence, there have been many attempts to describe a "dependence-prone" personality. Most studies have compared drug-dependent with non-dependent individuals. This is clearly an unsatisfactory approach because any difference may be the result of drug dependence rather than its cause. Often too, the drug-dependent individuals chosen for the study are from hospital or prison, where the process of institutionalisation may also affect observations on personality. Retrospective attempts to assess what the personality was like before dependence are difficult and unreliable.

It is quite understandable that environmental factors should be blamed for drug dependence, particularly when its prevalence starts to rise sharply, and poverty and unemployment are the usual candidates for blame. They may indeed be relevant, although it should always be remembered that not everyone in a particular environment becomes dependent on drugs, and that ultimately environmental factors are local and inapplicable to general and global theories of drug dependence. However, the immediate situation in which drug taking occurs, in other words the setting, may influence the effect of the drug and whether drug taking is a pleasurable experience likely to be repeated on another occasion.

In conclusion, when putting forward ideas and theories about drug dependence, it is important to remember that there is no single cause and that many factors may play a part, assuming different importance in different cases. A way of unifying the wide range of theories is to hypothesise that ultimately the different factors may share common or communicating pathways in the brain, the malfunctioning of which, for whatever reason(s), may lead to drug dependence.

## Criminality and Drug Abuse

**2.10**  Because the possession of controlled drugs is itself a criminal offence, there is an in-built statistical relationship between drug abuse and criminality. Each year, for example, there are many offenders against drug legislation (25,022 in 1984)[2] and many are given custodial sentences. Possession of cannabis accounts for 70% of all drug offences, and most of the drug offenders given a prison sentence have committed offences involving cannabis.

A study of drug offenders in prison seems, at first sight, to be a good starting point for finding out about the relationship between criminality and drug abuse. However, information about drug offenders in prison can be misleading, firstly, because some prisoners who are on remand may be acquitted, or may not receive a custodial sentence. Secondly, not all offenders against drug legislation are themselves drug abusers or dependent on drugs, and, thirdly, the majority of prisoners with drug problems have committed non-drug offences.

2  *Statistics of Misuse of Drugs in the United Kingdom 1984,* Home Office 18/84.

It is easy and perhaps tempting to assume that this criminal activity is somehow caused by drug abuse. There is certainly no pharmacological basis for this assumption as no drug has inherent criminogenic properties. It is true that intoxication with some drugs such as amphetamine or barbiturates may sometimes produce aggressive feelings, verbal abuse and occasionally, physical aggression, but as abuse of these drugs is rare in comparison with the frequency of violent crimes, no statistically significant relationship can be established. In fact, UK addicts are rarely involved in serious crime and violent offences are uncommon while crimes against property (theft, burglary) occur most often. It is often suggested that drug abusers steal to get money to buy their drugs and although this may be true, there is little evidence to support the hypothesis.

There is, however, some evidence that criminality often precedes drug abuse. For example, between a quarter and a third of male addicts are convicted of an offence before drug abuse starts and two-thirds have been convicted before they are notified to the Home Office.

It is perhaps not surprising that most research has concentrated on those dependent on opiates and follow-up studies have shown that crime and continued drug use go hand-in-hand, and that when drug use stops, so do illegal activities. It is interesting, and somewhat disappointing, that attendance at a clinic and receipt of a prescription for opiates does not bring about a halt in criminal activities, although these tend to become restricted to drug, rather than non-drug, offences. Frugal prescribing policies of the drug clinics have been blamed for continued drug-related offences by their patients, but more liberal prescriptions do not seem to lead to reduced use of illicit drugs.

Because so many addicts commit crimes and receive custodial sentences, it is interesting to examine the effect of a prison sentence on their drug dependence. It is a widely held belief, particularly by those ignorant of the complexities of drug dependence, that a period of compulsory abstinence from drugs would be the turning point for many addicts. As the new Mental Health Act[3] excludes drug dependence as a reason for compulsory admission to hospital, prison is the only situation in which drug withdrawal can be enforced. In fact, the chances of remaining abstinent after a prison sentence, are similar to those after treatment in hospital, and evidence from other countries also suggests that compulsory treatment is no more successful than voluntary treatment. Those findings are unsurprising—they reinforce the belief that drug withdrawal is merely the first stage of treatment and ineffective, unless followed by the all-important process of rehabilitation.

---

3 Mental Health Act 1983 s. 1(3).

**Pregnancy and Drug Abuse**

**2.11**   It is now not uncommon for drug abusers and drug dependent women to continue taking illicit drugs during pregnancy. Heavy drug use is likely to affect the mother's health, not only because of the direct effects of the drugs, but also because of the self-neglect and poor nutrition that are common features of a drug-abuser's life-style. These factors, combined with late and intermittent ante-natal care, may adversely affect the foetus, and heavy drug use in pregnancy is associated with prematurity and low birth weight.

Maternal drug use, however, has more specific effects on the foetus.

(1) *Withdrawal Effects.* Because opiates cross the placenta, the foetus is constantly exposed to them throughout pregnancy. After delivery, when the drugs are abruptly withdrawn from the foetus, a characteristic neonatal abstinence syndrome may occur in which the baby is hyperactive, restless and irritable and may suffer convulsions. The severity and duration of the abstinence syndrome depends on the duration of dependence, the daily dose of opiates consumed, the timing of the last dose before delivery etc. A neonatal abstinence syndrome also occurs after birth when the mother has been taking barbiturates and may be particularly dangerous because its onset is delayed, and may not become manifest until mother and baby have been discharged from hospital. Cases of benzodiazepine withdrawal in new-born babies have also been described.

(2) *Teratogenicity.* There have been reports that LSD and cannabis are teratogens, that is that they cause congenital abnormalities. The specific deformities with which they have been associated are ones with a high background incidence and it has therefore proved impossible to find a statistically significant relationship between the use of these drugs and congenital deformities.

**Dangers of Injection**

**2.12**   Many of the complications of drug dependence are due not to the direct effects of the drugs themselves but to the life-style of the addict and to the method of drug-administration. Self-injection of illicit drugs is particularly hazardous. Drugs may be injected intramuscularly, sub-cutaneously ("skin-popping") or intravenously ("mainlining"), when the total dose is delivered straight into the bloodstream.

Dirty injection techniques, using contaminated water and/or non-sterile syringes and needles, introduce infection, causing septic injection sites and abscesses. The infection may spread through the bloodstream and affect other organs such as the lungs and the heart. When syringes and needles are shared there is considerable risk of transmitting viral infections such as hepatitis and the notorious acquired immune deficiency syndrome (AIDS).

Linear scar marks ("tracks") develop over veins, usually in the forearms, used repeatedly for injection and the veins themselves become swollen and blocked (thrombosed). Other veins then have to be used and it may eventually become difficult or impossible to find an unoccluded, accessible vein.

Other complications of injection are due not to infection but to the contamination of illicit drugs with adulterants. Heroin, for example, is often "cut" with substances such as talc, which, if injected into a vein, is eventually filtered out of the blood in the lungs where the particles of talc may cause serious complications later.

The injection of drugs that were originally intended for oral consumption (e.g. the contents of capsules, crushed tablets) may cause serious problems. Barbiturates are often administered in this way and have a particularly irritant and destructive effect on the tissues; gangrene may occur if barbiturates are accidentally injected into an artery.

## STEREOISOMERISM

**2.13**   This arises when two or more compounds (isomers) are made up of the same atoms, joined together in the same order, but in different spatial, or three-dimensional configuration. One form of stereoisomerism is optical isomerism, in which the different stereoisomers rotate plane-polarised light differently. This is important in pharmacology because different optical isomers may possess different pharmacological properties. For example:

(1) *Morphine.* The natural alkaloids of opium, including morphine, occur only in the laevo-rotatory form. In other words, they rotate plane-polarised light to the left. This is identified by the symbol L− or (−); only L− forms of morphine and the synthetic drugs derived from it possess analgesic properties; synthetic dextrorotatory (d, (+)) forms of any of these drugs do not.

(2) *Amphetamine.* This exists in both dextro and laevo-rotatory isomers. It was first marketed as Benzedrine which contains equal parts of both isomers. This shows no resultant rotation of light, since the left-hand and right-hand contributions balance exactly, and is termed racemic amphetamine, written as dl or (±) amphetamine. The isolated d-isomer (dextroamphetamine) is approximately twice as powerful as racemic amphetamine as a cerebral stimulant.

CHAPTER 3

# Drugs of Dependence

## OPIATES

**3.01**  The parent drug of this class is opium, which has been known to man for thousands of years and is obtained from the opium poppy, *Papaver somniferum*, which grows in large areas of the East and Middle East (Turkey, Iran, Afghanistan, Pakistan, Burma, Thailand). It is obtained by incising the unripe seed capsule of the plant and allowing the milky exudate to dry into a brown, gummy mass which is scraped off by hand. This, dried further and powdered, is then crude opium which may be smoked in special pipes, chewed, or inserted as small pellets into cigarettes. In the UK it is sometimes available as sticks of opium, imported illegally from the Middle East. "Prepared" opium is a boiled-down aqueous solution of raw opium, prepared for opium smokers by repeated boilings and filtrations to extract all possible opium without impurities (such as leaves, stalks etc). The final boiling leaves a thick, sticky paste ready for smoking. It is not prescribed medically.

Crude opium contains a number of chemical compounds called alkaloids which possess the same or similar properties as opium and which are used clinically in preference to it. The most important is morphine, first isolated in 1803 and named after Morpheus, the Greek god of sleep and dreams. Other naturally occurring alkaloids are codeine, papaverine and thebaine.

### Effects of Opiates

**3.02**  The principal medical use of opiates is for the relief of pain, but they also have sedative effects on the nervous system causing inability to concentrate, drowsiness and sleep. In addition they depress the respiratory centre, the part of the brain that controls breathing, so that respiration becomes progressively slower and more shallow. Higher doses cause increasing respiratory depression, unconsciousness and death. They may also cause nausea and vomiting and characteristically a constricted "pin point" pupil (miosis). Their action on the intestines causes constipation, accounting for their use in anti-diarrhoeal preparations. Some opiates may induce a euphoric mood change, giving the consumer

32

an exaggerated sense of well-being, although the opposite, dysphoria, may sometimes occur.

Unfortunately, when opiates are administered regularly tolerance to their effects develops and there is a marked physical and psychological tolerance.

### Physical Dependence

**3.03**   There is no subjective or objective evidence of physical dependence on opiates during drug administration because opiates themselves have few adverse effects, even after a long period of administration. The complications often associated with opiate-dependence are usually due to the life style of the addict and the method of drug administration (if injection is used) rather than to any direct effect of the drug itself.

### Abstinence Syndrome

**3.04**   When drug administration ceases, the following symptoms and signs of the opiate abstinence syndrome develop: craving for drugs, anxiety, abdominal pain, yawning, irritability, cold sweats, goose flesh, restlessness, diarrhoea, increased pulse and respiration rates, tremor, runny nose and eyes and dilated pupils.

The timing of the abstinence syndrome, its onset, the peak of severity of symptoms, and its duration, all depend on which opiate was being taken, the dose and the duration of drug administration. For example, an abstinent heroin addict may be suffering from yawning and sweating only 8 hours after the last dose of heroin, whereas these features may not be apparent in a methadone addict until 34–48 hours after the last dose, because methadone is a longer-acting opiate and so remains in the body for longer.

Generally, withdrawal from heroin is more severe in the short term than withdrawal from methadone, which, however, lasts longer. If the dose of opiate has been reduced, by a doctor, or by the patient himself, the abstinence syndrome will be correspondingly milder. The severity of suffering also depends on the personality of individual addicts, some of whom appear to tolerate withdrawal better than others.

Although the abstinence syndrome is extremely unpleasant, it is rarely life-endangering in an otherwise healthy person. Consciousness remains unimpaired during withdrawal so that the addict is fully aware of what is happening, what is being said to him and of all the symptoms of abstinence. His general state of wretchedness at this time may lead him to say things that are not true or that he does not mean, if he believes that he will then receive earlier attendance from a doctor and quicker relief of his symptoms. The abstinence syndrome can be relieved immediately by administration of any opiate. Other sedative drugs may be administered; they cannot specifically reverse the symptoms and signs of withdrawal, as opiates can, but may partially relieve symptoms such as anxiety, restlessness and nausea.

The duration of the abstinence syndrome also varies enormously with different opiates, but it is now recognised that there are two phases that merge into each other. There is an early, acute phase in which the symptoms already described occur and a protracted abstinence syndrome lasting for up to 26 weeks during which certain observable signs remain abnormal (e.g. blood pressure, pulse rate, pupil diameter). The existence of a prolonged abstinence syndrome may help to explain why so many addicts relapse to opiate use after several months of abstinence.

### Tolerance to Opiates

**3.05**   Tolerance develops rapidly to many of the effects of opiates (both the desired ones and the undesired ones)—to analgesia, euphoria and dysphoria, sedation and sleep, respiratory depression and vomiting. Thus, just as a patient with continuing severe pain may require increasing doses of morphine to provide adequate analgesia, so an opiate-dependent individual requires increasing doses not only to obtain the desired euphoria, but also to prevent the development of the unpleasant symptoms of the abstinence syndrome— and this high dose does not cause drowsiness, vomiting or respiratory depression. The extent to which tolerance can develop is best illustrated by going back to the 1960s when a few physicians were prescribing large quantities of pharmaceutical heroin. Some addicts were then taking 300 to 600 mg daily, a dose which would kill an opiate-naive individual (the therapeutic dose is 5 to 10 mg repeated two or three times a day).

Tolerance is promoted and maintained by frequent administration of opiates and any period of abstinence leads to a loss of tolerance, so that a regular opiate user may be seriously intoxicated by a dose which before abstinence was well tolerated. This situation arises not infrequently when an addict, after a period of enforced abstinence, in prison, for example, resumes his former habit when he is released, sometimes with fatal consequences.

Cross-tolerance occurs between different opiates so that an addict, unable to obtain the drug of his choice, may substitute a more easily available opiate to prevent the abstinence syndrome.

Tolerance does *not* develop to the miotic effect of opiates so that opiate-dependent individuals characteristically have pin-point pupils.

Over the years there have been many attempts to separate the analgesic action of opiates from their dependence-producing liability by chemical modification and many new drugs have been synthesized. However, all of the clinically useful opiate analgesics share similar structural characteristics, and are remarkable more for their general similarity of action than for the differences between them, which tend to be differences of degree rather than of nature.

## Morphine (Class A)

**3.06**  Morphine (Class A) is widely used medicinally for the treatment of severe pain when it may be administered by injection or orally in a dose of 10–20 mg four-hourly. Although it is used illicitly, it is not particularly popular because it often produces nausea and vomiting. It may be taken by injection or sniffed or smoked. One kilo of opium produces 100 g morphine. The use of morphine spread rapidly in the 19th century, but as the dangers of dependence were recognised, the search began for a safer substitute.

## Heroin (Diacetylmorphine or Diamorphine) (Class A)

**3.07**  Heroin (Diacetylmorphine or diamorphine), which is prepared from morphine, was first marketed in 1898 when it was claimed to be the "heroic" cure for morphinism, providing a safe and effective cure with no danger of dependence. This claim was soon proved to be false and heroin is the drug of choice of most opiate-dependent individuals and is widely available in most places in the world. The process by which it is manufactured, although simple in theory, requires considerable skill and a quantity of equipment in practice. It is usually manufactured close to the source of opium and the object of the chemist is to obtain one kilo of heroin for every kilo of morphine put into the process. In the UK the geographical source of illicit heroin varies from time to time and is influenced by international politics.

Heroin is a white powder which is very easy to smuggle. As it passes down the distribution chain it is progressively diluted ("cut") with a variety of substances including sugar, starch, powdered milk, quinine, talc, etc. It can be taken orally or administered by intravenous or subcutaneous injection. A common way of taking it at present is called "chasing the dragon", in which the heroin, on a piece of foil, is heated by a flame, the resultant fumes being inhaled. When heroin is in short supply and, therefore, much more expensive than at present or if an individual's habit becomes large (and more expensive), it is then more likely to be taken by intravenous injection ("mainlining"), which delivers all of the available drug right into the blood stream. Injection, while providing the addict with a "kick" ("rush", "high"), is associated with a number of serious complications, mostly infective.[1] Inhaling heroin lacks these risks and is much less likely to be associated with overdose. However, it may encourage those reluctant to embark on injection to experiment with heroin. Medicinally, heroin is usually used in a dose of 5–10 mg four-hourly, either orally or by injection.

### Methadone (Class A)

**3.08** Methadone (Class A) is a synthetic opiate analgesic with a longer duration of action, so that once-daily administration to an addict prevents the development of the abstinence syndrome. It is the opiate most frequently prescribed by drug-dependence treatment units for the maintenance treatment of the opiate-dependent individual and is usually prescribed in the form of a mixture which has less black-market value than other opiates (see para. 4.04 *post*). It is occasionally prescribed in injectable form. Most addicts receive between 30 and 80 mg methadone daily.

### Pethidine (Class A)

**3.09** Pethidine (Class A) was the first wholly synthetic opiate. It is a very effective analgesic widely used post-operatively and during child-birth. It is used medically in a dose of 50–100 mg four hourly. Perhaps because of the frequency of its medical use it is a common drug of abuse by "professional" addicts (i.e. doctors and nurses) who have access to controlled drugs. Some pethidine is also available illicitly as a result of burglaries from pharmacies.

### Dipipanone (Class A) and Dextromoramide (Class A)

**3.10** Dipipanone (Class A) (marketed with cyclizine as Diconal), and dextromoramide (Class A) (Palfium) are synthetic opiates with a shorter duration of action than morphine. Diconal (dipipanone 10 mg with cyclizine 30 mg) is available as a small pink tablet for oral use. During the late 1970s and early 1980s it was prescribed in generous quantities to opiate-dependent individuals, mostly by independent doctors whom addicts had consulted because drug-dependence treatment clinics were unwilling to prescribe injectable opiates for them. Although intended for oral use, Diconal tablets were frequently crushed and injected by addicts, with the expected complications of self-injection, and those surplus to requirement were sold on the black market, usually to finance the cost of

1 See para. 2.12 *ante*.

a private consultation and prescription. Because of the increasing frequency of dependence on dipipanone, it was brought under the same control as heroin and cocaine. Dextromoramide tablets are used in similar ways, but now that heroin is widely available on the black market, both dextromoramide and dipipanone are less attractive to addicts.

## Codeine (Class B; Injectable Class A)

**3.11** This is another alkaloid that is found in crude opium. It is a less effective analgesic than morphine and is therefore used for the relief of mild to moderate pain and as a cough suppressant (15–60 mg four hourly). A derivative of codeine, dihyrocodeine (DF 118), is a more potent analgesic and like codeine is available as tablets, syrup (30 mg four-hourly) and for injection. Both of these drugs can cause dependence and may be taken by opiate-dependent individuals in the absence of preferred drugs (e.g. heroin, dipipanone) to relieve the symptoms of the abstinence syndrome.

## Opium Antagonists

**3.12** During the search for new and safer opiate analgesics some compounds were synthesised that prevented or abolished the respiratory depression caused by heroin or morphine. These compounds are called *opiate antagonists*, examples of which are naloxone (not controlled) and the longer-acting naltrexone (not yet marketed in the UK).

In the absence of opiates, naloxone has no important effects. If given to a non-dependent individual who has taken an opiate, the effects of opiates (e.g. respiratory depression, sedation, unconsciousness) will be abolished immediately. If it is given to an opiate-dependent individual, the signs and symptoms of the abstinence syndrome develop immediately. The latter observation is the basis of the use of naloxone in a diagnostic test for opiate dependence: If a small dose of naloxone (0·16 mg–0·4 mg intramuscularly) is given to an opiate dependent individual, dilatation of the (constricted) pupil occurs, while there is no change in pupil size in a non-dependent individual.

Naloxone and naltrexone are both described as "pure" antagonists, but other drugs have been synthesised which, while antagonising some of the effects of morphine, may possess some of its properties too. Nalorphine (not marketed in the UK), for example, is an opiate analgesic that can also precipitate the opiate abstinence syndrome if given to an addict. Such drugs are described as agonist-antagonists. At first, it was hoped that they might be free from dependence-producing liability, but earlier hopes have yet again been proved false.

*Pentazocine (not controlled) (Fortral)*
**3.13** Pentazocine (not controlled) (Fortral) is an opiate agonist-antagonist which may be administered orally (25–100 mg four-hourly) or by injection (30–60 mg four-hourly). There have been many reports of dependence on it and it is extensively abused in many areas of the USA, often together with another drug, tripelennamine, a combination known as "T's and blues". Repeated injections of pentazocine lead to severe muscle wasting.

*Buprenophine (not controlled) (Temgesic)*
**3.14** Buprenophine (not controlled) (Temgesic) is a comparatively new opiate agonist-antagonist, unusual because its abstinence syndrome is delayed for up to 14 days after drug withdrawal. It is being used in the treatment of opiate dependence, but it is probably too early to state categorically that it has no abuse potential, an optimistic claim made in error in the past for many opiate drugs. In fact there have recently been reports of its abuse in West Germany, New Zealand and Australia. Medically it is used in a dose of 200–400 micrograms sublingually (under the tongue) every 6–8 hours.

## COCAINE

**3.15** Cocaine is an alkaloid obtained from the coca shrub, *Erythroxylon coca*, that grows in South American countries such as Peru, Bolivia and Colombia. Traditionally, the leaves were (and are) chewed by the natives to relieve fatigue, apparently without ill-effect.

Cocaine itself was first isolated in 1858 and its pharmacological properties were investigated by Sigmund Freud, who was aware of its local anaesthetic and psychic actions. Because of its stimulant and euphoric effects it was used in the treatment of a number of psychiatric problems (including morphine dependence), but now it is available only in the form of eye-drops as an opthalmic local anaesthetic. Its use in other types of local anaesthesia is no longer recommended, because of the availability of safer alternatives. There are no other medical indications for its use.

The process by which the drug is extracted from the leaves is simple, and illegal factories are set up close to where the shrub grows. Cocaine hydrochloride of a high degree of purity is obtained in the form of a white powder that is easy to smuggle. It is diluted or "cut" with a variety of adulterants such as sugars, amphetamine or other local anaesthetics.

**Effects of Cocaine**
**3.16** Cocaine is a powerful stimulant of the nervous system, producing

increased wakefulness, activity, energy and confidence. It also gives the user a great feeling of well-being and an indefinable euphoria. Physically, there is an increased pulse rate and blood pressure and dilation of the pupils. It causes profound psychological dependence, manifested by the overwhelming compulsion to obtain the drug at whatever price or social or personal consequence. This interferes with, and ultimately completely disrupts the individual's normal life-style. However, there is no clear-cut withdrawal syndrome to confirm the existence of physical dependence, although depression and apathy (the "crash") may occur with drug abstinence after a severe bout of abuse. Regular users may consume massive amounts of cocaine, many times greater than that used by novices, but it is not clear whether this is due to the development of tolerance or to a search for greater euphoria. There is no cross-tolerance with amphetamine or any other nervous system stimulant.

*Cocaine Psychosis*
**3.17** A psychotic illness may occur with chronic, heavy use of cocaine. It is characterised by paranoid delusions and auditory, visual and, often, by tactile hallucinations—the latter is often described as feeling as if insects ("cocaine bugs") are crawling under the skin. Drug withdrawal usually leads to rapid improvement.

**Route of Administration**

**3.18** Cocaine may be administered by almost any route: the South American Indians, as described already, chew it and in the 1960s it was often self-injected, together with heroin ("speedball"). Sniffing ("snorting") cocaine leads to its absorption through the mucous membrane lining the nasal passages and a fairly rapid "high". However, because cocaine causes local constriction of blood vessels, continuous use of this method carries the risk of a perforated nasal septum. Recently, "freebasing" has become popular in USA; cocaine is separated or freed from its hydrochloride base and is then smoked. Absorption then occurs very rapidly via the lungs and the drug reaches the brain so quickly that the effect is akin to that of injection, while lacking all its disadvantages. As free-basing is associated with a rapidly rising level of cocaine, and hence intense euphoria, it seems likely to lead to greater psychological dependence.

## AMPHETAMINE (CLASS B)

**3.19** Amphetamine is a synthetic drug (phenylisopropylamine), first marketed as a nasal inhaler (Benzedrine) to relieve the congestion of a cold. It was soon realised that a side effect of Benzedrine was sleeplessness, and it was thus that the central stimulant effect of amphetamine first came to light. Benzedrine was a mixture of racemic dl amphetamine, and it was found that the dextro-rotatory stereoisomer, dextro-amphetamine, was approximately twice as powerful a central stimulant as the racemic compound (see para. 2.13 *ante*). The laevo-rotatory isomer, laevoamphetamine, affects the cardiovascular system (increased blood pressure, pulse rate, etc.,) more than dextroampheta-mine; the latter, however, is three to four times more potent as a stimulant of the central nervous system than laevoamphetamine. Methylamphetamine, an injectable amphetamine, is also a potent stimulant.

During the second world war, amphetamine was used by military personnel to alleviate fatigue. It was also prescribed very widely for the treatment of mild depression, and because of its appetite-suppressant effect, for the treatment of obesity. Increasing concern about the abuse of amphetamine led to a voluntary ban on its prescription by many doctors during the 1960s, and this concern now extends to related stimulants and appetite suppressants, such as methylphenidate (Ritalin), phenmetrazine, and diethylpropion. The only medical indications for prescribing amphetamine are the treatment of narcolepsy and, paradoxically, the treatment of hyperactivity in children. Nevertheless, some amphetamine still finds its way to the black market from slimming clinics. Illicit factories and illegal imports also contribute to the black market. It is taken orally, although methylamphetamine, when it was available, was injected.

*Amphetamine and related drugs*

| | |
|---|---|
| Dexamphetamine (Dexedrine) | Class B |
| Amphetamine with dexamphetamine (Durophet) | Class B |
| Methylamphetamine (Methedrine) | Class B |
| Pipradol | Class C |
| Diethylpropion (Tenuate Dospan, Apisate) | Class C |
| Phenmetrazine (Preludin) | Class B |
| Methylphenidate (Ritalin) | Class B |
| Chlorphentermine | Class C |
| Mephentermine | Class C |
| Benzphetamine | Class C |

**Effects of Amphetamine**
**3.20** Amphetamine is a powerful central stimulant producing an elevated mood and making the user feel energetic, alert and self-confident. Feelings of hunger and fatigue are reduced and there may be increased talkativeness, restlessness and sometimes agitation. Because

amphetamine is closely related chemically to adrenaline, a compound that occurs naturally in the body, it mimics many of its effects; thus amphetamine causes a raised heart rate, palpitations, raised blood pressure, dry mouth and sweating.

## Tolerance to Amphetamine

**3.21** Tolerance develops to some, but not all of the effects of amphetamine. Those people taking it for its euphoric, mood-elevating effect may take 250–1000 mg amphetamine daily (10–20 times the usual daily dose), but because tolerance also develops to its effect on the heart and circulation, they do not suffer from adverse cardio-vascular effects. Tolerance occurs to the appetite-suppressant effect of amphetamine, accounting for its ineffectiveness in the treatment of obesity, but not to its awakening effect, so that it remains useful for the treatment of the rare condition of narcolepsy. Cross-tolerance develops between different amphetamines, but not between amphetamine and cocaine, despite their many similarities.

Although chronic users may be taking very large quantities of amphetamine, the existence of physical dependence on it is disputed. When the drug is withdrawn, feelings of fatigue, depression and hunger ensue with prolonged periods of sleep. These symptoms could all be a normal reaction to the lack of sleep and food that occurs with chronic amphetamine use, but it is perhaps more likely that they represent a true withdrawal syndrome. Depression at this time may be so severe that suicidal attempts are made. Psychological dependence on amphetamine undoubtedly develops, and chronic users experience intense craving and exhibit drug-seeking behaviour. Laboratory experiments on animals confirm that it is a powerful primary reinforcer of drug-seeking behaviour.

The most serious consequence of amphetamine abuse is a psychotic illness characterised by paranoid delusions and auditory and visual hallucinations. It usually develops in a setting of chronic amphetamine use and is particularly common if methylamphetamine is injected. It can occur, however, with oral use and may even develop after a single dose of amphetamine. Symptoms usually remit within one week of drug withdrawal. Another complication is automatic, stereotyped behaviour in which some action, such as tidying a handbag, fiddling with a radio or searching compulsively for insects under the skin, continues compulsively for hours at a time.

## KHAT (NOT SUBJECT TO CONTROL)

**3.22** Khat is a tree, *Catha edulis*, that grows at high altitudes in East

Africa, Yemen and Democratic Yemen. The leaves and young shoots have been used for their stimulant effect, certainly for hundreds of years, and are still widely used in several countries, including Democratic Yemen, Ethiopia, Somalia, Yemen, and in parts of Kenya and Tanzania. Modern methods of transport make it easy to bring regular supplies of fresh khat to the towns where it is often sold in special markets. It is commonly used for social recreation and, occasionally, medicinally. In some areas it is estimated that 50–80 % of the male population use khat. Significantly fewer women use it. Nowadays, it is usually chewed, although in the past infusions of the leaves were prepared (Arabian or Ethiopian tea). The khat leaves are plucked from the twig and meticulously chewed, the juicy extract being swallowed while leafy residue is stored on one side of the mouth so that the cheek bulges.

The active principle of khat has been identified as an alkaloid called cathine. Other psychoactive constituents are probably present too. Khat is chewed because of its ability to produce cerebral stimulation. Because of this it was traditionally consumed by tribal people when travelling, and nowadays is taken by long-distance lorry drivers and students preparing for examinations. In Yemen, where it is often taken in a group setting, at special parties, it promotes social interaction, elevates the mood of the group, and induces a general sense of well-being. It may cause sleeplessness which in turn leads to the consumption of sedative-hypnotic drugs. Physical effects of khat include increased heart rate and blood pressure, palpitations and congestion of the face; anorexia and constipation have also been reported.

The ability of khat to cause dependence has not been thoroughly investigated. The general consensus is that it leads to a certain (probably mild) degree of psychological, but not physical, dependence. It has been said that it can cause psychotic illness, although in the apparently rare cases when it does, khat may be acting as the precipitating factor in a susceptible individual.


## LYSERGIC ACID DIETHYLAMIDE (LSD) (CLASS A)

**3.23**  LSD was first synthesised in 1938. It is derived from lysergic acid, a constituent of ergot which is a fungus that grows on rye grains. Poisoning from ergot was not uncommon in the Middle Ages and was called St. Anthony's fire, because the victims used to invoke the help of this saint; a convulsive form of the condition occurred, associated with mental changes, and one can only speculate on the role of LSD in causing these symptoms.

LSD was used medically in the 1950s and 60s, mostly as an aid to psychotherapy, particularly in those patients who had difficulty in freely communicating or associating. Probably because objective research in this area is difficult, there is no clear evidence of its therapeutic value and although a licensing system exists in the UK for doctors to prescribe it if they wish, there are no recognised medical indications for doing so.

During the 1960s, LSD was widely used by those interested in mysticism and exploration of consciousness and it became, together with other similar drugs, part of the hippy culture of that time. As it is very easy for a competent chemist to synthesise LSD, its illicit production and use is difficult to eliminate.

LSD is a white crystalline powder, soluble in water and effective in such minute quantities that doses are measured in micrograms ($\mu$g) (i.e. millionths of a gram). It is taken orally and its effects can be felt with a dose of only 25 $\mu$g, although a more usual dose would be 100 $\mu$g. Within a few minutes the physical effects of its consumption are experienced; they include nausea, headache, dilated pupils, raised pulse rate, a small and variable alteration of blood pressure, and perhaps an increase in body temperature.

### Effects of LSD

**3.24**   The drug is, of course, taken for its psychological effects which are also variable, depending on the expectations of the user and the setting in which drug consumption occurs. Characteristically, there are changes in perception, affecting all the senses and, particularly, vision, so that stationary objects appear to move and change shape, colours become more intense, some things become minute whereas a previously ignored detail looms large and assumes importance. There may be a crossing over of perceptions so that sounds are seen and colours are heard. Although LSD and similar drugs are commonly referred to as "hallucinogens", the experiences usually described are not true hallucinations; rather, they are the altered perception of an existing object and are more accurately described as illusions (and the drugs as psychotomimetics). More rarely, true hallucinations may occur. The perception of time is also altered and it often appears to pass very slowly. Emotional instability is common, with outbursts of weeping or laughter, and there are often mystical feelings of self awareness, of gaining true insight into the nature of life, of contact with God. Such profound experiences may be intensely rewarding or intensely frightening. The LSD user may be completely withdrawn, preoccupied with these experiences, and conversation, if any, may have a mystical and pseudo-philosophical content.

### Tolerance to LSD

**3.25**   Tolerance to the effects of LSD develops rapidly, so that a second dose taken within 24 hours has less effect than the first, and after 3 or 4 daily doses, subsequent administration has little or no effect. Tolerance is lost equally rapidly, and after 3 or 4 days' abstinence, full sensitivity to the effects of LSD is regained. Cross tolerance develops between LSD and similar drugs such as mescalin and psilocybin. There is no evidence that psychological or physical dependence on LSD develops and there is no abstinence syndrome on drug withdrawal.

However, LSD use can have serious adverse effects. Perhaps the most common is a "bad trip", in which the psychological experiences induced by LSD are so frightening that there is an acute panic reaction. "Flashbacks" are the spontaneous recurrence of LSD-induced experiences, without actually taking the drug again; they may also occur after using another drug, usually cannabis, after earlier exposure to LSD. A serious psychotic illness, closely resembling schizophrenia, may also develop occasionally; it is not clear whether this is caused by LSD or precipitated by drug use in a predisposed individual.

As well as LSD, there are many drugs that have similar psychological effects. Many are derived from plants and have a long history of being used in religious rituals. They include mescalin, (Class A), obtained from the peyote cactus, and psilocybin (Class A) from a particular species of mushroom in Mexico. Morning glory seeds also contain lysergic acid derivatives.

**Phencyclidine (Class A)**

**3.26** Phencyclidine (PCP) is a modern synthetic drug with psychoactive properties related to those of LSD. It was developed in 1959 for use in anaesthesia, making use of its property of causing patients to feel detached from bodily sensations and, therefore, unaware of pain. Its use in anaesthesia was abandoned because it so often made patients agitated and deluded. It became, however, a drug of abuse in the USA, where it is known as "angel dust" and where it is often smoked or snorted. It frequently causes unpleasant experiences and is more likely than LSD to cause a serious psychotic illness. It is rarely abused in the UK (yet).

## CANNABIS (CLASS B—LIQUID CANNABIS, CLASS A)

**3.27** Cannabis is another drug that has been known to man for thousands of years. It was used medicinally in the West in the 19th century for a variety of ailments, but now has no approved therapeutic indications and cannot be prescribed by doctors (except under licence from the Home Secretary).

Cannabis is obtained from the Indian hemp plant, *Cannabis sativa*, which is grown in many countries as a source of rope fibre. When the plant is fully grown its flowers and top leaves are covered with a sticky, fragrant resin which contains a number of psychoactive substances, collectively known as cannabinoids, that together make up the drug called cannabis. The most important cannabinoid is delta-9-tetrahydrocannabinol (THC). The THC content of the resin and therefore the potency of the cannabis obtained is affected by the particular variety of the plant that is grown, which part of the plant is gathered (e.g. flowers, leaves) and environmental factors such as climate. A special variety of *Cannabis sativa* is cultivated specifically for its resin in some tropical countries, including those of the Caribbean, S.E. Asia, the Indian sub-continent and Central and South America.

Various preparations of *Cannabis sativa* are available, known by different names in different countries.

(1) *Bhang* is the cheapest and least potent and comes from the cut tops of uncultivated plants with a low resin content.

(2) *Ganja* also comes from the flowering tops and leaves, but from specially cultivated plants, so that the resin content is higher.

Both of these herbal preparations (also known as "grass" or "weed") are usually smoked in hand-rolled cigarettes ("joints" or "reefers"). Potency is variable, with a THC content of between 1 and 10%.

(3) *Cannabis resin* (charas, hashish) is the resin itself in the form of a sticky, brownish cake. It may contain 8–15% THC. It may be smoked in cigarettes or in pipes, including elaborate water pipes such as the hookah. It can also be eaten.

(4) *Liquid cannabis* or hashish oil (Class A) is considerably more potent than cannabis resin and may contain up to 60% THC. It is obtained by subjecting cannabis resin to extraction with a non-aqueous solvent. After filtration and evaporation, a brown syrup-like substance is obtained and tobacco is dipped into this before smoking.

When herbal preparations of cannabis are smoked, each cigarette usually contains 300–500 mg of material, of which approximately 1% is THC. Even if smoked by an experienced user, only 50% of the available THC is absorbed, and so the estimated dose of THC from one cigarette is approximately 2·5 mg. It is absorbed very rapidly through the lungs into the bloodstream and because it is fat-soluble it is taken up rapidly by the tissues. THC and its metabolites may remain stored in body fats for long periods, being released only slowly back into the bloodstream, and traces of metabolites can be detected in the urine for days or even weeks after a single dose.

Although smoking is the usual way of consuming cannabis, it can also be eaten. The onset of action is then slower than if it is smoked and a larger dose is required to obtain the same effect, which then lasts longer.

## Effects of Cannabis

*Physical Effects*
**3.28** The most obvious effects of smoking cannabis are a raised heart rate and a reddening of the conjunctivae of the eyes. Other effects include nausea, vomiting, diarrhoea, yawning and coughing.

*Psychological Effects*
The effects of cannabis vary according to the dose consumed, whether the subject is naive or experienced in cannabis use, his expectations and the setting in which the drug is taken. The sought-after effect is a feeling of euphoria and self-confidence, accompanied by relaxation and perhaps sleepiness. This may be obtained with one cigarette of cannabis, although it appears that an experienced user "learns" how to achieve this high. With increasing dosage, changes in perception occur so that hearing, taste, touch and smell are subjectively (but not objectively) enhanced. There is often an altered perception of time. Concentration and short-term memory may be impaired, leading to difficulty in carrying out complex tasks. Although there is no conclusive evidence, it is likely that the ability to drive a car safely may be adversely affected.

## Tolerance to Cannabis

**3.29** The development of tolerance to the effects of cannabis has often been doubted, probably because in the West even "experienced" users smoke only one or two cigarettes, two or three times a week, and at this dose tolerance is not apparent. In Eastern countries, however, many users consume very high daily doses, suggesting that tolerance can develop, and in laboratory studies, regular cannabis users showed less impairment of performance on objective studies than naive subjects did. In summary, it would appear that there is now no doubt that tolerance to cannabis can and does develop, but it is much less obvious than the tolerance that develops to heroin and cocaine which enables vast doses to be taken without ill effect.

*Dependence*
It is not clear whether physical dependence on cannabis occurs or not. It does not seem to occur in the U.K., but as few people smoke it heavily, this is perhaps not surprising. In those countries where it is more readily available and heavy daily use is common, an inability to stop taking it—

the hall-mark of dependence—does occur, and regular administration of THC under laboratory conditions is followed by some discomfort on drug withdrawal. On the other hand, there is no evidence in terms of craving or drug-seeking behaviour that psychological dependence occurs and only weak evidence from animal studies that cannabis has primary reinforcing properties.

### Adverse Effects

**3.30**  It is not surprising that cannabis does not always induce pleasant psychological effects and that sometimes the sensations it induces are unpleasant and frightening. Adverse psychological effects vary from a mild panic attack to an acute psychotic reaction in which the customary perceptual changes become hallucinations, and the subject may become confused and disorientated and suffer paranoid delusions. Some authorities believe that when psychosis has occurred, cannabis has merely acted as a precipitating factor in a predisposed individual. However, as the occurrence of psychosis appears to be dose-related, it is probably a primary psychopharmacological effect of cannabis (although one that can be modified by personality, setting etc). Most psychotic reactions are transient, lasting only a few hours while the effects of the drug wear off, but a few last much longer and may require hospital admission.

"Flashbacks" are said to occur after cannabis use; this is a recurrence of hallucinations and perceptual disturbance similar to those described at the time of drug use but occurring in the abstinent state. They occur more often when drugs such as LSD have been used too and because of the difficulty of obtaining an accurate account, it is not clear whether they ever occur after the use of cannabis alone.

The long-term effects of chronic use are also a cause for concern; it has been suggested that heavy long-term use may lead to an "amotivational syndrome" with loss of ambition, apathy and social deterioration. There is no definite evidence either for this theory or to confirm that cannabis causes brain damage.

## SEDATIVE-HYPNOTICS (BARBITURATES) (CLASS B)

**3.31**  Barbiturates are chemical derivatives of barbituric acid. The first to be synthesised in 1883 was barbitone (Veronal) which, when it was marketed in 1903, was the first wholly synthetic drug with consciousness-altering properties. Many other barbiturates have since been produced by chemical modification.

Barbiturates act on the brain where they have a depressant or sedative effect. They relieve feelings of anxiety, inducing a sense of relaxation. They also cause drowsiness and, in higher doses, sleep, unconsciousness, general anaesthesia and death. Because they are so effective in relieving anxiety and insomnia, there is a tendency to continue taking them, but with longer-term use tolerance to their effects develops together with dependence, both physical and psychological.

*Hangover Effect*
After taking a barbiturate hypnotic the patient may experience residual drowsiness next day or perhaps some slowing of performance manifesting itself in daily life by an inability to concentrate, make quick decisions or carry out tasks as quickly and efficiently as usual.

## Tolerance to Barbiturates

**3.32** Tolerance develops very rapidly to some of the effects of barbiturates. For example, the first time that a patient takes a barbiturate sleeping tablet because of insomnia, he falls asleep rapidly and sleeps long and apparently soundly. After only a few days, however, he is again taking longer to get to sleep and there is a reduction in total sleep time, and to achieve the original improvement, the dose of barbiturate has to be increased. Thus after a while the habitual barbiturate user may show little sign of sedation and may be sleeping for only an hour or two more than usual on a daily dose of barbiturate that would make anyone not used to taking them deeply sedated. However, tolerance to barbiturate is limited; there comes a point at which even a regular user cannot increase the dose further without experiencing the ill-effects of intoxication, and when a further increase is as likely to be fatal for the regular user as for the non-dependent, occasional user. This is clearly quite different from the situation that arises with opiates, where there seems to be no upper limit to the dose that can be taken by dependent individuals as long as it is increased gradually.

*Physical dependence* on barbiturates is characterised by the manifestations of the abstinence syndrome, and by a state of chronic intoxication that often develops in heavy users. It is difficult to say precisely the dose of barbiturate and the duration of use necessary to cause physical dependence, because it depends on the criteria of dependence that are adopted. If the symptoms and signs of the abstinence syndrome (see para. 3.33 below) are taken as criteria of dependence, a dose of pentobarbitone (Nembutal) of 0·6–0·8 g day for about two months is required, but it is only when 1 g/day is being taken that the majority would suffer from fits and delirium on drug withdrawal.

**Abstinence Syndrome**

**3.33** The symptoms and signs of barbiturate withdrawal develop progressively and include weakness, anxiety, insomnia, nausea, vomiting, sweating, increased pulse rate and muscle twitching and tremor. The time of their onset and duration varies according to the barbiturate being taken, its dose and the period for which it has been taken, but the early symptoms of abstinence usually appear between 8 and 36 hours after the last dose, reach their peak of intensity on the second day, then gradually reduce over the next week or two. If large doses of barbiturates are being consumed, the abstinence syndrome may be more serious, even life-threatening, with epileptic fits and a psychotic mental state rather like alcohol delirium tremens, in which the sufferer is indeed delirious and suffers auditory and visual hallucinations. Convulsions may develop as soon as 12–16 hours after withdrawal, or as late as the 12th day.

**Chronic Intoxication**

**3.34** Because there is an upper limit to tolerance to barbiturates and because barbiturate-dependent individuals often increase their daily consumption beyond this limit, chronic intoxication is a common feature of barbiturate dependence. Again, it is difficult to define precisely the dose level at which signs of intoxication occur, but many barbiturate users at levels equivalent to 1·0–1·2 g pentobarbitone daily will be experiencing drowsiness, difficulty in thinking, emotional instability and agitation. Abusive and aggressive behaviour is also common. With higher levels of consumption, progressive signs of intoxication occur such as slurred speech, unsteadiness, falling, sleep and difficulty in arousing, respiratory depression and death. As the normal hypnotic dose of pentobarbitone is 100–200 mg, and severe intoxication is likely with daily doses of say 2 g, it will be appreciated that while an opiate-dependent subject can take a dose of opiate perhaps 100 times greater than the therapeutic dose without apparent ill-effect, the barbiturate-dependent subject can tolerate a dose only a few times greater than normal. Indeed, this is one of the main dangers of barbiturate-dependence—that tolerance reduces the gap between the dose that can be taken without ill-effect and the fatal dose.

During the late 1960s and 1970s it became common for opiate-dependent individuals and others to abuse barbiturates and other sedative-hypnotics, many of which were widely available on the black market. These tablets were sometimes taken orally, but were often crushed, dispersed in water and injected; the contents of capsules were emptied out and administered in the same way. This process is associated with a number of local complications due to the irritant action of these drugs, and often aggravated by infection. It should be emphasised that no cross-tolerance exists between barbiturates and opiates, so that the former are unable to relieve the withdrawal symptoms of the latter, and vice-versa. What happened was that many opiate addicts also became dependent on barbiturates and suffered the dangers of that condition as well. In particular, they were frequently in a condition of barbiturate intoxication, and barbiturate overdose was a common cause of death.

### Types of sedative-hypnotics

**3.35** A vast number of different barbiturates have been synthesised over the years. Very short-acting barbiturates (thiopentone, methohexitone— not subject to control) are used by intravenous injection for anaesthesia. Long-acting barbiturates (phenobarbitone and methylphenobarbitone— both Class B) are of value in epilepsy, and have not been involved in problems of abuse and dependence. Concern is centred on the barbiturates of medium duration of action prescribed for insomnia and the relief of anxiety. They include:

| | | |
|---|---|---|
| Amylobarbitone | (Amytal, Sodium Amytal) | Class B |
| Butobarbitone | (Soneryl) | Class B |
| Cyclobarbitone | (Phanodorm) | Class B |
| Heptabarbitone | (Medomin) | Class B |
| Pentobarbitone | (Nembutal) | Class B |
| Quinal barbitone | (Seconal sodium) | Class. B |
| Quinal barbitone/ Amylobarbitone | (Tuinal) | Class B |

It is perhaps not surprising that cross-tolerance develops between different barbiturates, and that any of these can be taken to prevent the onset of the abstinence syndrome caused by withdrawal of another. It is less obvious that a considerable degree of cross-tolerance also exists with other nervous system depressants such as alcohol, benzodiazepines and a host of other non-barbiturate hypnotics. Many of these drugs were synthesised in the course of the search for newer and safer drugs, lacking the dependence liability of barbiturates and their serious effects when taken in overdose. Although some of these drugs, particularly the benzodiazepines, do appear safer than barbiturates, any differences are of degree rather than a basic change in the properties of the drug. Thus their effects on the nervous system are similar to those of barbiturates (described above), tolerance develops to their effects, and physical and psychological dependence may also occur.

Before being largely replaced by benzodiazepines, other non-barbiturate hypnotics were widely prescribed and used. They include:

| | |
|---|---|
| Meprobamate (Equanil) | Not controlled |
| Glutethimide (Doriden) | Not controlled |
| Dichloralphenazone (Welldorm) | Not controlled |
| Methaqualone (Mandrax) | Class B |

When taken in overdose all of these drugs show features of poisoning similar to those of barbiturate overdose, although some, such as glutethimide, which is no longer marketed in the UK, were particularly dangerous. Methaqualone (Class B) was available, in combination with an antihistamine, as Mandrax, which became a very common drug of abuse; it too is no longer marketed in the UK.

**Benzodiazepines**

**3.36** Benzodiazepines were introduced into clinical practice in the 1960s and are now the most commonly prescribed minor tranquillisers; they are also used as hypnotics. They are only available on prescription but are not controlled drugs. They relieve feelings of anxiety and tension and relax muscles, as well as having a sedative effect, depressing mental activity and alertness; however they do not generally make people feel drowsy as much as barbiturates do.

Tolerance develops to the effects of benzodiazepines so that long-term treatment with them is not effective. Dependence, both physical and psychological, can also develop although the dependence liability is less than that of barbiturates. The withdrawal syndrome is similar to that of barbiturates; symptoms include insomnia, anxiety and tremor, and after high doses, convulsions and mental confusion. Benzodiazepines are much less likely to be fatal when taken in overdose than barbiturates. Among the many benzodiazepines currently available are:

Diazepam (Valium)
Chlordiazepoxide (Librium)
Flurazepam
Nitrazepam
Lorazepam

*Amnesia*
**3.37** A well-known effect of heavy drinking is transient periods of amnesia or impaired memory ("blackouts"). Sometimes this takes the form of a period of total amnesia, with no subsequent recall of any event during that period and sometimes the amnesia is "patchy" with retained

periods of memory. It is less well-known that impairment of memory may also occur after consumption of benzodiazepines. This effect varies among different benzodiazepines and appears to be related to the dose and route of administration, occuring most often after intravenous administration, less frequently after intra-muscular administration and rarely after oral consumption. Because of the nature of this symptom it is likely to be under-reported and may go unrecognised; memory acquisition, retention and recall may all be impaired and there is greater impairment if alcohol and benzodiazepines are used in combination than if either is used alone. The deleterious effect of this combination is greater if the subject has been taking benzodiazepines for some time and then consumes alcohol, perhaps because this causes an accumulation of the drug and its metabolites (break-down products) within the body.

## SOLVENT MISUSE

**3.38** In recent years, there has been considerable concern about the practice of "glue sniffing". Like most drug abuse problems, it is not a new phenomenon, rather a modern manifestation of the much older problem of inhaling gases or volatile substances such as nitrous oxide, ether, chloroform and petrol. The substances involved nowadays are a wide range of products such as paint-thinners, lighter fuel, glues, laquers and aerosols, all containing a variety of volatile organic compounds such as toluene, benzene, acetone, etc. These products are widely available, present in most homes and on sale in many shops and self-service supermarkets.

The usual method of sniffing is to put some of the substance into a small plastic bag that is then held over the mouth and nose while the fumes are inhaled. Alternatively, it may be inhaled directly from the original container, or some may be decanted into an empty bottle, or soaked on to a rag that is held near the mouth. Aerosols, which are particularly hazardous, may be sprayed directly into the mouth or through a piece of material, or into a plastic bag. Glue-sniffers often have a characteristic facial rash around the mouth and nose due to the repeated application of the plastic bag containing the solvent.

The general effect of inhalation is intoxication, similar to that obtained from alcohol, but achieved very rapidly, because these solvents are absorbed very quickly through the large surface area of the lung. It may last for about half an hour after sniffing, but can be prolonged by intermittent sniffing. Although the desired effect is euphoria, solvent inhalation may also cause giddiness, unsteadiness, slurred speech, impaired judgement, hallucinations and delusions. If inhalation continues it may also lead to loss of consciousness. Occasionally, impaired judgement, together with a euphoric feeling of omnipotence, leads to reckless and dangerous behaviour. Another risk is of suffocation if a plastic bag is put right over the head to retain fumes.

The prevalence of this practice in the UK is not known. It is common among younger teenagers, particularly boys, often as a temporary, local craze and usually as a group activity. Occasionally, one individual persists with the practice, even when his peers abandon it, and appears to become psychologically dependent on solvents. There is no evidence in the form of a withdrawal syndrome that physical dependence occurs, although it appears that tolerance can develop to particular solvents as increasing amounts are used to obtain the desired effect. Long-term use of these highly toxic substances is very dangerous and can result in damage to the liver, kidneys, nervous system and bone marrow.

## POLYDRUG ABUSE

**3.39**  Polydrug abuse, that is the abuse of more than one drug, is not a new phenomenon. During the early 1960s, for example, it was quite common for drug-dependent individuals to take heroin and cocaine simultaneously, often in the same syringe ("speedballs"). During the last 20 years, however, polydrug abuse has become more widespread, and now involves psychotropic drugs with which the general population is familiar, drugs such as antidepressants, hypnotics and tranquillisers. Different drugs may be taken together or separately at different times, according to availability and personal whim; sometimes they are taken in overdose, sometimes the individual concerned is dependent on one or more of these drugs which are also often taken by opiate-dependent subjects. In summary, polydrug abuse is characterised by its disorganised nature, and by the fact that the effects of the drugs being taken are often unpredictable when taken in combination with others, or, as frequently occurs, with alcohol.

The situation now is clearly very different to that in the 1960s when drug abuse and dependency involved drugs with which the general population were unfamiliar, so that those who took them were clearly set apart. Now, many people receive prescriptions from their general practitioners for the same psychotropic drugs that are abused by others. Although some prescriptions are for defined psychiatric illness, many are for personal and interpersonal problems, and many prescriptions are for more than one drug. The boundary between use and abuse is thus less clearly defined than it was formerly. Furthermore, in the context of polydrug abuse, a preoccupation with dependence on one particular substance is out-of-date. To describe the drug-dependent individual as a "heroin addict", and to attribute all of his problems to dependence on the drug for which he has been notified to the Home Office, when he may be dependent on and/or abusing a variety of other drugs, is to over-simplify a complex subject.

CHAPTER 4

# Treatment of Drug Dependence

## INTRODUCTION

**4.01** Drug dependence is a complicated condition resulting from the interaction of many factors and it is not surprising that its treatment is not simple. The details of treatment obviously depend on the nature of the dependence and the drug involved, but in general terms, two phases can be recognised.

### Drug Withdrawal

**4.02** The first is drug withdrawal, which is usually a fairly simple procedure, although for some drugs it requires careful medical supervision. Detoxification is, however, only the beginning; all of the interacting factors—the drug, the individual personality and society—are still present and unchanged by a brief period of drug withdrawal, so that there is a real possibility, even a likelihood, of relapse to drug-taking and drug-dependence. Furthermore, it has been shown for opiates, and the same may be true for other drugs, that minor symptoms of abstinence may persist for months after the last dose of opiate. In other words, subtle physiological and psychological changes may last long after drug withdrawal, predisposing the individual to relapse.

### Rehabilitation

**4.03** Drug withdrawal is therefore only the first phase of treatment and must be completed by a much longer-term response, summarised by the term "rehabilitation", which is the task of integrating the drug misuser into society, so that he can cope without drugs. Ideally these two phases of treatment should occur concurrently rather than sequentially so that rehabilitation starts, through counselling, psychotherapy and social work support, as soon as the individual presents himself for treatment. Unfortunately, and probably because drug withdrawal is the easier component of the package, more emphasis is placed on the provision of facilities for drug withdrawal and much less on the essential long-term planning for rehabilitation facilities. Indeed, a dichotomy has arisen in

55

the U.K. between "treatment", which is the medical component of the response and, therefore, the responsibility of the National Health Service, and "rehabilitation", which is the statutory responsibility of the social services.

## Maintenance

**4.04**   There is, of course, an alternative approach to the treatment of drug dependence when, instead of attempting drug withdrawal, drug maintenance is offered. In other words, the doctor prescribes the drug of dependence for the patient so that the unpleasant symptoms of the abstinence syndrome are avoided. The philosophy behind this approach dates back more than 50 years when the main problem was one of opiate dependence, involving perhaps a few hundred addicts, of whom a large proportion were members of the medical or nursing professions or those who had become addicted during the course of an illness and who did not form any sort of criminal subculture. The Rolleston Committee, which was set up to review and advise on the prescription of morphine and heroin to addicts,[1] did not perceive this respectable group as criminals, and recommended that heroin and morphine could be prescribed to addicts if complete withdrawal produced serious symptoms which could not be satisfactorily treated, or if the patient, while capable of leading a useful and fairly normal life so long as he took the drug of addiction, ceased to be able to do so if the regular allowance were withdrawn.

Thus the principle of maintenance treatment was born and for the next 30 years or so, the situation remained fairly stable, with addicts obtaining supplies of their drugs from their general practitioners. The situation in the USA, where maintenance was banned, was quite different; addiction increased rapidly and was associated with major crime, and these differences seemed to confirm the correctness of the British approach. Even when the number of heroin addicts in the U.K. increased rapidly during the 1960s, and the right to prescribe heroin and cocaine to addicts was limited to those doctors holding a special licence from the Home Office,[2] the basic principle of maintenance was not really questioned. Indeed, it was thought that the legal prescription of opiates for maintenance would undercut and eliminate the black market in drugs. Since then, doubts have been growing. Although the Rolleston Committee permitted more or less indefinite opiate maintenance, it is unlikely that they ever envisaged this as chronic "treatment" for the vast number of young opiate addicts that exist today. In the 1960s, certainly,

1   See para. 1.07 *ante.*
2   Under the Dangerous Drugs Act 1967; see para. 1.13 *ante.* For current Regulations see Chapter 22.

the intention and the hope was that addicts should attend the new drug treatment clinics where, after stabilisation, they would be weaned off drugs. In practice, this rarely occurred and a growing number remained on opiate (methadone) maintenance. More recently there has been a marked trend away from opiate maintenance for newly notified addicts, and strenuous (often repeated) attempts are made to effect opiate withdrawal and to encourage a drug-free lifestyle.

Even though it is used less frequently than before, the option of maintenance treatment for opiate dependence remains, whereas for other types of drug dependence it has rarely, if ever, been used or even considered. For drugs such as LSD and cannabis, which cannot be prescribed by doctors, maintenance is clearly impossible. In the 1960s, when many addicts took cocaine and heroin simultaneously, cocaine was sometimes prescribed when the addicts attended the newly-opened drug treatment clinics. However, this practice soon ceased, perhaps because it was realised that it did not stop addicts from buying more from the black market. Furthermore, as there is no clear-cut physical dependence on cocaine and, therefore, no serious abstinence syndrome, there is no logical reason for continuing to prescribe it. The same is true for amphetamine, but although it is not prescribed as maintenance treatment for dependence, some "slimming clinics" will prescribe amphetamine regularly for long periods for their clients who have undoubtedly become dependent on it.

The other group of drugs for which the question of maintenance treatment warrants discussion is the group of sedative-hypnotics. Barbiturates, in particular, cause a very unpleasant abstinence syndrome which may be of life-threatening severity, so that maintenance might seem a reasonable treatment option. However, because tolerance to the effects of barbiturates is limited, maintenance treatment would keep the patient in an unacceptable state of chronic intoxication, and incapable of leading a useful life.

# TREATMENT

## Treatment Services

### *Medical Practitioners*
**4.05** Any medical practitioner can treat patients with problems of drug dependence, although only those with a licence from the Home Office may prescribe heroin, cocaine or dipipanone to addicts. The patient's own general practitioner may be approached first, but many are unwilling to undertake the care of patients with drug problems whom

they regard as troublesome and time-consuming. A number of private independent practitioners are involved in the treatment of patients with drug problems.

*Drug Treatment Clinics*
Special clinics for the treatment of drug dependence were set up in 1967–68 to deal with the rapidly growing problem of heroin and cocaine abuse. In charge of each clinic is a consultant psychiatrist; other clinic staff may include junior doctors, nurses, social workers, a clinical psychologist and secretary. At first, most of these clinics were in or near London, but as the drug abuse problem has grown numerically and spread geographically, other clinics have opened, and in its recent report,[3] the Treatment and Rehabilitation Working Group of the Advisory Council on Misuse of Drugs has recommended that each Regional Health Authority should establish a multidisciplinary regional drug problem team based in an existing, or new treatment clinic. Soon, therefore, every Region should have at least one specialist drug treatment clinic.

Patients may be referred by their general practitioner or another doctor, or by a social worker, probation officer or other agency. Some refer themselves, although some clinics insist on a formal referral letter from another doctor.

Because the clinics were set up in response to an alarming increase in heroin addiction, the treatment of opiate dependence has always been their most important responsibility. Permanently under-staffed and under-financed, they have had neither the facilities nor the resources to deal with other types of drug dependence. The modern trend towards viewing substance abuse as a whole rather than in terms of individual drugs of abuse and dependence is, however, bringing about a change in the role of the clinics. Many clinics are now prepared to see and treat patients with other types of drug problems, such as solvent-sniffing or sedative-hypnotic abuse, usually in separate sessions to those attended by opiate-dependent individuals. It is hoped that the clinics will, in time, be perceived as a more ordinary place to seek help for all types of drug-related problems, rather than as the "end of the road" for long-term opiate addicts receiving maintenance prescriptions.

*In-patient Treatment*
In-patient facilities specifically for the treatment of drug-dependent patients are very limited. Patients may be admitted for assessment, for

3 *Treatment and Rehabilitation: Report of the Advisory Council on the Misuse of Drugs,* H.M.S.O., 1982.

stabilisation of dose, for detoxification, for treatment of the complications of drug dependence or for a general sorting out of chaos. They may remain in hospital for a period of rehabilitation which may be on or off drugs. In-patient detoxification is essential for barbiturate-dependent patients, because of the risks associated with barbiturate withdrawal.

## Rehabilitation Services

### Social Workers

**4.06** Although rehabilitation is the logical extension of treatment, little provision is made for it. Social workers are vitally important members of the multi-disciplinary team of the Drug Treatment Clinics, but usually have to deal with an unrealistic number of patients so that the long-term out-patient contact necessary for counselling and support is often difficult to maintain.

### Probation Service

Another source of help is the Probation and After-Care Service for the large proportion of drug misusers who have had contact with the criminal justice system. Like that of social workers, the work of probation officers involves care and support within the community and they are often instrumental in referring clients on to other rehabilitation agencies.

### Voluntary Agencies

Many religious and charitable institutions have perceived that the needs of drug-dependent individuals for rehabilitation are not being met, and with the strong tradition of voluntary work that exists in the U.K., have set out to fill this glaring deficiency. In so doing, they have gained skills and experience that cannot be matched by statutory services so that the government's role in the provision of rehabilitation has become confined to providing funding for the work of the voluntary agencies. Because rehabilitation services have developed in this way, they have done so in an unplanned, haphazard fashion, according to local interests, local skills, local needs and the money available.

*Drug-free Residential Rehabilitation Houses.* The provision of residential facilities by voluntary agencies is a very important component of rehabilitation, and there are a number of drug-free, residential houses. They can be divided into three categories—Christian-based hostels, therapeutic communities and community-based hostels, each with their own therapeutic style.

*ROMA.* In contrast, ROMA (Rehabilitation of Metropolitan Addicts) is a hostel that helps addicts to attain a stable life-style, but does not require them to give up drug-taking.

*City Roads (Crisis Intervention).* This centre was set up to provide assessment, detoxification and onward referral for multiple drug misusers, particularly those dependent on barbiturates. It offers short-term (three week) intervention at a time when the patient is likely to be responsive to such help.

In addition to the services out-lined above, there are a variety of counselling services working with young drug misusers, in different localities. Local self-help groups also exist in many areas, often for the parents of drug-dependent individuals. (See Appendix XIV.)

## Psychotherapy

**4.07**  Various types of psychotherapy may be used in the treatment of drug dependence. They include group therapy, family therapy, marital therapy and behavioural or cognitive therapy. Any of these approaches may be appropriate, regardless of the drug of dependence or abuse. In the drug treatment clinics, where the majority of patients are dependent on or abuse opiates, they are mostly used for this particular group. However, as the scope of the clinics widens, other types of drug dependence may be treated using similar techniques.

## Treatment of Opiate Dependence

**4.08**  Most patients contacting the drug treatment clinics for the first time either are, or say they are dependent on opiates. An accurate diagnosis of their dependence status is essential, as a regular prescription for opiates could convert an occasional user into an addict, or could be diverted to the black market. On the other hand, withholding a prescription because of doubts about the patient's dependent status often means that the patient will not attend the clinic. Assessment, therefore, needs to be thorough and usually takes 2–3 weeks. A careful history is taken, including age at first use, subsequent drug-taking, injecting, medical complications etc. The diagnosis of opiate dependence also relies heavily on urine tests being positive for opiates.

If the patient is diagnosed as being physically dependent on opiates, an opiate will be prescribed. This is usually an oral methadone mixture, because its long duration of action permits once daily administration, the complications of self-injection are avoided and it has less black market value than injectable opiates. The dose to be prescribed is decided individually, the aim being to prescribe the minimum dose so that the patient has to take it all personally to prevent the onset of withdrawal syndrome, and has no surplus to produce euphoria or to sell. In practice, most patients nowadays require 30–80 mg methadone daily. This is issued daily so that the patient does not have an excessive amount at any time to sell on the black market, or to overdose. The prescription form is posted direct to the retail pharmacist with whom a special arrangement has been made.

Although indefinite maintenance on prescribed opiates is permissible and theoretically possible, it condemns the patients, most of whom are young, to a state of chronic dependence. Clinic staff then seem to have little more to do than issue regular prescriptions and become frustrated by their therapeutic impotence, and by frequent confrontations with patients about which drug should be prescribed and in what dose. For these reasons many people have come to believe that all addicts should at least be offered the opportunity of coming off drugs, and a new approach is a treatment contract which is agreed between patients and staff before opiates are prescribed for the first time. Opiate prescription is only part of the contract, which includes weekly attendance, getting a job wherever possible and giving up illicit drug use. The dose of opiate is gradually reduced over an agreed period (a few months) and other goals are worked for simultaneously. This approach reduces confrontation between staff and patients about drug dosage and enables them to work together towards other goals, putting the drug abuse into its true perspective. Repeated contracts may be necessary.

In-patient detoxification permits a more rapid drug-withdrawal. Once the patient has been stabilised on methadone, the dose is reduced by 5 mg on alternate days. Careful observation is carried out to detect signs of the abstinence syndrome.

## Treatment of Barbiturate Dependence

**4.09** Those who abuse barbiturates and become dependent on them often have chaotic life styles and are often chronically intoxicated. Admission to hospital is usually necessary to sort out the chaos, and to stabilise them on a dose of pentobarbitone which is then gradually reduced. This has to be done in hospital so that the signs of withdrawal can be carefully monitored and the risk of withdrawal fits is minimised. Fits may occur up to 10 days after barbiturate withdrawal is completed. Serious overdoses are also frequent among these patients, causing unconsciousness and respiratory depression. They are treated medically and may require admission to an intensive care unit.

### Treatment of Benzodiazepine Dependence

**4.10**   Withdrawal of benzodiazepines, although less risky than barbiturate withdrawal, should also be carried out gradually. Symptoms of withdrawal often mimic the symptoms for which benzodiazepines were originally prescribed, encouraging the patient to believe that the drugs are still required.

### Treatment of LSD Abuse

**4.11**   There is no specific treatment for abuse of LSD. The panic attack associated with a "bad trip" is often best dealt with by someone experienced in LSD use who may be able to "talk down" the affected individual. Psychotic reactions usually improve with drug withdrawal. A phenothiazine drug (e.g. chlorpromazine) may sometimes be necessary and may also be helpful if flashbacks are frequent and troublesome. Phenothiazines are sedatives which relieve florid psychotic symptoms such as hallucinations and delusions, and are used for the treatment of serious mental disorders. They do not cause dependence and are rarely abused because of their unpleasant side-effects.

### Treatment of Cannabis Dependence

**4.12**   There is no specific treatment for cannabis dependence. Psychotic reactions are dealt with similarly to those caused by LSD.

### Treatment of Amphetamine Dependence

**4.13**   Although amphetamine-dependent individuals may be consuming large quantities of the drug, the symptoms and signs of withdrawal, if present at all, are mild and do not require treatment. A depressive reaction can develop, however, and should not be ignored because suicide may be attempted. Amphetamine-induced psychosis usually responds to drug-withdrawal. Phenothiazines may be necessary.

### Treatment of Cocaine Dependence

**4.14**   There is no specific treatment for cocaine dependence or for managing drug-withdrawal. Psychotic reactions may require treatment with phenothiazines.

## Treatment of Solvent Misuse

**4.15** Specific treatment is rarely needed except in cases of psychotic reaction. Advice and support to the family of the young solvent misuser may be valuable as it prevents panic and over-reaction. Counselling by one experienced in the problems of adolescence is often all that is required. The rare case in which solvent misuse persists after the peer-group has given it up may be difficult to treat, requiring long-term counselling and support.

# PART II
# *CUSTOMS AND EXCISE ACTS*

CHAPTER 5

# Offences Relating to Importation and Exportation of Controlled Drugs

Relevant provisions of the Customs and Excise Management Act 1979 are set out in Appendix I.

## The Prohibitions

**5.01** The import and export of controlled drugs except under a licence issued by the Home Secretary is prohibited by section 3(1) of the Misuse of Drugs Act 1971. (Controlled drugs and their classification are dealt with in Chapter 9.) Certain medicines containing a limited proportion of controlled drugs are specified in Schedule 1 to the Misuse of Drugs Regulations 1973 (S.I. no. 797)[1] and (together with poppy straw) are exempted from the prohibition. The exemption would cover such medicines as aspirin/codeine compounds for headaches and kaolin and morphine for diarrhoea. It is an offence to contravene a term of a licence (section 18(2) Misuse of Drugs Act 1971).

## THE OFFENCES

**5.02** The prohibitions are effected by sections 50, 68 and 170 of the Customs and Excise Management Act 1979 (the relevant sections are set out in Appendix I).

Section 50 is concerned with importation and makes it an offence for any person to import or be concerned in importing prohibited goods, whether or not the goods are unloaded, with intent to evade the prohibition. Section 68 is concerned with exportation and makes it an offence for any person to be knowingly concerned in the exportation or attempted exportation of prohibited goods, with intent to evade the prohibition. Section 170 is concerned with the fraudulent evasion of both prohibitions. Subsection (1) makes it an offence to knowingly acquire possession of prohibited goods or to be knowingly concerned in removing, harbouring or concealing such goods with intent to evade the prohibition. Subsection (2) makes it an offence to be in any way knowingly concerned in any fraudulent evasion or attempted evasion of

1 Set out in Appendix IV.

the prohibition. The predecessor of section 170, section 304 of the Customs and Excise Act 1952, was described by Lord Salmon in *D.P.P. v Doot* (1973) 57 Cr.App.R. 600 at p. 623 as being a longstop for sections 45 or 46 of that Act to catch anyone against whom actual importing and exporting could not be proved although it was wide enough to cover importing and exporting also. In practice prosecutions for importing or exporting controlled drugs are brought under subsection (2) of section 170. (For penalties see para. 8.01). The offences arise from the combination of the two Acts and not from the Misuse of Drugs Act 1971 alone, but the offence can be described or charged as an offence arising under either or both Acts. However the underlying offences are offences under the Customs and Excise Acts (*R v Whitehead* (1982) 75 Cr.App.R. 389) so that the relevant procedural and consequential provisions of those Acts are applicable.

## Postal Packets

**5.03** Section 16(1) of the Post Office Act 1953 (set out in Appendix II) applies the provisions of the Customs and Excise Acts to importations and exportations by post. However Regulation 5(*h*) of the Postal Packets (Customs and Excise) Regulations 1975[2] has the effect that exportation is deemed to take place when the goods are posted or re-directed. (The relevant regulations are set out in Appendix II.) Postal traffic from abroad is routed through Overseas Mail Offices. Customs officers are stationed at such offices and they have power to open packets for examination (Regulation 12). If controlled drugs are discovered in a packet it is handed over by the Post Office (Regulation 17) to Customs officers who remove the drugs. The packet is then re-packed with an innocuous substance and delivered by the Post Office in co-operation with customs officers. This procedure was followed in , for example, *R v Williams* (1971) 55 Cr.App.R. 275.

## Knowledge

**5.04** Sections 68(2) and 170(2) use the words "knowingly concerned", section 170(1) uses the words "knowingly acquires possession", whereas section 50(2) uses the words "with intent to defraud". In the case of a prosecution under any of these provisions it is necessary to prove that the defendant knew he was dealing with the goods and that he knew that they were prohibited: *Frailey v Charlton* [1920] 1 K.B. 147. It is not necessary to prove that he knew the precise category of the prohibited goods. In the case of *Hussain* (1969) 53 Cr.App.R. 448 Lord Justice

2   S.I. no. 1992.

Widgery gave judgement in the following terms (p. 451):

> "It seems perfectly clear that the word 'knowingly' in the section in question is concerned with knowing that a fraudulent evasion of a prohibition in respect of goods is taking place. If, therefore, the accused knows what is on foot is the evasion of a prohibition against importation and he knowingly takes part in that operation, it is sufficient to justify his conviction, even if he does not know precisely what kind of goods are being imported. It is, of course, essential that he should know that the goods which are being imported are goods subject to a prohibition. But it is not necessary he should know the precise category of the goods the importation of which has been prohibited."

The case of *Hussain* was concerned with Section 304 of the Customs and Excise Act 1952. That Act was amended by section 26 of the Misuse of Drugs Act 1971 to provide increased penalties for persons convicted of offences in relation to controlled drugs. Maximum penalties were dependent on whether the drugs belonged to Class A, B or C. (Sections 304 and 26 have in effect been re-enacted by section 170 and Schedule 1 of the Customs and Excise Management Act 1979.) This amendment could produce difficulties for a sentencer. If, for example, a defendant who pleaded guilty to an indictment for importing heroin claimed that he believed it was pipradol the judge would need to hear evidence on oath to enable him to decide the basis on which to sentence, since the maximum sentence applicable to heroin (a Class A drug) is fourteen years[3] whilst that for pipradol (a Class C drug) is five years.

In *R v Hennessey and Others* (1978) 68 Cr.App.R. 419 the defendant claimed that he believed he was involved in smuggling blue films—the importation of which is prohibited. The trial judge directed the jury that that was not a defence. The Court of Appeal held the judge correct to base his summing up on the decision in *Hussain*. The court's attention was not drawn to the possible change in the position following the enactment of section 26 of the Misuse of Drugs Act 1971.

There the law rested in what would seem a satisfactory state from the point of view of Her Majesty's Customs and Excise until the trial and appeals of Mr. Taaffe.[4] At his trial at the Crown Court the defendant claimed that he believed he was importing money, not cannabis as turned out to be the case. He was under the mistaken impression that there was a prohibition on the importation of currency. The trial judge ruled that the fact that he was mistaken in his belief that currency was a prohibited substance did not afford him a defence and the defendant pleaded guilty. The Court of Appeal allowed his appeal, holding that the goods which

3　Increased to life imprisonment by the Controlled Drugs (Penalties) Act 1985 for offences committed after 16 September 1985.
4　*R v Taaffe* (1983) 77 Cr.App.R. 82 C.A.; (1984) 78 Cr.App.R. 301 H.L.

the appellant believed himself to be concerned with had to be in fact prohibited goods. He had to be judged against the facts as he believed them to be. His mistaken belief concerning the law could not turn what was not an offence into an offence. The Crown appealed to the House of Lords, which upheld the decision of the Court of Appeal. In so doing, however, Lord Scarman cast doubt on the present effectiveness of the decision in *Hussain* (*supra*) although it was rightly decided at the time. Lord Scarman drew attention to the decision in *Courtie* (below) and to the fact that section 26 of the Misuse of Drugs Act 1971 had substituted several different offences for one offence (for penalties see para. 8.01 *post*). In his opinion the decision in *Hennessey* (above) needed to be reconsidered.

*R v Courtie* (1984) 78 Cr.App.R. 292 was concerned with an act of buggery contrary to section 12 of the Sexual Offences Act 1956 on a male person aged nineteen years. By section 3(1) of the Sexual Offences Act 1967 different penalties apply according to whether or not it is proved that the victim did or did not consent. The indictment was silent on this factor in the offence. The appellant pleaded guilty but claimed that the victim did consent. The trial judge heard evidence and then passed sentence on the basis that the victim did not consent. The Court of Appeal held that Section 12 read with Section 3(1) of the later Act created two separate offences.

It seems that it is only a matter of time before the Court of Appeal is asked to rule that each of sections 50, 68 and 170 of the Customs and Excise Management Act 1979 read with Schedule 1 create a number of different offences which must be separately indicted according to (a) the Act imposing the prohibition, and (b), if that Act is the Misuse of Drugs Act, the Class of drug involved. The Customs and Excise Management Act does not contain a provision equivalent to section 28(3)(*a*) of the Misuse of Drugs Act 1971, which would appear to preclude to some extent the decision in *Courtie* from affecting prosecutions under that Act. On the other hand it is already the practice to specify in Customs prosecutions the class of drug involved (see model indictment at para. 26.06 *post*) so that a defendant has no doubt what he is pleading to. It may be that the situation under the Sexual Offences Acts is not on all fours with that under the Customs and Excise Acts. In each case the offence-creating provisions of the latter refer to "any prohibition or restriction for the time being in force with respect to the goods under or by virtue of any enactment".

Where a defendant has revealed his defence in the depositions it might be possible for the prosecution to draft alternative counts on the indictment, leaving it for the jury to decide whether the alleged mistaken belief was a genuine one. This course would hardly be a satisfactory one where the defence was not that the defendant was mistaken as to the nature of the drugs, but that he believed he was importing something quite different such as blue films. The maximum penalty for smuggling blue films is two years' imprisonment.

### Evidence of Knowledge

**5.05** It must be proved by the prosecution that at the time when he was involved with the goods the defendant knew that they were prohibited goods. This is proved either directly by the words or admissions of the defendant or circumstantially by proving that the defendant concealed them or denied their being in his possession. In the case of *R v Fernandez* [1970] Crim.L.R. 277 the defendant was charged with possession of cannabis under the Drugs (Prevention of Misuse) Act 1964 rather than with importation under the Customs and Excise Acts. He was a seaman who was given a package to bring to England. He was told it contained sticks for smoking, he saw the contents and appreciated that he might get into trouble with the Customs. However he claimed he did not know the package contained drugs. The Court of Appeal, in applying *Warner v Metropolitan Police Commissioner* [1968] 2 All E.R. 356, held that if the defendant took a package into his possession in a situation in which he should certainly have been put on inquiry as to the nature of what he was carrying and yet he deliberately failed to pursue an inquiry and accepted the goods in circumstances which must have pointed the finger of suspicion at their nature and the propriety of his carrying them, then it was a proper inference that he accepted them whatever they were. It was not open to him to say that he was not in possession of the goods because he did not know what they were.

Assistance may be obtained from decisions concerning handlers of stolen goods. It is not conclusive to show that the defendant received or was involved with the goods in circumstances which should have put a reasonable man on inquiry. The test is a subjective one. A jury may be directed that in common sense and in law they may find that the defendant knew the goods to be prohibited because he deliberately closed his eyes to the circumstances. They may not be directed that the offence is proved if the defendant, suspecting that the goods were prohibited, deliberately shut his eyes to the circumstances: *R v Griffiths* (1975) 60 Cr.App.R 14. In other words they may draw an inference from a "blind eye" but the "blind eye" is not, in itself, proof of knowledge.[5]

## DEFINITIONS

### Fraudulent Evasion—Intent to Defraud

**5.06** "Defraud" does not mean cause economic loss in this context. It

5 See also paras. 11.04 and 13.04 *post*.

means causing a person performing public duties to act contrary to his public duty (*per* Lord Diplock in *Scott v Metropolitan Police Commissioner* (1975) 60 Cr.App.R. 124 at p. 131 and see *R v Borro and Abdullah* [1973] Crim.L.R. 513). In *Attorney-General's Reference (No. 1 of 1981)* (1982) 75 Cr.App.R. 45 the Court of Appeal considered the meaning of the words "fraudulent evasion". The facts of the reference were that drugs were unloaded from a ship in the early hours when there was no Customs officer on regular duty at the port. The trial judge held that since no Customs officer had been deceived, the facts did not come within the definition of fraudulent evasion. The Court of Appeal held that it is inappropriate to import narrow definitions of the word "fraudulent" from branches of the law concerned with fraud practised on other persons. In the context of smuggling offences the word has the meaning of "intentional and deliberate, that is to say without mistake". An offence can be committed by avoiding Customs control altogether. There is no necessity for the prosecution to prove acts of deceit practised on a Customs officer in his presence. If goods are not unloaded or remain within the Customs area, there is nevertheless a fraudulent evasion of a prohibition: *R v Smith* (1973) 57 Cr.App.R. 737. A person who knowingly comes into the possession of uncustomed cigarettes and "uses" them by smoking them and giving them away is guilty of the offence of keeping uncustomed goods with intent to defraud the revenue: *Sayce v Coup* [1953] 1 Q.B. 1. "Evade" means "to get around" or "to avoid"—it does not necessarily carry a connotation of fraud or dishonesty: *R v Hurford-Jones and Others* (1977) 65 Cr.App.R. 263.

*Possession*
**5.07**   See "Meaning of Possession" at para. 11.03 *post.*

**Time of Importation and Exportation**

**5.08**   This is defined in section 5. Goods are imported when the ship carrying them comes within the limits of a port,[6] when the aircraft carrying them lands in the United Kingdom or the goods are unloaded (presumably by parachute) whichever is the earlier, or when the goods are brought by land across the boundary into Northern Ireland. Passengers' baggage, however, is imported when the ship carrying it enters the port at which it is discharged.

Goods are exported by sea or by air when the exporting ship or aircraft departs from the last port or Customs and Excise airport at which it is cleared. They are exported by land when they are cleared by

6   By a series of statutory instruments made under the Customs and Excise Acts the whole coastline of the United Kingdom is brought within such limits.

the proper officer at the last Customs and Excise station on their way to the boundary. Goods sent by post are deemed to be exported when they are posted (see para. 5.03).

## Meaning of "Importation"

**5.09** Prohibited goods are, subject to the exception below, imported when they arrive in the United Kingdom. The action is complete without the goods having to clear customs control. Goods in an aeroplane that lands at Heathrow are imported even though it is intended that they should remain in the Customs area and be re-loaded onto an aeroplane bound for Bermuda. It is clear that the Customs and Excise Acts comtemplate that goods can be imported before they are either landed from a ship or unloaded from an aircraft: *R v Smith* [1973] 2 All E.R. 1161 C.A. It is no defence that the route taken necessitated a stop in the United Kingdom: *R v Borro and Abdullah* [1973] Crim.L.R. 513.

Passengers' baggage brought in by ship is in a slightly different situation. This is deemed to be imported when the ship carrying it comes within the limits of the port at which the goods are discharged. If passengers' baggage were to remain on board a ship which called at a United Kingdom port *en route* for other destinations, then small quantities of controlled drugs in the baggage would be part of the baggage and would not be imported. However, if the quantities were such that they clearly indicated that the passenger had a commercial purpose in mind, they would be merchandise rather than passengers' baggage and their presence would amount to an importation within the meaning of the Customs and Excise Acts: *Buckland v The Queen* [1933] 1 K.B. 767.

## Meaning of "Exportation"

**5.10** Prohibited goods are exported even if it is intended to bring them back to this country: *R v Berner and Others* (1953) 37 Cr.App.R. 113. Goods are exported if the aircraft carrying them lands in the United Kingdom and they are transferred to an aeroplane which takes off for a foreign destination without the goods being removed from the Customs area: *R v Smith* [1973] 2 All E.R. 1161.

## "*Concerned In*"
**5.11** A person who arranges to sell prohibited goods that are despatched to him from abroad is concerned in their importation: *R v Williams* (1971) 55 Cr.App.R. 275.

A person who is a party to importing prohibited goods into the United

Kingdom as a staging post for their onward transmission to another country is concerned in the fraudulent evasion of the prohibition: *R v Smith* [1973] 2 All E.R. 1161.

A person who took luggage containing cannabis onto an aeroplane in Lagos but *en route* changed her mind, tore up the baggage tickets and failed to collect the baggage in England, was nevertheless concerned in its importation: *R v Jakeman* (1983) 76 Cr.App.R 223.

A person can be concerned in the exportation of goods by doing things in advance of the time when the aircraft leaves. Delivering articles to another knowing that he is going to export them amounts to being concerned in their exportation: *Garrett v Arthur Churchill (Glass) Ltd* [1970] 1 Q.B. 92.

In the case of *Martin John King* C.A. 11 May 1984 (unreported) the appellant was a passenger in a car entering the U.K. which his co-defendant had packed with cannabis. He claimed that although he knew the cannabis was there, it was nothing to do with him. He was asked why he did not get out of the car and come back alone and he replied "I don't know". On the ferry his co-defendant gave the appellant £100 and told him to go ashore on foot. If the co-defendant failed to clear Customs, the appellant was to telephone an accomplice. He appealed against his conviction on the grounds that he was not concerned (i) because the importation was not a consequence of anything that he did and (ii) because to tell an accomplice that the importation had failed could not assist the importation. The Court allowed the appeal on another ground concerning corroboration of an accomplice but applied the proviso to section 2 of the Criminal Appeal Act 1968 by which the conviction was maintained on the ground that no miscarriage of justice had actually occurred. The grounds set out above were rejected. Purchas L. J. held:

> "Providing acts take place and the actors are knowingly concerned in acts which form part of the whole scheme, then in our judgement it matters not that the scheme is doomed to failure if at the time when the act upon which the prosecution relies is carried out, the accused person is knowingly concerned in an expedition whose object is the fraudulent evasion . . . . . . . When the appellant agreed to take part in the telephoning it was all part of the execution of the enterprise itself."[7]

## EVASION OR ATTEMPT AT EVASION

**5.12** The Customs and Excise Management Act 1979 section 170(2) creates separate offences of committing the full offence and of attempting the offence: *R v Miller and Hanoman Ltd* [1959] Crim.L.R. 51—see para.

7   See also para. 7.05 *post.*

26.06 *post*. Attempt at evasion under section 170(2) is now an attempt under a special statutory provision to which subsections (3), (4) and (5) of section 3 of the Criminal Attempts Act 1981 apply. Subsection (3) provides that a person is guilty of such an offence if, with intent to commit the full offence, he does an act which is more than merely preparatory. Subsection (4) makes it an offence to attempt the impossible. Subsection (5) provides that if, had the facts been as the defendant believed them to be, his intention would have amounted to an intent to commit the full offence, then he is to be regarded as having that intent. It would therefore seem to follow that if a defendant concealed sand in his petrol tank and failed to declare it in the belief that he had concealed heroin, he would be guilty of attempted evasion of the prohibition. This topic is discussed in paragraph 5.15 *post*.

Since controlled drugs are prohibited, importation takes place as soon as the goods arrive in the United Kingdom (5.08 *ante*). It follows that even if the drugs are discovered at Customs control, the full offence has been committed. (If goods are merely subject to duty, evasion is not completed until Customs control has been evaded).

The *actus reus* of section 170(2)(*b*) is being knowingly concerned in evasion or attempted evasion in respect of prohibited goods—not the successful evasion of the prohibition. Evasion is a continuing offence and it does not cease when the goods are seized by the authorities. Evasion continues until the goods cease to be prohibited goods—for example when they are destroyed. These propositions were expressed by the Court of Appeal in the course of its judgement in the case of *R v Green* [1976] 1 Q.B. 985. The facts of that case were that a crate arrived at the docks with an inventory indicating that it contained goods such as a child's desk. It was opened by Customs officers and found to contain bags of cannabis. The cannabis was replaced by peat and the crate allowed to continue to its destination. It was taken by haulage contractors to a garage rented by the defendant. He was indicted for being knowingly concerned in the fraudulent evasion of the prohibition and for conspiracy to evade the prohibition. It was argued for the defendant that the seizure of the cannabis by the Customs rendered the offences thereafter ones that it was impossible to commit. The Court of Appeal held that (1) fraudulent evasion was a continuing offence and the defendant could be convicted of the substantive offence even if he had nothing to do with the crate until after the cannabis had been removed, and (2) only the lifting of the prohibition would prevent the conspiracy being unlawful. The re-enacting of section 304 of the Customs and Excise Act 1952 as section 170 of the Customs and Excise Management Act 1979 has not affected the validity of the decision in *Green* and nor has the definition of the time of importation in section 5: *R v Nesbitt and Others*, C.A. 10 July 1981 (unreported), where an attempt to argue that the enactment of section 5 invalidated the decision was dismissed as frivolous and vexatious.

A similar situation to that in *Green* had been considered by the Court of Appeal in relation to a count of conspiracy to acquire possession of prohibited goods contrary to section 304 of the Customs and Excise Act 1952, the predecessor of section 170(1). That was the case of *R v Ardalan and Others* [1972] 2 All E.R. 257. The facts were that the Customs intercepted a cargo of cannabis at Heathrow. They followed their usual practice of removing the cannabis and re-packing the containers with an innocuous substance. Thereafter the defendant conspired with other defendants to take delivery and arrangements were made for the containers to be delivered. It was argued that since all the activities in connection with the conspiracy were remote from Heathrow and remote in time from the importation, no offence took place. The Court dismissed the appeal, holding that (1) there was no distinction between uncustomed goods and prohibited goods, and (2) there was no limit in time or place on the commission of an offence provided that the goods are the subject of a prohibition.

The decision in *Green* (*supra*) is merely a development in a line of cases concerning possession of dutiable goods. For example in the case of *Beck v Binks* [1949] 1 K.B. 250 Lord Goddard held that a person knowingly carrying uncustomed goods is assisting in the smuggling of the goods: "for while goods are no doubt smuggled when they are brought into the country, it is no good bringing smuggled goods into the country unless something can be done with them. Such a person is intending to defraud His Majesty as much as anybody else."

When Customs officers suspect the presence of prohibited goods they exercise the power conferred on them by section 159 Customs and Excise Management Act 1979 (set out in Appendix I) to open containers and examine goods and remove any prohibited goods. They then frequently repack the containers with an innocuous substance and allow the containers to be collected or delivered in order to arrest the recipients, as in the case of *Green* (*supra*). This is also their practice with postal packets (see para. 5.03).

In the case of *R v Neal and Others* (1983) 77 Cr.App.R. 283 it was held (in a prosecution under section 170(2)) that there was no necessity to establish a link between concealing prohibited goods and the actual importation. This case is discussed further at para. 6.02 *post*.

**Acts Done Abroad**

**5.13**   Acts done abroad in order to further the fraudulent evasion of the prohibition on importing controlled drugs into the United Kingdom are punishable in the U.K. Taking part in despatching drugs from abroad to England is triable here because the evasion or attempted evasion takes place in England: *R v Wall* [1974] 2 All E.R. 245 C.A., applying *R v Baxter* [1971] 2 All E.R. 359 C.A.—a case which concerned attempts to obtain property by means of letters posted in Ireland which contained false pretences. Even if the goods fail to arrive in the United Kingdom the offence of attempt is triable here (Criminal Attempts Act 1981, section 1(4)), although it would be wise to indict under section 50 rather than 170(2) (and see para. 5.15 *post*).

## Conspiracies made Abroad

**5.14**  In the leading case of *D.P.P. v Doot* (1973) 57 Cr.App.R. 600 the House of Lords considered the question whether an agreement made outside the jurisdiction of the English courts to import a dangerous drug into England is a conspiracy which can be tried in England. The facts were that a number of American citizens agreed to bring cannabis resin into England and transport it across the country for export to Canada. The agreement was made in Belgium or Morocco. Three defendants were arrested in England with quantities of cannabis hidden in secret compartments in their Volkswagen vans and two with only a small quantity for their own use. All of them were indicted with conspiracy to import dangerous drugs.

The Court of Appeal (1973) 57 Cr.App.R. 13 had held that the essence of conspiracy is the agreement to do an unlawful act. The offence is completed when the agreement is made. Acts in furtherance of it are evidence of it but are not constituent parts of it. The Court therefore, although with reluctance, held that there was no jurisdiction to try the case. The Court certified that the following question involved a point of law of general public importance: whether an agreement made outside the jurisdiction of the English Courts to import a dangerous drug into England and carried out by importing it into England is a conspiracy that can be tried in England.

The House of Lords, however, were unanimous in reversing the decision and holding that such a conspiracy could be tried in England but their reasoning differed:

(1) Lord Pearson described the three stages in the existence of a conspiracy as: (a) making or formation; (b) performance or implementation; (c) discharge or termination. When the agreement has been made the conspirators can be prosecuted but the fact that the offence is complete does not mean that it is finished with. If it is being performed it

is still very much alive. It continues in operation until it is discharged. Where an agreement is entered into abroad to commit in England an offence against English law and it is wholly or partly carried out in England, Lord Pearson held that it has been carried out with the consent and authority of all the conspirators and therefore it has been committed in England personally or through an agent or agents by *all* the conspirators (p. 619). Lord Wilberforce expressed his agreement with Lord Pearson's judgement (p. 604).

(2) Lord Wilberforce went on to hold that in the normal case of a conspiracy carried out or partly carried out in this country, the location of the formation of the agreement is irrelevant: the attack on the laws of this country is identical wherever the conspirators happen to meet (p. 606). Lord Salmon held that a conspiracy to commit a crime in England is an offence against the common law even when entered into abroad, certainly if acts in furtherance of the conspiracy are done in this country (p. 626). He would not express an opinion on the position of a member of such a conspiracy coming to England for an entirely innocent purpose unconnected with it.

(3) Viscount Dilhorne based his opinion on the fact that a conspiracy is a continuing offence giving the English courts jurisdiction only if the conspiracy, wherever it was formed, was in existence when the accused were in England (p. 614).

It is clear from their Lordships' speeches that there is jurisdiction to try persons who enter into a conspiracy abroad to commit an offence in England if one or more of them comes to England to act in furtherance of the conspiracy or if it is carried out in England by agents such as an airline or a shipping company. Lord Salmon seems to go further by saying that such a conspiracy on its own amounts to an offence at common law but he weakens his position by refusing to express an opinion on the position of a conspirator who enters the country for a purpose unconnected with the conspiracy. Viscount Dilhorne founds jurisdiction on the continuance of the conspiracy in England even though it was formed abroad—this would appear to require that two or more of the conspirators should be in England at the same time.

An attempt was made to distinguish the position of the appellants in *R v Borro and Abdullah* [1973] Crim.L.R. 513 from that of the appellants in *D.P.P. v Doot*. The facts were that the appellants brought cannabis from Beirut *en route* for Antigua. They had to stay overnight in London but their baggage remained in the custody of the airline. It was argued on their behalf *inter alia* that (1) the route taken necessitated a stop in London, and (2) since the baggage remained in the control of the airline the appellants did nothing in England to implement the conspiracy. The

Court of Appeal found no factor or combination of factors which took the case outside the decision in *Doot*.[8]

## Attempt

**5.15** An attempt to breach a prohibition (which constitutes an indictable offence) effected by a provision of the Customs and Excise Acts (other than an offence under a special statutory provision such as section 170(2)) is now an offence under section 1 of the Criminal Attempts Act 1981. The Act is intended to reverse the decision in *Haughton v Smith* [1975] AC 476 which decided that it was not an offence to attempt the impossible. Subsection (1) provides that a person is guilty of an attempt to commit an offence if, with intent to commit the full offence, he does an act which is more than merely preparatory. Subsection (2) makes it an offence to attempt the impossible. Subsection (3) is in the following terms:

> "(3) In any case where—
>    (*a*) apart from this subsection a person's intention would not be regarded as having amounted to an intent to commit an offence; but
>    (*b*) if the facts had been as he believed them to be, his intention would be so regarded;
> then, for the purposes of subsection (1) above, he shall be regarded as having had an intent to commit that offence."

Subsection (4) provides that the section applies to any offence which, if it were completed, would be triable in England and Wales as an indictable offence. Similar provisions apply to attempts under section 170(2) by virtue of section 3.

The Court of Appeal in *R v Shivpuri* (1984) 80 Cr.App.R. 241 held that subsection (4) clearly suggested that the prosecution no longer had to establish that the substantive offence would have been committed if the accused's acts had not been interrupted. In that case the appellant believed that a suitcase which he had agreed whilst in India to look after contained heroin. The suitcase was delivered to him in England. It did not contain heroin but some vegetable matter akin to snuff. He was charged with attempting to deal with and attempting to harbour a controlled drug contrary to section 170(1)(*b*). The Court held that the fact that the commission of the full offence was impossible was irrelevant (subsection (2)) and that the appellant had the requisite intent because he believed that the substance was a controlled drug (subsection (3)).

In *Shivpuri* the Court of Appeal judged that the Criminal Attempts Act 1981 had achieved its intention of reversing the decision in *Haughton v*

---

8   For a case of a conspiracy in England to send drugs to the U.S.A. see para. 15.02 *post*.

*Smith,* but the House of Lords in *Anderton v Ryan* (1985) 81 Cr.App.R. 166 has since decided that Parliament has failed. The situation is further complicated by the fact that the Court of Appeal in *Shivpuri* referred to its own decision in *Anderton v Ryan* (1985) 80 Cr.App.R. 235 which has now been reversed by the House of Lords. The facts in *Anderton v Ryan* were that on a count of attempting to handle particular stolen goods the prosecution were unable to prove that they were in fact stolen. The appeal therefore proceeded on the basis that the goods were not stolen. In his judgement in the House of Lords Lord Roskill held that subsection (2) had achieved the effect that a man who tried to pick an empty pocket would be guilty of attempted theft, but that subsection (3) did not make a man guilty where he had an erroneous belief in facts which, if they were true, would have made his completed act a crime. Lord Roskill concluded:

> "Subsection (3) covered the case of a defendant possessed of a specific criminal attempt which he erroneously believed to be possible of achievement but which in fact was not possible of achievement. It did not however make a defendant liable to conviction for an attempt to commit an offence when, whatever his belief on the true facts, he could never have committed an offence had he gone beyond his attempt so as to achieve fruition."[9]

His Lordship criticised the drafting of the Criminal Attempts Act but his judgement has certainly created just as many difficulties. Does it mean that a man who intends to import heroin but is mistaken in the material he purchases abroad is not guilty of attempt? Perhaps the answer is that there is nothing impossible about importing heroin. He was not concerned about the particular quantity he brought with him, unlike the defendant in *Anderton v Ryan,* who, it may be supposed, did not go out intending to purchase any stolen goods, but when a particular video recorder was offered to her, took it in spite of the fact that it was stolen. Whatever the importer in fact brought in with him, he intended to bring in heroin. Only the means adopted prevented the completion of the offence. His position is closer to that of the unsuccessful pickpocket.

It would seem from an examination of Lord Scarman's judgement in *D.P.P. v Nock* (1978) 67 Cr.App.R. 116 (discussed at para. 10.08 *post*) that the answer may lie in an examination of whether the defendant had a general intention to smuggle heroin or a specific intention to smuggle the particular substance with which he was caught.

A recent case which discusses the tests to be applied in judging whether acts are merely preparatory is *R v Mohammed Ilyas* (1984) 79 Cr.App.R. 17. The Court of Appeal appears to approve either of two tests:

9    As reported in *The Times,* 13 May 1985.

(1) The offender must have crossed the Rubicon and burnt his boats. He must have done all the physical acts lying within his power to complete the offence (*D.P.P. v Stonehouse* (1977) 65 Cr.App.R. 192 at p. 208); or

(2) The *actus reus* is complete if the offender does an act which is a step toward the commission of the specific crime, which is immediately and not merely remotely connected with the commission of it, and the doing of which cannot reasonably be regarded as having any other purpose than the commission of the specific crime: *Davey v Lee* (1967) 51 Cr.App.R. 303.

So far as trials on indictment are concerned every allegation of an offence includes an allegation of attempting to commit that offence (section 6(4) Criminal Law Act 1967).

## Defence of Duress

**5.16**   It is a defence that the defendant agreed to bring drugs to England under threat of death or serious injury. In *R v Valderrama-Vega* [1985] Crim.L.R. 220 it was so held but the proviso to section 2 of the Criminal Appeal Act 1968 was applied by which the conviction is maintained on the ground that no miscarriage of justice has actually occurred. The proper direction would appear to be: "It is a defence that the defendant acted as the result of threats of death or serious injury to himself or members of his family operating on his mind at the time of his act and of such gravity that they might well have caused a reasonable man placed in the same situation to act as he did." The word "solely" which has been used in such directions should be omitted. If the defence of duress is raised then the burden of proof rests upon the prosecution to disprove it because the defendant is not required to establish his innocence—see for example *Bullard v The Queen* (1957) 42 Cr.App.R. 1.

# CHAPTER 6

# Evidential and Procedural Provisions

## EVIDENCE

### Proof of Certain Matters

**6.01** Section 154(1) Customs and Excise Management Act 1969 makes provision for the proof of matters averred in proceedings under the Customs and Excise Acts. These matters are specified in the subsection and include averments that (1) proceedings were instituted by the orders of the Commissioners, (2) a person was an officer of Customs and Excise or a constable, (3) a person was appointed or authorised by the Commissioners to discharge any duty, (4) the Commissioners have or have not been satisfied as to any matter as to which they are required by any provision of the Acts to be satisfied and (5) goods destroyed or thrown overboard were so dealt with to avoid seizure. The fact that such matters are averred is, until the contrary is proved, sufficient evidence of the matter in question.

### Burden of Proof on Defendant

**6.02** Section 154(2) provides that where proceedings are brought by or against the Commissioners, their officers, or other persons in relation to the Customs and Excise Acts, then if any question arises as to the place from which goods have been brought or as to such matters as whether or not duty has been paid, goods have been lawfully imported or are subject to any prohibition on their importation or exportation, the burden of proof shall lie upon the other party to the proceedings.

This statutory provision is in addition to the normal rule of law that the prosecution do not have to negative the possession by the defendant of licences or consents or prove that he does not come within statutory exceptions or exemptions. If the true construction of an enactment is that it prohibits the doing of a certain act save in specified circumstances, it is not for the prosecution to prove a *prima facie* case of lack of excuse or qualification because the onus of proof shifts and it is for the defendant to prove that he is entitled to do the prohibited act. It follows that even if the prosecutor has access to a register of licences it is not incumbent on him to prove that the defendant does not have one: *R v Edwards* [1974] 3 W.L.R. 285 C.A. (A case under the Licensing Acts).

In the case of *R v Cohen* [1951] 1 K.B. 505 the Court of Appeal considered the effect of section 259 of the Customs Consolidation Act 1876 which contained the words:

> "If in any prosecution in respect of any goods seized for non-payment of duties . . . . . . . . . . . any dispute shall arise whether the duties of customs have been paid in respect of such goods . . . . . . . . . then and in every such case the proof thereof shall be on the defendant in such prosecution . . . . . . . . ."

Customs officers visited the defendant at his home where he showed the officers some watches and denied that he had any more. The search revealed many more watches, the subject of prosecution for knowingly harbouring uncustomed goods (now contrary to section 170(1) 1979 Act). Lord Goddard C.J. held that to prove a conscious harbouring it would usually be enough to show that goods which were subject to duty were found in the possession of the accused. If they were found in his house, warehouse or other place under his control that would establish a *prima facie* case that he knowingly harboured them. Once it was established that the accused knowingly harboured the goods, section 259 threw on him the onus of proving that the goods were in fact customed. If he gave no explanation he might be convicted of harbouring. If he did give an explanation, the jury should be told that if it either satisfies them that he did not know the goods were uncustomed or leaves them in doubt whether he knew, he should be acquitted. Another case dealing with uncustomed watches is *Beck v Binks* [1949] 1 K.B. 250 (see para. 5.12). No distinction can be drawn between uncustomed goods and prohibited goods in this respect: *R v Ardalan* [1972] 2 All E.R. 257 at p. 261.

The decision in *Cohen* (above) does not appear to have been considered by the Court of Appeal in reaching its decision in *R v Watts and Stack* (1979) 70 Cr.App.R. 187. In that case, which was concerned with dealing in a prohibited drug, the prosecution proved that the defendants were in possession of cocaine. They did not prove, as they could easily have done, that the coca shrub does not grow in England and that cocaine is not manufactured in England. They relied on section 290 of the Customs and Excise Act 1952 (which is identical to section 154 of the 1979 Act) to reverse the burden of proof on the question of whether or not the goods had been lawfully imported. They contended:

(a)   that it was an offence to possess any prohibited substance even if it had been grown in England; and

(b)   that section 290 cast on the defendants the burden of proving that the goods had not been imported.

Contention (a) was obviously wrong and the Court of Appeal allowed the appeal on that ground. However they then delivered (*obiter*) the opinion that section 290(2)(*c*) (now section 154(2)(*c*)) was not apt to refer to an issue of whether the goods have been imported or not. Lord Justice Bridge went on to direct that prosecutions should not be brought under section 304 (now section 170) where the prosecution is unable to establish a link between any prohibited importation and the dealing. If this decision were effective in reducing the scope of section 170, the Customs and Excise would have to rely on the relevant provisions of the Misuse of Drugs Act 1971.

The decision in *Watts and Stack* was not followed by the Court of Appeal in *R v Neal and Others* (1983) 77 Crim.App.R. 283, which held that the direction in *Watts and Stack* was *obiter*. The facts of this case were that two defendants, Anthony Cardwell and D'Antone, visited Neal at his farmhouse and arranged for him to receive and conceal some 6 cwt of cannabis resin. Anthony Cardwell then recruited his brother. The two Cardwells and D'Antone played parts in the delivery of the resin to Neal, who concealed it behind a wall which he built inside his barn. Neal admitted that he knew the resin was imported. He said, "Obviously it has been imported but I do not know how, where or when and I do not want to know." The prosecution called evidence that the resin was Lebanese in origin. The trial judge rejected submissions based on the judgement in *Watts and Stack* and all four defendants were convicted and appealed. The appeals were unsuccessful. The Court of Appeal held that section 170(2) was inserted by the draftsman with the intention of casting his net as widely as words enabled him. Following the judgement in *Ardalan*, they held that section 170(2) cannot be considered as applying only to those engaged upon the initial importation.

**Proof of Documents**

**6.03**   Section 153(1) is concerned with the proof of certain documents signed or authorised by the Commissioners. Subsections (2) and (3) apply the Documentary Evidence Act 1868 to documents issued by the Commissioners. This means that such documents may be proved by the production of a copy printed by the government printer. Subsection (4), which was added by the Finance Act 1981, makes a certified photocopy of a document delivered to the Commissioners admissible in any proceedings to the same extent as the document itself.

## OFFENCES BY BODIES CORPORATE

**6.04**   Where it is proved that an offence has been committed by a body corporate with the consent or connivance of, or to be attributable to any neglect by, a director, manager, secretary or other similar officer, then that officer, as well as the body corporate, shall be guilty of that offence (section 171(4). There does not appear to be any decision on the bearing of this provision on drug offences but the whole scheme of drugs legislation would appear to indicate that knowledge of the facts of the offence must be proved before anybody can be convicted of it. Section 21 of the Misuse of Drugs Act 1971 is similar (see para. 15.03).

## PROCEDURE

### Institution of Proceedings and Place of Trial

**6.05** By section 145 prosecutions and proceedings for condemnation under the Customs and Excise Acts may only be instituted by order of the Commissioners or in the name of a Law Officer, except that, where a person has been arrested for an offence under the Acts, a court may proceed to deal with him although it has not been so instituted. If the process avers that the proceedings are instituted by the Commissioners, that is sufficient evidence that they are so instituted (see para. 6.01 *ante*). Proceedings instituted in a magistrates' court are to be brought in the name of a Customs officer. In the case of the death or absence of the officer, another officer authorised by the Commissioners may continue the proceedings. The whole section applies equally to a prosecution for conspiracy to evade a prohibition by virtue of section 4(3) of the Criminal Law Act 1977. Where police officers detained the appellants for conspiracy to evade the prohibition, the Court of Appeal held that there was no need for the prosecution to obtain an order from the Commissioners before bringing a prosecution: *R v Whitehead* (1982) 75 Cr.App.R. 389.

In effect proceedings may be commenced in any court in that part of the United Kingdom where the offence was committed (section 148(1)). This means that if an offence is committed anywhere in England and Wales, the Customs and Excise may commence proceedings in any magistrates' court in England and Wales. If the offence was committed outside the jurisdiction, it is deemed to have been committed within the jurisdiction of the courts in that part of the United Kingdom where the offender is found (section 148(2)).

### Limitation of Time

**6.06** Proceedings for an offence under the Acts must be instituted within three years of the date of the offence, except that where it was not practicable to arrest a defendant at the time of the commission of the offence or he escaped from arrest, time will run from the date when he is finally arrested (section 138(2) and section 147(1)). This provision in effect excludes the usual rule that summary proceedings must be commenced within six months from the time when the offence was committed. The limitation does not apply to civil proceedings such as forfeiture proceedings.

### Magistrates may not Change Mode of Trial

**6.07** Where a magistrates' court has begun to enquire into any information proffered under the Customs and Excise Acts, they may not proceed under section 25(3) of the Criminal Law Act 1977 to try the information summarily without the consent of the prosecutor (section 147(2)).

### *Prosecution's Right of Appeal*

**6.08** The prosecutor may appeal to the Crown Court against any decision of a magistrates' court in proceedings under the Customs and Excise Acts (section 147(3)).

### Procedural and Evidential Provisions of Customs and Excise Acts Apply

**6.09** Prosecutions under sections 50, 68 and 170 are prosecutions under the Customs and Excise Acts and the various provisions of those Acts rather than the provisions of the Misuse of Drugs Act 1971 apply to such prosecutions. This is the effect of the decision in *R v Williams* (1971) 55 Cr.App.R. 275, where the Court of Appeal decided that it was not necessary to obtain the leave of the Attorney-General under section 20 of the Dangerous Drugs Act 1965 for a prosecution under section 304 of the Customs and Excise Act 1952 (section 304 is the predecessor of section 170). This decision was followed by the Court of Appeal in *R v Whitehead* (1982) 75 Cr.App.R. 389 on the grounds that the "underlying offence" is an offence under the Customs and Excise Acts.

### Evidence of Value

**6.10** Section 171(3) is concerned with fixing the value of goods for the purpose of calculating penalties (see para. 8.02 *post*). The question sometimes arises of whether the prosecution is entitled to prove the street-level value of goods seized as part of their case to prove the guilt of accused persons. Very often the defence are willing to make a formal admission of the value.[1] If the defence challenges the relevance of such evidence, it is submitted that the following considerations arise:

1 For proof of value see para. 11.10 *post*.

(1) Does the value help to explain the steps that the accused are alleged to have taken to smuggle in the drug? These may include sending watchers on separate flights to countries such as India, elaborate chains of meetings between couriers, watchers and the ultimate receivers of the drug and complicated and expensive methods of concealment. Steps that might seem fantastic in relation to a few thousand pounds may become credible when it is realised that millions of pounds are at stake.

(2) Does the value help to explain steps that accused persons have taken to space themselves from other accused persons or to lie to investigators?

## Witness Statements made outside the United Kingdom

**6.11**　A witness statement taken outside the United Kingdom can be used at committal proceedings under section 102 of the Magistrates' Courts Act 1980. Section 46(2) of the Criminal Justice Act 1972 provides that section 102 applies to such a statement but that it need not include the usual declaration that it is true to the best of the witnesses knowledge and belief etc. If the witness is made the subject of a conditional witness order, the statement may be read at the trial in the Crown Court in pursuance of section 13(3) of the Criminal Justice Act 1925. But if the witness is not subject to a conditional witness order, his statement cannot be read on the grounds that he is dead, unable to travel etc., because subsection (7) of section 102 is excepted from application to statements taken abroad by section 46(2).

Where a statement taken outside the United Kingdom is served on the defence too late for it to be used at committal proceedings, it can only be read at the trial under section 9 of the Criminal Justice Act 1967 if various conditions are satisfied. Subsection (2)(*b*) requires the statement to contain the usual declaration. This may be of practical significance where evidence is taken abroad in pursuance of a Commission Rogotoire (see para. 6.12 below). In some countries a witness statement is made in a prescribed form which does not include a declaration which satisfies the requirement. In such circumstances the statement can only be read if the defence will admit that it is true under section 10 of the Criminal Justice Act 1967. If the defence will not make such an admission, the witness must be called in person.

*Commissions Rogatoires and the Naples Convention*
**6.12**　A Commission Rogatoire is an authority granted by one country to another for the obtaining of witness statements from persons resident in that country. A request for a Commission Rogatoire is made by the Customs (or the police) in the United Kingdom to the Foreign Office,

who forward it to the Embassy or High Commission of the relevant country. When it is granted, Customs officers (or police officers) go to the country concerned and, accompanied by police officers of that country, interview the witness. The form of the statement may be dictated by the laws of the host country. (The provisions applying to foreign requests to obtain witness statements in the United Kingdom are section 5 of the Extradition Act 1873 and section 5 of the Evidence (Proceedings in Other Jurisdictions) Act 1975.)

The United Kingdom acceded to the Convention of 7 September 1967 between the Member States of the E.E.C. on the Provision of Mutual Assistance by Customs Authorities (the Naples Convention) on 23 January 1974. The Convention provides for exchange of information and mutual assistance to prevent contraventions of customs law. Article 12 is concerned with officials appearing as witnesses before the courts of another contracting state and Article 13 with the examination of witnesses, experts and persons wanted for contravention of customs laws. The contracting states are Belgium, the Federal Republic of Germany, France, Italy, Luxembourg, the Netherlands, Denmark, the United Kingdom and the Republic of Ireland. The provisions of the Convention are set out in Appendix XIII.

The Council of the European Community has issued regulations and directives concerning customs co-operation.

*Foreign Documents—Copies*
**6.13**   Copies of foreign documents are admissible to the extent that the original would be if it is impossible to bring the original within the jurisdiction.

A Customs officer went to Morocco where he made a photostat copy of a hotel register—the hotel refusing to part with the original. The register showed that the defendant's name had been entered as staying the night of 13 to 14 October. Lord Justice Lane, sitting in the Queen's Bench Division of the High Court, applied the reasoning in *R v Nowaz* [1976] 3 All E.R. 5 C.A. where it was held that if it was impossible to enforce the production of a document because the person in possession of the original was beyond the jurisdiction of the court, secondary evidence as to the contents of the documents was admissible. That rule applied to criminal as well as civil proceedings. Although it was not necessary for the Divisional Court to make a final pronouncement on this means of satisfying the requirements of section 1(1) of the Criminal Evidence Act 1965, Lord Lane did say that it seemed highly likely that the contentions of Counsel for the Customs and Excise were correct: *R v Ipswich Justices ex parte Edwards* (1979) 143 J.P. 699.

## Some Cases On Evidence

**6.14** Whilst the evidence against a courier bringing drugs into the country rarely presents legal problems, questions of relevance and admissibility arise in pressing a charge against parties one or more steps removed from the courier.

The appellant in *R v Diana Kay Willis* C.A. 29 January 1979 (unreported) came through the customs with two photograph albums. Concealed in the covers was opium and heroin. She denied any knowledge of the drugs. In the loft of her flat was found a teaspoon on which were detected traces of heroin. In a chest of drawers was found 80 mg of heroin. She appealed against her conviction on the ground that the evidence discovered in her flat was irrelevant and inadmissible. Lawton L.J. gave judgement holding that the finding of the spoon and the heroin in the flat was relevant to the issue of knowledge. It tended to show that the appellant was connected with heroin in the United Kingdom. This decision was applied in the appeal of *Christakis Peter Alexiou* C.A. 14 November 1983 (unreported). The facts of the case were that a consignment of chandeliers was examined at Heathrow Airport. The packing boxes had false bottoms in which were concealed slabs of cannabis resin. The slabs were removed and the consignment left in the K.L.M. freight shed. They were addressed to a Mr. Shipton. The appellant's co-defendant, Mr. Andriotis, hired a van, collected the consignment and took it to 67 Clonmell Road where the appellant was waiting. He helped to carry the boxes into the house. Once they were inside the house, customs officers arrested both men. Inside the house were various articles including a jigsaw which was contaminated with cannabis. Subsequently the appellant's house in Romilly Road was searched and a suitcase and scales found on both of which were detected traces of cannabis. Inside a bread-bin was £600 and documents were found covering the purchase of the jigsaw. The appellant explained his presence at Clonmell Road by saying that he had let the house to his co-defendant and met him there to give him the keys. He was going to be paid for helping to carry in the boxes. It was submitted that the evidence concerning Romilly Road went to show that the appellant might have been involved in previous importations but that it was irrelevant to the current importation. Mr. Justice McCowan gave judgement that the evidence was relevant to the question of knowledge of the fact that cannabis had been hidden in the boxes and to rebut the defence that his presence at Clonmell Road was innocent. His Lordship referred to the decision in *Willis* and held that it was binding upon the court.

In *R v John Phillip Ypres Thrussel* C.A. 30 November 1981 (unreported) the appellant and his co-defendant, Hardy, travelled from London to Chicago, Miami and Peru in May 1980. The appellant had made a similar journey in January. On 25th May Hardy left Peru, went through Heathrow and on to Paris. He then returned to England by sea. In a false compartment in his suitcase the customs found 2.93 kilograms of cocaine. The appellant left Peru on 26th May and followed a similar route. Within minutes of his arrival at his home customs officers arrived and searched his premises. In his house was found a book entitled "Cocaine Consumers' Handbook" and $27,500. Another $17,900 was also discovered. He admitted taking Hardy to Peru but claimed that he needed someone to look after him because he had been ill and also because he was collecting large sums of money; he knew nothing about the cocaine trade. He said that he had found the book when he had been renovating a hotel. The book contained a chapter about the cocaine trade. It was argued that the evidence of the finding of the book was irrelevant and inadmissible. The Court of Appeal held that the possession of the book was something that would require explanation in anybody's hands. It was relevant to the issue of knowledge and provided the last link in the chain of evidence.

# CHAPTER 7

# Powers of Detention and Search

Section 114(2)(9) of the Police and Criminal Evidence Act 1984 empowers the Treasury by order to direct that any provision of that Act which relates to investigation of offences by police officers and to detention of persons by the police shall apply to investigations and detentions by customs officers. It is likely that such an order will be made in the near future. Relevant provisions of the Act are set out in Appendix IX and see Chapter 16 *post.*

## DETENTION OF PERSONS

**7.01**   Any person who has committed an offence under sections 50(2) or (3), 68(2) or 170(1) or (2) of the Customs and Excise Management Act 1979 or whom there are reasonable grounds to suspect of having committed such an offence may be arrested by a Customs officer, coastguard or member of H.M. Armed Forces within three years of the commission of the offence (section 138(1)).[1] This provision extends to conspiracy to commit such an offence: *R v Whitehead* [1982] 75 Cr.App.R. 389.

Any offence for which a person may be arrested under the Customs and Excise Acts is an arrestable offence for the purpose of the Police and Criminal Evidence Act 1984 (section 24(2)).[2] It would appear also to be a "serious arrestable offence"—see para. 16.07 *post.*

The arrest will not be lawful unless the arrested person is informed at the earliest opportunity of the charge or suspicion which is the ground for his detention: *Christie v Leachinsky* [1947] A.C. 573 and section 28 of the Act of 1984 (set out in Appendix IX).

A person held in custody is entitled, if he so requests, to consult a solicitor under section 58 of the Act of 1984 and to have a friend or relative informed (section 56).

## POWERS OF SEARCH

### Power to Examine Goods

**7.02**   An officer of Customs and Excise has power to examine any goods

1   For limitation of time see para. 6.06 *ante.*
2   Conspiracy to commit, attempting, inciting, aiding etc. such an offence are also arrestable offences (S. 24(3)).

which are imported or in a warehouse and may require that containers should be opened or unpacked (1979 Act, section 159). "Queen's warehouse" and "warehouse" are defined in section 1.

## Power to Search Premises

**7.03**   An officer in possession of a writ of assistance may, where there are reasonable grounds to suspect that anything liable to forfeiture is kept or concealed in any building or place, enter and search and as far as is reasonably necessary break open doors, windows and containers. (Forfeiture is dealt with in para. 8.05). A writ of assistance is a prerogative writ issued to a named officer and valid for the reign in which it is granted and for six months thereafter (section 161(6)). The only limitation on this power is that if it is exercised at night the officer must be accompanied by a constable (section 161(2)). In addition, a Justice of the Peace may issue a search warrant containing similar powers and subject to the same limitation if it is to be exercised at night (section 161(3) and (4)).

It is likely that Part II of the Police and Criminal Evidence Act 1984 will be applied by order to customs investigations. It is set out in Appendix IX. It is further likely that section 114(2)(b) of the Act will be brought into force, amending the Customs and Excise Management Act 1979 by the addition of a new section 14A which is also set out in Appendix IX.

## Power to Search Vehicles and Vessels

**7.04**   Officers of the Customs and Excise, constables, members of the armed forces and coastguards are empowered by section 163 to stop and search vehicles and vessels where they have reasonable grounds to suspect the presence of goods liable to forfeiture. There is a penalty on summary conviction of £100 for refusing to stop. They have powers to board ships within the limit of a port, (by a series of statutory instruments made under the Customs and Excise Acts the whole coastline of the United Kingdom is within such limits), aircraft within customs airports and vehicles crossing the border with Eire and rummage them (section 27) without any need to justify their action. They can lock up, seal and mark goods, or break open containers (section 28). Any goods found concealed in such circumstances are liable to forfeiture.

## Power to Search Persons

**7.05**   Section 164 empowers an officer of Customs and Excise to search any person whom he suspects of carrying prohibited goods. Such a person has a right to require that he should be taken before a Justice of the Peace or a superior officer who shall decide whether there are sufficient grounds for suspicion to order a search. This power is restricted to the categories of person set out in subsection (4). These include persons who are on board ships or aircraft or who have landed from them, persons entering or leaving the United Kingdom and persons in the dock areas of ports and at airports. The section is relied on as authority to carry out, *inter alia*, intimate body searches. The suspect must be informed of the reason for the search—see para. 16.03 *post*.

Whatever provisions of the Police and Criminal Evidence Act 1984 may be applied by order to the Customs, the exercise of section 164 will not be limited (section 114(3)). If section 55 (see para. 16.08 *post*) is applied, the order applying it may limit it in its application to intimate body searches for objects likely to cause injury (section 114(2)(*b*)(ii)), leaving the Customs to operate section 164 for intimate body searches for drugs. Section 55 does, however, apply to searches in relation to the export of drugs (section 55(17)).

## Obstruction of Officers

**7.06**   Section 16 makes it an offence punishable with a maximum of two years' imprisonment to obstruct or hinder a person engaged in the performance of duties under the Customs and Excise Acts. This includes impeding a search, destroying goods liable to forfeiture or doing anything calculated to prevent the procuring or giving of evidence.

# CHAPTER 8

# Penalties and Forfeiture

## PENALTIES

**8.01**   Penalties for offences under sections 50, 68 and 170 of the Customs and Excise Management Act 1979 are provided for in Schedule 1 to the Act (set out in Appendix I) by way of variation of those sections. The maximum penalty varies according to the classification of the drug in respect of which the offence was committed. On trial upon indictment the maximum penalty in respect of Class A drugs is life imprisonment;[1] in respect of Class B drugs it is 14 years' imprisonment; in respect of Class C drugs, 5 years; and in respect of all classes of drug an unlimited fine. On summary trial the maximum period of imprisonment is six months and three times the value of the goods or the "prescribed sum", whichever is the greater. (The "prescribed sum" is provided by section 171(2) and is at present £1,000 in respect of Classes A and B drugs). In respect of Class C drugs the maxima are 3 months' imprisonment and three times the value of the goods or £500, whichever is the greater. By section 149, where a magistrates' court imposes a term of imprisonment in default of paying a fine, that period, together with any period of imprisonment imposed in respect of that offence shall not exceed fifteen months.

The court is required by Article 36(*a*)(iii) of the Single Convention on Narcotic Drugs 1961[2] to take account of foreign convictions for drug offences as establishing recidivism when passing sentence. It would seem that this requirement, whilst not incorporated in the Act, can be given full weight: *Trawnik v Ministry of Defence* [1984] 2 All E.R. 791.

### Market Value

**8.02**   Section 171(3) provides that where a penalty is to be fixed by reference to the value of the goods, that value is the value in the open market. In arriving at such a value the court is not constricted by the distinction between a so-called black market and white market. What is being sought is the price which a willing seller would accept from a

---

1   Imposed by the Controlled Drugs (Penalties) Act 1985 for offences committed on or after 16 September 1985.
2   Set out in Appendix XI.

willing buyer for these goods: *Byrne v Low* [1972] 3 All E.R. 526. In the case of *Barr v Nuez*, heard on 14 May 1982 in the Court of Appeal (unreported), the accused was convicted of smuggling cocaine in the form of cocaine paste which would need to be converted into cocaine hydrochloride before the drug was sold on the streets. The value was nevertheless given as the potential value after conversion and this approach was upheld by the Court of Appeal, which said, "The proper approach to take is the potential street value of this material."
(For proof of value see para. 11.10 *post*.)

## Drugs Intended for Use in a Foreign Country

**8.03** The fact that drugs are not intended for consumption in the United Kingdom does not constitute a mitigation. The courts cannot look with indifference or leniency on conduct which has the object of introducing into a foreign country drugs that are prohibited there: *R v Winter* [1973] Cr.L.R. 63 C.A.

*Guidelines on Sentence*

**8.04** Guidelines to sentencers were laid down in December 1982 by the Lord Chief Justice in *R v Aramah* (1983) 76 Cr.App.R. 190. After describing the evils of the trade and the profits that could be earned, his Lordship said that consequently anything which the courts of this country could do by way of deterrent sentences on those found guilty of crimes involving these Class A drugs should be done. The appropriate sentences suggested are summarised as follows:

(1) *Class A*[3]

| Importation | — £1 million or more | — 12 to 14 years |
|---|---|---|
| | £100,000 or more | — upwards of 7 years |
| | appreciable | |
| | quantities | — at least 4 years |

(2) *Class B*  (with particular reference to cannabis)

| Importation | — large-scale or | |
|---|---|---|
| | massive | — 10 years |
| | 20 kilos or more | — 3 to 6 years |
| | up to 20 kilos | — 18 months to 3 years |

The Lord Chief Justice further stated that the personal circumstances and character of an offender was of less importance than in other cases because traffickers seek as couriers persons who would have a powerful

---

3 The maximum penalty is increased to life imprisonment by the Controlled Drugs (Penalties) Act 1985 for offences committed on or after 16 September 1985.

mitigation if they were caught. Hoever, where couriers have given information or been of considerable assistance to the police and have pleaded guilty, this conduct should be marked by a substantial reduction in what would otherwise be the proper sentence.

The considerations applicable to sentences for offences in relation to heroin apply equally to other Class A drugs. Any idea that those who import cocaine or LSD should be treated more leniently is wrong. The Lord Chief Justice so held in dismissing an appeal against a sentence of four years' imprisonment for importing 23·7 grams of cocaine worth about £3,000 at street level: *R v Martinez* [1985] Crim.L.R. 109.

## FORFEITURE

### Forfeiture of Prohibited Goods

**8.05** Any prohibited goods that are imported (section 49(1)) or exported or brought to any place for the purpose of being exported (section 68(1)) are liable to forfeiture. Such goods may be seized or detained by any Customs officer, constable or member of Her Majesty's armed forces or coastguard (section 139). The procedure to be followed is prescribed by section 139 and Schedule 3 to the 1979 Act. In practice controlled drugs are forfeited automatically because they are normally seized in the presence of a person whose offence or suspected offence occasioned the seizure (para. 2(*a*) of Schedule 3) and no notice claiming that the goods are not liable to forfeiture is given within the prescribed period of one month.[4]

### Forfeiture of Ships, Vehicles, etc.

**8.06** Ships, aircraft, vehicles and containers used for carriage or concealment of goods liable to forfeiture and anything mixed or packed with such goods are also liable to forfeiture (section 141(1)). In addition the owners or masters of such aircraft, ships not exceeding 100 tons and hovercraft are liable on summary conviction to a penalty equal to the value of the craft or £500, whichever is the less (section 141(2)). With certain exceptions ships exceeding 250 tons are not liable to forfeiture (section 142) but penalties may be imposed in lieu (section 143). Ships, aircraft and vehicles constructed or adapted to conceal goods are liable to forfeiture (section 88). The procedure to be followed is prescribed by section 139 and Schedule 3 of the Act. The Commissioners have power under paragraph 16 of Schedule 3 to agree to accept a payment in lieu of forfeiture.

4 See para. 8.07 below.

A vessel used for the importation of goods is liable to forfeiture notwithstanding that the goods are transferred to another vessel outside territorial waters and the other vessel carries them within the limits of a United Kingdom port: *Attorney-General v Hunter* [1949] 2 K.B. 111 (a case concerning section 172 of the Customs Consolidation Act 1876).

## Forfeiture Proceedings

**8.07** Schedule 3 provides for proceedings to be taken in the High Court or in a magistrates' court. They are civil proceedings (paragraph 8). The fact, form and manner of a seizure are taken to be as set out in the process unless the contrary is proved (paragraph 13). The Commissioners must give notice of seizure to any person who was, to their knowledge, owner or part owner of the thing seized unless the seizure was made in his presence or that of his agent (paragraph 1). The owner has one month in which to claim that the thing was not liable to forfeiture and, if no notice in proper form is given, the thing shall be deemed to be forfeited (paragraphs 3 and 5). The only relevant time limit is the month during which the owner must give notice of his claim: no time limit is imposed on seizures: *Commissioners of Customs and Excise v Sokolow's Trustees* [1954] 2 Q.B. 336.

If the goods are liable to forfeiture the Court has no discretion—it must order forfeiture. This was the decision of the King's Bench Division in *de Keyser v British Railway Traffic and Electric Company Ltd* [1936] 1 K.B. 224, a case concerning a tank wagon which had been used to carry oils which had been forfeited.

Forfeiture proceedings are proceedings *in rem* and not proceedings *in personam*. If goods are liable to forfeiture, then those proceedings are not interested in the identity of the owner or the importer of the goods: *Denton v John Lister Ltd* [1971] 3 All E.R. 669.

## Forfeiture of Money

**8.08** The Customs and Excise Acts do not make any provision for the forfeiture of money used for the purpose of offences or resulting from offences under the Acts, although section 43 of the Powers of Criminal Courts Act 1973 is available where money was in the possession or control of a convicted defendant at the time of his apprehension for the purpose of committing offences. Section 27 of the Misuse of Drugs Act 1971 (see paras 17.04 and 17.05 *post*) would be effective to order the forfeiture of the profits of an offence if it were available. On a conviction for importing cannabis Mr Justice Caulfield sitting at the Central

Criminal Court ordered the forfeiture of money which was part of the proceeds of dealing with drugs: *R v Beard* [1974] 1 W.L.R. 1549. In the case of *R v Menocal* (1978) 69 Cr.App.R. 148 the Court of Appeal decided that there was a power to order forfeiture of money under the section following a conviction for smuggling cocaine and the House of Lords[5] agreed, although at that stage their Lordships' opinions upon the point were *obiter*. These decisions appear to conflict with that in *R v Williams* (1971) 55 Cr.App.R. 275 discussed at para. 6.09. The Court of Appeal in *R v Whitehead* (1982) 75 Cr.App.R. 389 declared that the decisions were not inconsistent with each other. Lord Diplock in *R v Cuthbertson* [1980] 2 All E.R. 401 at p. 404 had expressed the view that section 25 and Schedule 4 of the Misuse of Drugs Act 1971 contained a comprehensive list of all offences under that Act. It would follow from his reasoning that importing drugs is not an offence under the Act. The situation awaits clarification by the Court of Appeal.

### Protection of Officers

**8.09**  Where the owner of property seized by the Commissioners succeeds in an action to recover it he shall not be entitled to any damages or costs if the Court is satisfied that there were reasonable grounds for seizing or detaining that thing under the Customs and Excise Acts (section 144 1979 Act). This provision does not affect the owner's right to compensation if the property has been damaged or destroyed while in the custody of the Customs and Excise.

### Mitigation of Penalties

**8.10**  The Commissioners have very wide powers under section 152 to mitigate or remit pecuniary penalties, to restore things that have been seized or forfeited and to order that persons who have been imprisoned for offences under the Customs and Excise Acts be discharged before the expiration of their sentences. They have similar powers under paragraph 16 of Schedule 3 in respect to forfeiture proceedings.

### Extradition

**8.11**  Offences under the Customs and Excise Acts relating to controlled drugs and conspiracy to commit such offences are extraditable—see Chapter 24 *post*.

---

5  (1979) 69 Cr.App.R. 157.

PART III

# MISUSE OF DRUGS ACT AND REGULATIONS

CHAPTER 9

# Controlled Drugs and Their Classification

## DEFINITION AND CLASSIFICATION

**9.01** By section 2 Misuse of Drugs Act 1971[1] "controlled drug" is defined as any substance or product specified in Parts I, II and III of Schedule 2 to the Act. The Schedule classifies the substances listed as Class A, Class B and Class C according to their relative harmfulness. Schedule 4 provides for a range of punishments which is related to the class of drug in connection with which an offence has been committed. Schedule 2 can be amended by Order in Council after consultation with the Advisory Council set up in accordance with section 1. For example the Misuse of Drugs Act 1971 (Modification) Order 1984 (S.I. no. 859) makes adjustments to Schedule 2 with effect from 1 January 1985 and in particular brings certain barbiturates under control. This is a step towards complying with the Convention on Psychotropic Substances 1971.[2] "Cannabis", "cannabis resin" and "prepared opium" are defined in section 37(1). Prepared opium includes dross left over after smoking. Part IV of Schedule 2 also contains definitions.

Drugs are also scheduled for other purposes in the Misuse of Drugs Regulations 1973—see Chapters 19 and 20. The drugs scheduled in the Misuse of Drugs (Designation) Order 1977 (S.I. no. 1379)[3] are drugs which, under subsection (4) of section 7 of the Act, it is wholly unlawful to produce, supply or possess except for research or other special purposes and they are not covered by the authorisations in the 1973 Regulations.[4] Misusing a drug means misusing it by taking it by way of self-administration—section 37(2).

*Not necessary to Prove Exact Nature or Form of Drug*
**9.02** Each part of Schedule 2 specifies in paragraph 1 a list of drugs. It then goes on to list in succeeding paragraphs various forms which those drugs can take such as salts, esters or stereoisomeric forms. The reason

1 The whole Act is set out in Appendix III. Relevant Regulations are set out in Appendices IV–VIII.
2 Schedule 2 is set out in Appendix III (incorporating the amendments that have been made since the Act came into force in July 1973; other amendments will take effect on 1 April 1986—see Appendix XV), and the Convention in Appendix XII.
3 The Schedule (as amended) is set out in appendix VII.
4 S.I.s nos. 797, 798, 799.

for including salts is that, for example, diamorphine (heroin) is normally sold in the form of a salt, diamorphine hydrochloride, which is readily soluble. The reason for including stereoisomeric forms is that in the manufacture of a compound a proportion of the molecules produced may have the pattern of their atomic make-up reversed. The chemical constitution of isomers is identical; they may differ, however, in their pharmacological properties. This matter is explained in para. 2.13 *ante*.

Unfortunately the draftsman did not use the word "includes" and lawyers have used what were designed as longstop provisions as escape routes where the prosecution have failed to prove whether a substance was or was not in a particular stereoisomeric form. In fact it could be very difficult and time-consuming to distinguish a stereoisomer, especially if only a small quantity of the drug was available. However this escape route would appear to have been blocked by the decision in *R v Greensmith* (1983) 77 Cr.App.R. 202. In that case the analyst stated that the substance in the possession of the defendant was cocaine. He did not test to discover if it was a stereoisomeric form of cocaine or whether it was a salt of cocaine. He said "whatever it is, it still is cocaine". The trial judge rejected a submission that the prosecutor had to prove whether the cocaine was in a stereoisomeric form or a mixture form or salt form. The Court of Appeal upheld the ruling of the trial judge and held that the word "cocaine" as used in paragraph 1 of Part I of Schedule 2 is a generic word which includes within its ambit both the direct extracts of the coca leaf, the natural form and whatever results from a chemical transformation.

The same point was again argued before a differently constituted Court of Appeal in *R v Watts* (1984) 79 Cr.App.R. 127, when no reference was made in the judgement to the decision in *Greensmith*. On this occasion the analyst stated that the substance in the possession of the defendant was a mixture of 2/1 ephedrine and amphetamine. He could not determine whether there was present a specific amount of dexamphetamine and it was possible that the powder was wholly laevoamphetamine. Ephedrine is not a controlled drug; dexamphetamine and laevoamphetamine are stereoisomeric forms of amphetamine of which dexamphetamine is specifically mentioned in Part II of Schedule 2. It was argued for the appellant that the maxim "*expressio unius exclusio alterius est*" applied, that the inclusion of dexamphetamine excluded laevoamphetamine and that the appeal should be allowed because the possibility could not be excluded that the whole of the substance was laevoamphetamine. The Court of Appeal treated the appeal on the basis that the whole of the substance was laevoamphetamine but decided that the word "amphetamine" in Part II embraces both stereoisomers and that the inclusion by the draftsman of dexamphetamines in the Schedule was unnecessaary. (See paras 2–13 and 3.19 *ante*.)

## Naturally Occuring Material

**9.03**    Certain substances which occur naturally or as the primary result of cultivation are included in Schedule 2. These include coca leaf and poppy straw. "Cannabis" was originally defined in section 37(1) as "the flowering or fruiting tops of any plant of the genus *Cannabis* from which the resin has not been extracted".[6] This definition of cannabis gave difficulty because the psycho-active ingredients occur in other parts of the plant as well as in the flowering or fruiting tops. Prosecutors tried to get round the difficulty by charging possession of a "cannabinol derivative" which is a Class A drug. This stratagem was eventually brought to the attention of the House of Lords in the case of *D.P.P. v Goodchild* (1978) 67 Cr.App.R. 56, when it was held that the offence of unlawful possession of any controlled drug described in schedule 2 is not established by proof of possession of naturally occuring material of which the described drug is one of the constituents, unseparated from the other constituents. In arriving at this decision their Lordships were influenced by the fact that cannabis was a Class B drug, whereas a cannabinol derivative came into Class A.

A new definition of "cannabis" was substituted in section 37 by section 52 of the Criminal Law Act 1977 so as to include any part of a plant of the genus *Cannabis*; so that particular problem no longer exists.

Mr Goodchild suffered two trials in the Crown Court, two appeals and an Attorney-General's Reference before the appeal to the House of Lords in respect of his possession of some leaves and stalk of a cannabis plant.[7] It is only necessary to consider further the answer to the Attorney-General's Reference (No. 1 of 1977) 65 Cr.App.R. 165. The question posed was "whether possession of some leaves and stalk only from a plant of the genus *Cannabis*, which leaves and stalk have been separated from the plant, amounts to possession of cannabis resin . . . . ." The Court of Appeal held that the words in section 37 "separated resin" did not apply to the separation of leaves from a plant but to the separation of the resin in effect from the other plant material.

A decision tending in the opposite direction is *Stevens* [1981] Crim.L.R. 568 which concerned powdered mushrooms. The defendant

---

5    Dexamphetamine is omitted from the Schedule with effect from 1 April 1986—see Appendix XV.
6    International conventions since 1924 have referred to "flowering or fruiting tops of the pistillate plant *Cannabis sativa*"—see Article 1 of the 1961 Convention (set out in Appendix XI).
7    See Table of Cases for citations.

was found in the possession of powdered mushrooms containing a naturally occurring derivative of psilocybin and appealed on the ground that "preparation" had a technical pharmaceutical meaning. The Court of Appeal rejected the appeal, holding that in order for the mushrooms to be prepared they merely had to cease to be in their natural growing state and be in some way altered by the hand of man to put them into a condition in which they could be used for human consumption.

In the case of *R v Thomas* [1981] Crim.L.R. 496 the Court of Appeal had to consider the definition of cannabis resin in section 37. The defendant possessed a morphious brown substance which had been produced by compacting the shakings or scrapings of part of a cannabis plant. Under a microscope the substance was shown to contain cannabis oil bearing glandular trichomes from which the cannabis had not been removed. It was held that the presence of trichome husks did not prevent the substance from being cannabis resin. Sufficient separation from the plant had taken place. It is rather strange that the Court of Appeal was troubled with this problem, since it had held in *R v Best* (1979) 70 Crim.App.R. 21 that "cannabis" and "cannabis resin" can be charged or indicted in the alternative because they are described in Part II of Schedule 2 as "cannabis and cannabis resin". Where therefore it was impossible to say which the substance was, the indictment could say "possession of a controlled drug being either cannabis or cannabis resin" without offending against the rules of duplicity. *Muir v Smith*, (1978) *The Times*, 17 February D.C. is wrongly cited as having decided that if the prosecution can prove only that a substance is either cannabis or cannabis resin the defendant is entitled to be acquitted. In that case the charge before the magistrates was one of possession of cannabis resin. 20 micrograms of resin in a pipe were used as evidence of earlier possession of a larger quantity of either cannabis or cannabis resin. Neither the Crown Court nor the Appeal Court could amend the charge which had been before the magistrates and the Divisional Court therefore ordered an acquittal on a technicality.

### Expert Evidence

**9.04**   In *Goodchild (No. 2)* (1977) 65 Cr.App.R. 165 the Lord Chief Justice stated (p. 171) that the court required expert evidence to understand the structure of the plant, the nature of the plant and to understand the language which is peculiar to the expertise of the particular subject. He went on to say that the experts should be called rather than have written statements submitted to the Court. It is submitted that when questions are going to arise as to the nature or effect of a drug it is inappropriate to read the statements of analysts as conditional witnesses. The defence should give the prosecution notice that the witnesses' attendance will be required. A practical difficulty arises in that analysts are frequently unable or unwilling to give evidence as to the effect, rather than the composition, of a substance. This can be relevant to the question of whether or not a quantity of drugs in a defendants possession are for his own consumption or for supply to others. It is also difficult to establish what a "normal" dose is likely to be. This evidence can be obtained by calling a witness who is medically qualified and has experience in the field of drug abuse.

Whereas an expert witness may refer to results of experiments and analyses and tables made up from such results carried out and tabulated by other experts working in his field and described in learned publications, he cannot refer to experiments or analyses carried out by other people, even by members of his staff, on the actual subject-matter of his evidence unless they are also called to give evidence. Evidence of such experiments or analyses would have to be established by the persons who carried them out unless the expert witness actually supervised them and checked the results step by step and can vouch for their accuracy from his own observation. This position would appear to be established by the decisions in *R v Abadom* [1983] Crim.L.R. 254 and *R v Tate* [1977] R.T.R. 17; 66 Cr.App.R. 48.

Section 81 of the Police and Criminal Evidence Act 1984 (set out in Schedule IX *post*) makes provision for Crown Court Rules requiring advance disclosure of such evidence by the defence.

### Admission of Nature of Drugs by Defendant

**9.05** Normally the prosecution proves that a substance is a controlled drug by the evidence of a qualified analyst.

In circumstances where the drug is not available to be analysed, the prosecution has sought to rely on admissions made by the defendant. The evidential value of such an admission depends on the source of the defendant's knowledge—hearsay evidence does not prove facts merely because it has been embodied in a confession: *Surujpaul* (1958) 42 Cr.App.R. 266 P.C. at p. 273. On the other hand a defendant who is familiar with the controlled drug, and especially one who uses it, may very well be able to recognise it and, indeed, distinguish between different grades and qualities. His admission is *prima facie* evidence of the nature of the drug: *R v Chatwood* [1980] 1 All E.R. 467 (where previous decisions on the subject are also set out and discussed). The admission of a dealer in LSD (*Bird v Adams* [1972] Crim.L.R. 174 D.C.) and of consumers of heroin and amphetamine (*Chatwood, supra*) have founded convictions. Cases to the contrary concerning cannabis and decided on facts before section 52 of the Criminal Law Act 1977 took effect, are, it is submitted, no longer of any value (see para. 9.03). *R v Abbott* (unreported), discussed in para. 13.04 *post*, was concerned with an admission that cannabis was smoked on the appellant's premises.

## CHAIN OF EVIDENCE

**9.06**  It is vital for the prosecution to establish the chain of evidence. This means that they must establish that the drugs analysed are the same drugs as were found in possession of the defendant. Statements must be served to establish every movement of the drugs together with the fact that they were in safe custody between moves. In a case where there is not much of a defence one of the best lines to take is to probe the chain for weak links. A similar chain may exist for the transmission of documents.

However, in recent years the courts do seem to have relaxed their attitude to some extent. An example is *Tremlett v Fawcett* (1984) *The Times*, 9 October Q.B. In that case it appears that the transmission of a sample of urine from the police station to the analyst was not proved. Stephen Brown L.J. held that there was ample evidence from the police officer that the urine sample had been marked, the officer's signature placed over the seal of the envelope and the appellant's name written on the envelope, and of the certification by the analyst that the specimen had been received in a sealed container.

## CONTROLLED DRUGS EXCEPTED FROM PROHIBITION

**9.07**  Sections 7 and 22 empower the Secretary of State to make regulations excluding the application of the offence provisions of the Act and of the Customs and Excise Management Act 1979 (see para. 19.02 *post*). The relevant regulations are set out in Appendices IV, V and VI. He can issue licences under section 3 or under regulations. Section 18 makes it an offence to contravene a regulation or the terms of a licence. If a defendant wishes to rely on an exception under section 7 and a relevant regulation or on a licence, the onus is on him—see para. 19.03.

Section 30 deals with the issuing of licences.

# CHAPTER 10

# *Production and Supply*

## The Prohibition

**10.01** Section 4(1) Misuse of Drugs Act 1971 makes it unlawful to produce, supply or offer to supply controlled drugs to another unless authorised by regulations under section 7 of the Act. Subsections (2) and (3) make it an offence to contravene subsection (1) or to be concerned in such a contravention. "Contravene" includes failure to comply (section 37(1)). Lack of knowledge may be a defence—see Chapter 14. Penalties are prescribed by Schedule 4 and dealt with in Chapter 17. Regulations are dealt with in Chapter 19.

## DEFINITIONS

### The Meaning of Produce

**10.02** "Produce" means producing a controlled drug by manufacture, cultivation or any other method (section 37). The amendment to the definition of "cannabis" in section 37(1) by section 52 of the Criminal Law Act 1977 (see para. 9.03 *ante*) has the effect that persons cultivating cannabis plants can be prosecuted under section 4 rather than under section 6 (the penalties are identical). It follows that it becomes an offence under section 8 for the occupier of premises to permit the cultivation of cannabis on his premises: *Taylor v Chief Constable of Kent* (1981) 72 Cr.App.R. 318 (see Chapter 13).

Drying and powdering mushrooms would, it appears, amount to producing a preparation containing psilocybin—a Class A drug (see *R v Stevens*, para. 9.03 *ante*).

### The Meaning of Supply

**10.03** The Court of Appeal has twice found it necessary to point out that the recipient of the supply must be "another". In *Brian William Smith* C.A. 14 February 1983 (unreported) it was held that A and B could not be indicted for conspiracy to supply B. In *Ferrara* C.A. 17 July 1984 (unreported) the Court of Appeal held that the trial judge had been wrong to direct the jury that a co-defendant could be the recipient. It follows that a recipient or proposed recipient can be charged with possession or attempted possession but not with being a party to the offence of supplying himself. It may be that he can be charged with inciting another person to supply him (see section 19, discussed at para. 15.01 *post*).

Supplying includes distributing (section 37(1)). Where one person purchases drugs on behalf of others or holds drugs on their behalf, he nevertheless "supplies" them when he shares them out or "distributes" them among their owners: *Holmes v Chief Constable of Merseyside* [1976] Crim.L.R. 125 D.C.; *R v Buckley* (1979) 69 Cr.App.R. 371. In another context the Court of Appeal gave its opinion that "supply" denotes the passing of possession from one person to another: *R v Mills* [1963] 1 Q.B. 522 at p. 527. The meaning of the word "supply" was considered by the Court of Appeal in the case of *R v Delgado* (1984) 78 Cr.App.R. 175, which was a case cncerning possession with intent to supply (dealt with at para. 11.08). The defendant, who admitted being in possession of 6.31 kg of cannabis belonging to two friends, gave evidence that he was transporting it in order to return it to them. The trial judge (Judge West Russell) then ruled that returning cannabis to a friend was an act of supplying and the defendant changed his plea to guilty. The Court of Appeal held that questions of transfer of legal ownership or legal possession were irrelevant. The Court considered the *Shorter Oxford English Dictionary* definitions and concluded that they had a common feature in presupposing that inherent in "supply" was the furnishing or providing of something that was wanted. "Supply" covered a wide range of transactions with the common feature of transfer of physical control of a drug from one person to another. The defendant was rightly convicted.

To inject into a person's arm his own drug is merely assisting him and, as a matter of common sense, it is impossible to say that a person administering heroin in those circumstances is supplying the heroin. If the heroin belonged to the person administering the injection, that would be supplying: *R v Harris* [1968] 1 W.L.R. 769 C.A.

Whether or not allowing others to "take a puff" at a "reefer" containing cannabis amounts to supplying cannabis has been the subject of conflicting decisions at first instance. In *R v King* [1978] Crim.L.R. 228 Judge Finlay held that the smoke inhaled was not the material in the cigarette as it existed in the possession of the defendant. This decision is logical, since what was inhaled was smoke containing cannabinol—a Class A drug. In *R v Moore* [1979] Crim.L.R. 789 Judge Baker declined to follow *King* and held that "supply" should not be given too narrow a definition. In the unreported case of *Chief Constable of Cheshire v Hunt and Others* Q.B.D. 25 April 1983 both Goff L.J. and Mann J. expressed reservations about the case of *King*. It is likely that the Court of Appeal would follow Judge Baker's commonsense approach. In any event possession and control of the "reefer" passes temporarily to the person who is smoking it: *Chief Constable of Cheshire v Hunt and Others* (see para. 11.06 *post*).

In the appeal of *Mieras v Rees* [1975] Crim.L.R. 224 the Divisional Court held that supplying a drug which the defendant believed to be a controlled drug but which had not been proved to be a controlled drug could not amount to an attempt to supply. This is no longer the law as a result of the Criminal Attempts Act 1981 (see Chapter 15)—in any case, it is unlikely to have been preceded by an offer.

**Offer to Supply**

**10.04**  It is a complete offence to offer to supply a controlled drug, whether or not the offeror is able to complete the transaction by handing over the drug. The Queen's Bench Division in *Haggard v Mason* [1976] 1 W.L.R. 187 had to consider the position of a defendant who mistakenly believed that he possessed a quantity of LSD, a controlled drug. He offered to sell it to a purchaser and at the time of the transaction both believed it to be LSD. He was convicted by the Justices under section 4(3)(a). The Divisional Court held that the offence was completed at the time when the offer was made. It mattered not that the substance subsequently supplied pursuant to the offer was not in fact a controlled drug.

Inviting people to a flat where another person has cannabis available can amount to an offer to supply—see *Blake and O'Connor* below.

**Meaning of "Concerned in"**

**10.05**  Section 4(3) has been particularly widely drawn to involve people who may be at some distance from the making of the offer. The Court of Appeal so held in rejecting the appeals of *Blake and O'Connor* (1978) 68 Cr.App.R. 1. The facts in the case were that O'Connor offered to take some people he met in the street to a flat where they could obtain cannabis. He discussed with them the price and their ability to pay. He took them to Blake's flat where Blake said to O'Connor, "Is it shit they want?" This evidence was sufficient for the jury to draw the inference that there was some previous arrangement of understanding between the appellants. The offence of being concerned in the making to another of an offer does not require a specific and close involvement in the particular offer charged (see also para. 5.11 *ante*).

Allowing somebody to use a kitchen in his house to produce a drug does not apparently go so far as to "be concerned in" the production of controlled drugs, although it would amount to an offence under section 8 as an occupier of premises (see Chapter 13). There must be some identifiable participation in the process: *R v Farr* [1982] Crim.L.R. 745 C.A. In reaching this decision the Court of Appeal does not appear to have been referred to *R v Blake and O'Connor* (*supra*) but, in any event, it would appear that providing premises knowing that they were to be used for an unlawful act would amount to aiding and abetting that act.

## RESTRICTION ON CULTIVATION OF CANNABIS

**10.06**   Section 6 makes it an offence to cultivate any plant of the genus *Cannabis*.[1] Since the definition of cannabis in section 37 was amended by section 52 of the Criminal Law Act 1977 (see para. 9.03 *ante*) prosecutions for growing cannabis have tended to be brought under section 4. Section 37(1) defines "produce" as including cultivation. The Divisional Court has confirmed that section 6 overlaps section 4 and that cultivation can now be equated with production: *Taylor v Chief Constable of Kent* (1981) 72 Cr.App.R. 318. (Licences for cultivation are dealt with in para. 19.04 *post* and a decision on cultivation and the defence under section 28 is *R v Champ* [1982] Crim.L.R. 108 C.A., discussed in para. 14.02 *post*).

A method of "cultivation" sometimes practised is to place seeds in a gro-bag which is then abandoned in a ditch or weed patch until the resulting plants are ready for harvest. There might be room for argument as to whether these actions amount to cultivation or whether some care of the plant, such as weeding, staking or watering, is required to constitute cultivation. In the old days nothing more went into the cultivation of wheat or other cereals. On the other hand there can be little doubt that the gro-bag method is a method of production.

In the Scottish case of *Tudhope v Robertson* 1980 S.L.T. 60 fifteen cannabis seedlings were found growing indoors lit by a nearby window. A packet of seeds was also found on the premises. The High Court of Justiciary held that cultivation lay in the positioning of the plants to catch the light, the presence of seeds and the objective of having living plants in the house at all. There was no need to prove possession of objects such as watering cans etc.—any jug, fork or spoon would serve.

## SUPPLY AND MANSLAUGHTER

**10.07**   Where one addict injected heroin which was unlawfully in his

---

1   When Indian hemp was originally prohibited in 1925 it was defined as "the dried flowering or fruiting tops of the pistillate plant known as *Cannabis sativa* from which the resin has not been abstracted by whatever name such tops are called". In order to avoid arguments about species and cultivars the wider definition "genus" has been substituted.

*Cannabis plant (Photo—Metropolitan Police)*

possession into the arm of another who died as a result, his conviction of manslaughter and of administering a noxious thing so as to endanger life contrary to section 23 of the Offences against the Person Act 1861 was upheld: *R v Cato, Morris and Dudley* (1976) 62 Cr.App.R. 41. The injection was an unlawful act and the victim's consent to it was irrelevant.

Where one addict, who had a quantity of dipipanone in his possession which he had obtained lawfully upon prescription, supplied some of it unlawfully to another addict who injected it into himself and died as a result, his appeal against conviction of manslaughter was allowed: *R v Dalby* (1982) 74 Cr.App.R. 348. Supplying the dipipanone was not an intrinsically dangerous act—the danger arose from the amount of the drug that the victim took and from the fact that he injected it rather than taking it orally. The Court of Appeal held that where a charge of manslaughter is based on an unlawful and dangerous act, the act must be directed at the victim and be likely to cause immediate injury, however slight. It is submitted that the position would have been different if the drug itself had been dangerous because of adulteration or contamination and that fact was known to the defendant. See also *R v Hill* [1985] Crim.L.R. 386, a case concerning "intent to injure" within the meaning of section 24 of the Act of 1861.

## CONSPIRACY TO PRODUCE

**10.08**  The question of impossibility rendering a conspiracy to produce drugs non-criminal has been considered twice in recent years by the Court of Appeal and the House of Lords.

In *D.P.P. v Nock* (1978) 67 Cr.App.R. 116 the appellants thought that they could extract cocaine from a substance which did not in fact contain cocaine. The House of Lords held that *Haughton v Smith* [1975] A.C. 476 applied to conspiracy and that what had been proved against the appellants was not a general agreement to produce cocaine but a limited agreement to produce cocaine by a method which was frustrated by impossibility. The appeal was allowed and the conviction quashed. It would seem that such a conspiracy would now be indictable under the Criminal Law Act 1977 since section 1(1) (as amended by the Criminal Attempts Act 1981) reads as follows (emphasis added):

"1.—(1) Subject to the following provisions of this Part of the Act, if a person agrees with any other person or persons that a course of conduct shall be pursued which, if the agreement is carried out in accordance with their intentions, either—

(a) *will necessarily amount to or involve the commission of any offence or offences* by one or more of the parties to the agreement, or

[(*b*) would do so but for the existence of facts which render the
commission of the offence or any of the offences impossible],[2]
he is *guilty of conspiracy to commit the offfence or offences in question.*"

However, it may be that everything is now put back in the melting pot by
the decision in *Anderton v Ryan* (discussed at para. 5.15 *ante*).

In *R v Harris* (1979) 69 Cr.App.R. 122 the appellants attempted to
make amphetamine by a method which would have succeeded had they
known how to carry it out properly. The Court of Appeal held that the
agreement was possible of consummation and it was not within the
boundaries of the decision in *Nock*.

The fact that a conspirator believes that it was impossible to achieve
the object does not afford him a defence: *R v Anderson* (1985) *The Times*
12 July C.A.

---

**2**   Words added by 1981 Act.

# CHAPTER 11

# Possession and Possession with Intent to Supply

## The Prohibition

**11.01**  Section 5(1) Misuse of Drugs Act 1971 makes it unlawful to possess a controlled drug unless authorised by regulations under section 7 of the Act. Subsection (2) makes it an offence to contravene subsection (1) and subsection (3) makes it an offence to possess controlled drugs, whether lawfully or not, with intent to supply in contravention of section 4(1). "Contravene" includes failure to comply (section 37(1)). Lack of knowledge may be a defence—see Chapter 14. Penalties are prescribed by Schedule 4 and dealt with in Chapter 17; the penalty for possession alone is less than that for possession with intent to supply—see Schedule 4. Defences under regulations for doctors, nurses etc. and persons to whom drugs are prescribed are dealt with in Chapter 19 *post*.

Where a count on an indictment alleges possession of a number of drugs, a verdict of guilty is justified if the jury is satisfied that the defendant possessed any of them: *R v Peevy* (1973) 57 Cr.App.R. 554 C.A.

*Special Defence*

**11.02**  Section 5(4) provides that it shall be a defence for the accused to prove that he took possession of a controlled drug to prevent another committing a crime or for the purpose of delivering it into lawful custody. He must also prove that as soon as possible after taking possession he took all such steps as were reasonably open to him to destroy it or to deliver it into lawful custody. (As to the burden of proof, see para. 14.02 *post*).

## DEFINITIONS

### The Meaning of "Possession"

**11.03**  Section 37(3) provides that the things which a person has in his possession shall be taken to include any thing subject to his control which is in the custody of another, e.g. at a left luggage office. If the other knows the nature of thing under his control, there is no need of this provision since both parties would be guilty of joint possession.

114

A clear definition of "possession" was given by the Privy Council in the Jamaican case of *D.P.P. v Brooks* [1974] A.C. 862. The words of the relevant Jamaican ordinance were "Every person who . . . . . . has in his possession any . . . . . ganja . . . . . shall be guilty of an offence against this law" and this was held to mean:

"In the ordinary use of the word 'possession' one has in one's possession whatever is to one's own knowledge, physically in one's custody or under one's physical control. This is obviously what was intended to be prohibited in the case of dangerous drugs . . . . . These technical doctrines of the civil law about possession are irrelevant to this field of criminal law."

This definition was cited by the House of Lords in *R v Boyesen* (1982) 75 Cr.App.R. 51, at p. 57, and ties in with the decision in *Delgado* (see para. 10.03), where the Court of Appeal held that questions of the transfer of ownership or legal possession of drugs were irrelevant to the issue whether or not there was an intent to supply.

"Physical possession" was defined by Lord Pearce in *Warner* (1968) 52 Cr.App.R. 373[1] at p. 427: "By physical possession or control I include things in his pocket, in his car, in his room and so forth." Where a person ordered a supply of amphetamine to be sent through the post, he was in possession of it as soon as it arrived through the letterbox of the house in which he had a bed-sitter. The Court of Appeal so held in *R v Peaston* (1978) 69 Cr.App.R. 203, in which the Court of Appeal quoted a passage from the case of *Cavendish* (1961) 45 Cr.App.R. 374, a case concerning the recovery of stolen goods, where the Lord Chief Justice, Lord Parker, had said:

"The sole question . . . . . is whether a case was made out at the end of the case for the prosecution which called for an answer. Certain propositions are quite clear. It is quite clear, without referring to authority, that for a man to be found to have possession, actual or constructive, of goods, something more must be proved than that the goods have been found at his premises. It must be shown either, if he was absent, that on his return he has become aware of them and exercised some control over them or . . . . . that the goods had come, albeit in his absence, at his invitation or by arrangement. It is also clear that a man cannot be convicted of receiving goods of which delivery has been taken by his servant unless there is evidence that he, the employer, had given the servant authority or instructions to take the goods."[2]

If a woman is found in her flat with a quantity of cannabis on her bed and makes no comment, there is a *prima facie* case that she possesses it. If she gives an explanation to the police which would exculpate her, that unsworn statement would not entitle the judge to withdraw the case from the jury: *R v Storey and Anwar* (1968) 52 Cr.App.R. 334 C.A.

1  See also para. 11.04 below.
2  See also Ribeiro and Perry, "Possession and Section 28 of the Misuse of Drugs Act 1971" [1979] Crim.L.R. 90.

A person given a "reefer" in order that he may inhale it has possession of the "reefer"—see *Chief Constable of Cheshire v Hunt and Others*,[3] para. 11.06 *post*.

### Knowledge of Presence of Substance

**11.04**   The prosecution must prove that the defendant knew he possessed the substance—once that has been proved it is up to the defendant to prove that he did not believe or suspect that it was a controlled drug (knowledge of the nature of the substance and section 28 are discussed in Chapter 14). The judgements in *Warner v Metropolitan Police Commissioner* (1968) 52 Cr.App.R. 373 and *R v Ashton-Rickhardt* (1977) 65 Cr.App.R. 67 make it clear that the prosecution must prove knowledge of the presence of the "thing" in question. Section 28 of the present Act has not altered the position. In the course of his judgement in *Ashton-Rickhardt* Lord Justice Roskill said:

> ". . . . . in *Warner v Metropolitan Police Commissioner* . . . . . it was laid down by the highest tribunal that there could not be possession of a controlled drug unless the accused person knew that the 'thing' which was alleged to contain the controlled drug was in his possession, that knowledge of the presence of the 'thing' in question was an essential prerequisite to proof of possession and that therefore the Crown had to prove, as part of its proof of possession of the controlled drug, knowledge that the 'thing' (which was in fact a controlled drug) was there. As was pointed out, and indeed had been pointed out earlier by Lord Parker C.J.— how can you have possession of something of the existence of which you do not know?"

The law in Scotland is identical: *McKenzie v Skeen* 1983 S.L.T. 121.

*Containers—Indirect Knowledge*

Where the drug is inside a container the prosecution has to prove (a) that the defendant knew that he possessed the container and that he came into possession of it in circumstances which had enabled him to know or discover (or would have enabled him, had he so wished, to know or discover) what it was that he had before assuming control of it or continuing to be in control of it; and (b) that, whether the accused knew this or not, the article or thing or substance or package or container, consisted of, or contained, a prohibited substance (Lord Morris in *Warner* at p. 414; and see *Fernandez* (1970) Crim.L.R. 277 C.A. and other cases discussed in para. 5.05 *ante*). It is wrong to direct the jury that if a defendant is knowingly in possession of a bottle he is also deemed to be in possession of the contents. The Court of Appeal so held where the defence was that an amphetamine tablet in a bottle containing the defendant's stomach pills must have been one of his wife's which she put in by mistake: *R v Irving* [1970] Crim.L.R. 642. It seems as though the

3   Unreported.

Court strained the interpretation of possession to help the defendant in this case—it is the sort of situation which section 28(3)(*b*)(1) of the 1971 Act was designed to meet. (See also *Lockyer v Gibb* [1967] 2 Q.B. 243.)

Where the passenger in a car was handed a container and told to throw it out of the window, which he did immediately, he was not in possession of the contents. In the case of *Brian Lloyd Wright* (1975) 62 Cr.App.R. 169 the appellant realised as soon as he was told to throw the container away that it must contain drugs. The Court of Appeal held that when the container was handed to the defendant he did not have possession of the cannabis, since he had not examined it and that by throwing it away before he had the opportunity to examine it he did not come into possession of the cannabis inside even though at that stage he suspected that something was wrong.

In another case decided on the earlier legislation but which would still appear to be good law it was held that the possession of a knife to which adhered 0·03 of a gram of cannabis did not amount to possession of a controlled drug unless the possessor was, at the least, aware of the presence of some foreign matter: *R v Marriott* (1971) 55 Cr.App.R. 82 C.A. (see para. 11.05 below as to the "usability test"). On the other hand where the prosecution proved that the defendant had picked up and pocketed 36 cigarette ends, one of which contained 3 milligrams of cannabis and two others traces, the Divisional Court held that the difference between a cigarette containing cannabis and an ordinary one was similar to that between an aspirin and a heroin tablet. The prosecution did not have to prove that the defendant knew it contained cannabis: *Searle v Randolph* [1972] Crim.L.R. 779 D.C. The defendant would now have available the defence provided by section 28—see para. 14.01 *post*.[4]

In *Young* (1984) 78 Cr.App.R. 288 the Courts-Martial Appeal Court upheld a direction that the Court need only be satisfied that the appellant knew he was in possession of something which turned out to be or to contain the controlled drug in question.

### "Usable Quantity"—de Minimis

**11.05**  The courts have gone round in a circle on the question of whether there is a *de minimis* rule which applies to possession of very small quantities of controlled drugs. The test has been defined as whether there is a "usable quantity" but the issue has been confused with (1) that of knowledge by the defendant of the presence of the drug, and (2) the use of small quantities as evidence of prior possession of larger quantities. The

---

4   See also para. 5.05 ante and in particular *R v Fernandes* [1970] Crim.L.R. 277 C.A.

the test is now established as whether the quantity is sufficient to permit the drug's presence to be detected and its nature identified.[5]

*(1) The Usability Test*
In the case of *Worsell* (1969) 53 Cr.App.R. 322 the defendant was convicted of possession of "a few droplets of heroin" in an apparently empty tube—they were invisible to the naked eye and could not be poured out. The Court of Appeal allowed the appeal on the grounds that whatever the tube contained it obviously could not be used and could not be sold. There was nothing in reality in the tube. The case of *Worsell* was distinguished in *Graham* [1970] 1 W.L.R. 113, where it was held that the defendant was properly convicted when scrapings from his pockets contained very small quantities of cannabis that were capable of being measured. This was followed in *Bocking v Roberts* [1973] 3 W.L.R. 465 D.C., in which the defendant possessed a pipe containing a quantity of cannabis resin that could not be measured but that was determined by chemical tests to be at least 20 micrograms. Lord Widgery held that the *de minimis* maxim did not apply and that the magistrates had not gone beyond the legal limits of determination in convicting the appellant of possessing cannabis resin.

However in *Colyer* [1974] Crim.L.R. 242 Judge Stinson, sitting at Ipswich Crown Court, did not consider himself bound by the decision of the Divisional Court. The facts were that the defendant, Colyer, had a used pipe. Chemical tests revealed the presence of at least 20 micrograms of cannabis. The judge held that this was not a measurable quantity and that the prosecution had not proved that the defendant knew that the pipe contained cannabis.

The usability test was restated by the Court of Appeal in *Carver* (1978) 67 Cr.App.R. 352, where the defendant was in possession of a roach end (a filter made of cardboard) containing 20 micrograms of cannabis resin and an empty box from which 2 milligrams of resin were scraped. In allowing the defendant's appeal Davies J. stated:

> "However the court is of the opinion that, whilst it would be inappropriate to rely upon the ordinary maxim of *de minimis*, if the quantity of the drug found is so minute as in the light of common sense to amount to nothing or, even if that cannot in a particular case be said, if the evidence be that the quantity is so minute that it is not usable, in any manner which the Misuse of Drugs Act 1971 was intended to prohibit, then a conviction for being in possession of the minute quantity of the drug would not be justified. Of course, it remains open to the prosecution in an appropriate case to rely upon the possession of a minute quantity as evidence in support of possession at some earlier time. But no doubt rarely would such evidence alone enable a charge of possession at an earlier time to be justified."

5   See the House of Lords' decision in *R v Boyesen* discussed in (2) below.

*(2) The Identifiability Test*

The judgement in *Carver* was the Indian summer of the usability test, although the Scottish courts refused to be led into this backwater: *Keane v Gallacher* 1980 S.L.T. 144. It was followed by the Court of Appeal in *R v Boyesen* (1980) 72 Cr.App.R. 43, where the Court held that it was offensive that the mechinery of law should be brought into operation to prosecute a man for allegedly possessing five milligrams of cannabis resin and criticised both the prosecuting authorities and the trial judge. However the House of Lords took a different view ((1982) 75 Cr.App.R. 51). Their Lordships approved the ruling of the trial judge and the conduct of the prosecuting authority. Lord Scarman held that the plain unqualified words of the subsection simply refer to a controlled drug, and *ex facie* anything which is capable of being identified as a controlled drug is struck at by the subsection. The "usability" test is incorrect in law. Lord Scarman went on (p. 57):

> "The question is not usability but possession. Quantity is, however, of importance in two respects when one has to determine whether or not an accused person has a controlled drug in his possession. First, is the quantity sufficient to enable a court to find as a matter of fact that it amounts to something? If it is visible, tangible, and measurable, it is certainly something. The question is one of fact for the common sense of the tribunal . . . . .
> Secondly, quantity may be relevant to the issue of knowledge."

In the case of *Frederick* [1970] 1 W.L.R. 107 the defendant was charged with possession of 307 grains of cannabis resin and of traces in a pouch and a pipe. The jury returned a general verdict of guilty. The Court of Appeal in rejecting the appeal said that the inclusion of the traces introduced an unnecessary complication. It would have been sufficient to rely on the presence of the traces to support the case on the 307 grains of resin.

The position now would seem to be that the quantity of a drug found in a person's possession is relevant only to his knowledge. It does not matter how minute the quantity may be—and no question arises of usability or otherwise. If a minute quantity indicates previous possession of a larger quantity—then the question arises of whether the evidence as a whole indicates knowledge by the accused. For example minute quantities in the bowl of a pipe in the defendant's room would probably result in there being a case to answer unless there was evidence of recent acquisition by him of the pipe.

**Evidence of Prior Possession**

**11.06** In *Worsell* (para. 11.05 *ante*) the Court of Appeal—having said that a tube containing a few droplets of heroin was in reality empty—went on to say that if the defendant had been charged with a prior possession of the drug, the evidence of the tube put together with his admission of having had a "fix" would have been conclusive evidence against him. A passage from the judgement in *Carver* (quoted in para. 11.05 *ante*) refers to the possibility of the prosecution relying on possession of a minute quantity as evidence in support of possession at some earlier time.

In the case of *Chief Constable of Cheshire v Hunt and Others*, Q.B.D. 25 April 1983 (unreported) the question stated for the answer of the Court was: "If a person smokes cannabis resin belonging to another, does that person commit the offence of possessing cannabis resin contrary to section 5(2) of the Misuse of Drugs Act 1971?" The answer was, "If a person smokes cannabis resin, he must have cannabis resin in his possession at the time of smoking, otherwise he would not be able to smoke it."

*Urine Samples*

Once drugs have been consumed their character alters and the consumer is no longer in possession of a controlled drug; the Divisional Court so held in regard to traces of amphetamine detected in a urine sample (*Hambleton v Callinan* [1968] 2 Q.B. 427) but Lord Parker C.J. went on:

> ". . . . . I can see no reason why in another case the time when the possession is said to have taken place should not be a time prior to the consumption, because as it seems to me the traces of, in this case, amphetamine powder in the urine is at any rate *prima facie* evidence—which is all the prosecution need—that the man concerned must have had it in his possession . . . . ."

The case of *Tansley v Painter* [1969] Crim.L.R. 139 D.C. gave Lord Parker the opportunity to develop this theory concerning urine tests but in fact his judgement as reported takes the matter no further.

In the case of *Beet* (1977) 66 Cr.App.R. 188 the defendant was required to provide a sample of urine. The sample contained amphetamine and methylamphetamine. Upon the trial judge ruling that evidence of the analysis of the sample was admissible the defendant pleaded guilty to possessing quantities of amphetamine and methylamphetamine. Although the report does not say so, the offences charged must have related to drugs possessed by the defendant before he was arrested. The defendant appealed on the grounds (1) that the police ought to have given him a specific caution before inviting him to give a sample, (2) that they should have offered him a portion for his own analyst if he desired to instruct one, and (3) that the trial judge should have exercised his discretion to exclude the evidence as unfair. The Court of Appeal rejected the appeal and held that the trial judge had correctly exercised his discretion. There was nothing improper in asking for a specimen of urine, even if it was put in terms that it was required, without giving a caution, having regard to what happened in the case. Further there was nothing improper in failing to offer a portion—if the defendant requires one he can ask for it. There was no analogy to be drawn from the legislation regarding road safety.

Morphine would be identifiable in the blood and urine of a person who had recently smoked opium or inhaled heroin as would cocaine if he had ingested that drug (see para. 2.10 *ante*).

The decision in *Beet* has clearly opened the door to the admission of evidence of urine tests. It would however be fairer if there were some obligation on the police to offer a prospective defendant a portion of the sample. It is unlikely that many persons in a police station suffering from the shock of arrest would have the foresight to ask for a portion on their own initiative. Indeed Lord Parker indicated in his judgement in *Hambleton* (*supra*) that the police should act fairly and that would entail enabling the accused, if he desired it, to have a part of the sample taken.

**Joint Possession—Common Pool**

**11.07** The mere fact that a defendant knows that someone else has drugs in premises or a car that he shares is not enough to make him a participator in the offence of possessing them. Joint possession has to be proved. In such a situation the jury should be directed to consider whether the drugs constituted a common pool from which each defendant could draw at will. If there was a joint enterprise to consume drugs together, then the possession of drugs by one of them in pursuance of that common purpose might well be possession on the part of all of them: *R v Searle* [1971] Crim.L.R. 592; and see also *R v Irala-Prevost* [1965] Crim.L.R. 606 C.A.

## INTENT TO SUPPLY

**11.08** Section 5(3) prohibits possession of a controlled drug with intention to supply another. The intent can make an otherwise lawful possession unlawful. The offence of supplying controlled drugs to another includes returning drugs to their owner or sharing out drugs held on behalf of others (see para. 10.03 *ante* on the meaning of "supply").

In the case of *Greenfield* 1984 78 Cr.App.R. 179 the defendant was found with a bag of cannabis in his car. He claimed that the cannabis belonged to an unnamed person who had left it in the car; it was to be handed back to that person who intended to supply it to others. The defendant was charged (1) with an offence under section 5(3) of possession with intent to supply, and (2) with an offence under section 5(2) of simple possession. The case proceeded on the basis that the supplying was intended to be done *by* the unnamed person, not on the basis that the offence would be committed by the intent to return the drugs *to* the unnamed person. The defendant was found guilty of count (1) and appealed. The Court of Appeal held that the intent to supply must be an intent for the person charged to do the supplying—not an intent that a third person should supply. A conviction on count (2) was substituted. If the case had proceeded on the basis of supply to the unnamed person there would have been no answer: *R v Delgado* (1984) 79 Cr.App.R. 175, discussed in para. 10.03 *ante.*

*Greenfield* was followed by the Court of Appeal in *Downes* [1984] Crim.L.R. 552. In that case the appellant was alleged to be in joint possession of drugs found in her flat with intent to supply. The trial judge directed the jury that they had to be satisfied that the appellant was in possession of the drug and that either she intended to supply it to another or she knew full well that her co-defendant was going to supply it to others. The Court of Appeal in allowing the appeal held that it was not enough to direct the jury that it would be sufficient if the appellant knew full well that the co-defendant intended to supply the cannabis; for the mere fact of such knowledge without herself being involved in any joint venture with him was not enough to establish the necessary intent. The report does not say why a verdict of simple possession was not substituted.

In neither of the above cases does the Court of Appeal appear to have considered whether or not the successful appellant was aiding and abetting another in possessing the drugs with intent to supply another. An aider or abettor may, by virtue of section 8 of the Accessories and Abettors Act 1861, be tried and indicted as a principal.

## Evidence of Intent to Supply

**11.09**   An intent to supply may be proved by an admission or by the circumstances of the possession or by the accused person having made an offer to a witness. Very often it is inferred from the fact that the defendant possessed a larger quantity than he would be expected to consume on his own.

In the Scottish case of *Morrison v Smith* 1983 S.C.C.R. 171 the appellant, who was a heroin addict, pleaded guilty to possessing methadone contrary to section 5(2) and not guilty to possessing substantial quantities of Class A and Class B drugs with intent to supply contrary to section 5(3). The facts proved were that (1) convicted drugs users were observed to visit the appellant's premises, (2) on entry there were a number of men present who were searched but had no drugs, (3) the appellant had a quantity of methadone concealed in her pants, (4) a plastic bag on the floor near one of the men contained 100 Dromaran tablets (Class A) with a street value of £200 or £300 and 64 Ritalin tablets (Class B) with a street value of £64 to £128, and (5) the appellant said, "Thats all I've got. That stuff . . . in the bag and the stuff that was on me. I swear it on my bairn's life." The report is silent on how the street value of the drugs was established. The sheriff convicted her on the basis that: "Their value, quantity and diversity [referring to the drugs] convinced me that her possession was with the intention of supplying others and I therefore convicted her of contraventions of section 5(3) of the Misuse of Drugs Act 1971." The Lord Justice-General upheld the conviction, stating:

> "Now that was the sole basis upon which the sheriff proceeded to convict on the first two charges in their first alternative form, and in presenting this appeal, which is directed to conviction on charges (1) and (2) only, Mr Mitchell has argued that in the circumstances of this case there was not enough to support the inference which the sheriff drew from the quantity of the drugs, their variety or their value. In this case it has to be borne in mind that it was found as a fact that the appellant was a registered heroin addict and in all the circumstances she would have to be found in possession of larger quantities of drugs of greater value before the sheriff could have taken the leap which he did from possession to possession with intent. We have to reject that submission. In this case the starting-point was the finding of the appellant in possession of a substantial quantity of assorted drugs—four different drugs of substantial value.[6] The appellant offered no explanation for her possession, negativing the idea that it was possession with intent. Her evidence was that she knew nothing about them and that evidence the sheriff rejected. In these circumstances the sheriff was perfectly entitled, in our judgement, to draw the inference which he did from the matters to which he paid attention, and in the result the appeal against conviction on charges (1) and (2) fails . . . ."

If the quantity of drugs found is large—say a kilo of heroin— the inference of intent to supply may be obvious. If it is not obvious, expert evidence will be required. An analyst is unlikely to be willing to give evidence of a person's daily requirement of a drug because of problems of tolerance and dependence: see paras. 2.04–06 *ante*, although he will say, for example, how much cannabis resin is usually found in a "reefer". Indeed an addict may become so habituated to his chosen drug that he can take a quantity which might kill the uninitiated. Very often a police officer can say from his experience that a drug is usually retailed in packets of a certain size but it may be necessary to call a witness who

---

6   It is not clear from the report what the four different drugs were.

combines medical qualifications with experience of treating addicts. Evidence of the street level value of the drug may also be relevant. With heroin and cocaine costing upwards of £50 per gram not many people can afford to buy more than a gram for their own consumption. (As to proving the street level value, see para. 11.10 *post*.)

The fact that drugs have been split into small packages or the presence of scales may also lead to the inference that drugs are to be supplied to others.

## PROOF OF VALUE

**11.10**   Evidence is frequently called in order to prove that the value of drugs in the possession of an accused person is such that it can be inferred that the drugs are not for his personal use. This is done by calling a police officer who can say from his own experience what the street level price of certain drugs is likely to be. He may also wish to refer to the latest information from the National Drugs Intelligence Unit. The National Drugs Intelligence Unit is situated at Metropolitan Police Headquarters, New Scotland Yard, London SW1. It is a national unit staffed by officers from various forces. It receives and collates reports on the availability and prices of drugs from police and customs officers all over the country.[7] Prices vary according to the availability of drugs. It is hoped that large-scale seizures by the Customs will put up street level prices.

The knowledge of the officer who gives evidence, and of the officers reporting to the National Drugs Intelligence Unit, will be drawn from various sources—from actual observation of illegal transactions, from questioning addicts as to the prices they have paid for recent supplies, and from interrogation of arrested suppliers. Such evidence is often admitted without challenge but it is sometimes challenged on the ground that it amounts to hearsay.

Evidence of value, whether it be of horses, houses or motor cars, must always be based on a collation of facts, many of which cannot be known first-hand to the expert. The court has to evaluate the degree of expertise of the witness and the reliability of the material on which he bases his opinion. It is submitted that such evidence is admissible on the grounds of necessity, because there is no other way of establishing a black-market price. Once the witness is established as an expert on the basis of his experience in the drugs field, it is submitted that he may refer to prices as established by the National Drugs Intelligence Unit in the same way as doctors are permitted to refer to tables or stockbrokers to prevailing prices as ascertained from *The Times* list of closing prices of stocks and shares or from a Stock Exchange journal.

7   The Drugs Indicators Project at University College Hospital, London also monitors drugs prices.

Surprisingly there does not appear to be reported authority on the admissibility of evidence of the street level value of controlled drugs. A decision on experts giving evidence of value in another field is to be found in *English Exporters (London) Ltd v Eldonwall Ltd* [1973] 1 Ch. 415, where Megarry J stated (at p. 420):

> "As an expert witness, the valuer is entitled to express his opinion about matters within his field of competence. In building up his opinions about values, he will no doubt have learned much from transactions in which he has himself been engaged, and of which he could give first-hand evidence. But he will also have learned much from many other sources, including much of which he could give no first-hand evidence. Textbooks, journals, reports of auctions and other dealings, and information obtained from his professional brothers and others, some related to particular transactions and some more general and indefinite, will all have contributed their share. Doubtless much, or most, of this will be accurate, though some will not; and even what is accurate so far as it goes may be incomplete, in that nothing may have been said of some special element which affects values. Nevertheless, the opinion that the expert expresses is not the worse because it is in part derived from the matters of which he could give no direct evidence. Even if some of the extraneous information which he acquires in this way is inaccurate or incomplete, the errors and omissions will often tend to cancel each other out; and the valuer, after all, is an expert in this field, so that the less reliable the knowledge that he has about the details of some reported transaction, the more his experience will tell him that he should be ready to make some discount from the weight that he gives it in contributing to his overall sense of values. Some aberrant transactions may stand so far out of line that he will give them little or no weight. No question of giving hearsay evidence arises in such cases; the witness states his opinion from his general experience."

In the case of *R v Bryan*, C.A. 8 November 1984 (unreported) a police officer with some two years' experience in a drugs squad was allowed to give evidence that the usual quantity of cannabis "pushed" in a street deal is 1–2 g at a cost of about £5. The Court of Appeal rejected the appellant's argument that this evidence was hearsay and that the officer was not an expert. Mr Justice Wood gave judgement:

> "The view of this court is that police officers with their experience of dealing with these problems, being on the streets and with their knowledge and meeting those having a drug problem and those pushing the drugs, have a very wide experience and can give evidence of fact of what takes place on many occasions on the street."

# CHAPTER 12

# Special Offences Relating to the Use of Opium

Section 9 Misuse of Drugs Act 1971 makes it an offence to smoke or use prepared opium, to frequent a place used for that purpose (an opium divan) or to possess pipes made or adapted for use in that connection or which have been used or are intended to be used in that connection. It is also an offence to possess any utensils which have been used in connection with the preparation of opium for smoking. (A typical set of equipment would be a jar of liquid opium, a needle to dip in the opium, a pipe with a hole in which the needle can be scraped, and a small oil lamp over which the pipe is held).[1] Knowledge is an ingredient of the possession offences but not of the offence of frequenting an opium den. The defences under section 28 (para. 14.01 *post*) apply. "Prepared opium" is defined in section 37(1) and includes dross which may give a high concentration of morphine on re-use.

This is the only provision making it an offence to ingest a drug. It reproduces provisions originally contained in section 5 of the Dangerous Drugs Act 1920.

The word "frequent" involves the notion of something which is to some degree continuous or repeated: *Nakhla v the Queen* [1976] A.C. 1 P.C.; *Rawlings v Smith* [1938] 1 K.B. 675 at p. 686.

(Offences by occupiers of premises are dealt with in Chapter 13.)

---

1   This is for the Chinese method of smoking.

# CHAPTER 13

# *Offences of Occupiers of Premises*

## The Prohibition

**13.01** It is an offence for the occupier of premises or any person concerned in their management knowingly to permit or suffer to take place on those premises the production or supply of controlled drugs, the preparation of opium for smoking or the smoking of opium, cannabis or cannabis resin (section 8 Misuse of Drugs Act 1971). "Produce" extends to include the cultivation of cannabis—see para. 10.02 *ante*.

The wording of section 8 should be contrasted with that of earlier provisions because it may be dangerous to rely on decisions relating to those provisions. Section 5 of the Dangerous Drugs Act 1965 was in the following terms:

> "if a person—(a) being the occupier of any premises, permits those premises *to be used for the purpose* of smoking cannabis or cannabis resin, of dealing in cannabis or cannabis resin . . . . . , or (b) is concerned in the management of any premises *used* for any such purpose as aforesaid . . . . ."[1]

Of significance is the fact that the word "knowingly" does not appear. The offence under that section did not apply to a casual smoke, but only when the premises were used for the purpose of smoking (*per* Lord Morris in *Sweet v Parsley* (1969) 53 Cr.App.R. 221 at p. 233). That case also decided that knowledge was an ingredient of section 5(*b*). However, the word "knowingly" now appears in section 8 of the 1971 Act.

## DEFINITIONS

### The Meaning of "Occupier"

**13.02** The phrase "the occupier" in section 8 should be given a common-sense interpretation. It means someone who, on the facts of the particular case, can be fairly said to be "in occupation" of the premises so as to have the requisite degree of control over them and be able to exclude from them those who might otherwise intend to carry on the forbidden activities set out in the section. The Court of Appeal so held in the case of *R v Ben Nien Tao* (1976) 63 Cr.App.R. 163. The defendant was

---

1 Emphases added.

an undergraduate living in a room in a student hostel—in his waste-paper basket the police found 8 cigarette ends containing 10 milligrams of cannabis and elsewhere in his room two pipes containing 2 milligrams. He was convicted of permitting his room to be used for the purpose of smoking cannabis—the draftsman of the indictment apparently ignoring the change in the definition of the offence. He appealed on the ground that he was not the occupier. The Court of Appeal held that the correct legal analysis of the appellant's right of occupation of his room in the hostel was: he had an exclusive contractual licence from the college to use the room; he was entitled to retain the use of that room to live in, sleep in, eat in and work in; he paid the college for the use of the room. It was a licence which gave him not merely a right of use but a sufficient exclusivity of possession so that he was an "occupier" within the meaning of section 8.

In the case of *Mogford* [1970]1 W.L.R. 988, parents went away on holiday leaving their young daughters at home. The girls were charged with being occupiers permitting the use of the house for smoking cannabis. Mr Justice Nield, the trial judge, decided that they were not the "occupiers" in their parents absence. He held that they had to be proved to be the "legal" occupiers. The Court of Appeal in *Tao* (above) agreed with the judge's conclusion that the girls were not occupiers but disagreed with his reasoning and his equating "legal possession" with "possession".[2] This does not leave the law in a satisfactory situation. It is difficult to see why the daughters did not have the requisite degree of control to exclude possible offenders; however *Mogford* was followed at first instance in *Campbell* ([1982] Crim.L.R. 595), where sons held a party whilst their mother slept elsewhere.

One occupier can be guilty of permitting another occupier to use the premises of which they are joint tenants for the smoking of cannabis. The Court of Appeal so held in *Ashdown and others* (1974) 59 Cr.App.R. 193, where the conviction of four joint tenants for, in effect, permitting each other to smoke in the premises was upheld. The Court of Appeal did not discuss the question of what degree of control one co-tenant could be expected to exercise over another. (The meaning of "knowingly permits" is dealt with in para. 13.04 *post*).

**Meaning of "Concerned in the Management"**

**13.03**   The meaning of this phrase was discussed by the House of Lords in *Sweet v Parsley* (1969) 53 Cr.App.R. 221 while considering the earlier provision[3] set out in para. 13.01 *ante*, and much discussion turned on the

---

2   (1976) 63 Cr.App.R. 163 at p. 168.
3   S. 5 Dangerous Drugs Act 1965.

words "used for the purpose of" which have been omitted from section 8. Nevertheless the following passage from the judgement of Lord Wilberforce (at p. 241) may be helpful:

> "The words 'concerned in the management' are not, on the face of them, very clear, but at least they suggest some technical or acquired meaning, some meaning other than one which refers merely to such common transactions as letting or licensing the occupation of premises. For if it had been intended to penalise anyone who lets or licences premises on which cannabis comes to be smoked, it would have been easy to do so in simple language. The impression is strengthened when the following words of the paragraph are read ['use for the purpose of']. They reflect what I would think to be logically correct, namely, that one does not 'manage' the inert subject of a conveyance or a lease, but rather some human activity on the premises which the manager has an interest in directing."

It would seem therefore that section 8 applies to a person who is concerned in the management of activities on the premises although not necessarily, on the present law, the illegal activity itself. Thus it would apply to someone concerned in the management of a public house or a restaurant if he knowingly permitted cannabis to be smoked on the premises. There is authority for this view in *R v Josephs and Christie* (1977) 65 Cr.App.R. 253, where squatters ran a card school in the basement of a house owned by a local authority. Cannabis was found on a man in the premises. The squatters appealed unsuccessfully against conviction for being concerned in the management of the premises on the grounds that they had no legal authority to be there. The Court of Appeal held that there was no principle that required a person charged with management of premises to have any sort of lawful title to be on the premises. If he is managing them in the sense that he is running them, organising them and planning them, then the fact that he has no right to them and is a mere squatter does not prevent him from coming within the terms of the section.

The Lord Chief Justice in *Josephs and Christie* referred to a defendant managing premises in the sense of running them. Presumably a person is concerned in the management if he participates to some extent in a managerial role. It is submitted that a waiter or bar-tender does not participate in the management of premises unless, for example, he is left in charge of them at a time when activities are being carried out. In *Gorman v Standen* (1963) 48 Cr.App.R. 30, a case concerning a brothel, the Lord Chief Justice said (at p.35):

> "I take it that it must be right that the mere fact that a woman participates in the activities being conducted in the brothel does not make her a person assisting in the management of a brothel. 'Assisting in the management of a brothel' seems to me to contemplate in the ordinary way the case of a man

> who runs a brothel not living there himself; he keeps and manages it, but he has on the premises a woman who assists in the management."

and he went on to refer to her having "a part at any rate of the say of what goes on at the house".

A person who lets premises knowing that they will be used for an activity mentioned in section 8 would not appear to commit an offence as a person concerned in their management, but he would be liable to be prosecuted as an aider and abettor of the offence which he knew his letting the premises would facilitate.

### Meaning of "Knowingly Permits"

**13.04** The words "permits" and "suffers" mean the same thing. The word "knowingly" adds nothing to the meaning of "permits" so that the directions in the case of *Souter* still apply: *R v Thomas and Thomson* (1976) 63 Cr.App.R. 65. In the case of *Souter* (1971) 55 Cr.App.R. 403 the Court of Appeal held that the word "permits", used to define the prohibited act, in itself connotes as a mental element of the prohibited conduct: (1) knowledge or grounds for reasonable suspicion on the part of the occupier that the premises will be used for that purpose; and (2) unwillingness on his part to take means available to him to prevent it. The court adopted as applicable to prosecutions under section 5 of the Dangerous Drugs Act 1965 (see para 13.01) the test indicated by Lord Parker in *Grays Haulage Co. v Arnold* [1966] 1 W.L.R.534, where he said:

> "Knowledge is not imputed by mere negligence, but by something more than negligence, something which can describe as reckless, sending out a car not caring what happens . . . . . 'permitting' . . . . . . [implies] actual knowledge or knowledge of circumstances which fixed them, as it were, with a suspicion or knowledge of circumstances so that it could be said that they had shut their eyes to the obvious, or had allowed something to go on not caring whether an offence was committed or not."

In the case of *Thomas and Thomson* (*supra*) the appellant had been charged with knowingly permitting or suffering the smoking of cannabis resin to take place at his home. Thomas, through his counsel, admitted (i) that the appellant was one of the occupiers of the premises, (ii) that the smoking of cannabis resin took place on those premises, and (iii) that he knew that smoking took place. There was dispute as to whether the third admission applied to the actual smoking during the period alleged in the charge. The defence was that the appellant knew that cannabis smoking had taken place when he was not at home and that he could not stop it happening behind his back. He said: "I have asked him not to smoke in my house but what can you do? He is a good mate and I could not kick him out." The appeal was rejected. From the judgments it may be inferred the proper direction would be:

"Knowledge is really of two kinds, actual knowledge and knowledge which arises either from shutting ones eyes to the obvious or, what is much the same thing put in another way, failing to do something or doing something not caring whether contravention takes place or not. Of course if a person knows that smoking is taking place and is unwilling to take means available to him to prevent the prohibited act, then, members of the jury, he is at the very least shutting his eyes to what is happening. The best indication of such unwillingness is proof of failure to take reasonable steps readily available to prevent the prohibited activity. Conversely all steps taken by the accused to prevent it have a direct bearing on the charge [they should then be enumerated by the Judge].

You must decide whether if you let someone reside in and smoke in premises of which you are the occupier and in partial control, knowing perfectly well what they are doing, because they are a friend, taking no positive action other than saying 'Please do not do it', whether or not in those circumstances you are not permitting the smoking of cannabis resin to take place as those premises".

In the unreported case of *R v Abbott* C.A. 16 July 1982 Farquharson J. emphasised the necessity for the judge to identify the steps taken by the defendant and to relate them to the issue. In this case the prosecution relied on the admission of the appellant that he knew that other people smoked cannabis in his cottage in his absence. It was submitted that this admission amounted to hearsay in the absence of any direct evidence that any person other than the appellant had in fact smoked on the premises. The Court of Appeal applied *R v Chatwood* [1980] All E.R. 467 (para. 9.05 *supra*) and held that the appellant had experienced the smoking of cannabis so that he could establish from what he saw and smelled that cannabis had been smoked. His admission could suffice to ground a conviction.[4]

## Meaning of "Premises"

**13.05** Decisions on the meaning of expressions in the Act appear to be against too strict or legalistic an interpretation—see *Tao* (1976) 63 Cr.App.R. 163 (para. 13.02) and *D.P.P. v Brooks* [1974] A.C. 862 (para. 11.03 *ante*), cited with approval in *Boyesen* (1982) 75 Cr.App.R. 51 H.L. Where a house is described as "premises" the term has been held to include the yard and the garden but it is doubtful if decisions on other legislation have much relevance. For what it is worth a caravan on a permanent site has been held to be premises for the purpose of the Rent

---

4   See also *R v Ashdown and Others* (1974) 59 Cr.App.R. 193, discussed at para. 13.02 above, which is concerned with joint tenants permitting each other to smoke.

Act 1965 (*Norton v Knowles* [1969] 1 Q.B. 572) but a moveable petrol tanker from which petrol is sold retail is not premises for the purposes of the Petroleum (Consolidation) Act 1928 (*Grandi v Milburn*[1966] 2 Q.B. 263). A houseboat on a permanent mooring is premises within the meaning of the Water Act 1945 (*West Mersea U.D.C. v Fraser* [1950] 2 K.B. 119). This decision turned on the degree of permanency; which might be the logical test to apply to the meaning of the word in section 8.

CHAPTER 14

# Knowledge—the Statutory Defence

Knowledge has already been dealt with at some length in paragraphs 5.05, 11.04 and 13.04 *ante*.[1]

## PROOF OF LACK OF KNOWLEDGE

**14.01**  Section 28 Misuse of Drugs Act 1971 provides a possible defence to charges under sections 4, 5, 6 and 9. It does not prejudice any other defences open to a defendant (subsection (4)).

Subsection (2) makes it a defence for the defendant to prove that he neither knew nor suspected nor had reason to suspect the existence of some fact alleged by the prosecution which it is necessary for the prosecution to prove.

Subsection (3) provides that where it is necessary for the prosecution to prove that a substance was a particular controlled drug and it is so proved the defendant shall not be acquitted if he proves that he did not know or suspect that it was the particular drug; but he shall be acquitted if he proves (i) that he did not believe or suspect or have reason to suspect that the substance was a controlled drug at all, or (ii) that believing it was such a drug, he believed that in the circumstances at the material time he would not have been committing any offence in relation to it. The use of the words 'have reason to suspect' introduces an objective test—see *R v Young* (para. 14.03 *post.*)

If a person is given a bottle of what he thinks is aspirin which in fact turns out to be morphine he has a possible defence under subsection (2) and (3). If he thinks he has a box of cannabis which turns out to be heroin the effect of subsection (3) is that he has no defence.

### The Burden of Proof on the Defendant

**14.02**  The prosecution has to prove that the defendant possessed (or whatever the offence charged alleges) the relevant controlled drug and

1  See also Don Mathias, "The application of Section 28 of the Misuse of Drugs Act 1971 to Possession" [1980] Crim.L.R. 689.

that he knew he possessed something which turned out to be or to contain the drug in question.

If the defence is that the defendant did not know that he had the drug at all, that it was planted on him, or that the container came into his possession in circumstances in which he could not know what it contained—then the prosecution has the usual burden of proof in criminal trials and has to disprove the defence: *R v Ashton Rickhardt* (1977) 65 Cr.App.R. 67, discussed in para. 11.04 *ante.*

Once it is proved to the satisfaction of the jury that the defendant possessed the drug, then they must consider any defences under section 28 put forward by the defendant.[2] He does not thereby shoulder the same burden of proof as the prosecutor. He has to prove his defence on the balance of probabilities—that it is more probable than not that he did not know that the substance in question was a controlled drug. The proper direction was laid down by the Court of Appeal in *R v Carr-Briant* (1943) 29 Cr.App.R. 76 at p. 87:

" . . . . . the jury should be directed that . . . . . the burden of proof required is less than that required at the hands of the prosecution in proving the case beyond a reasonable doubt; and that the burden may be discharged by evidence satisfying the jury of the probability of that which the accused is called upon to establish."

Where a herbalist cultivated a plant of the genus *Cannabis* in her windowbox it was incumbent on the defendant to prove that she did not know that the plant was cannabis. The appellant apparently gave evidence that she thought she was cultivating hemp which was good for certain ailments. Considering this evidence, the Court of Appeal held that she had failed to establish her defence under section 28: *R v Champ* (1982) Crim.L.R. 108 C.A.

**Drunkenness**

**14.03**  Not surprisingly the Courts-Martial Appeal Court looked with disfavour on the proposition that self-induced intoxication could render the defendant so disabled in his mind that he would not have reason to suspect that he had a controlled drug in his possession: *R v Young* (1984) 78 Cr.App.R. 288. Drunkeness was relevant to subjective consideration of the defendant's knowledge or suspicion but not to the objective consideration of whether he had reason for suspicion under section 28(3)(*b*)(i).

2   The defence of duress is considered at para. 5.16 *ante.*

## NEGATIVE AVERMENTS

**14.04**   The prosecution does not have to prove that the defendant did not have a licence etc: see *R v Edwards* (1974) 3 W.L.R. 285 (para. 6-02 *ante* and also paras. 19.02 and 19.03 *post*). The defendant has to prove that he *did* have one—he has to prove that he had a licence upon the balance of probabilities.

# CHAPTER 15

# Special Provisions Relating to Offences

## Attempting and Inciting Commission of Offences

**15.01**   Attempt to commit an indictable offence is now a statutory offence by virtue of the Criminal Attempts Act 1981 (see para. 5.15 *ante*) and section 19 Misuse of Drugs Act 1981 has had its reference to attempt repealed. It is probable that the Criminal Attemps Act has had the effect of reversing the decision in *Kyprianou v Reynolds* [1969] Crim.L.R. 657. In that case the appellant approached a pedlar and said, "What you got tonight boys—hash or heroin? I got money upstairs," then, seeing the police officers, said, "Not now, push off, law." The Court of Appeal held that some further step was required to complete the attempt—the appellant's words were no more than an invitation to treat. This decision imports terms from civil law which in other circumstances the Court of Appeal has held to be undesirable—see for example *R v Delgado* (1984) 78 Cr.App.R 175, discussed in para. 10.03. A recent decision on the test of whether or not an act is merely preparatory is *Ilyas* (1984) 78 Cr.App.R. 17, discussed in para 5.15 *ante*, where the troublesome decision in *Anderton v Ryan* is also considered.

Section 19 of the Misuse of Drugs Act makes it an offence to incite another to commit an offence under any provision of the Act. To incite somebody to do something is to urge him to do it. The incitement does not have to succeed. To send a letter inciting a boy to commit a criminal act completes the offence even if he does not read the letter. The sending of the letter with a criminal intent is the criminal act: *R v Ransford*, 13 Cox 9. Section 25(3) provides that an offence under section 19 shall be subject to the same punishments and mode of trial as the relevant substantive offence.

## Assisting and Inducing Offences Outside the United Kingdom

**15.02**   Section 20 makes it an offence for a person within the United Kingdom to assist in or induce the commission of an offence in a place outside the United Kingdom providing that that offence is punishable under the provisions of a corresponding law in force in that place. The penalties are set out in Schedule 4—the maximum sentence is fourteen years' imprisonment.[1]

Section 36 defines a "corresponding law" as a law certified by a government outside the United Kingdom to be a law for the regulation of controlled drugs in that country in accordance with the Single Convention on Narcotic Drugs of 1961[2] or a law for the regulation of controlled drugs in pursuance of any treaty to which the government of that country and Her Majesty's Government are for the time being parties. By sub-section (2) a statement in such a certificate to the effect that any facts constitute an offence against the law mentioned in the certificate shall be evidence of the matters stated. This important provision gives effect to the Single Convention on Narcotic Drugs of 1961[2] and the Convention on Psychotropic Substances 1971.[3] It is of the utmost importance that the battle against the traffic in controlled drugs should be world-wide. A parochial attitude to drug traffic is as ineffective as it would be towards an epidemic of an infectious disease.

Parliament chose the plain English phrase "assists in . . . . . the commission . . . . . of" so as to leave to a jury the opportunity of exercising a common-sense judgement upon the facts of a particular case. The Court of Appeal so held in the case of *R v Vickers* (1975) 1 W.L.R. 811[4] which concerned conspiracy to take from England speaker cabinets which were to be filled in Italy with cannabis and shipped thence to the United States. The appellant's role was to collect the cabinets in England and transport them to Italy. He knew the object of the exercise. The trial judge ruled that on these facts the offence was made out and the appellant pleaded guilty. He appealed unsuccessfully on the grounds that his role did not amount to an agreement to assist in the commission of the offence of importing drugs into the U.S.A. since it was not sufficiently proximate to the American offence. The court held that there was a case to answer; in ordinary English one who assists knows what he is doing and the defendant knew the purpose of the operation.

The maximum sentence under the corresponding law is irrelevant to sentences passed in the United Kingdom; The Court of Appeal so held in *Faulkner and Thomas* (1976) 63 Cr.App.R. 295, a case which concerned a "hashish run" between Pakistan and Denmark.

**Offences by Corporations**

**15.03** Section 21 provides that where an offence is proved to have been committed by a body corporate, then if it is proved to have been

---

1   The maximum penalty is increased to imprisonment for life for offences committed after 16 September 1985 by the Controlled Drugs (Penalties) Act 1985.
2   Set out in Appendix XI.
3   Set out in Appendix XII.
4   Applied in *R v Evans* (1977) 64 Cr.App.R. 237.

committed with the consent or connivance of, or to be attributable to any neglect of any director, manager, secretary or other similar officer, he as well as the body corporate shall be guilty of that offence. This provision also appears in the Customs and Excise Acts as section 171(4) (see para. 6.04 *ante*).

### Limitation of Time of Trial at a Magistrates Court

**15.04** Subsections (4), (5) and (6) of section 25 provide that a magistrates' court may try an information under the Act provided that it was laid within 12 months from the commission of the offence.

### Mode of Trial

**15.05** Almost all offences under the Act and Regulations are triable summarily or on indictment. Column 3 of Schedule 4 sets out the modes of trial for each offence. The sentences being passed by Crown Court judges for comparatively small-scale supply indicate that magistrates' courts should generally refuse to try cases of supplying Class A or B drugs or possessing Class A or B drugs with intent to supply.

# CHAPTER 16

# Powers of Search and Arrest

## POWERS OF SEARCH

### Power to Inspect Books etc. of Producers and Suppliers

**16.01**   Section 23(1) Misue of Drugs Act 1971 empowers a constable or person duly authorised by the Secretary of State to enter the premises of a person carrying on business as a producer or supplier of controlled drugs and to inspect books and records and stocks of such drugs. Chapters 20 and 21 deal with the required records and the safe custody of drugs.

*Obstruction*

**16.02**   Section 23(4) makes it an offence to obstruct a person in the exercise of his powers under section 23 and, in particular, to conceal or fail to produce books for inspection under section 23(1). Penalties are provided in Schedule 4 and are six months' imprisonment or £2,000 on summary trial, and two years' on indictment.

### Power to Search Persons and Vehicles

**16.03**   Section 23(2) empowers a constable who has reasonable grounds to suspect that any person is in possession of a controlled drug to search that person and detain him for the purpose and to stop vehicles or vessels and to search them. He will also have powers to search an arrested person under section 32 of the Police and Criminal Evidence Act 1984 (set out in Appendix IX). He may seize anything which appears to be evidence of an offence. Sections 2 and 3 of the Police and Criminal Evidence Act 1984 apply to such searches; they cover the exercise of powers of search and records of searches.

Obviously the power to detain must imply a power to stop. The Court of Appeal considered the extent of the power in *R v Green* [1982] Crim.L.R. 604, where a policewoman told a suspect that she wished to question him. The Court held that the right to detain in order to search must necessarily involve the right to detain and question and search. It is unlikely that this means more than ask questions incidental to the search because the word "question" does not appear in section 23(2)(*a*). In the case of *Farrow v Tunnicliffe* [1976] Crim.L.R. 126 the Divisional Court held that the word "detain" empowered a police officer to take a suspect to a police station for the purpose of searching him without there being any need for an arrest. On the other hand where an officer did arrest a suspect in order to search her, a Scottish court held that the subsequent search was illegal and acquitted the suspect of assault on the police officers: *Wither v Reid* 1979 S.L.T. 192. The Lord Justice Clerk dissented from this decision, arguing that an error in the word used did not make it illegal to take the suspect to a police station to search her. A search or attempted search must be explained before-hand to the subject, who is entitled to know the reason for the search. If no such explanation is given, the officer carrying out the search is not acting in execution of his duty and the subject is entitled to resist: *Brazil v Chief Constable of Surrey* (1983) 77 Cr.App.R. 237.

The power to stop and search vehicles seems to be governed by the requirement for the officer to have reasonable grounds to suspect that a person is in possession of a controlled drug. Where an officer had information that a car was suspected of being involved in drug trafficking but had no reason for suspecting that the person in charge was in possession of drugs, Judge Stephen at Doncaster Crown Court held that the search was illegal, although he admitted the evidence so gained: *R v Littleford* [1978] Crim.L.R. 48. This decision must be based on the necessity to establish knowledge as a constituent of possession (see para. 11.03 *ante*). It would appear to follow that a police officer cannot search an unattended car. These conclusions are verging on the fantastic. The officer only requires to have reasonable grounds for suspicion—it must be logical to suspect that the possessor of a motor car knows what it contains. The officer is not required at this stage to be able to prove knowledge.

Where a constable called out to the defendant to stop and the defendant, as soon as the constable caught up with him swallowed something, he was rightly convicted of obstruction of the constable in the execution of his duty under section 23(2)(*a*). The Court of Appeal held that so far as the constable was concerned, it must be established that he had the necessary belief and that he had reasonable grounds for that belief. It must then be established that the defendant knew that the constable wished to detain him in order to search him for drugs and that he intentionally obstructed him. Intentional obstruction is an act which does in fact obstruct the officer and which is intended by the defendant to have that effect: *R v Forde* [1985] Crim.L.R. 323, 81 Cr.App.R. 19.

## Power to Search Premises

**16.04**   Section 23(3) provides that a justice of the peace may issue a warrant authorising a constable to search premises for controlled drugs or documents relating to a prohibited transaction. Sections 9 to 16 of the Police and Criminal Evidence Act 1984 apply. (These are set out in Appendix IX.) They provide a special procedure for items subject to legal privilege or otherwise specially defined in those sections. Sections 15 and 16 are concerned with application for and execution of warrants to search premises.

Where a warrant was made out for Flat 45 whereas the defendant's flat was Flat 30, it did not empower the police to enter Flat 30, and the defendant was wrongly convicted of obstructing them. The Court of Appeal stated that their decision did not apply to trivial errors or misspellings, but that here the warrant applied to quite different premises: *R v Atkinson* [1976] Crim.L.R. 307.

## Evidence Obtained by Illegal Search

**16.05**   Where evidence has been obtained as the result of illegal searches the courts have nevertheless admitted it. The leading case on the subject is *Kuruma v The Queen* [1955] A.C. 197, where the Privy Council held that the test to be applied in considering whether evidence is admissible is whether it is relevant. If it is, the court is not concerned with how it was obtained, although a judge has a discretion to exclude it if the rules of admissibility would operate unfairly. (See also section 78 of the Police and Criminal Evidence Act 1984, set out in Appendix IX).

Where the defendant was arrested for stealing a sandwich and the police took him to his room and searched it, discovering in the process a quantity of cannabis, the justices excluded the evidence and dismissed the charge. The Divisional Court held that although the search was unlawful, the justices had exercised their discretion wrongly by excluding the evidence; although obtained in an irregular manner, it was admissible. The discretion to exclude evidence should only be exercised where the police had acted in a reprehensible manner: *Jeffrey v Black* [1978] 1 Q.B. 490.

## POWERS OF ARREST

**16.06**   Special powers under the 1971 Act[1] have been repealed by the Police and Criminal Evidence Act 1984. Sections 24 and 25 of that Act contain the powers which will now apply to drug offences as to other

1   Formerly contained in s. 24.

offences. These are set out in Appendix IX. A constable must inform the
arrested person at the earliest opportunity of the grounds for his arrest:
*Christie v Leachinsky* [1947] A.C. 573 and section 28 of the Act of 1984.

### Arrestable Offences

**16.07**   Arrestable offences are defined by section 24(1) of the Police and
Criminal Evidence Act 1984 as offences for which the sentence is fixed by
law or for which a person of 21 years of age (not previously convicted)
may be sentenced to imprisonment for a term of five years or more. The
effect of section 8 of the Accessories and Abettors Act 1861, section 3 of
the Criminal Law Act 1977 and section 2 of the Criminal Attempts Act
1981 is to include aiding and abetting, conspiracies and attempts which
carry the required penalties among arrestable offences.

The following offences under the Misuse of Drugs Act are arrestable
offences:

*Section*

4(2)   production
4(3)   supplying
5(2)   possession of Class A or Class B drugs
5(3)   possession with intent to supply (all Classes of controlled
       drugs)
6(2)   cultivation of cannabis plants
8      offences as occupiers of premises etc.
9      special offences relating to opium
12(6) ⎰ contravention of a direction to a
13(3) ⎱ practitioner

*Serious Arrestable Offences*

An offence under the Misuse of Drugs Act (or the Customs and Excise
Acts) which involves any quantity of a Class A drug or considerable
quantity of a Class B or Class C drug would appear to be a "serious
arrestable offence" within the meaning of section 116(6)(*d*) and (*e*) of the
Police and Criminal Evidence Act of 1984, since these are offences which
are likely to have the consequence of serious injury to any person, and the
criterion for prohibiting drugs is that they are dangerous or otherwise
harmful or that they are being or are likely to be misused (section 1(2)
and (3) of the Misuse of Drugs Act).

## TREATMENT, SEARCHES ETC. OF DETAINED PERSONS

**16.08**   This is not the place for a detailed consideration of Part V of the

Police and Criminal Evidence Act 1984, although certain provisions particularly relevant to those accused of drug offences are set out in Appendix IX and are briefly considered below.

Section 54 is concerned with searches of arrested persons and the recording of their property. Section 55 is concerned with intimate searches. "Intimate search" is defined in section 118 as a search which consists of the physical examination of a person's body orifices. Section 55(1)(*b*) (read with subsection (17)) authorises such searches where a superintendent has reasonable grounds for suspecting that a person may have a Class A drug concealed on him and was in possession of it before his arrest with intent to commit an offence contrary to section 5(3) (possession with intent to supply) of the Misuse of Drugs Act 1971 or section 68(2) (exportation) of the Customs and Excise Management Act 1979. An importer will also be committing an offence under section 5(3) if he brings in any quantity of drug, since it must have been his intent, before he was arrested, to pass it on to others. An intimate search for a drug may only be carried out by a registered medical practitioner or by a nurse (subsection (4)). Such a search may not be carried out at a police station (subsection (9)).

Section 62 is concerned with the taking of intimate samples which include blood, semen, urine or saliva. Section 63 is concerned with the taking of non-intimate samples such as of hair, or a toe or finger nail, or a footprint, Scrapings from under fingernails will often reveal whether somebody has been engaged in packing a drug such as heroin in powder form.

Section 65 contains definitions.

The Customs and Excise are likely to continue to operate section 164 of the Customs and Excise Management Act 1979 (see para. 7.05 *ante*).

# CHAPTER 17

# *Penalties*

## PUNISHMENT

**17.01** Section 25 and Schedule 4 prescribe the punishment and mode of trial for the various offences under the Misuse of Drugs Act.[1] In the case of all the more serious offences the maximum penalty varies according to the class of drug in relation to which the offence was committed.

The court is required by Article 36(*a*)(iii) of the Single Convention on Narcotic Drugs 1961[2] to take account of foreign convictions for drug offences as establishing recidivism when passing sentence. It would seem that this requirement, whilst not incorporated in the Act, can be given full weight: *Trawnik v Ministry of Defence* [1984] 2 All E.R. 791 Q.B.D.

### Contravention of Regulations and Licences and False Statements

**17.02** Section 18 makes it an offence to contravene regulations or the terms of a licence or authority under the Act with the exception of regulations made in pursuance of Section 10(2)(*h*) or (*i*) or licences issued under section 10(2)(*l*). (Section 10(2)(*h*) and (*i*) are concerned with doctors treating addicts). Subsection (3) makes it an offence for a person to give information required from him under any regulation falsely or recklessly and subsection (4) relates to false statements etc. used for the purpose of obtaining a licence or authority. Schedule 4 prescribes the penalties.

## GUIDELINES ON SENTENCE

**17.03** The guidance given to the sentencers by the Lord Chief Justice in *R v Aramah* (1983) 76 Cr.App.R. 190 is described in para 8.04 in relation to importers. Guidance was also given in relation to offences under the Misuse of Drugs Act. This guidance is subject to the increase in the maximum penalty in relation to Class A drugs to life imprisonment.[3]

---

1  Life imprisonment applies to certain offences committed after 16 September 1985: Schedule 4, Misuse of Drugs Act 1971 as amended by the Controlled Drugs (Penalties) Act 1985 (for the amended text of the 1971 Act see Appendix III).
2  Set out in Appendix XI.
3  See n. 1 above.

*For supplying Class A drugs* the penalty should seldom be less than three years imprisonment—the nearer the source the longer the term. "Big fish" should receive sentences similar to those imposed on importers. For possession of such drugs the circumstances of the offender are more important but imprisonment must be a possibility. "Beginners or not, anyone who trades in dangerous drugs, particularly heroin, must expect very severe sentences;" the Court of Appeal so stated when confirming sentences of seven years' imprisonment for supplying heroin and ten years' for offering to supply heroin. The first defendant was in possession of 52 grams with a street value of £5,200, the second defendant was in possession of 45 grams: *Ashraf and Huq* [1981] 3 Cr.App.R. (S) 287.

*For supplying Class B drugs* (with particlar reference to cannabis) offenders should receive one to four years' imprisonment. "Big fish" should receive sentences of up to ten years'. Supplying a number of smaller sellers comes at the top of the scale. At the lower end comes the retailer of small quantities to consumers. For possession a fine should be appropriate but imprisonment may be required for persistent offenders.

The penalty under the corresponding law of another country is irrelevant to a sentence in this country under section 20: *Faulkner and Thomas* (1976) 63 Cr.App.R. 295. It seems that the court should apply the same considerations as it would if the offence were committed in the United Kingdom.

A series of decisions seems to establish that the penalty for supplying very small quantities of Class A drugs should be in the region of four years imprisonment although this tariff may well be increased if the menace of heroin abuse continues to increase: *R. v Gee* (1984) 6 Cr.App.R. (S) 86 and *R v Guiney* [1985] Crim.L.R. 751.

*Addicts*

There is no specific power in the Act to require an addict to submit to treatment for his addiction. However a probation order can be made with a requirement that the offender shall submit to treatment: section 3, Powers of Criminal Courts Act 1973. This would normally be at a drug dependence clinic under the supervision of a doctor licenced under Regulation 4 of the Misuse of Drugs (Notification of and Supply to Addicts) Regulations 1973[4]—see para. 22.04 *post* and Chapter 4 (Treatment of Drug Dependence).

Supplying to young persons must call for a heavy penalty: *Williams* [1969] Crim.L.R. 497; and *Macauley* (1967) 52 Cr.App.R. 230, where the maximum sentence of ten years' imprisonment was upheld in the case of

---

4   S.I. no. 799; set out in Appendix VI.

supply of ten heroin tablets to a fifteen-year-old boy.

Section 1(3) of the Mental Health Act 1983 excludes dependence on drugs from the definition of "mental disorder". This means that hospital orders are not available to the courts in the case of addicts unless they suffer from mental disorder as a result of their addiction.


## FORFEITURE

**17.04** Subject to the rights of any other person interested in the property, a court is empowered by section 27 to order forfeiture of any thing proved to relate to an offence under the Act of which a person before the court has been convicted. Subsection (2) gives an owner a right to apply to the court to show cause why an order should not be made. This provision does not apply to convictions for conspiracy to commit an offence under the Act (*R v Cuthbertson and others.*[1980] 2 All E.R. 401, the "Operation Julie" case, discussed below) but it does apply to attempts (section 2 Criminal Attempts Act 1981). Forfeiture is part of the sentence of the court and section 11 of the Courts Act 1971 applies to it. It cannot be varied nor can it be added to a sentence outside the twenty-eight days allowed by section 11(2): *R v Menocal* (1979) 69 Cr.App.R.156 H.L.

Mr Justice Caulfield, sitting at the Central Criminal Court, construed the words "any thing" as not applying to real property: *R v Beard* [1974] 1 W.L.R. 1549. A similar construction was apparently given to the words by the House of Lords in *Cuthbertson* (*supra*) where Lord Diplock said (at p. 483):

> "I would apply a purposive construction to the section considered as a whole. What does it set out to do? Its evident purpose is to enable things to be forfeited so that they may be destroyed or dealt with in some other manner as the court thinks fit. The words are apt and, as it seems to me, are only apt to deal with things that are tangible, things of which physical possession can be taken by a person authorised to do so by the court and which are capable of being physically destroyed by that person or disposed by him in some other way. To ascribe to the section any more extended ambit would involve putting a strained construction on the actual language that is used, and, so far from there being any grounds for doing so, it seems to me that if it were attempted to extend the subject-matter of orders of forfeiture to choses in action or other intangibles, this would lead to difficulties and uncertainties in application which it can hardly be supposed that Parliament intended to create . . . . . . .
>
> So one limitation on the subject-matter of an order for forfeiture is that it must be something tangible."

This passage was construed by Lord Justice Dunn as indicating that a forfeiture order under section 27 (or section 43 of the Powers of Criminal

Courts Act 1973) could not be made in respect of real property: *R v Khan* [1982] 3 All E.R. 969.

### Forfeiture of Money—Bank Balances etc.

**17.05**   Money may be the subject of an order under section 27: *R v Beard* [1974] 1 W.L.R. 1549. Where the appellant was arrested with drugs in his possession for the purpose of supplying them to others and with £393 in cash, the money was ordered to be forfeited. In quashing the order the Court of Appeal held that the money was part of his working capital. The court evidently was not satisfied that it was sufficiently closely connected with the offences of which he was convicted: *R v Morgan* [1977] Crim.L.R. 488.[5] It is also wrong to impose a disproportionate fine in order to get at the proceeds of drug trading: *R v Johnson* [1984] Crim.L.R. 691.

Section 27 is not intended to be used to strip drug traffickers of their profits. To quote again from Lord Diplock in *Cuthbertson* [1980] 2 All E.R. 401 (*supra*) at p.406:

> "On any charge of a substantial offence by a sole offender . . . . . it is not disputed that it would be necessary to connect the specific thing sought to be forfeited with the particular substantive offence to which it is related. In such a case it could not plausibly be suggested that the section authorises the court (so to speak) 'to follow the assets' by applying a process of reasoning such as this, for instance: the offender received £1000 in cash out of this particular transaction of which he was convicted; he paid the cash into his bank account; six months later out of the balance of that account, then standing at £4,500, he bought a car worth £4000, leaving £500 remaining in the account; the court therefore has jurisdiction to order the forfeiture of either a one quarter share in the car or a one-eighth share together with the bank's debt to the offender to the amount of £500 standing to his credit in the bank account."

It seems probable that legislation will be enacted following the report of the Hodgson Committee[6] to make it possible to trace and seize assets acquired as a result of offences against the Misuse of Drugs Act and the offence of importing or evading the prohibition on importing controlled drugs. The present position is that such assets must be tangible and relate closely to the offence of which the possessor is convicted, for it to be possible for them to be seized.

### Notices etc. to be Served by Post

**17.06**   Section 29 makes provision for the service of notices and other

---

5   Followed in *R v Llewellyn* [1985] Crim.L.R. 750.
6   *Profits of Crime and their Recovery*, Cambridge Studies in Criminology Vol. LII, Heinemann.

documents either by delivery or by post. The address of a person shall be taken to be the last such address known to the Secretary of State.

Subsection (4) is concerned with service of the following documents:

(1) a notice under section 11(1) (special precautions for safe custody—para. 21.01 *post*);

(2) a notice under section 15(6) (temporary directions to a practitioner—para. 23.04 *post*)

(3) a direction under section 12(2) (prohibitions on convicted practitioners—para. 23.01 *post*);

(4) a direction under section 13(1) or (2) (prohibitions on irresponsible practitioners—para.23.02 *post*);

(5) a direction under section 16(3) (cancelling of directions under sections 14(7) and 15).

They are assumed to have been served at the time when the letter containing the document(s) would be delivered in the ordinary course of post.

# CHAPTER 18

# Power to Make Regulations

Sections 7, 10, and 22 Misuse of Drugs Act 1971 empower the Secretary of State (the Home Secretary) to make regulations. His power is amplified by section 31(1). Before making any regulations the Secretary of State must first consult the Advisory Council on the Misuse of Drugs[1] (section 31(3)). The power to make regulations must be exercised by statutory instrument subject to annulment in pursuance of a resolution of either House of Parliament (section 31(2)).

Section 7 authorises the Secretary of State to make lawful activities which would otherwise be prohibited under the Act. In particular he is required by subsection (3) to make lawful the use of controlled drugs by medical practitioners etc. which they need for their legitimate activities. Section 7(4) permits him to exclude from legitimisation such drugs as he so designates in the public interest. The drugs scheduled to the Misuse of Drugs (Designation) Order 1977 (as amended by S.I. 1984/1144) are excluded from such legitimisation, although possession etc. may be permitted by special licence.

The following statutory instruments are set out in their amended form as follows:

The Misuse of Drugs Regulations 1973 (S.I. no. 797)—Appendix IV

The Misuse of Drugs (Safe Custody) Regulations 1973 (S.I. no. 798)—Appendix V

The Misuse of Drugs (Notification of and Supply to Addicts) Regulations 1973 (S.I. no. 799)—Appendix VI

The Misuse of Drugs (Designation) Order 1977 (S.I. no. 1379)—Appendix VII.

Contravention of the regulations and making of false statments are dealt with in para. 17.02 *ante*.

There is a strong argument that in all the exceptions introduced by the Misuse of Drugs Regulations the burden of proof rests on the defendant. It is the burden of persuasion: *R v Hunt, Times* 24 November 1985 C.A.

---

1   See para. 1.15 *ante*.

# CHAPTER 19

# *Authority to Administer, Prescribe, Supply or Possess Drugs*

### General Authority to Possess Drugs

**19.01** Regulation 6 of the Misuse of Drugs Regulations 1973 (S.I. no. 797) authorises constables, carriers, employees of the Post Office, customs officers, forensic scientists and persons conveying drugs to an authorised person to possess controlled drugs in the course of their duties.

### Administration and Supply etc. of Drugs Specified in Schedules

**19.02** Schedules 1, 2, 3 and 4 of the Misuse of Drugs Regulations 1973 list various drugs. These schedules do not coincide with the classifications in Schedule 2 to the 1971 Act.

*Schedule 1* is concerned with preparations which contain a very small proportion of a controlled drug, such as aspirin and codeine compounds of Kaolin and morphine. Controls over such preparations are relaxed by Regulations 4 and 7(1). It is no offence under the Misuse of Drugs Act 1971 to import them, or to possess them or to administer them to others. The burden of proof that a drug is one of those specified in Schedule 1 rests upon the defendant. It is the burden of persuasion (see para. 14.02): *R v Hunt*, *Times*, 24 November 1985 C.A.

*Schedule 2* lists a large number of Class A and Class B drugs (but not cannabis or opium).

*Schedule 3* lists a number of Class B and Class C drugs.

*Schedule 4* lists a number of drugs which are not normally used in medicine such as cannabis, coca-leaf, LSD and raw opium. No general exemptions apply to these drugs which form the same list of drugs as are scheduled to the Misuse of Drugs (Designation) Order 1977.

Regulation 5 makes provision for special licences to be issued in respect of such controlled drugs.

Paragraphs (2) and (3) of Regulation 7 authorise doctors or dentists to administer drugs listed in Schedule 2 and 3 and provide that any person may administer them in accordance with the directions of a doctor or dentist. Regulations 8 and 9 are concerned with the manufacture or compounding of drugs by doctors and pharmacists and the supply of such drugs by a practitioner (defined in section 37(1) of the Act), a matron, sister or nurse and by other specified categories of person.

Regulation 11 authorises midwives to administer pethidine.

## Lawful Possession of Drugs listed in Schedules 2 and 3

**19.03**   Regulation 10(1) authorises a person specified in regulations 8(2) and 9(2) to have in his possession drugs specified in schedule 2 or 3 respectively for the purpose of acting in his official capacity. Regulation 10(2) authorises other persons to have such drugs in their possession for administration for medical, dental or veterinary purposes in accordance with the directions of a practitioner (defined in section 37(1) of the Act) subject to such a person not having obtained the prescription without disclosing that he was also obtaining prescriptions from another doctor or by making a false statement to obtain the prescription. Regulation 10(5) is concerned with the masters of ships and managers of offshore installations.

If an accused person wishes to rely on an exception under section 7 and the relevant regulations the onus of establishing that defence is on him. The facts whether he comes within an excepted category lie peculiarly within his own knowledge. He must produce *prima facie* evidence that he is within such a category. If the jury thinks that the evidence is true or may reasonably be true, then he is entitled to be acquitted: *R v Ewens* [1967] 1 Q.B. 322. The standard of proof appears to be on the balance of probabilities: *R v Carr-Briant* (para. 14.02 *ante*).

Where the defence rely on a prescription they must establish the existence at the relevant time of a lawful prescription complying with the requirements of the relevant regulations. Regulation 15 (*post*, para. 20.02) is concerned with the form to be followed in drawing up a prescription. A remark by a doctor that tablets might be useful for a certain purpose cannot amount to a prescription: *R v Jagger* (1967) 51 Cr.App.R. 473.

Once a person is in lawful possession of drugs prescribed for him by a doctor, the possession does not become unlawful because he has finished his course of treatment. Nor does the possession become unlawful because he has become unaware of their existence because he has forgotten them or believed, mistakenly, that they had been destroyed: *R v Buswell* [1972] 1 All.E.R. 75, C.A.

In the case of *Ian Dunbar* (1982) 74 Cr.App.R. 88 the Court of Appeal considered the position of a doctor who obtained Class A drugs for the purpose of administering them to himself. The trial judge ruled that in such circumstances he did not have the drugs for the purpose of acting in his capacity as a doctor as required by Regulation 10 and was therefore not provided with a defence under section 7 of the Act. The Court Appeal held that a doctor can act in his capacity as a doctor when treating himself. It is a matter for the jury to decide whether he is acting in good faith as a doctor or not.

These regulations do not authorise possession of drugs listed in Schedule 4.

**Permission to Cultivate and Smoke Cannabis**

**19.04**　Regulation 12 provides for the issue of licences for the cultivation of cannabis plants. Regulation 13 permits the use of cannabis for the purpose of research in premises approved by the Secretary of State.

CHAPTER 20

# Requirements as to Documentation and Record-Keeping

## DOCUMENTS

### Documents to be Obtained by Supplier

**20.01**  Regulation 14 of the Misuse of Drugs Regulations 1973 (S.I. no. 797) is concerned with persons supplying controlled drugs other than on prescription. It provides that such drugs may only be supplied on the production of signed requisition from a person authorised to have them and, if they are collected by an agent, a statement in writing signed by the recipient to the effect that he is empowered by the recipient to collect the drugs.

### Form of Prescriptions

**20.02**  Regulation 15 prescribes the manner in which a prescription for a controlled drug (other than a drug specified in Schedule 1) is to be drawn and its contents. In particular it must be written and signed in ink, contain the date, the address of the person issuing it (unless it is a National Health Service prescription) and the name and address of the recipient and specify the dose and the total quantity to be supplied. It may specify that the drug is to be dispensed in instalments. Pheno-barbitone is excepted from the requirements of Regulation 15 by paragraph 2(A) (added by S.I. 1984/1143). There is, of course, no provision for repeat prescriptions.

### Supply on Prescription

**20.03**  Regulation 16 provides that a controlled drug shall only be supplied (a) in accordance with a prescription which complies with Regulation 15, and (b) where the supplier recognises the signature or takes steps to satisfy himself that it is genuine. The address of the practitioner must be an address within the United Kingdom. The container must be marked with the date of issue, which must be within thirteen weeks of the date of the prescription. Unless it is a National Health Service prescription it is to be retained on the premises. Regulation 18 is concerned with the marking of bottles and other containers.

153

**Registers**

**20.04**  Regulation 19 provides for the keeping of registers by persons supplying drugs listed in Schedules 2 or 4. Regulations 19 and 20 prescribe the form and contents of such registers. Regulation 22 requires such registers to be preserved for two years.

*Records of Schedule 1 Drugs*

**20.05**  Regulation 23 requires producers, wholesalers and retailers of drugs specified in Schedule 1 to keep invoices and records of such drugs for two years. The requirement imposed on retailers is limited to records of receipt by the retailer.

*Destruction of Drugs*

**20.06**  Regulation 24 makes provision for the keeping of records concerning the destruction of drugs listed in Schedules 2 and 4. Such drugs may only be destroyed in the presence of a person authorised by the Secretary of State.


## SUPPLY ON PRESCRIPTION UNDER MEDICINES ACT 1968

**20.07**  The provisions relating to controlled drugs may be contrasted with those that apply to the sale of prescription-only medicines. Section 58 of the Medicines Act 1968 empowers the appropriate ministers by order to specify medicines. No person may supply such medicines by retail sale without a prescription by a doctor, dentist or veterinary practitioner. (A practitioner may supply his own patients.) No person other than an appropriate practitioner or a person acting in accordance with the directions of an appropriate practitioner may administer such medicines except to himself. The maximum penalty for contravention is two years' imprisonment. Sale or supply other than in accordance with a prescription is an offence of strict liability: *Pharmaceutical Society of Great Britain v Storkwain Ltd* (1985) *The Times*, 9 May.

Medicines are specified in Schedule 1 to the Medicines (Products other than Veterinary Drugs) (Prescription Only) Order 1983 (S.I. no.1212). Article 12 lays down conditions for the sale of such medicines. A prescription must (1) be signed in ink by the practitioner, (2) be indelible (but, if it does not relate to controlled drugs, it may be written by means of carbon paper), (3) give the address and the capacity of the practitioner, (4) give the date, (5) give the name and address of the patient, and (6) not be older than six months unless it is a repeat prescription, in which case paragraphs (*d*) and (*e*) lay down special conditions.

## SUPPLY BY RETAIL OF POISONS

**20.08** Poisons are listed in Part I and Part II of the Poisons List Order 1978 (S.I. no. 2) made under the Poisons Act 1972. Part I substances may only be sold by pharmacists; Part II substances may be sold by pharmacists and by persons entered on a list maintained by local authorities. In general terms poisons can only be sold to authorised purchasers and the sale must be entered in a book kept for the purpose and signed by the purchaser. The Poisons Rules 1982 (S.I. no. 218) supplement the requirements of the Poisons Act.

# CHAPTER 21

# *Safe Custody of Drugs*

The Misuse of Drugs (Safe Custody) Regulations 1973 (S.I. no.798), set out in Appendix V, provide for the safe custody of controlled drugs kept by retail dealers (defined in Regulation 2), nursing homes and hospitals. Drugs are to be kept in locked safes, cabinets or rooms which comply with the requirements of Schedule 2 to the Regulations unless a certificate is issued by a chief officer of police stating that security is adequate. Regulation 5 provides that when the drugs are not in a locked safe etc. they shall be kept in a locked receptacle which can only be opened by the owner or a person authorised by him.

In addition to the general requirements imposed by the Regulations, the Secretary of State may by notice give specific directions to the occupier of any premises where drugs are kept. This power is contained in section 11 of the Misuse of Drugs Act 1971, and the penalty for contravention of directions is specified in Schedule 4. Drugs listed in Schedule 1 to the Regulations are exempted. These include some barbiturates and amphetamines.

A medical practitioner who left drugs in an unlocked case inside a locked up motor car did not leave them in a locked receptacle; Lord Goddard held that a motor car is not a receptacle within the meaning of the predecessor of Regulation 5: *Rao v Wyles* [1949] 2 All E.R. 685 K.B.

# CHAPTER 22

# Notification of and Supply to Addicts

## Relevant Drugs

**22.01** The Misuse of Drugs (Notification of and Supply to Addicts) Regulations 1973 (S.I. no. 799), set out in Appendix VI, apply to the controlled drugs specified in the Schedule—these include all the more notorious drugs of addiction such as cocaine and heroin. Contravention of these regulation or of a licence issued in pursuance of them is not in itself an offence (Section 13(3) Misuse of Drugs Act 1971) but doctors contravening the regulations may be subjected to directions under section 13 (see para. 23.02 *post*).

## Definition of Addict

**22.02** Regulation 2(2) defines an addict as:

"a person shall be regarded as being addicted to a drug if, and only if, he has as a result of repeated administration become so dependent upon the drug that he has an overpowering desire for the administration of it to be continued."

(Features of addiction are described in Chapter 2.)

## Notification to Home Office

**22.03** Regulation 3 requires any doctor who attends an addict to furnish within seven days a written notification to the Chief Medical Officer at the Home Office of the personal particulars of the addict, unless the controlled drug is required for the purpose of treating organic disease or injury. This requirement is limited to persons addicted to one of the drugs listed in the Schedule to the Regulations.

## Administration of Heroin, Cocaine and Dipipanone

**22.04** The effect of Regulation 4 is to prevent a doctor from administering or supplying heroin, cocaine or dipipanone[1] except for the treatment of organic disease or injury unless he is licenced to do so by the Secretary of State.

1 Added by S.I. 1983/1909.

# CHAPTER 23

# Powers of Control over Practitioners and Pharmacists

## Prohibition of Prescribing after Conviction

**23.01**   Section 12 of the Misuse of Drugs Act 1971 provides that where a practitioner (defined in section 37) or a pharmacist has, after the date of coming into operation of the section (1st July 1973), been convicted of an offence under the Act or under relevant provisions of the Customs and Excise Acts, the Secretary of State may give a direction prohibiting him from prescribing, possessing or supplying such controlled drugs as may be specified in the direction. It is an offence to contravene such a direction; the penalty is specified in Schedule 4.

## DIRECTIONS

### Directions to Doctors Treating Addicts and to Irresponsible Practitioners

**23.02**   Section 13(1) is concerned with contraventions by a doctor of the requirements of the Misuse of Drugs (Notification of and Supply to Addicts) Regulations 1973 (S.I. no. 799—see Chapter 22 *ante*) and of licences issued to doctors under those regulations. Such contraventions are not in themselves offences (section 13(3)). Section 13(2) is concerned with practitioners (defined in Section 37) who supply or authorise the supply of controlled drugs in an irresponsible manner.

In either case the Secretary of State may give directions prohibiting a practitioner from prescribing, administering or supplying such drugs as may be specified in the direction. Such a direction takes effect when a copy is served (section 16(2)). It is a serious offence to contravene such a direction; the penalty is specified in Schedule 4. The Secretary of State is required to refer the matter to a tribunal before giving a direction unless in the case of irresponsible behaviour under subsection (2) he considers that it is a matter of urgency (see para. 23.04).

A doctor who issues prescriptions for heroin substitutes irresponsibly is likely to be struck off the Medical Register for serious professional misconduct.

### Investigation of Grounds for a Direction

**23.03**   Section 14 provides that if the Secretary of State considers that

158

there are grounds for giving a direction he may refer the case to a tribunal constituted in accordance with Schedule 3, Part I.[1] The procedure to be followed is prescribed in the Schedule and by the Misuse of Drugs Tribunal (England and Wales) Rules 1974 (S.I. no. 85), set out in Appendix VIII. The practitioner is entitled to be legally represented. The tribunal will consider the case and report on it to the Secretary of State. Where the tribunal finds that a case has been made out and that a direction under section 13 is appropriate, it should indicate the controlled drugs that should be specified in the direction. The Secretary of State shall thereupon serve a notice on the practitioner stating whether or not he proposes to give a direction and, if he proposes to give one, the terms. The practitioner may make representations within a period of twenty-eight days.

If the practitioner does make representations, they will be referred to an advisory body constituted in accordance with Schedule 3, Part II. The practitioner is entitled to be legally represented. The advisory body may regulate its own procedure. It is the duty of the advisory body to advise the Secretary of State whether it considers a direction is appropriate. After the expiry of the twenty-eight days, or after receiving the advice of the advisory body, the Secretary of State may give a direction, refer the matter back to a tribunal or order that no further proceedings shall be taken.

The tribunal is subject to the supervision of the Council on Tribunals in accordance with the Tribunals and Enquiries (Misuse of Drugs Tribunals) Order 1973 (S.I. no. 1600).

## Temporary Directions

**23.04** Section 15 empowers the Secretary of State in a case of urgency under section 13(2) to refer the matter to a professional panel constituted in accordance with Schedule 3, Part III. The practitioner is entitled to legal representation. The professional panel may regulate its own procedure.

Where the panel reports that there are reasonable grounds for thinking that there has been such conduct as is mentioned in section 13(2) the Secretary of State may give a direction under the section. He must forthwith refer the matter to a tribunal. The period of such a direction shall be six weeks but it may be extended by notice in writing for further periods of twenty-eight days.

---

1   There were three references in 1983 and three in 1984. In each case the doctor was prohibited from supplying some or all controlled drugs.

## SOCIAL PROBLEMS IN ANY AREA

**23.05**   If it appears to the Secretary of State that there exists in any area a social problem caused by extensive misuse of dangerous or harmful drugs, he is empowered by section 17 to serve notice on any doctor or pharmacist in the area requiring him to furnish to the Secretary of State such particulars as may be specified in the notice. Such a notice may require a pharmacist to name a doctor on whose prescription such drugs were supplied, but shall not require the names or particulars of any person for or to whom such drugs were prescribed or supplied. It is an offence to fail to comply with such a notice or to furnish false particulars; the penalties are set out in Schedule 4

This provision is not restricted in its application to controlled drugs but it has no application to such materials as solvents or others which are not sold by pharmacists.

# CHAPTER 24

# *Extradition*

## Drug Offences Extraditable

**24.01** Section 1 of the Extradition Act 1932 provides that the Extradition Act 1870 shall be construed as if offences against any enactment for the time being in force relating to dangerous drugs, and attempts to commit such offences, were included in the list of crimes in Schedule 1 to the Act of 1870.

Article 36(2) of the Single Convention on Narcotic Drugs 1961 provides that serious offences listed in that article shall be prosecuted by the party in whose territory the offender is found if extradition is not acceptable in conformity with the law of the party to which application is made.

## Conspiracy Extraditable

**24.02** Section 33 of the Misuse of Drugs Act 1971 includes conspiracy to commit any offence against any dangerous drugs legislation in Schedule 1 to the Act of 1870.

# CHAPTER 25

# The Intoxicating Substances (Supply) Act 1985

## Offence of Supply of Intoxicating Substance

**25.01**  Section 1(1) of the Intoxicating Substances (Supply) Act 1985 makes it an offence to supply a substance which is not a controlled drug to a person under the age of eighteen if the supplier knows or has reasonable cause to believe that the recipient is likely to inhale it for the purpose of causing intoxication ("glue sniffing"). It is also an offence to supply such a substance to a person acting on behalf of a person under the age of eighteen if the supplier knows or has reasonable cause to believe that it will be used for such a purpose. (For the medical effects of solvent abuse see para. 3.38 *ante*). The only definition in the Act is in subsection (4) of section 1, where "controlled drug" is given the same meaning as in the Misuse of Drugs Act 1971. The Act is set out in Appendix X and came into effect on 13 August 1985.

## Special Defence

**25.02**  Section 1(2) makes it a defence for a supplier to show that at the time of making the supply he was under eighteen and was not acting in the course of furtherance of a business. The defendant would have to establish both legs of the defence on the balance of probabilities (see para. 14.02 *ante*).

## Penalties and Mode of Trial

**25.03**  Section 1(3) provides for a maximum penalty upon summary trial of six months' imprisonment or a fine not exceeding level 5 on the standard scale (at present £1,000).

# CHAPTER 26

# *Drafting the Charge*

## GENERAL

### Indictments

**26.01** In drafting an indictment the provisions of the Indictment Act 1915 and the Indictment Rules 1971[1] must be complied with. In general the indictment must identify the offence and (unless a common law offence) the statutory provision contravened and give sufficient particulars to enable the accused to know what is alleged against him so that he can prepare his defence. Where the exact quantity of a drug involved is known, it is sensible to specify it in the indictment. If the defence is embarrassed by lack of details, it should apply to the prosecution for further particulars. If these are refused an application should be made to the Crown Court for a practice direction. The Practice Rules of the Central Criminal Court make provision for a judge to rule upon such an application (Rule 6)—other Crown Courts proceed by analogy.

### Informations

**26.02** The rules for drafting informations leading to appearances in magistrates' courts are less specific. Rule 4 of the Magistrates Courts Rules 1981[2] and Forms 1 and 2 require the accused to be given "short particulars and statute". It is submitted that natural justice entitles an accused at a magistrates' court to have sufficient particulars to enable him to prepare his defence or, as least, to be clear about the charge which is made against him.

### Duplicity

**26.03** Rule 4(2) of the Indictment Rules 1971 requires that where more than one offence is charged in an indictment the statement and particulars of each shall be set out in a separate count. Rule 12 of the Magistrates' Courts Rules 1981 provides that the Court shall not proceed to the trial of an information that charges more than one offence.

1  S.I. no. 1253.
2  S.I. no. 552.

*Alternatives*

**26.04** Rule 7 of the Indictment Rules 1971 allows the prosecution to allege the committal of an offence in the alternative. There is no equivalent of Rule 7 applying to informations in the magistrates' courts, which means that decisions on indictments may not be applicable to informations and *vice versa*. Rule 7 is in the following terms:

> "Where an offence created by or under an enactment states the offence to be the doing or the omission to do any one of any different acts in the alternative, or the doing or the omission to do any act in any one of the different capacities, or with any one of any different intentions, or states any part of the offence in the alternative, the acts, omissions, capacities or intentions, or other matters stated in the alternative in the enactment or subordinate instrument may be stated in the alternative in an indictment charging the offence."

For example section 8 of the Misuse of Drugs Act 1971 creates a number of separate offences: "A person commits an offence if, being the occupier or concerned in the management of any premises . . . . ." Rule 7 has the effect that it is permissible to indict a person in those various capacities in the alternative. However the Divisional Court has decided that in the case of summary trials these words create two offences that cannot be included in one information: *R v Ware and Fox* [1967] 1 All E.R. 100. The Divisional Court also held that using premises for supplying drugs was a different offence from using premises for smoking: *Fox v Dingley and Another* [1967] 1 All E.R. 103 and it would seem that this would also apply to indictments under section 8, which does not set out those activities as alternatives. (The cases cited concerned section 5 of the Dangerous Drugs Act 1965).

It is permissible to indict for possession of either cannabis or cannabis resin because the definition in Schedule 2 to the Act of 1971 links the two substances. In *R v Best* [1979] Crim.L.R. 787 the Court Appeal specifically did not rely on Rule 7 and it is submitted that the decision applies equally to informations. It is further submitted that a count or information would be a good one if it alleged possession either of a drug or its stereoisomer or salt (*R v Watts* (1984) 79 Cr.App.R. 127, discussed in para. 9.02 *ante*).

*Separate Quantities*

**26.05** A search of premises often reveals drugs hidden in different places. The question then arises whether they should be aggregated, set out separately in one count or given separate counts. If the drugs belong to different classes or are distinct from each other in their nature, e.g. cocaine and heroin, they should be put into different counts or informations. If the drugs are the same or similar, e.g. cannabis and cannabis resin, it is submitted that the course to be taken must depend on the circumstances. Obviously if it is likely that the accused might have a different defence in respect of a quantity found in one place from that in respect of a quantity found in another, or if the evidence differs in respect of each, they should be specified in different counts. The question has, however, been much reduced in importance since the "usable quantity" test has been held irrelevant (see para. 11.05 *ante*). In the case of *Peevey* (1973) 57 Cr.App.R. 554 C.A. the defendant was charged with possessing drugs, some of which were found in his wallet and a larger quantity under the driving seat of his car. It is unclear whether they were particularised or aggregated but the Court of Appeal found no fault with the indictment. It was held that proof of possession of any of the tablets was sufficient to justify a verdict of guilty. In the unreported case of *R v Bryan* C.A. 8 November 1984 it was held that a count charging possession with intent to supply of two packets of cannabis—one of 19 grams and one of 2 grams—was not bad for duplicity. A charge before a magistrates' court would not be bad for duplicity solely on the grounds that it alleged possession of a number of separate quantities: *R v Bristol Crown Court ex parte Willets* [1985] Crim.L.R. 219, a case concerning obscene articles; see also *Bullen v Jardine* [1985] Crim.L.R. 668 where one information correctly charged unlawful felling of 90 trees.

*Section 170(2) of the Customs and Excise Management Act*
**26.06** This section creates at least two offences. These are (1) being knowingly concerned in a fraudulent evasion, and (2) being knowingly concerned in an attempted evasion. In *Miller and Hanoman Ltd* [1959] Crim.L.R. 50 the statement of offence was wrong in alleging both an attempt and the wrong offence but the particulars were correct and the Court of Appeal applied the proviso to section 4(1) of the Criminal Appeal Act 1907 and dismissed the appeal. This decision is of little significance when drafting an indictment because the full offence can be charged if there is any doubt and the jury may still convict of attempt (section 6(4) Criminal Law Act 1967).

*Conspiracies*
**26.07** Care should be taken in deciding whether one or more conspiracies are revealed by the evidence. If several defendants each conspire with one accused, then if there is a common purpose there will be one conspiracy, but if each conspirator has his own purpose there will be several conspiracies: *R v Griffiths* (1965) 49 Cr.App.R. 279; *R v Greenfield* (1973) 57 Cr.App.R. 849:

**Exceptions, Exemptions and Excuses**

**26.08** Rule 6(c) of Indictment Rules 1971 provides that it is not necessary to specify or negative an exception, proviso, excuse or qualification. Rule 4(3) of the Magistrates' Court Rules 1981 is in similar terms.

## MODEL INDICTMENTS

### 26.09 (1) Customs and Excise Management Act 1979

*Importation*

#### Statement of Offence

Being knowingly concerned in the fraudulent evasion of the prohibition on importation of a controlled drug, contrary to section 170(2) of the Customs and Excise Management Act 1979.

#### Particulars of Offence

A.B. was, on 26 November 1984 in relation to a Class A controlled drug, namely 372 grams of a powder containing diamorphine, knowingly concerned in the fraudulent evasion of the prohibition on importation imposed by section 3(1) of the Misuse of Drugs Act 1971.

*Conspiracy to Import*

#### Statement of Offence

Conspiracy, contrary to section 1(1) of the Criminal Law Act 1977.

#### Particulars of offence

A.B., C.D. and E.F., on divers days between 1 September 1984 and 30 November 1984, conspired together and with G.H. and others unknown to evade the prohibition on the importation of diamorphine imposed by section 3(1) of the Misuse of Drugs Act 1971 in contravention of section 170(2) of the Customs and Excise Management Act 1979.

*Attempt to Import*[4]

#### Statement of Offence

Being knowingly concerned in an attempted fraudulent evasion of the prohibition on importation of a controlled drug contrary to section 170(2) of the Customs and Excise Management Act 1979.

---

4 This would only apply if the drugs never came within the limits of a port or airport; see para. 5.08 *ante*.

*Particulars of Offence*

A.B. was on 1 November 1984 in relation to a Class B controlled drug, namely cannabis or cannabis resin, knowingly concerned in an attempt at fraudulent evasion of the prohibition on importation imposed by section 3(1) of the Misuse of Drugs Act 1971.

*Attempt to Export*

*Statement of Offence*

Attempting to export a controlled drug contrary to section 1(1)[5] of the Criminal Attempts Act 1981.

*Particulars of Offence*

A.B. on 20 December 1984 attempted to export a controlled drug of Class A, namely one kilogram of diamorphine, in contravention of section 3 of the Misuse of Drugs Act 1971 and section 68(1)(a) of the Customs and Excise Management Act 1979.

**(2) Misuse of Drugs Act 1971**

*Possession*

*Statement of Offence*

Possession of a controlled drug, contrary to section 5(2) of the Misuse of Drugs Act 1971.

*Particulars of Offence*

A.B. on 20 January 1985 was in possession of a controlled drug of Class B, namely one gram of cannabis or cannabis resin.[6]

*Possession with Intent to Supply*

*Statement of Offence*

Possession of a controlled drug with intent to supply contrary to section 5(3) of the Misuse of Drugs Act 1971.

*Particulars of Offence*

A.B. and C.D., on 20 January 1983, were in possession of a controlled drug of Class B, namely 303 grams of cannabis, with intent to supply it to another.

5   This could also be framed as an offence under s. 170(2).
6   It is possible to indict for possession of either because the definition in Sch. 2 of the 1971 Act links the two substances: *R v Best* [1979] Crim.L.R. 787; see paras. 9.03 and 26.04 *ante*.

*Offering to Supply*

### Statement of Offence

Offering to supply drugs, contrary to section 4(3)(*a*) of the Misuse of Drugs Act 1971.

### Particulars of Offence

A.B. on 5 November 1984, offered to supply a controlled drug of Class A, namely diamorphine, to C.D.

*Permitting Premises to be used for Supply*

### Statement of Offence

Permitting premises to be used for the supply of controlled drugs, contrary to section 8(*b*) of the Misuse of Drugs Act 1971.

### Particulars of Offence

A.B.,in the month of January 1983, being the occupier of premises known as 21 Winsley House, Wades Place, N.W.10, knowingly permitted C.D. to supply a controlled drug of Class B, namely cannabis resin, on those premises to other persons.

*Conspiracy to Possess*

### Statement of Offence

Conspiracy to possess a controlled drug contrary to section 1(1) of the Criminal Law Act 1977.

### Particulars of Offence

A.B. and C.D., between 1 May 1984 and 10 June 1984, conspired together and with others unknown to possess controlled drugs of Class A, namely diamorphine, in contravention of section 5(2) of the Misuse of Drugs Act 1971.

*Attempt to Produce*

### Statement of Offence

Attempting to produce a controlled drug, contrary to section 1(1) of the Criminal Attempts Act 1981.

### Particulars of Offence

A.B. and C.D., between 1 March 1985 and 10 March 1985, attempted to produce a controlled drug of Class A, namely diamorphine, in contravention of section 4(2)(*a*) of the Misuse of Drugs Act 1971.

## MODEL INFORMATIONS

### 26.10   (1)   Customs and Excise Management Act 1979

*Importation*

A.B. was, on 26 November 1984 at Dover in the County of Kent, knowingly concerned in the fraudulent evasion of the prohibition on importation of a controlled drug, namely one kilo of heroin, a Class A drug, imposed by section 3(1) of the Misuse of Drugs Act 1971 contrary to section 170(2) of the Customs and Excise Management Act 1979.[7]

### (2)   Misuse of Drugs Act 1971

*Possession*

A.B. was, on 20 January 1985 in the County of Oxford, in possession of a controlled drug of Class B, namely 375 grams of methaqualone, contrary to section 5(2) of the Misuse of Drugs Act 1971.

(Other informations can be drafted by adapting the model indictments.)

---

7   As to place of trial, see s. 148 1979 Act and para. 6.05 *ante*.

# APPENDIX I

# Customs and Excise Management Act 1979

(CHAPTER 2)

## ARRANGEMENT OF SECTIONS PRINTED

**Part I: Preliminary**

**Part II: Administration**

**Part III: Customs and Excise Control Areas**

**Part IV: Control of Importation**

*Forfeiture, offences, etc. in connection with importation*

**Part V: Control of Exportation**

*Offences in relation to exportation*

*Miscellaneous*

174. Removal from or to Isle of Man not to be importation or exportation, (subsections (1) and (2)).
178. Citation and commencement, (subsections (1) and (3)).

**Schedules:**

Schedule 1—Controlled drugs: variation of punishments for certain offences under this Act.
Schedule 3—Provisions relating to forfeiture.

## Part I

### Preliminary

*Interpretation.*

**1.**—(1) In this Act, unless the context otherwise requires—

"aerodrome" means any area of land or water designed, equipped, set apart or commonly used for affording facilities for the landing and departure of aircraft;

"approvad route" has the meaning given by section 26 below; . . .

"armed forces" means the Royal Navy, the Royal Marines, the regular army and the regular air force, and any reserve or auxiliary force of any of those services which has been called out on permanent service, or called into actual service, or embodied;

"assigned matter" means any matter in relation to which the Commissioners are for the time being required in pursuance of any enactment to perform any duties;

"boarding station" means a boarding station for the time being appointed under section 19 below;

"boundary" means the land boundary of Northern Ireland;

"British ship" means a British ship within the meaning of the Merchant Shipping Act 1894, so, however, as not to include a ship registered in any country other than the United Kingdom, the Channel Islands, the Isle of Man or a colony within the meaning of the British Nationality Act 1948;

"claimant", in relation to proceedings for the condemnation of any thing as being forfeited, means a person claiming that the thing is not liable to forfeiture;

"coasting ship" has the meaning given by section 69 below;

"commander", in relation to an aircraft, includes any person having or taking the charge or command of the aircraft;

"the Commissioners" means the Commissioners of Customs and Excise; . . .

"container" includes any bundle or package and any box, cask or other receptacle whatsoever;

"the customs and excise Acts" means the Customs and Excise Acts 1979 and any other enactment for the time being in force relating to customs or excise;

"the Customs and Excise Acts 1979" means—

    this Act,

    the Customs and Excise Duties (General Reliefs) Act 1979,

    the Alcoholic Liquor Duties Act 1979,

the Hydrocarbon Oil Duties Act 1979,
the Matches and Mechanical Lighters Duties Act 1979,
    and
the Tobacco Products Duty Act 1979;
"customs warehouse" means a place of security approved by the Commis-
    sioners under subsection (2) (whether or not it is also approved under
    subsection (1)) of section 92 below;
"customs and excise airport" has the meaning given by section 21(7) below;
"customs and excise station" has the meaning given by section 26 below; . . .
"examination stapion" has the meaning given by section 22 below; . . .
"exporter", in relation to goods for exportation or for use as stores, includes the
    shipper of the goods and any person performing in relation to an aircraft
    functions corresponding with those of a shipper;
"goods" includes stores and baggage;
"holiday", in relation to any part of the United Kingdom, means any day that
    is a bank holiday in that part of the United Kingdom under the Banking
    and Financial Dealings Act 1971, Christmas Day, Good Friday and the
    day appointed for the purposes of customs and excise for the celebration
    of Her Majesty's birthday;
"hovercraft" means a hovercraft within the meaning of the Hovercraft Act
    1968;
"importer", in relation to any goods at any time between their importation and
    the time when they are delivered out of charge, includes any owner or
    other person for the time being possessed of or beneficially interested in
    the goods and, in relation to goods imported by means of a pipe-line,
    includes the owner of the pipe-line;
"justice" and "justice of the peace" in Scotland includes a sheriff and in
    Northern Ireland, in relation to any powers and duties which can under
    any enactment for the time being in force be exercised and performed
    only by a resident magistrate, means a resident magistrate;
"land" and "landing", in relation to aircraft, include alighting on water;
"law officer of the Crown"means the Attorney General or in Scotland the Lord
    Advocate or in Northern Ireland the Attorney General for Northern
    Ireland;
"licence year", in relation to an excise licence issuable annually, means the
    period of 12 months ending on the date on which that licence expires in
    any year;
"master", in relation to a ship, includes any person having or taking phe charge
    or command of the ship;
"nautical mile" means a distance of 1,852 metres;
"night" means the period between 11 pm and 5 am; . . .
"officer" means, subject to section 8(2) below, a person commissioned by the
    Commissioners;
"owner", in relation to an aircraft, includes the operator of the aircraft; . . .
"port" means a port appointed by the Commissioners under section 19 below;
"prescribed area" means such an area in Northern Ireland adjoining the
    boundary as the Commissikners may by regulations prescribe;
"prescribed sum", in relation to the penalty provided for an offence, has the
    meaning given by section 171(2) below;
"prohibited or restricted goods" means goods of a class or description of which
    the importation, exportation or carriage coastwise is for the time being

prohibited or restricted under or by virtue of any enactment;

"proper", in relation to the person by, with or to whom, or the place at which, anything is to be done, means the person or place appointed or authorised in that behalf by the Commissioners;

"proprietor", in relation to any goods, includes any owner, importer, exporter, shipping or other person for the time being possessed of or beneficially interested in those goods;

"Queen's warehouse" means any place provided by the Crown or appointed by the Commissioners for the deposit of goods for security thereof and of the duties chargeable thereon; . . .

"ship" and "vessel" include any boat or other vessel whatsoever (and, to the extent provided in section 2 below, any hovercraft);

"shipment" includes loading into an aircraft, and "shipped" and cognate expressions shall be construed accordingly;

"stores" means, subject to subsection (4) below, goods for use in a ship or aircraft and includes fuel and spare parts and other articles of equipment, whether or not for immediate fitting;

"tons register" means the tons of a ship's net tonnage as ascertained and registered according to the tonnage regulations of the Merchant Shipping Act 1894 or, in the case of a ship which is not registered under that Act, ascertained in like manner as if it were to be so registered;

"transit goods", except in the expression "Community transit goods", means imported goods entered on importation for transit or transhipment;

"transit or transhipment", in relation to the entry of goods, means transit through the United Kingdom or transhipment with a view to the re-exportation of the goods in question;

"transit shed" has the meaning given by section 25 below;

"vehicle" includes a railway vehicle;

"warehouse", except in the expressions "Queen's warehouse" and "distiller's warehouse", means a place of security approved by the Commissioners under subsection (1) or (2) or subsections (1) and (2) of section 92 below and, except in that section, also includes a distiller's warehouse; and "warehoused" and cognate expressions shall, subject to subsection (4) of that section, be construed accordingly;

"warehousing regulations" means regulations under section 93 below.[1]

(2) This Act and the other Acts included in the Customs and Excise Acts 1979 shall be construed as one Act but where a provision of this Act refers to this Act that reference is not to be construed as including a reference to any of the others.

(3) Any expression used in this Act or in any instrument made under this Act to which a meaning is given by any other Act included in the Customs and Excise Acts 1979 has, except where the context otherwise requires, the same meaning in this Act or any such instrument as in that Act; . . .

(4) Subject to section 12 of the Customs and Excise Duties (General Reliefs) Act 1979 (by which goods for use in naval ships or establishments may be required to be treated as exported), any goods for use in a ship or aircraft as merchandise for sale by retail to persons carried therein shall be treated for the purposes of the customs and excise Acts as stores, and any reference in those Acts to the consumption of stores shall, in relation to goods so treated, be construed as referring to the sale thereof as aforesaid. . . .

1  Definitions irrelevant to the subject of this work have been omitted.

(6) In computing for the purpose of this Act any period expressed therein as a period of clear days no account shall be taken of the day of the event from which the period is computed or of any Sunday or holiday. . . .

*Application to hovercraft*

**2.**—(1) This Part, Parts III to VII and Parts X to XII of this Act shall apply as if references to ships or vessels included references to hovercraft, and the said Parts III to VII shall apply in relation to an approved wharf or transit shed which is not in a port as if it were in a port.

(2) All other provisions of the customs and excise Acts shall apply as if references (however expressed) to goods or passengers carried in or moved by ships or vessels included references to goods or passengers carried in or moved by hovercraft.

(3) In all the provisions of the customs and excise Acts "landed", "loaded", "master", "shipped", "shipped as stores", "transhipment", "voyage", "waterborne" and cognate expressions shall be construed in accordance with subsections (1) and (2) above.

(4) References in the customs and excise Acts to goods imported or exported by land, or conveyed into or out of Northern Ireland by land, include references to goods imported, exported or conveyed across any part of the boundary of Northern Ireland; and it is hereby declared that in those Acts references to vehicles include references to hovercraft proceeding over land or water or partly over land and partly over water.

(5) Any power of making regulations or other instruments relating to the importation or exportation of goods conferred by the customs and excise Acts may be exercised so as to make provision for the importation or exportation of goods by hovercraft which is different from the provision made for the importation or exportation of goods by other means.

*Time of importation, exportation, etc.*

**5.**—(1) The provisions of this section shall have effect for the purposes of the customs and excise Acts.

(2) Subject to subsections (3) and (6) below, the time of importation of any goods shall be deemed to be—

    (*a*)  where the goods are brought by sea, the time when the ship carrying them comes within the limits of a port;

    (*b*)  where the goods are brought by air, the time when the aircraft carrying them lands in the United Kingdom or the time when the goods are unloaded in the United Kingdom, whichever is the earlier;

    (*c*)  where the goods are brought by land, the time when the goods are brought across the boundary into Northern Ireland.

(3) In the case of goods brought by sea of which entry is not required under section 37 below, the time of importation shall be deemed to be the time when the ship carrying them came within the limits of the port at which the goods are discharged.

(4) Subject to subsections (5) and (7) below, the time of exportation of any goods from the United Kingdom shall be deemed to be—

    (*a*)  where the goods are exported by sea or air, the time when the goods are shipped for exportation;

(*b*)   where the goods are exported by land, the time when they are cleared by the proper officer at the last customs and excise station on their way to the boundary.

(5) In the case of goods of a class or description with respect to the exportation of which any prohibition or restriction is for the time being in force under or by virtue of any enactment which are exported by sea or air, the time of exportation shall be deemed to be the time when the exporting ship or aircraft departs from the last port or customs and excise airport at which it is cleared before departing for a destination outside the United Kingdom.

(6) Goods imported by means of a pipe-line shall be treated as imported at the time when they are brought within the limits of a port or brought across the boundary into Northern Ireland.

(7) Goods exported by means of a pipe-line shall be treated as exported at the time when they are charged into that pipe-line for exportation.

(8) A ship shall be deemed to have arrived at or departed from a port at the time when the ship comes within or, as the case may be, leaves the limits of that port.

## Part II

### Administration

#### Appointment and duties of Commissioners, officers, etc.

*Exercise of powers and performance of duties.*
**8.**—(1) Any act or thing required or authorised by or under any enactment to be done by the Commissioners or any of them may be done—

(*a*)   by any one or more of the Commissioners; or
(*b*)   if the Commissioners so authorise, by a secretary or assistant secretary to the Commissioners; or
(*c*)   by any other person authorised generally or specially in that behalf in writing by the Commissioners.

(2) Any person, whether an officer or not, engaged by the orders or with the concurrence of the Commissioners (whether previously or subsequently expressed) in the performance of any act or duty relating to an assigned matter which is by law required or authorised to be performed by or with an officer, shall be deemed to be the proper officer by or with whom that act or duty is to be performed.

(3) Any person deemed by virtue of subsection (2) above to be the proper officer shall have all the powers of an officer in relation to the act or duty performed or to be performed by him as mentioned in that subsection.

*Assistance to be rendered by police, etc.*
**11.** It shall be the duty of every constable and every member of Her Majesty's armed forces or coastguard to assist in the enforcement of the law relating to any assigned matter.

#### Offences in connection with Commissioners, officers, etc.

*Unlawful assumption of character of officer, etc.*
**13.** If, for the purpose of obtaining admission to any house or other place, or of

doing or procuring to be done any act which he would not be entitled to do or procure to be done of his own authority, or for any other unlawful purpose, any person falsely assumes the name, designation or character of a Commissioner or officer or of a person appointed by the Commissioners he may be detained and shall, in addition to any other punishment to which he may have rendered himself liable, be liable—

(a) on summary conviction, to a penalty of the prescribed sum, or to imprisonment for a term not exceeding 3 months, or to both; or

(b) on conviction on indictment, to a penalty of any amount, or to imprisonment for a term not exceeding 2 years, or to both.

*Bribery and collusion.*

**15.**—(1) If any Commissioner or officer or any person appointed or authorised by the Commissioners to discharge any duty relating to an assigned matter—

(a) directly or indirectly asks for or takes in connection with any of his duties any payment or other reward whatsoever, whether pecuniary or other, or any promise or security for any such payment or reward, not being a payment or reward which he is lawfully entitled to claim or receive; or

(b) enters into or acquiesces in any agreement to do, abstain from doing, permit, conceal or connive at any act or thing whereby Her Majesty is or may be defrauded or which is otherwise unlawful, being an act or thing relating to an assigned matter,

he shall be guilty of an offence under this section.

(2) If any person—

(a) directly or indirectly offers or gives to any Commissioner or officer or to any person appointed or authorised by the Commissioners as aforesaid any payment or other reward whatsoever, whether pecuniary or other, or any promise or security for any such payment or reward; or

(b) proposes or enters into any agreement with any Commissioner, officer or person appointed or authorised as aforesaid,

in order to induce him to do, abstain from doing, permit, conceal or connive at any act or thing whereby Her Majesty is or may be defrauded or which is otherwise unlawful, being an act or thing relating to an assigned matter, or otherwise to take any course contrary to his duty, he shall be guilty of an offence under this section.

(3) Any person committing an offence under this section shall be liable on summary conviction to a penalty of £500 and may be detained.

*Obstruction of officers, etc.*

**16.**[2]—(1) Any person who—

(a) obstructs, hinders, molests or assaults any person duly engaged in the performance of any duty or the exercise of any power imposed or conferred on him by or under any enactment relating to an assigned matter, or any person acting in his aid; or

---

2   Amended by the Police and Criminal Evidence Act 1984.

(*b*)  does anything which impedes or is calculated to impede the carrying out of any search for any thing liable to forfeiture under any such enactment or the detention, seizure or removal of any such thing; or

(*c*)  rescues, damages or destroys any thing so liable to forfeiture or does anything calculated to prevent the procuring or giving of evidence as to whether or not any thing is so liable to forfeiture; or

(*d*)  prevents the [arrest] of any person by a person duly engaged or acting as aforesaid or rescues any person so [arrested,]

or who attempts to do any of the aforementioned things, shall be guilty of an offence under this section.

(2) Any person guilty of an offence under this section shall be liable—

(*a*)  on summary conviction, to a penalty of the prescribed sum, or to imprisonment for a term not exceeding 3 months, or to both; or

(*b*)  on conviction on indictment, to a penalty of any amount, or to imprisonment for a term not exceeding 2 years, or to both.

(3) Any person committing an offence under this section and any person aiding or abetting the commission of such an offence may be [arrested.]

## Part III

### Customs and Excise Control Areas

*Appointment of ports, etc.*

**19.**—(1) The Commissioners may by order made by statutory instrument appoint and name as a port for the purposes of customs and excise any area in the United Kingdom specified in the order.

(2) The appointment of any port for those purposes made before 1st August 1952 may be revoked, and the name or limits of any such port may be altered, by an order under subsection (1) above as if the appointment had been made by an order under that subsection.

(3) The Commissioners may in any port from time to time appoint boarding stations for the purpose of the boarding of or disembarkation from ships by officers.

*Control of movement of aircraft, etc. into and out of the United Kingdom.*

**21.**—(1) Save as permitted by the Commissioners, the commander of an aircraft entering the United Kingdom from a place outside the United Kingdom shall not cause or permit the aircraft to land—

(*a*)  for the first time after its arrival in the United Kingdom; or

(*b*)  at any time while it is carrying passengers or goods brought in that aircraft from a place outside the United Kingdom and not yet cleared,

at any place other than a customs and excise airport.

(2) Sava as permitted by the Commissioners, no person importing or concerned in importing any goods in any aircraft shall bring the goods into the United Kingdom at any place other than a customs and excise airport.

(3) Save as permitted by the Commissioners—

(a) no person shall depart on a flight to a place or area outside the United Kingdom from any place in the United Kingdom other than a customs and excise airport; and

(b) the commander of any aircraft engaged in a flight from a customs and excise airport to a place or area outside the United Kingdom shall not cause or permit it to land at any place in the United Kingdom other than a customs and excise airport specified in the application for clearance for that flight.

(4) Subsections (1) to (3) above shall not apply in relation to any aircraft flying from or to any place or area outside the United Kingdom to or from any place in the United Kingdom which is required by or under any enactment relating to air navigation, or is compelled by accident, stress or weather or other unavoidable cause, to land at a place other than a customs and excise airport; but, subject to subsection (5) below,—

(a) the commander of any such aircraft—

( i) shall immediately report the landing to an officer or constable and shall on demand produce to him the journey log book belonging to the aircraft,

( ii) shall not without the consent of an officer permit any goods carried in the aircraft to be unloaded from, or any of the crew or passengers to depart from the vicinity of, the aircraft, and

(iii) shall comply with any directions given by an officer with respect to any such goods; and

(b) no passenger or member of the crew shall without the consent of an officer or constable leave the immediate vicinity of any such aircraft.

(5) Nothing in subsection (4) above shall prohibit—

(a) the departure of passengers or crew from the vicinity of an aircraft; or

(b) the removal of goods from an aircraft,

where that departure or removal is necessary for reasons of health, safety or the preservation of life or property.

(6) Any person contravening or failing to compy with any provision of this section shall be liable on summary conviction to a penalty of £200, or to imprisonment for a term not exceeding 3 months, or to both.

(7) In this Act "customs and excise airport·' means an aerodrome for the time being designated as a place for the landing or departure of aircraft for the purposes of the customs and excise Acts by an order made by the Secretary of State with the concurrence of the Commissioners which is in force under an Order in Council made in pursuance of section 8 of the Civil Aviation Act 1949.

*Approval of examination stations at customs and excise airports.*

**22.**—(1) The Commissioners may, in any customs and excise airport, approve for such periods and subject to such conditions and restrictions as they think fit a part of, or a place at, that airport for the loading and unloading of goods and the embarkation and disembarkation of passengers; and any such part or place so approved is referred to in this Act as an "examination station".

MOD-N

(2) The Commissioners may at any time for reasonable cause revoke or vary the terms of any approval given under this section.

(3) Any person contravening or failing to comply with any condition or restriction imposed by the Commissioners under this section shall be liable on summary conviction to a penalty of £100.

*Control of movement of hovercraft.*

**23.**—(1) The Commissioners may by regulations impose conditions and restrictions as respects the movement of hovercraft and the carriage of goods by hovercraft, and in particular—

(a) may prescribe the procedure to be followed by hovercraft proceeding to or from a port or any customs and excise airport or customs and excise station, and authorise the proper officer to give directions as to their routes; and

(b) may make provision for cases where by reason of accident, or in any other circumstance, it is impracticable to comply with any conditions or restrictions imposed or directions given as respects hovercraft.

(2) Subsection (1) above shall apply to hovercraft proceeding to or from any approved wharf or transit shed which is not in a port as if it were a port.

(3) If any person contravenes or fails to comply with any regulation made under subsection (1) above, or with any direction given by the Commissioners or the proper officer in pursuance of any such regulation, he shall be liable on summary conviction to a penalty of £100 and any goods in respect of which the offence was committed shall be liable to forfeiture.

*Power to regulate movements of goods into and out of Northern Ireland by land.*

**26.**—(1) The Commissioners may, for the purpose of safe-guarding the revenue and for the better enforcement of any prohibition or restriction for the time being in force under or by virtue of any enactment with respect to the importation or exportation of any goods, make regulations—

(a) prohibiting the importation or exportation by land of all goods or of any class or description of goods except within such hours and by such routes within Northern Ireland (referred to in this Act as "approved routes") as may be prescribed by the regulations;

(b) appointing places for the examination and entry of and payment of any duty chargeable on any goods being imported or exported by land (referred to in this Act as "customs and excise stations").

(2) If any person contravenes or fails to comply with any regulation made under subsection (1) above he shall be liable on summary conviction to a penalty of £100, and any goods in respect of which the offence was committed shall be liable to forfeiture.

*Officers' powers of boarding.*

**27.**—(1) At any time while a ship is within the limits of a port, or an aircraft is at a customs and excise airport, or a vehicle is on an approved route, any officer and any other person duly engaged in the prevention of smuggling may board the ship, aircraft or vehicle and remain therein and rummage and search any part thereof.

(2) The Commissioners may station officers in any ship at any time while it is within the limits of a port, and if the master of any ship neglects or refuses to provide—

    (*a*) reasonable accommodation below decks for any officer stationed therein; or

    (*b*) means of safe access to and egress from the ship in accordance with the requirements of any such officer,

the master shall be liable on summary conviction to a penalty of £50.

*Officers' powers of access, etc.*

**28.**—(1) Without prejudice to section 27 above, the proper officer shall have free access to every part of any ship or aircraft at a port or customs and excise airport and of any vehicle brought to a customs and excise station, and may—

    (*a*) cause any goods to be marked before they are unloaded from that ship, aircraft or vehicle;

    (*b*) lock up, seal, mark or otherwise secure any goods carried in the ship, aircraft or vehicle or any place or container in which they are so carried; and

    (*c*) break open any place or container which is locked and of which the keys are withheld.

(2) Any goods found concealed on board any such ship, aircraft or vehicle shall be liable to forfeiture.

*Power to inspect aircraft, aerodromes, records, etc.*

**33.**—(1) The commander of an aircraft shall permit an officer at any time to board the aircraft and inspect—

    (*a*) the aircraft and any goods loaded therein; and

    (*b*) all documents relating to the aircraft or to goods or persons carried therein;

and an officer shall have the right of access at any time to any place to which access is required for the purpose of any such inspection.

(2) The person in control of any aerodrome shall permit an officer at any time to enter upon and inspect the aerodrome and all buildings and goods thereon.

(3) The person in control of an aerodrome licensed under any enactment relating to air navigation and, if so required by the Commissioners, the person in control of any other aerodrome shall—

    (*a*) keep a record in such form and manner as the Commissioners may approve of all aircraft arriving at or departing from the aerodrome;

    (*b*) keep that record available and produce it on demand to any officer, together with all other documents kept on the aerodrome which relate to the movement of aircraft; and

    (*c*) permit any officer to make copies of and take extracts from any such record or document.

(4) If any person contravenes or fails to comply with any of the provisions of this section he shall be liable on summary conviction to a penalty of £200 or to imprisonment for a term not exceeding 3 months, or to both.

*Power to prevent flight of aircraft.*

**34.**—(1) If it appears to any officer or constable that an aircraft is intended or likely to depart for a destination outside the United Kingdom from—

(*a*)  any place other than a customs and excise airport; or

(*b*)  a customs and excise airport before clearance outwards is given,

he may give such instructions and take such steps by way of detention of the aircraft or otherwise as appear to him necessary in order to prevent the flight.

(2) Any person who contravenes any instructions given under subsection (1) above shall be liable on summary conviction to a penalty of £200, or to imprisonment for a term not exceeding 3 months, or to both.

(3) If an aircraft flies in contravention of any instruction given under subsection (1) above or notwithstanding any steps taken to prevent the flight, the owner and the commander thereof shall, without prejudice to the liability of any other person under subsection (2) above, each be liable on summary conviction to a penalty of £200, or to imprisonment for a term not exceeding 3 months, or to both, unless he proves that the flight took place without his consent or connivance.

# Part IV

## Control of Importation

**Forfeiture, offences, etc. in connection with importation**

*Forfeiture of goods improperly imported.*

**49.**—(1) Where—

(*a*)  except as provided by or under the Customs and Excise Acts 1979, any imported goods, being goods chargeable on their importation with customs and or excise duty, are, without payment of that duty—

(i)  unshipped in any port,

(ii)  unloaded from any aircraft in the United Kingdom,

(iii)  unloaded from any vehicle in, or otherwise brought across the boundary into, Northern Ireland, or

(iv)  removed from their place of importation or from any approved wharf, examination station or transit shed; or

(*b*)  any goods are imported, landed or unloaded contrary to any prohibition or restriction for the time being in force with respect thereto under or by virtue of any enactment; or

(*c*)  any goods, being goods chargeable with any duty or goods the importation of which is for the time being prohibited or restricted by or under any enactment, are found, whether before or after the unloading thereof, to have been concealed in any manner on board any ship or aircraft or, while in Northern Ireland, in any vehicle; or

(*d*)  any goods are imported concealed in a container holding goods of a different description; or

(*e*)  any imported goods are found, whether before or after delivery, not to correspond with the entry made thereof; or (*f*) any imported goods are concealed or packed in any manner appearing to be intended to deceive an officer,

those goods shall, subject to subsection (2) below, be liable to forfeiture.

(2) Where any goods, the importation of which is for the time being prohibited or restricted by or under any enactment, are on their importation either—

(*a*) reported as intended for exportation in the same ship, aircraft or vehicle; or
(*b*) entered for transit or transhipment; or
(*c*) entered to be warehoused for exportation or for use as stores,

the Commissioners may, if they see fit, permit the goods to be dealt with accordingly.

*Penalty for improper importation of goods.*

**50.**[3]—(1) Subsection (2) below applies to goods of the following descriptions, that is to say—

(*a*) goods chargeable with a duty which has not been paid; and
(*b*) goods the importation, landing or unloading of which is for the time being prohibited or restricted by or under any enactment.

(2) If any person with intent to defraud Her Majesty of any such duty or to evade any such prohibition or restriction as is mentioned in subsection (1) above—

(*a*) unships or lands in any port or unloads from any aircraft in the United Kingdom or from any vehicle in Northern Ireland any goods to which this subsection applies, or assists or is otherwise concerned in such unshipping, landing or unloading; or
(*b*) removes from their place of importation or from any approved wharf, examination station, transit shed or customs and excise station any goods to which this subsection applies or assists or is otherwise concerned in such removal,

he shall be guilty of an offence under this subsection and may be [arrested.]

(3) If any person imports or is concerned in importing any goods contrary to any prohibition or restriction for the time being in force under or by virtue of any enactment with respect to those goods, whether or not the goods are unloaded, and does so with intent to evade the prohibition or restriction, he shall be guilty of an offence under this subsection and may be [arrested.]

(4) Subject to subsection (5) below, a person guilty of an offence under subsection (2) or (3) above shall be liable—

(*a*) on summary conviction, to a penalty of the prescribed sum or of three times the value of the goods, whichever is the greater, or to imprisonment for a term not exceeding 6 months, or to both; or
(*b*) on conviction on indictment, to a penalty of any amount, or to imprisonment for a term not exceeding 2 years, or to both.

(5) In the case of an offence under subsection (2) or (3) above in connection with a prohibition or restriction on importation having effect by virtue of section

3   Amended by the Police and Criminal Evidence Act 1984

3 of the Misuse of Drugs Act 1971, subsection (4) above shall have effect subject to the modifications specified in Schedule 1 to this Act.

(6) If any person—

   (a) imports or causes to be imported any goods concealed in a container holding goods of a different description; or
   (b) directly or indirectly imports or causes to be imported or entered any goods found, whether before or after delivery, not to correspond with the entry made thereof,

he shall be liable on summary conviction to a penalty of three times the value of the goods or £100, whichever is the greater.

(7) In any case where a person would, apart from this subsection, be guilty of—

   (a) an offence under this section in connection with the importation of goods contrary to a prohibition or restriction; and
   (b) a corresponding offence under the enactment or other instrument imposing the prohibition or restriction, being an offence for which a fine or other penalty is expressly provided by that enactment or other instrument,

he shall not be guilty of the offence mentioned in paragraph (a) of this subsection.


## Part V

### Control of Exportation

#### Offences in relation to exportation

*Offences in relation to exportation of prohibited or restricted goods.*
   **68.**[4]—(1) If any goods are—

   (a) exported or shipped as stores; or
   (b) brought to any place in the United Kingdom for the purpose of being exported or shipped as stores,

and the exportation or shipment is or would be contrary to any prohibition or restriction for the time being in force with respect to those goods under or by virtue of any enactment, the goods shall be liable to forfeiture and the exporter or intending exporter of the goods and any agent of his concerned in the exportation or shipment or intended exportation or shipment shall each be liable on summary conviction to a penalty of three times the value of the goods or £100, whichever is the greater.

(2) Any person knowingly concerned in the exportation or shipment as stores, or in the attempted exportation or shipment as stores, of any goods with intent to evade any such prohibition or restriction as is mentioned in subsection (1) above shall be guilty of an offence under this subsection and may be [arrested.]

(3) Subject to subsection (4) below, a person guilty of an offence under subsection (2) above shall be liable—

4 Amended by the Police and Criminal Evidence Act 1984

(*a*) on summary conviction, to a penalty of the prescribed sum or of three times the value of the goods, whichever is the greater, or to imprisonment for a term not exceeding 6 months, or to both; or

(*b*) on conviction on indictment, to a penalty of any amount, or to imprisonment for a term not exceeding 2 years, or to both.

(4) In the case of an offence under subsection (2) above in connection with a prohibition or restriction on exportation having effect by virtue of section 3 of the Misuse of Drugs Act 1971, subsection (3) above shall have effect subject to the modifications specified in Schedule 1 to this Act.

(5) If by virtue of any such restriction as is mentioned in subsection (1) above any goods may be exported only when consigned to a particular place or person and any goods so consigned are delivered to some other place or person, the ship, aircraft or vehicle in which they were exported shall be liable to forfeiture unless it is proved to the satisfaction of the Commissioners that both the owner of the ship, aircraft or vehicle and the master of the ship, commander of the aircraft or person in charge of the vehicle—

(*a*) took all reasonable steps to secure that the goods were delivered to the particular place to which or person to whom they were consigned; and

(*b*) did not connive at or, except under duress, consent to the delivery of the goods to that other place or person.

(6) In any case where a person would, apart from this subsection, be guilty of—

(*a*) an offence under subsection (1) or (2) above; and

(*b*) a corresponding offence under the enactment or instrument imposing the prohibition or restriction in question, being an offence for which a fine or other penalty is expressly provided by that enactment or other instrument,

he shall not be guilty of the offence mentioned in paragraph (*a*) of this subsection.

## Part VII

### Customs and Excise Control: Supplementary Provisions

#### Additional provisions as to information

*Information in relation to goods imported or exported.*

77.—(1) An officer may require any person—

(*a*) concerned with the importation, exportation or shipment for carriage coastwise of goods of which an entry or specification is required for that purpose by or under this Act; or

(*b*) concerned in the carriage, unloading, landing or loading of goods which are being or have been imported or exported,

to furnish in such form as the officer may require any information relating to the goods and to produce and allow the officer to inspect and take extracts from or make copies of any invoice, bill of lading or other book or document whatsoever relating to the goods.

(2) If any person without reasonable cause fails to comply with a requirement imposed on him under subsection (1) above he shall be liable on summary conviction to a penalty of £50.

(3) Where any prohibition or restriction to which this subsection applies, that is to say, any prohibition or restriction under or by virtue of any enactment with respect to—

(a) the exportation of goods to any particular destination; or
(b) the exportation of goods of any particular class or description to any particular destination,

is for the time being in force, then, if any person about to ship for exportation or to export any goods or, as the case may be, any goods of that class or description, in the course of making entry thereof before shipment or exportation makes a declaration as to the ultimate destination thereof, and the Commissioners have reason to suspect that the declaration is untrue in any material particular, the goods may be detained until the Commissioners are satisfied as to the truth of the declaration, and if they are not so satisfied the goods shall be liable to forfeiture.

(4) Any person concerned in the exportation of any goods which are subject to any prohibition or restriction to which subsection (3) above applies shall, if so required by the Commissioners, satisfy the Commissioners that those goods have not reached any destination other than that mentioned in the entry delivered in respect of the goods.

(5) If any person required under subsection (4) above to satisfy the Commissioners as mentioned in that subsection fails to do so, then, unless he proves—

(a) that he did not consent to or connive at the goods reaching any destination other than that mentioned in the entry delivered in respect of the goods; and
(b) that he took all reasonable steps to secure that the ultimate destination of the goods was not other than that so mentioned,

he shall be liable on summary conviction to a penalty of three times the value of the goods or £100, whichever is the greater.

*Customs and excise control of persons entering or leaving the United Kingdom.*
**78.**—(1) . . .

(2) Any person entering or leaving the United Kingdom shall answer such questions as the proper officer may put to him with respect to his baggage and any thing contained therein or carried with him, and shall, if required by the proper officer, produce that baggage and any such thing for examination at such place as the Commissioner may direct.

(3) Any person failing to declare any thing or to produce any baggage or thing as required by this section shall be liable on summary conviction to a penalty of three times the value of the thing not declared or of the baggage or thing not produced, as the case may be, or £100, whichever is the greater.

(4) Any thing chargeable with any duty or tax which is found concealed, or is not declared, and any thing which is being taken into or out of the United Kingdom contrary to any prohibition or restriction for the time being in force with respect thereto under or by virtue of any enactment, shall be liable to forfeiture.

*Power to require evidence in support of information.*

**79.**—(1) The Commissioners may, if they consider it necessary, require evidence to be produced to their satisfaction in support of any information required by or under Parts III to VII of this Act to be provided in respect of goods imported or exported.

(2) Without prejudice to subsection (1) above, where any question as to the duties chargeable on any imported goods, or the operation of any prohibition or restriction on importation, depends on any question as to the place from which the goods were consigned, or any question where they or other goods are to be treated as grown, manufactured or produced, or any question as to payments made or relief from duty allowed in any country or territory, then—

(a) the Commissioners may require the importer of the goods to furnish to them, in such form as they may prescribe, proof of—

(i) any statement made to them as to any fact necessary to determine that question, or

(ii) the accuracy of any certificate or other document furnished in connection with the importation of the goods and relating to the matter in issue,

and if such proof is not furnished to their satisfaction, the question may be determined without regard to that statement or to that certificate or document; and

(b) if in any proceedings relating to the goods or to the duty chargeable thereon the accuracy of any such certificate or document comes in question, it shall be for the person relying on it to furnish proof of its accuracy.

## Forfeiture of ships, etc. for certain offences

*Forfeiture of ship, aircraft or vehicle constructed, etc. for concealing goods.*

**88.** Where—

(a) a ship is or has been within the limits of any port or within 3 or, being a British ship, 12 nautical miles of the coast of the United Kingdom; or

(b) an aircraft is or has been at any place, whether on land or on water, in the United Kingdom; or

(c) a vehicle is or has been within the limits of any port or at any aerodrome or, while in Northern Ireland, within the prescribed area,

while constructed, adapted, altered or fitted in any manner for the purpose of concealing goods, that ship, aircraft or vehicle shall be liable to forfeiture.

*Forfeiture of ship jettisoning cargo, etc.*

**89.**—(1) If any part of the cargo of a ship is thrown overboard or is staved or destroyed to prevent seizure—

(a) while the ship is within 3 nautical miles of the coast of the United Kingdom; or

(b) where the ship, having been properly summoned to bring to by any vessel in the service of Her Majesty, fails so to do and chase is given, at any time during the chase,

the ship shall be liable to forfeiture.

(2) For the purposes of this section a ship shall be deemed to have been properly summoned to bring to—

(*a*) if the vessel making the summons did so by means of an international signal code or other recognised means and while flying her proper ensign; and

(*b*) in the case of a ship which is not a British ship, if at the time when the summons was made the ship was within 3 nautical miles of the coast of the United Kingdom.

*Forfeiture of ship or aircraft unable to account for missing cargo.*
**90.** Where a ship has been within the limits of any port, or an aircraft has been in the United Kingdom, with a cargo on board and a substantial part of that cargo is afterwards found to be missing, then, if the master of the ship or commander of the aircraft fails to account therefor to the satisfaction of the Commissioners, the ship or aircraft shall be liable to forfeiture.

*Ships failing to bring to.*
**91.**—(1) If, save for just and sufficient cause, any ship which is liable to forfeiture or examination under or by virtue of any provision of the Customs and Excise Acts 1979 does not bring to when required to do so, the master of the ship shall be liable on summary conviction to a penalty of £50.

(2) Where any ship liable to forfeiture or examination as aforesaid has failed to bring to when required to do so and chase has been given thereto by any vessel in the service of Her Majesty and, after the commander of that vessel has hoisted the proper ensign and caused a gun to be fired as a signal, the ship still fails to bring to, the ship may be fired upon.


## Part XI

## Detention of Persons, Forfeiture and Legal Proceedings

**Detention of persons**

*Provisions as to arrest of persons.*
**138.**[5]—(1) Any person who has committed, or whom there are reasonable grounds to suspect of having committed, any offence for which he is liable to be [arrested] under the customs and excise Acts may be [arrested] by any officer [ . . . ] or any member of Her Majesty's armed forces or coastguard at any time within 3 years from the date of the commission of the offence.

(2) Where it was not practicable to [arrest] any person so liable at the time of the commission of the offence, or where any such person having been then or subsequently [arrested] for that offence has escaped, he may be [arrested] by any officer [ . . . ] or any member of Her Majesty's armed forces or coastguard at any time and may be proceeded against in like manner as if the offence had been committed at the date when he was finally [arrested].

(3) Where any person who is a member of the crew of any ship in Her Majesty's employment or service is [arrested] by an officer for an offence under the customs

**5** Amended by the Police and Criminal Evidence Act 1984

and excise Acts, the commanding officer of the ship shall, if so required by the detaining officer, keep that person secured on board that ship until he can be brought before a court and shall then deliver him up to the proper officer.

[(4) Where any person has been arrested by a person who is not an officer—

(a) by virtue of this section; or
(b) by virtue of section 24 of the Police and Criminal Evidence Act 1984 in its application to offences under the customs and excise Acts, the person arresting him shall give notice of the arrest to an officer at the nearest convenient office of customs and excise.]⁶

## Forfeiture

*Provisions as to detention, seizure and condemnation of goods, etc.*

**139.**—(1) Any thing liable to forfeiture under the customs and excise Acts may be seized or detained by any officer or constable or any member of Her Majesty's armed forces or coastguard.

(2) Where any thing is seized or detained as liable to forfeiture under the customs and excise Acts by a person other than an officer, that person shall, subject to subsection (3) below, either—

(*a*) deliver that thing to the nearest convenient office of customs and excise; or
(*b*) if such delivery is not practicable, give to the Commissioners at the nearest convenient office of customs and excise notice in writing of the seizure or detention with full particulars of the thing seized or detained.

(3) Where the person seizing or detaining any thing as liable to forfeiture under the customs and excise Acts is a constable and that thing is or may be required for use in connection with any proceedings to be brought otherwise than under those Acts it may, subject to subsection (4) below, be retained in the custody of the police until either those proceedings are completed or it is decided that no such proceedings shall be brought.

(4) The following provisions apply in relation to things retained in the custody of the police by virtue of subsection (3) above, that is to say—

(*a*) notice in writing of the seizure or detention and of the intention to retain the thing in question in the custody of the police, together with full particulars as to that thing, shall be given to the Commissioners at the nearest convenient office of customs and excise;
(*b*) any officer shall be permitted to examine that thing and take account thereof at any time while it remains in the custody of the police;
(*c*) nothing in the Police (Property) Act 1897 shall apply in relation to that thing.

(5) Subject to subsections (3) and (4) above and to Schedule 3 to this Act, any thing seized or detained under the customs and excise Acts shall, pending the determination as to its forfeiture or disposal, be dealt with, and, if condemned or deemed to have been condemned or forfeited, shall be disposed of in such manner as the Commissioners may direct.

(6) Schedule 3 to this Act shall have effect for the purpose of forfeitures, and of

6  Substituted by the Police and Criminal Evidence Act 1984

proceedings for the condemnation of any thing as being forfeited, under the customs and excise Acts.

(7) If any person, not being an officer, by whom any thing is seized or detained or who has custody thereof after its seizure or detention, fails to comply with any requirement of this section or with any direction of the Commissioners given thereunder, he shall be liable on summary conviction to a penalty of £50.

(8) Subsections (2) to (7) above shall apply in relation to any dutiable goods seized or detained by any person other than an officer notwithstanding that they were not so seized as liable to forfeiture under the customs and excise Acts.

*Forfeiture of ships, etc. used in connection with goods liable to forfeiture.*
**141.**—(1) Without prejudice to any other provision of the Customs and Excise Acts 1979, where any thing has become liable to forfeiture under the customs and excise Acts—

> (a) any ship, aircraft, vehicle, animal, container (including any article of passengers' baggage) or other thing whatsoever which has been used for the carriage, handling, deposit or concealment of the thing so liable to forfeiture, either at a time when it was so liable or for the purposes of the commission of the offence for which it later became so liable; and
> (b) any other thing mixed, packed or found with the thing so liable,

shall also be liable to forfeiture.

(2) Where any ship, aircraft, vehicle or animal has become liable to forfeiture under the customs and excise Acts, whether by virtue of subsection (1) above or otherwise, all tackle, apparel or furniture thereof shall also be liable to forfeiture.

(3) Where any of the following, that is to say—

> (a) any ship not exceeding 100 tons register;
> (b) any aircraft; or
> (c) any hovercraft,

becomes liable to forfeiture under this section by reason of having been used in the importation, exportation or carriage of goods contrary to or for the purpose of contravening any prohibition or restriction for the time being in force with respect to those goods, or without payment having been made of, or security given for, any duty payable thereon, the owner and the master or commander shall each be liable on summary conviction to a penalty equal to the value of the ship, aircraft or hovercraft or £500, whichever is the less.

*Special provision as to forfeiture of larger ships.*
**142.**—(1) Notwithstanding any other provision of the Customs and Excise Acts 1979, a ship of 250 or more tons register shall not be liable to forfeiture under or by virtue of any provision of the Customs and Excise Acts 1979, except under section 88 above, unless the offence in respect of or in connection with which the forfeiture is claimed—

> (a) was substantially the object of the voyage during which the offence was committed; or
> (b) was committed while the ship was under chase by a vessel in the service of Her Majesty after failing to bring to when properly summoned to do so by that vessel.

(2) For the purpose of this section, a ship shall be deemed to have been properly summoned to bring to—

(a) if the vessel making the summons did so by means of an international signal code or other recognised means and while flying her proper ensign; and

(b) in the case of a ship which is not a British ship, if at the time when the summons was made the ship was within 3 nautical miles of the coast of the United Kingdom.

(3) For the purposes of this section, all hovercraft (of whatever size) shall be treated as ships of less than 250 tons register.

(4) The exemption from forfeiture of any ship under this section shall not affect any liability to forfeiture of goods carried therein.

*Penalty in lieu of forfeiture of larger ship where responsible officer implicated in offence.*

**143.**—(1) Where any ship of 250 or more tons register would, but for section 142 above, be liable to forfeiture for or in connection with any offence under the customs and excise Acts and, in the opinion of the Commissioners, a responsible officer of the ship is implicated either by his own act or by neglect in that offence, the Commissioners may fine that ship such sum not exceeding £50 as they see fit.

(2) For the purposes of this section, all hovercraft (of whatever size) shall be treated as ships of less than 250 tons register.

(3) Where any ship is liable to a fine under subsection (1) above but the Commissioners consider that fine an inadequate penalty for the offence, they may take proceedings in accordance with Schedule 3 to this Act, in like manner as they might but for section 142 above have taken proceedings for the condemnation of the ship if notice of claim had been given in respect thereof, for the condemnation of the ship in such sum not exceeding £500 as the court may see fit.

(4) Where any fine is to be imposed or any proceedings are to be taken under this section, the Commissioners may require such sum as they see fit, not exceeding £50 or, as the case may be, £500, to be deposited with them to await their final decision or, as the case may be, the decision of the court, and may detain the ship until that sum has been so deposited.

(5) No claim shall lie against the Commissioners for damages in respect of the payment of any deposit or the detention of any ship under this section.

(6) For the purposes of this section—

(a) "responsible officer", in relation to any ship, means the master, a mate or an engineer of the ship and, in the case of a ship carrying a passenger certificate, the purser or chief steward and, in the case of a ship manned wholly or partly by Asiatic seamen, the serang or other leading Asiatic officer of the ship;

(b) without prejudice to any other grounds upon which a responsible officer of any ship may be held to be implicated by neglect, he may be so held if goods not owned to by any member of the crew are discovered in a place under that officer's supervision in which they could not reasonably have been put if he had exercised proper care at the time of the loading of the ship or subsequently.

*Protection of officers, etc. in relation to seizure and detention of goods, etc.*

**144.**—(1) Where, in any proceedings for the condemnation of any thing seized as liable to forfeiture under the customs and excise Acts, judgment is given for the claimant, the court may, if it sees fit, certify that there were reasonable grounds for the seizure.

(2) Where any proceedings, whether civil or criminal, are brought against the Commissioners, a law officer of the Crown or any person authorised by or under the Customs and Excise Acts 1979 to seize or detain any thing liable to forfeiture under the customs and excise Acts on account of the seizure or detention of any thing, and judgement is given for the plaintiff or prosecutor, then if either—

(a) a certificate relating to the seizure has been granted under subsection (1) above; or

(b) the court is satisfied that there were reasonable grounds for seizing or detaining that thing under the customs and excise Acts,

the plaintiff or prosecutor shall not be entitled to recover any damages or costs and the defendant shall not be liable to any punishment.

(3) Nothing in subsection (2) above shall affect any right of any person to the return of the thing seized or detained or to compensation in respect of any damage to the thing or in respect of the destruction thereof.

(4) Any certificate under subsection (1) above may be proved by the production of either the original certificate or a certified copy thereof purporting to be signed by an officer of the court by which it was granted.

## General provisions as to legal proceedings

*Institution of proceedings*

**145.**[7]—(1) Subject to the following provisions of this section, no proceedings for an offence under the customs and excise Acts or for condemnation under Schedule 3 to this Act shall be instituted except by order of the Commissioners.

(2) Subject to the following provisions of this section, any proceedings under the customs and excise Acts instituted in a magistrates' court, and any such proceedings instituted in a court of summary jurisdiction in Northern Ireland, shall be commenced in the name of an officer.

(3) Subsections (1) and (2) above shall not apply to proceedings on indictment in Scotland.

(4) In the case of the death, removal, discharge or absence of the officer in whose name any proceedings were commenced under subsection (2) above, those proceedings may be continued by any officer authorised in that behalf by the Commissioners.

(5) Nothing in the foregoing provisions of this section shall prevent the institution of proceedings for an offence under the customs and excise Acts by order and in the name of a law officer of the Crown in any case in which he thinks it proper that proceedings should be so instituted.

(6) Notwithstanding anything in the foregoing provisions of this section, where any person has been [arrested] for any offence for which he is liable to be [arrested] under the customs and excise Acts, any court before which he is brought may proceed to deal with the case although the proceedings have not been instituted by order of the Commissioners or have not been commenced in the name of an officer.

7 Amended by the Police and Criminal Evidence Act 1984

*Service of process.*

**146.**—(1) Any summons or other process issued anywhere in the United Kingdom for the purpose of any proceedings under the customs and excise Acts may be served on the person to whom it is addressed in any part of the United Kingdom without any further endorsement, and shall be deemed to have been duly served—

(a) if delivered to him personally; or

(b) if left at his last known place of abode or business or, in the case of a body corporate, at their registered or principal office; or

(c) if left on board any vessel or aircraft to which he may belong or have lately belonged.

(2) Any summons, notice, order or other document issued for the purposes of any proceedings under the customs and excise Acts, or of any appeal from the decision of the court in any such proceedings, may be served by an officer.

In this subsection "appeal" includes an appeal by way of case stated.

(3) This section shall not apply in relation to proceedings instituted in the High Court or Court of Session.

*Proceedings for offences.*

**147.**—(1) Save as otherwise expressly provided in the customs and excise Acts and notwithstanding anything in any other enactment, any proceedings for an offence under those Acts—

(a) may be commenced at any time within 3 years from the date of the commission of the offence; and

(b) shall not be commenced later than 3 years from that date.

(2) Where, in England or Wales, a magistrates' court has begun to inquire into an information charging a person with an offence under the customs and excise Acts as examining justices the court shall not proceed under section 25(3) of the Criminal Law Act 1977 to try the information summarily without the consent of—

(a) the Attorney General, in a case where the proceedings were instituted by his order and in his name; or

(b) the Commissioners, in any other case.

(3) In the case of proceedings in England or Wales, without prejudice to any right to require the statement of a case for the opinion of the High Court, the prosecutor may appeal to the Crown Court against any decision of a magistrates' court in proceedings for an offence under the customs and excise Acts.

(4) In the case of proceedings in Northern Ireland, without prejudice to any right to require the statement of a case for the opinion of the High Court, the prosecutor may appeal to the county court against any decision of a court of summary jurisdiction in proceedings for an offence under the customs and excise Acts.

(5) In the application of the customs and excise Acts to Scotland, and subject to any express provision made by the enactment in question, any offence which is made punishable on summary conviction—

(a) shall if prosecuted summarily be prosecuted in the sheriff court;

(b) may be also prosecuted by any other method.

*Place of trial for offences.*

**148.**—(1) Proceedings for an offence under the customs and excise Acts may be commenced—

(*a*) in any court having jurisdiction in the place where the person charged with the offence resides or is found; or

(*b*) if any thing was detained or seized in connection with the offence, in any court having jurisdiction in the place where that thing was so detained or seized or was found or condemned as forfeited; or

(*c*) in any court having jurisdiction anywhere in that part of the United Kingdom, namely—

    (i) England and Wales,

    (ii) Scotland, or

    (iii) Northern Ireland,

in which the place where the offence was committed is situated.

(2) Where any such offence was committed at some place outside the area of any commission of the peace, the place of the commission of the offence shall, for the purposes of the jurisdiction of any court, be deemed to be any place in the United Kingdom where the offender is found or to which he is first brought after the commission of the offence.

(3) The jurisdiction under subsection (2) above shall be in addition to and not in derogation of any jurisdiction or power of any court under any other enactment.

*Power of Commissioners to mitigate penalties, etc.*

**152.** The Commissioners may, as they see fit—

(*a*) stay, sist or compound any proceedings for an offence or for the condemnation of any thing as being forfeited under the customs and excise Acts; or

(*b*) restore, subject to such conditions (if any) as they think proper, any thing forfeited or seized under those Acts; or

(*c*) after judgment, mitigate or remit any pecuniary penalty imposed under those Acts; or

(*d*) order any person who has been imprisoned to be discharged before the expiration of his term of imprisonment, being a person imprisoned for any offence under those Acts or in respect of the non-payment of a penalty or other sum adjudged to be paid or awarded in relation to such an offence or in respect of the default of a sufficient distress to satisfy such a sum;

but paragraph (*a*) above shall not apply to proceedings on indictment in Scotland.

*Proof of certain documents.*

**153.**—(1) Any document purporting to be signed either by one or more of the Commissioners, or by their order, or by any other person with their authority, shall, until the contrary is proved, be deemed to have been so signed and to be made and issued by the Commissioners, and may be proved by the production of a copy thereof purporting to be so signed.

(2) Without prejudice to subsection (1) above, the Documentary Evidence Act 1868 shall apply in relation to—

(*a*) any document issued by the Commissioners;

(*b*) any document issued before 1st April 1909, by the Commissioners of Customs or the Commissioners of Customs and the Commissioners of Inland Revenue jointly;

(*c*) any document issued before that date in relation to the revenue of excise by the Commissioners of Inland Revenue,

as it applies in relation to the documents mentioned in that Act.

(3) That Act shall, as applied by subsection (2) above, have effect as if the persons mentioned in paragraphs (*a*) to (*c*) of that subsection were included in the first column of the Schedule to that Act, and any of the Commissioners or any secretary or assistant secretary to the Commissioners were specified in the second column of that Schedule in connection with those persons.

[(4) A photograph of any document delivered to the Commissioners for any customs or excise purpose and certified by them to be such a photograph shall be admissible in any proceedings, whether civil or criminal, to the same extent as the document itself.][8]

*Proof of certain other matters.*

**154.**—(1) An averment in any process in proceedings under the customs and excise Acts—

(*a*) that those proceedings were instituted by the order of the Commissioners; or

(*b*) that any person is or was a Commissioner, officer or constable, or a member of Her Majesty's armed forces or coastguard; or

(*c*) that any person is or was appointed or authorised by the Commissioners to discharge, or was engaged by the orders or with the concurrence of the Commissioners in the discharge of, any duty; or

(*d*) that the Commissioners have or have not been satisfied as to any matter as to which they are required by any provision of those Acts to be satisfied; or

(*e*) that any ship is a British ship; or

(*f*) that any goods thrown overboard, staved or destroyed were so dealt with in order to prevent or avoid the seizure of those goods,

shall, until the contrary is proved, be sufficient evidence of the matter in question.

(2) Where in any proceedings relating to customs or excise any question arises as to the place from which any goods have been brought or as to whether or not—

(*a*) any duty has been paid or secured in respect of any goods; or

(*b*) any goods or other things whatsoever are of the description or nature alleged in the information, writ or other process; or

(*c*) any goods have been lawfully imported or lawfully unloaded from any ship or aircraft; or

(*d*) any goods have been lawfully loaded into any ship or aircraft or lawfully exported or were lawfully waterborne; or

(*e*) any goods were lawfully brought to any place for the purpose of being loaded into any ship or aircraft or exported; or

(*f*) any goods are or were subject to any prohibition of or restriction on their importation or exportation,

**8** Added by Finance Act 1981, Sch. 8

then, where those proceedings are brought by or against the Commissioners, a law officer of the Crown or an officer, or against any other person in respect of anything purporting to have been done in pursuance of any power or duty conferred or imposed on him by or under the customs and excise Acts, the burden of proof shall lie upon the other party to the proceedings.

*Persons who may conduct proceedings.*

**155.**—(1) Any officer or any other person authorised in that behalf by the Commissioners may, although he is not a barrister, advocate or solicitor, conduct any proceedings before any magistrates' court in England or Wales or court of summary jurisdiction in Scotland or Northern Ireland or before any examining justices, being proceedings under any enactment relating to an assigned matter or proceedings arising out of the same circumstances as any proceedings commenced under any such enactment, whether or not the last mentioned proceedings are persisted in.

(2) Any person who has been admitted as a solicitor and is employed by the Commissioners may act as a solicitor in any proceedings in England, Wales or Northern Ireland relating to any assigned matter notwithstanding that he does not hold a current practising certificate.

## Part XII

### General and Miscellaneous

**General powers, etc.**

*Power to examine and take account of goods.*

**159.**—(1) Without prejudice to any other power conferred by the Customs and Excise Acts 1979, an officer may examine and take account of any goods—

    (a) which are imported; or
    (b) which are in a warehouse or Queen's warehouse; or
    (c) which have been loaded into any ship or aircraft at any place in the United Kingdom; or
    (d) which are entered for exportation or for use as stores; or
    (e) which are brought to any place in the United Kingdom for exportation or for shipment for exportation or as stores; or
    (f) in the case of which any claim for drawback, allowance, rebate, remission or repayment of duty is made;

and may for that purpose require any container to be opened or unpacked.

(2) Any examination of goods by an officer under the Customs and Excise Acts 1979 shall be made at such place as the Commissioners appoint for the purpose.

(3) In the case of such goods as the Commissioners may direct, and subject to such conditions as they see fit to impose, an officer may permit goods to be skipped on the quay or bulked, sorted, lotted, packed or repacked before account is taken thereof.

(4) Any opening, unpacking, weighing, measuring, repacking, bulking, sorting, lotting, marking, numbering, loading, unloading, carrying or landing of goods or their containers for the purposes of, or incidental to, the examination by an officer, removal or warehousing thereof shall be done, and any facilities or assistance required for any such examination shall be provided, by or at the expense of the proprietor of the goods.

(5) If any imported goods which an officer has power under the Customs and Excise Acts 1979 to examine are without the authority of the proper officer removed from customs and excise charge before they have been examined, those goods shall be liable to forfeiture.

(6) If any goods falling within subsection (5) above are removed by a person with intent to defraud Her Majesty of any duty chargeable thereon or to evade any prohibition or restriction for the time being in force with respect thereto under or by virtue of any enactment, that person shall be guilty of an offence under this subsection and may be detained.

(7) A person guilty of an offence under subsection (6) above shall be liable—

(a) on summary conviction, to a penalty of the prescribed sum or of three times the value of the goods, whichever is the greater, or to imprisonment for a term not exceeding 6 months, or to both; or

(b) on conviction on indictment, to a penalty of any amount, or to imprisonment for a term not exceeding 2 years, or to both.

(8) Without prejudice to the foregoing provisions of this section, where by this section or by or under any other provision of the Customs and Excise Acts 1979 an account is authorised or required to be taken of any goods for any purpose by an officer, the Commissioner may, with the consent of the proprietor of the goods, accept as the account of those goods for that purpose an account taken by such other person as may be approved in that behalf by both the Commissioners and the proprietor of the goods.

*Power to take samples.*
**160.**—(1) An officer may at any time take samples of any goods—

(a) which he is empowered by the Customs and Excise Acts 1979 to examine; or

(b) . . .

*Power to search premises.*
**161.**[9]—(1) Without prejudice to any other power conferred by the Customs and Excise Acts 1979 but subject to subsection (2) below, where there are reasonable grounds to suspect that any thing liable to forfeiture under the customs and excise Acts is kept or concealed in any building or place, any officer having a writ of assistance may—

(a) enter that building or place at any time, whether by day or night, on any day, and search for, seize, and detain or remove any such thing; and

(b) so far as is reasonably necessary for the purpose of such entry, search, seizure, detention or removal, break open any door, window or container and force and remove any other impediment or obstruction.

(2) No officer shall exercise the power of entry conferred on him by subsection (1) above by night unless he is accompanied by a constable.

(3) Without prejudice to subsection (1) above or to any other power conferred by the Customs and Excise Acts 1979, if a justice of the peace is satisfied by information upon oath given by an officer that there are reasonable grounds to suspect that any thing liable to forfeiture under the customs and excise Acts is kept or concealed in any building or place, he may by warrant under his hand

**9** Amended by the Police and Criminal Evidence Act 1984

given on any day authorise [any officer and any person accompanying an officer to enter and search the building or place named in the warrant within one month from that day.]⁸

(4) An officer or [other person so authorised]⁸ shall thereupon have the like powers in relation to the building or place named in the warrant, subject to the like conditions as to entry by night, as if he were an officer having a writ of assistance and acting upon reasonable grounds of suspicion.

(5) Where there are reasonable grounds to suspect that any still, vessel, utensil, spirits or materials for the manufacture of spirits is or are unlawfully kept or deposited in any building or place, subsections (3) and (4) above shall apply in relation to any constable as they would apply in relation to an officer.

(6) A writ of assistance shall continue in force during the reign in which it is issued and for 6 months thereafter.

*Power to search vehicles or vessels.*
**163.**—(1) Without prejudice to any other power conferred by the Customs and Excise Acts 1979, where there are reasonable grounds to suspect that any vehicle or vessel is or may be carrying any goods which are—

(a) chargeable with any duty which has not been paid or secured; or
(b) in the course of being unlawfully removed from or to any place; or
(c) otherwise liable to forfeiture under the customs and excise Acts,

any officer or constable or member of Her Majesty's armed forces or coastguard may stop and search that vehicle or vessel.

(2) If when so required by any such officer, constable or member the person in charge of any such vehicle or vessel refuses to stop or to permit the vehicle or vessel to be searched, he shall be liable on summary conviction to a penalty of £100.

*Power to search persons.*
**164.**—(1) Where there are reasonable grounds to suspect that any person to whom this section applies is carrying any article—

(a) which is chargeable with any duty which has not been paid or secured; or
(b) with respect to the importation or exportation of which any prohibition or restriction is for the time being in force under or by virtue of any enactment,

any officer or any person acting under the directions of an officer may, subject to subsections (2) and (3) below, search him and any article he has with him.

(2) A person who is to be searched in pursuance of this section may require to be taken before a justice of the peace or a superior of the officer or other person concerned, and the justice or superior shall consider the grounds for suspicion and direct accordingly whether or not the search is to take place.

(3) No woman or girl shall be searched in pursuance of this section except by a woman.

(4) This section applies to the following persons, namely—

(a) any person who is on board or has landed from any ship or aircraft;
(b) any person entering or about to leave the United Kingdom;
(c) any person within the dock area of a port;

(*d*) any person at a customs and excise airport;

(*e*) any person in, entering or leaving any approved wharf or transit shed which is not in a port;

(*f*) in Northern Ireland, any person travelling from or to any place which is on or beyond the boundary.

*Power to pay rewards.*

**165.** Subject to any directions of the Treasury as to amount, the Commissioners may at their discretion pay rewards in respect of any service which appears to them to merit reward rendered to them by any person in relation to any assigned matter.

## General offences

*Untrue declarations etc.*

**167.**—(1) If any person either knowingly or recklessly—

(*a*) makes or signs, or causes to be made or signed, or delivers or causes to be delivered to the Commissioners or an officer, any declaration, notice, certificate or other document whatsoever; or

(*b*) makes any statement in answer to any question put to him by an officer which he is required by or under any enactment to answer,

being a document or statement produced or made for any purpose of any assigned matter, which is untrue in any material particular, he shall be guilty of an offence under this subsection and may be detained; and any goods in relation to which the document or statement was made shall be liable to forfeiture.

(2) Without prejudice to subsection (4) below, a person who commits an offence under subsection (1) above shall be liable—

(*a*) on summary conviction, to a penalty of the prescribed sum, or to imprisonment for a term not exceeding 6 months, or to both; or

(*b*) on conviction on indictment, to a penalty of any amount, or to imprisonment for a term not exceeding 2 years, or to both.

(3) If any person—

(*a*) makes or signs, or causes to be made or signed, or delivers or causes to be delivered to the Commissioners or an officer, any declaration, notice, certificate or other document whatsoever; or

(*b*) makes any statement in answer to any question put to him by an officer which he is required by or under any enactment to answer,

being a document or statement produced or made for any purpose of any assigned matter, which is untrue in any material particular, then, without prejudice to subsection (4) below, he shall be liable on summary conviction to a penalty of £300.

(4) Where by reason of any such document or statement as is mentioned in subsection (1) or (3) above the full amount of any duty payable is not paid or any overpayment is made in respect of any drawback, allowance, rebate or repayment of duty, the amount of the duty unpaid or of the overpayment shall be recoverable as a debt due to the Crown or may be summarily recovered as a civil debt.

*Counterfeiting documents, etc.*

**168.**[10]—(1) If any person—

 (a) counterfeits or falsifies any document which is required by or under any enactment relating to an assigned matter or which is used in the transaction of any business relating to an assigned matter; or

 (b) knowingly accepts, receives or uses any such document so counterfeited or falsified; or

 (c) alters any such document after it is officially issued; or

 (d) counterfeits any seal, signature, initials or other mark of, or used by, any officer for the verification of such a document or for the security of goods or for any other purpose relating to an assigned matter,

he shall be guilty of an offence under this section and may be [arrested].

(2) A person guilty of an offence under this section shall be liable—

 (a) on summary conviction, to a penalty of the prescribed sum, or to imprisonment for a term not exceeding 6 months, or to both; or

 (b) on conviction on indictment, to a penalty of any amount, or to imprisonment for a term not exceeding 2 years, or to both.

(3) Any person committing an offence under this section shall be liable on summary conviction to a penalty of £200 and any false or unjust scales, and any article in connection with which the offence was committed, shall be liable to forfeiture.

(4) In this section "scales" includes weights, measures and weighing or measuring machines or instruments.

*Penalty for fraudulent evasion of duty, etc.*

**170.**[11]—(1) Without prejudice to any other provision of the Customs and Excise Acts 1979, if any person—

 (a) knowingly acquires possession of any of the following goods, that is to say—

  (i) goods which have been unlawfully removed from a warehouse or Queen's warehouse;

  (ii) goods which are chargeable with a duty which has not been paid;

  (iii) goods with respect to the importation or exportation of which any prohibition or restriction is for time being in force under or by virtue of any enactment; or

 (b) is in any way knowingly concerned in carrying, removing, depositing, harbouring, keeping or concealing or in any manner dealing with any such goods,

and does so with intent to defraud Her Majesty of any duty payable on the goods or to evade any such prohibition or restriction with respect to the goods he shall be guilty of an offence under this section and may be [arrested].

(2) Without prejudice to any other provision of the Customs and Excise Acts 1979, if any person is, in relation to any goods, in any way knowingly concerned in any fraudulent evasion or attempt at evasion—

10 Amended by the Police and Criminal Evidence Act 1984
11 Amended by the Police and Criminal Evidence Act 1984

   (*a*) of any duty chargeable on the goods;

   (*b*) of any prohibition or restriction for the time being in force with respect to the goods under or by virtue of any enactment; or

   (*c*) of any provision of the Customs and Excise Acts 1979 applicable to the goods,

he shall be guilty of an offence under this section and may be [arrested].

(3) Subject to subsection (4) below, a person guilty of an offence under this section shall be liable—

   (*a*) on summary conviction, to a penalty of the prescribed sum or of three times the value of the goods, whichever is the greater, or to imprisonment for a term not exceeding 6 months, or to both; or

   (*b*) on conviction on indictment, to a penalty of any amount, or to imprisonment for a term not exceeding 2 years, or to both.

(4) In the case of an offence under this section in connection with a prohibition or restriction on importation or exportation having effect by virtue of section 3 of the Misuse of Drugs Act 1971, subsection (3) above shall have effect subject to the modifications specified in Schedule 1 to this Act.

(5) In any case where a person would, apart from this subsection, be guilty of—

   (*a*) an offence under this section in connection with a prohibition or restriction; and

   (*b*) a corresponding offence under the enactment or other instrument imposing the prohibition or restriction, being an offence for which a fine or other penalty is expressly provided by that enactment or other instrument,

he shall not be guilty of the offence mentioned in paragraph (*a*) of this subsection.


*General provisions as to offences and penalties.*

   **171.**—(1) . . .

(3) Where a penalty for an offence under any enactment relating to an assigned matter is required to be fixed by reference to the value of any goods, that value shall be taken as the price which those goods might reasonably be expected to have fetched, after payment of any duty or tax chargeable thereon, if they had been sold in the open market at or about the date of the commission of the offence for which the penalty is imposed.

(4) Where an offence under any enactment relating to an assigned matter which has been committed by a body corporate is proved to have been committed with the consent or connivance of, or to be attributable to any neglect on the part of, any director, manager, secretary or other similar officer of the body corporate or any person purporting to act in any such capacity, he as well as the body corporate shall be guilty of that offence and shall be liable to be proceeded against and punished accordingly.

In this subsection "director", in relation to any body corporate established by or under any enactment for the purpose of carrying on under national ownership any industry or part of an industry or undertaking, being a body corporate whose affairs are managed by the members thereof, means a member of that body corporate.

   (5) . . .

**Miscellaneous**

*Removal from or to Isle of Man not to be importation or exportation.*
**174.**—(1) For the purpose of the customs and excise Acts, subject to section 6(2) and (3) of the Customs and Excise Duties (General Reliefs) Act 1979 and subsection (2) below, goods removed into the United Kingdom from the Isle of Man shall be deemed not to be imported into the United Kingdom.

(2) Subsection (1) above shall not apply to the removal of—

(a) any explosives within the meaning of the Explosives Act 1875 on the unloading or landing of which any restriction is for the time being in force under or by virtue of that Act; or

(b) copies of copyright works to which section 22 of the Copyright Act 1956 applies.

(3) For the purposes of the Customs and Excise Acts, subject to subsection (4) below, goods removed from the United Kingdom to the Isle of Man shall be deemed not to be exported from the United Kingdom.

*Citation and Commencement*
**178.**—(1) This Act may be cited as the Customs and Excise Management Act 1979.

(2) . . .

(3) This Act shall come into operation on 1st April 1979.


SCHEDULE 1
(Sections 50(5), 68(4) and 170(4).)

CONTROLLED DRUGS: VARIATION OF PUNISHMENTS FOR CERTAIN OFFENCES UNDER THIS ACT

**1.** Sections 50(4), 68(3) and 170(3) of this Act shall have effect in a case where the goods in respect of which the offence referred to in that subsection was committed were a Class A drug or a Class B drug as if for the words from "shall be liable" onwards there were substituted the following words, that is to say—

"shall be liable—

(a) on summary conviction, to a penalty of the prescribed sum or of three times the value of the goods, whichever is the greater, or to imprisonment for a term not exceeding 6 months, or to both;
[(b) on conviction on indictment—

(i) where the goods were a Class A drug, to a penalty of any amount, or to imprisonment for life, or to both; and
(ii) where they were a Class B drug, to a penalty of any amount, or to imprisonment for a term not exceeding 14 years, or to both.][12]

**2.** Sections 50(4), 68(3) and 170(3) of this Act shall have effect in a case where the goods in respect of which the offence referred to in that subsection was committed were a Class C drug as if for the words from "shall be liable" onwards there were substituted the following words, that is to say—

**12** Substituted by Controlled Drugs (Penalties) Act 1985 with effect from 16 September 1985 "shall be liable—

   (a) on summary conviction in Great Britain, to a penalty of three times the value of the goods or £500, whichever is the greater, or to imprisonment for a term not exceeding 3 months, or to both;

   (b) on summary conviction in Northern Ireland, to a penalty of three times the value of the goods or £100, whichever is the greater, or to imprisonment for a term not exceeding 6 months, or to both;

   (c) on conviction on indictment, to a penalty of any amount, or to imprisonment for a term not exceeding 5 years, or to both."

**3.** In this Schedule "Class A drug", "Class B drug" and "Class C drug" have the same meanings as in the Misuse of Drugs Act 1971.

## SCHEDULE 3
### (Sections 139, 143 and 145.)

#### PROVISIONS RELATING TO FORFEITURE

*Notice of seizure*

**1.**—(1) The Commissioners shall, except as provided in sub-paragraph (2) below, give notice of the seizure of any thing as liable to forfeiture and of the grounds therefor to any person who to their knowledge was at the time of the seizure the owner or one of the owners thereof.

(2) Notice need not be given under this paragraph if the seizure was made in the presence of—

   (a) the person whose offence or suspected offence occasioned the seizure; or

   (b) the owner or any of the owners of the thing seized or any servant or agent of his; or

   (c) in the case of any thing seized in any ship or aircraft, the master or commander.

**2.** Notice under paragraph 1 above shall be given in writing and shall be deemed to have been duly served on the person concerned—

   (a) if delivered to him personally; or

   (b) if addressed to him and left or forwarded by post to him at his usual or last known place of abode or business or, in the case of a body corporate, at their registered or prinicipal office; or

   (c) where he has no address within the United Kingdom, or his address is unknown, by publication of notice of the seizure in the London, Edinburgh or Belfast Gazette.

*Notice of claim*

**3.** Any person claiming that any thing seized as liable to forfeiture is not so liable shall, within one month of the date of the notice of seizure or, where no such notice has been served on him, within one month of the date of the seizure, give notice of his claim in writing to the Commissioners at any office of customs and excise.

**4.**—(1) Any notice under paragraph 3 above shall specify the name and address of the claimant and, in the case of a claimant who is outside the United Kingdom, shall specify the name and address of a solicitor in the United Kingdom who is authorised to accept service of process and to act on behalf of the claimant.

(2) Service of process upon a solicitor so specified shall be deemed to be proper service upon the claimant.

*Condemnation*

**5.** If on the expiration of the relevant period under paragraph 3 above for the giving of notice of claim in respect of any thing no such notice has been given to the Commissioners, or if, in the case of any such notice given, any requirement of paragraph 4 above is not complied with, the thing in question shall be deemed to have been duly condemned as forfeited.

**6.** Where notice of claim in respect of any thing is duly given in accordance with paragraphs 3 and 4 above, the Commissioners shall take proceedings for the condemnation of that thing by the court, and if the court finds that the thing was at the time of seizure liable to forfeiture the court shall condemn it as forfeited.

**7.** Where any thing is in accordance with either of paragraphs 5 or 6 above condemned or deemed to have been condemned as forfeited, then, without prejudice to any delivery up or sale of the thing by the Commissioners under paragraph 16 below, the forfeiture shall have effect as from the date when the liability to forfeiture arose.

*Proceedings for condemnation by court*

**8.** Proceedings for condemnation shall be civil proceedings and may be instituted—

    (a)  in England or Wales either in the High Court or in a magistrates' court;
    (b)  in Scotland either in the Court of Session or in the sheriff court;
    (c)  in Northern Ireland either in the High Court or in a court of summary jurisdiction.

**9.** Proceedings for the condemnation of any thing instituted in a magistrates' court in England or Wales, in the sheriff court in Scotland or in a court of summary jurisdiction in Northern Ireland may be so instituted—

    (a)  in any such court having jurisdiction in the place where any offence in connection with that thing was committed or where any proceedings for such an offence are instituted; or
    (b)  in any such court having jurisdiction in the place where the claimant resides or, if the claimant has specified a solicitor under paragraph 4 above, in the place where that solicitor has his office; or
    (c)  in any such court having jurisdiction in the place where that thing was found, detained or seized or to which it is first brought after being found, detained or seized.

**10.**—(1) In any proceedings for condemnation instituted in England, Wales or Northern Ireland, the claimant or his solicitor shall make oath that the thing seized was, or was to the best of his knowledge and belief, the property of the claimant at the time of the seizure.

(2) In any such proceedings instituted in the High Court, the claimant shall give such security for the costs of the proceedings as may be determined by the Court.

(3) If any requirement of this paragraph is not complied with, the court shall give judgement for the Commissioners.

**11.**—(1) In the case of any proceedings for condemnation instituted in a magistrates' court in England or Wales, without prejudice to any right to require the statement of a case for the opinion of the High Court, either party may appeal against the decision of that court to the Crown Court.

(2) In the case of any proceedings for condemnation instituted in a court of summary jurisdiction in Northern Ireland, without prejudice to any right to require the statement of a case for the opinion of the High Court, either party may appeal against the decision of that court to the county court.

**12.** Where an appeal, including an appeal by way of case stated, has been made against the decision of the court in any proceedings for the condemnation of any thing, that thing shall, pending the final determination of the matter, be left with the Commissioners or at any convenient office of customs and excise.

*Provisions as to proof*

**13.** In any proceedings arising out of the seizure of any thing, the fact, form and manner of the seizure shall be taken to have been as set forth in the process without any further evidence thereof, unless the contrary is proved.

**14.** In any proceedings, the condemnation by a court of any thing as forfeited may be proved by the production either of the order or certificate of condemnation or of a certified copy thereof purporting to be signed by an officer of the court by which the order or certificate was made or granted.

*Special provisions as to certain claimants*

**15.** For the purposes of any claim to, or proceedings for the condemnation of, any thing, where that thing is at the time of seizure the property of a body corporate, of two or more partners or of any number of persons exceeding five, the oath required by paragraph 10 above to be taken and any other thing required by this Schedule or by any rules of the court to be done by, or by any person authorised by, the claimant or owner may be taken or done by, or by any other person authorised by, the following persons respectively, that is to say—

(a) where the owner is a body corporate, the secretary or some duly authorised officer of that body;

(b) where the owners are in partnership, any one of those owners;

(c) where the owners are any number of persons exceeding five not being in partnership, any two of those persons on behalf of themselves and their co-owners.

*Power to deal with seizures before condemnation, etc.*

**16.** Where any thing has been seized as liable to forfeiture the Commissioners may at any time if they see fit and notwithstanding that the thing has not yet been condemned, or is not yet deemed to have been condemned, as forfeited—

(a) deliver it up to any claimant upon his paying to the Commissioners such sum as they think proper, being a sum not exceeding that which in their opinion represents the value of the thing, including any duty or tax chargeable thereon which has not been paid;

(b) if the thing seized is a living creature or is in the opinion of the Commissioners of a perishable nature, sell or destroy it.

**17.**—(1) If, where any thing is delivered up, sold or destroyed under paragraph 16 above, it is held in proceedings taken under this Schedule that the thing was not liable to forfeiture at the time of its seizure, the Commissioners shall, subject to any deduction allowed under sub-paragraph (2) below, on demand by the claimant tender to him—

(a) an amount equal to any sum paid by him under sub-paragraph (a) of that paragraph; or

(b) where they have sold the thing, an amount equal to the proceeds of sale; or

(c) where they have destroyed the thing, an amount equal to the market value of the thing at the time of its seizure.

(2) Where the amount to be tendered under sub-paragraph (1)(a), (b) or (c) above includes any sum on account of any duty or tax chargeable on the thing which had not been paid before its seizure the Commissioners may deduct so much of that amount as represents that duty or tax.

(3) If the claimant accepts any amount tendered to him under sub-paragraph (1) above, he shall not be entitled to maintain any action on account of the seizure, detention, sale or destruction of the thing.

(4) For the purpose of sub-paragraph (1)(c) above, the market value of any thing at the time of its seizure shall be taken to be such amount as the Commissioners and the claimant may agree or, in default of agreement, as may be determined by a referee appointed by the Lord Chancellor (not being an official of any government department), whose decision shall be final and conclusive; and the procedure on any reference to a referee shall be such as may be determined by the referee.

# Provisions from Post Office Act 1953 and Postal Packets (Customs and Excise) Regulations 1975

## POST OFFICE ACT 1953 (c. 36)

*Application of Customs Acts to postal packets*

**16.**—(1) Subject to the provisions of this section, the enactments for the time being in force relating to customs [or excise][1] shall apply in relation to goods contained in postal packets to which this section applies brought into or sent out of the United Kingdom by post from or to . . . the Isle of Man or any place outside the British postal area as they apply in relation to goods otherwise imported, exported or removed into or out of the United Kingdom from or to [that Isle] or any such place.

(2) The Treasury, on the recommendation of the Commissioners of Customs and Excise and [the Minister], may by statutory instrument make regulations—

(a) for specifying the postal packets to which this section applies;

(b) for making modifications or exceptions in the application of the said enactments to such packets;

(c) for enabling officers of the Post Office to perform for the purposes of the said enactments and otherwise all or any of the duties of the importer, exporter or person removing the goods;

(d) for carrying into effect any arrangement with the government or postal administration of any other country with respect to foreign postal packets;

(e) for securing the observance of the said enactments and, without prejudice to any liability of any person under those enactments, for punishing any contravention of the regulations;

and different regulations may be made for foreign and inland postal packets respectively.

(3)[2] [. . .]

(4) Without prejudice to section thirty-eight of the Interpretation Act, 1889 (which relates to the effect of repeal and re-enactment), sub-paragraph (2) of paragraph 1 of Part III of the Fifth Schedule to the Exchange Control Act, 1947, shall be construed as if—

(a) any reference therein to section fourteen of the Post Office (Parcels) Act, 1882, were a reference to this section; and

(b) the reference therein to section three of the Post Office (Amendment) Act, 1935, were a reference to paragraph (a) of subsection (2) of this section.

---

1 Inserted by S.I. 1969/1368 and Post Office Act 1969
2 Repealed by Post Office Act 1969 s. 141

## THE POSTAL PACKETS (CUSTOMS AND EXCISE) REGULATIONS 1975

### (S.I. No.1992)

| | |
|---|---|
| *Made* - - - | *3rd December 1975* |
| *Coming into Operation* | *1st January 1976* |

**1.** These Regulations may be cited as the Postal Packets (Customs and Excise) Regulations 1975, and shall come into force on 1st January 1976.

**2.**—(1) In these Regulations—

"Post Office" has the meaning assigned to those words by the Post Office Act 1969;

"Commissioners" means Commissioners of Customs and Excise;

"datapost packet" means a postal packet containing goods which is posted in the United Kingdom as a datapost packet for transmission to a place outside the United Kingdom in accordance with the terms of a contract entered into between the Post Office and the sender of the packet; or which is received at a post office in the United Kingdom from a place outside the United Kingdom for transmission and delivery in the United Kingdom as if it were a datapost packet;

"dutiable goods" has the meaning assigned to those words by section 307(1) of the Customs and Excise Act 1952 but includes goods chargeable with value added tax and goods subject to any other charge on importation;

"duty" and "duty of customs or excise" include value added tax and any other charge on imported goods;

"exporter" and "importer" have the meanings assigned to them by section 307(1) of the Customs and Excise Act 1952;

"inland post" means the post for transmission of those postal packets to which the Post Office Inland Scheme 1975 applies;

"letter packet" means a packet transmitted as the letter rate of postage and containing goods;

"prescribed" means prescribed by the provisions of the Universal Postal Convention and Detailed Regulations made thereunder which are for the time being in force:

"proper" in relation to an officer means appointed or authorised by the Commissioners or the Post Office to perform any duty in relation to a postal packet.

(2) In these Regulations (except in relation to the inland post) the expressions "printed packet" and "small packet" have the same meanings as in the Post Office Overseas Letter Post Scheme 1971 and "parcel" has the same meaning as in the Post Office Overseas Parcel Post Scheme 1971.

(3) In these Regulations, in relation to the inland post, the expression "parcel" has the same meaning as in the Post Office Inland Post Scheme 1975, and references to printed packets, small packets, and datapost packets shall, in relation to the inland post, be deemed to be omitted.

(4) Any reference in these Regulations to the provisions of any enactment or regulation or Post Office Scheme shall be construed, unless the context otherwise requires, as a reference to those provisions as amended, re-enacted or replaced by any subsequent enactment or regulation or scheme.

(5) The Interpretation Act 1889 shall apply for the interpretation of these Regulations as it applies for the interpretation of the Act of Parliament and as if these Regulations and the Regulations hereby revoked were Acts of Parliament.

**3.** The Postal Packets (Customs and Excise) Regulations 1971 and the Postal Packets (Customs and Excise) Amendment (No. 1) Regulations 1973 are hereby revoked.

**4.** Section 16 of the Post Office Act 1953, as amended pursuant to section 87 of the Post Office Act 1969 by Article 9 of the Postal Services (Channel Islands Consequential Provisions) Order 1969 and Article 11 of the Postal Services (Isle of Man Consequential Provisions) Order 1973 shall apply to all postal packets, other than postcards and telegrams, which are posted in the United Kingdom for transmission to any place outside it or which are brought by post into the United Kingdom.

**5.** In their application to goods contained in such postal packets, the following provisions of the Customs and Excise Act 1952 shall be subject to the following modifications and exceptions:—. . .

(*d*)   In the application of section 44,[3] paragraph (*a*) of that section shall be omitted. . . .

(*g*)   Section 65(1)[4] shall apply to goods brought by post into the United Kingdom, or posted in the United Kingdom for transmission to any place outside it, if an entry or specification is required of such goods when they are imported or exported otherwise than by post.

(*h*)   In the application of section 79[5] the proviso to subsection (2) shall be omitted and subsection (3) shall apply with the modification that the time of exportation of goods shall be the time when they are posted (or re-directed) in the United Kingdom for transmission to a place outside it. . . .

(*n*)   Paragraph 1 of Schedule 7[6] shall, in the case of a thing brought by post into the United Kingdom, apply with the substitution, for the words "to any person who to their knowledge was at the time of seizure the owner or one of the owners thereof", of the words "to the person to whom the postal packet containing the thing is addressed", and paragraph 10(1) of the said Schedule shall not apply.

**6.** Dutiable goods shall not be brought by post into the United Kingdom from a place situated outside the United Kingdom and the Isle of Man for delivery in the United Kingdom or the Isle of Man, except:—

(*a*)   in a parcel, a letter packet, a small packet or a datapost packet: or

(*b*)   in a printed packet, provided that the goods are of such a description as to be transmissible in such a packet under paragraph 22 of the Post Office Overseas Letter Post Scheme 1971.

3   Now s. 49, Customs and Excise Management Act 1979
4   Now s 77, 1979 Act
5   Now s. 5, 1979 Act
6   Now paras. 1 and 10, Sch. 3, 1979 Act

**7.**—(1) This Regulation relates to:—

(a) parcels brought by post into the United Kingdom:

(b) packets brought by post into the United Kingdom, being printed packets containing or consisting of dutiable goods, small packets, letter packets or datapost packets, where the value of any such packet exceeds £50;

(c) packets brought by post into the United Kingdom, being printed packets containing or consisting of dutiable goods, small packets, letter packets or datapost packets, where the value of any such packet does not exceed £50.

(2) Every parcel referred to aragraph (1)(a) of this Regulation shall have affixed to it, or be accompanied by, a customs declaration fully and correctly stating the nature, quantity and value of the goods which it contains or of which it consists, and such other particulars as the Commissioners or the Post Office may require:

Provided that the Commissioners may, at the request of the Post Office, relax the requirements of this paragraph by allowing the bringing in by post into the United Kingdom of any number of parcels accompanied by a single customs declaration containing the particulars prescribed above if the parcels are brought in together, sent by or on behalf of the same person and addressed to a single addressee.

(3) Every packet referred to in paragraph (1)(b) of this Regulation shall have attached to it a full and correct customs declaration of the kind described in paragraph (2) of this Regulation and, in addition, shall bear on the outside the top portion of a green label in the prescribed form:

Provided than any packet referred to in this paragraph, being a registered letter packet containing any article of value, may have the customs declaration referred to in this paragraph enclosed in it.

(4) Every packet referred to in paragraph (1)(c) of this Regulation shall either—

(a) bear on the outside a green label in the prescribed form, in which the declaration as to the description, net weight and value of the contents shall be fully and correctly completed: or

(b) bear on the outside the top portion of a green label in the prescribed form and, in addition, have attached to it a full and correct customs declaration of the kind described in paragraph (2) of this Regulation:

Provided that any packet referred to in this paragraph, being a registered letter packet containing any article of value, may have the customs declaration referred to in sub-paragraph (b) of this paragraph enclosed in it.

**8.**—(1) This Regulation relates to:—

(a) parcels posted in the United Kingdom for transmission to any place outside it:

(b) packets posted in the United Kingdom for transmission to any place outside it, being printed packets containing or consisting of goods which are dutiable in the country of destination, small packets, letter packets or datapost packets, where the value of any such packet exceeds £50:

(c) packets posted in the United Kingdom for transmission to any place outside it, being printed packets containing or consisting of goods which are dutiable in the country of destination, small packets, letter packets or datapost packets, where the value of any such packet does not exceed £50.

(2) Every parcel referred to in paragraph (1)(*a*) of this Regulation shall have affixed to it, or be accompanied by, a customs declaration fully and correctly stating the nature, quantity and value of the goods which it contains or of which it consists, and such other particulars as the Commissioners or the Post Office may require:

Provided that the Commissioners may, at the request of the Post Office, relax the requirements of this paragraph by allowing the exportation by post of any number of parcels accompanied by a single customs declaration containing the particulars prescribed above if the parcels are posted simultaneously at the same post office by or on behalf of the same person and are addressed to a single addressee.

(3) Every packet referred to in paragraph (1)(*b*) of this Regulation shall bear on the outside the top portion of a green label in the prescribed form and, in addition, shall have attached to it, or, if the postal administration of the country of destination so required, enclosed in it, a full and correct customs declaration of the kind described in paragraph (2) of this Regulation:

Provided that any packet referred to in this paragraph, being a registered letter packet containing any article of value, may have the customs declaration referred to in this paragraph enclosed in it if the sender so prefers.

(4) Every packet referred to in paragraph (1)(*c*) of this Regulation shall either—

(*a*) bear on the outside a green label in the prescribed form, in which the declaration as to the description, net weight and value of the contents shall be fully and correctly completed; or, if the sender so prefers,

(*b*) bear on the outside the top portion of a green label in the prescribed form and, in addition, have attached to it or, if the postal administration of the country of destination so requires, enclosed in it, a full and correct customs declaration of the kind described in paragraph (2) of this Regulation:

Provided that any packet referred to in this paragraph, being a registered letter packet containing any article of value, may have the customs declaration referred to in sub-paragraph (*b*) of this paragraph enclosed in it if the sender so prefers.

**9.**—(1) Without prejudice to the application of Regulations 7(1)(*b*) and (*c*), (3) and (4), and 8(1)(*b*) and (*c*), (3) and (4) of these Regulations to any printed packet contained in it, every mail bag containing printed packets containing or consisting of goods which are dutiable in the country of destination, brought by post into the United Kingdom or posted in the United Kingdom for transmission to any place outside it under the provisions of paragraph 30 of the Post Office Overseas Letter Post Scheme 1971, shall have affixed to the bag label a green label in the prescribed form.

(2) Regulations 7 and 8 of these Regulations and paragraph (1) of this Regulation shall not apply to a postal packet or mail bag which, having been posted in the Isle of Man, is brought by post to the United Kingdom for delivery there, or which is posted in the United Kingdom for delivery in the Isle of Man, or which is posted in a place situated outside the United Kingdom and the Isle of Man for delivery in a place so situated. . . .

**11.** The proper officer of the Post Office is hereby authorised to perform in relation to any postal packet or the goods which it contains such of the duties required by virtue of the customs enactments to be performed by the importer or exporter of goods as the Commissioners may require.

**12.** In such cases or classes of case as the Commissioners may so require, the proper officer of the Post Office shall produce to the proper officer of Customs and Excise postal packets arriving in the United Kingdom or about to be despatched from the United Kingdom, and, if the proper officer of Customs and Excise so requires, shall open for the customs examination any packet so produced. . . .

**14.**—(1) If goods are brought by post into the United Kingdom, and an officer of Customs and Excise sends to the addressee of the packet in which they are contained, or to any other person who is for the time being the importer of the goods, a notice requiring entry to be made of them or requiring a full and accurate account of them to be delivered to the proper officer of Customs and Excise but entry is not made or such account is not delivered within 28 days of the date of such notice or within such longer period as the Commissioners may allow, then unless the Commissioners have required the packet to be delivered to them under Regulation 17 of these Regulations the Post Office shall—

    (*a*) return the goods to the sender of the packet in which they were contained, or otherwise export them from the United Kingdom in accordance with any request or indication appearing on the packet; or

    (*b*) deliver the goods to the proper officer of Customs and Excise; or

    (*c*) with the permission of the Commissioners, and under the supervision of the proper officer of Customs and Excise, destroy them.

(2) Where goods have been delivered to him in accordance with paragraph 1(*b*) of this Regulation, the proper officer of Customs and Excise may cause the goods to be deposited in a Queen's Warehouse, and section 31(3) of the Customs and Excise Act 1952 shall apply to the goods as it applies to goods so deposited under the said section 31. . . .

**16.** If dutiable goods are brought by post into the United Kingdom in any postal packet contrary to Regulation 6 of these Regulations, or if any postal packet or mail bag to which Regulations 7, 8 and 9 of these Regulations or any of them apply does not contain, does not have affixed or attached to it, or is not accompanied by, the declaration, or does not bear the green label, required by those Regulations or any of them, or if the contents of any postal packet do not agree with the green label or customs declaration affixed or attached to the packet, or by which it is accompanied, or if the other requirements of those Regulations or any of them are not complied with in every material respect, then in every such case the packet or mail bag and all its contents shall be liable to forfeiture.

**17.** If the Commissioners require any postal packet to be delivered to them on the ground that any goods contained in it are liable to forfeiture under the customs enactments (including these Regulations) or under the Exchange Control Act 1947, then the proper officer of the Post Office shall deliver the packet to the proper officer of Customs and Excise.

# APPENDIX III

# *Misuse of Drugs Act 1971*

## (CHAPTER 38)

## ARRANGEMENT OF SECTIONS PRINTED

*Law enforcement and punishment of offences*
23. Powers to search and obtain evidence.
24. [Repealed]
25. Prosecution and punishment of offences.
26. [Repealed]
27. Forfeiture.

*Miscellaneous and supplementary provisions*
28. Proof of lack of knowledge etc. to be a defence in proceedings for certain offences.
29. Service of documents.
30. Licences and authorities.
31. General provisions as to regulations.
32. Research.
33. Amendment of Extradition Act 1870.
34. [Repealed]
35. Financial provisions.
36. Meaning of "corresponding law", and evidence of certain matters by certificate.
37. Interpretation.
38. Special provisions as to Northern Ireland.
39. Savings and transitional provisions, repeals, and power to amend local enactments.
40. Short title, extent and commencement.

**Schedules:**

Schedule 1—Constitution etc. of Advisory Council on the Misuse of Drugs.
Schedule 2—Controlled drugs.
Schedule 3—Tribunals, advisory bodies and professional panels.
Schedule 4—Prosecution and punishment of offences.
Schedule 5—Savings and transitional provisions.
Schedule 6—Repeals.

**The Advisory Council on the Misuse of Drugs**

*The Advisory Council on the Misuse of Drugs.*

**1.**—(1) There shall be constituted in accordance with Schedule 1 to this Act an Advisory Council on the Misuse of Drugs (in this Act referred to as "the Advisory Council"); and the supplementary provisions contained in that Schedule shall have effect in relation to the Council.

(2) It shall be the duty of the Advisory Council to keep under review the situation in the United Kingdom with respect to drugs which are being or appear to them likely to be misused and of which the misuse is having or appears to them capable of having harmful effects sufficient to constitute a social problem, and to give to any one or more of the Ministers, where either the Council consider it expedient to do so or they are consulted by the Minister or Ministers in question, advice on measures (whether or not involving alteration of the law) which in the opinion of the Council ought to be taken for preventing the misuse of such drugs or dealing with social problems connected with their misuse, and in particular on measures which in the opinion of the Council, ought to be taken—

(a) for restricting the availability of such drugs or supervising the arrangements for their supply;

(b) for enabling persons affected by the misuse of such drugs to obtain proper advice, and for securing the provision of proper facilities and services for the treatment, rehabilitation and after-care of such persons;

(c) for promoting co-operation between the various professional and community services which in the opinion of the Council have a part to play in dealing with social problems connected with the misuse of such drugs;

(d) for educating the public (and in particular the young) in the dangers of misusing such drugs, and for giving publicity to those dangers; and

(e) for promoting research into, or otherwise obtaining information about, any matter which in the opinion of the Council is of relevance for the purpose of preventing the misuse of such drugs or dealing with any social problem connected with their misuse.

(3) It shall also be the duty of the Advisory Council to consider any matter relating to drug dependence or the misuse of drugs which may be referred to them by any one or more of the Ministers and to advise the Minister or Ministers in question thereon, and in particular to consider and advise the Secretary of State with respect to any communication referred by him to the Council, being a communication relating to the control of any dangerous or otherwise harmful drug made to Her Majesty's Government in the United Kingdom by any organisation or authority established by or under any treaty, convention or other agreement or arrangement to which that Government is for the time being a party.

(4) In this section "the Ministers" means the Secretary of State for the Home Department, the Secretaries of State respectively concerned with health in England, Wales and Scotland, the Secretaries of State respectively concerned with education in England, Wales and Scotland, the Minister of Home Affairs for Northern Ireland, the Minister of Health and Social Services for Northern Ireland and the Minister of Education for Northern Ireland.

## Controlled drugs and their classification

*Controlled drugs and their classification for purposes of this Act.*

**2.**—(1) In this Act—

(a) the expression "controlled drug" means any substance or product for the time being specified in Part I, II, or III of Schedule 2 to this Act; and

(b) the expressions "Class A drug", "Class B drug" and "Class C drug" mean any of the substances and products for the time being specified respectively in Part I, Part II and Part III of that Schedule;

and the provisions of Part IV of that Schedule shall have effect with respect to the meanings of expressions used in that Schedule.

(2) Her Majesty may by Order in Council make such amendments in Schedule 2 to this Act as may be requisite for the purpose of adding any substance or product to, or removing any substance or product from, any of Parts I to III of that Schedule, including amendments for securing that no substance or product is for the time being specified in a particular one of those Parts or for inserting any substance or product into any of those Parts in which no substance or product is for the time being specified.

(3) An Order in Council under this section may amend Part IV of Schedule 2 to this Act, and may do so whether or not it amends any other Part of that Schedule.

(4) An Order in Council under this section may be varied or revoked by a subsequent Order in Council thereunder.

(5) No recommendation shall be made to Her Majesty in Council to make an Order under this section unless a draft of the Order has been laid before Parliament and approved by a resolution of each House of Parliament; and the Secretary of State shall not lay a draft of such an Order before Parliament except after consultation with or on the recommendation of the Advisory Council.

## Restrictions relating to controlled drugs etc.

*Restriction of importation and exportation of controlled drugs.*
 3.—(1) Subject to subsection (2) below—

  (a) the importation of a controlled drug; and
  (b) the exportation of a controlled drug,
   are hereby prohibited.

 (2) Subsection (1) above does not apply—

  (a) to the importation or exportation of a controlled drug which is for the time being excepted from paragraph (a) or, as the case may be, paragraph (b) of subsection (1) above by regulations under section 7 of this Act; or
  (b) to the importation or exportation of a controlled drug under and in accordance with the terms of a licence issued by the Secretary of State and in compliance with any conditions attached thereto.

*Restriction of production and supply of controlled drugs.*
 4.—(1) Subject to any regulations under section 7 of this Act for the time being in force, it shall not be lawful for a person—

  (a) to produce a controlled drug; or
  (b) to supply or offer to supply a controlled drug to another.

 (2) Subject to section 28 of this Act, it is an offence for a person—

  (a) to produce a controlled drug in contravention of sub-section (1) above; or
  (b) to be concerned in the production of such a drug in contravention of that subsection by another.

 (3) Subject to section 28 of this Act, it is an offence for a person—

  (a) to supply or offer to supply a controlled drug to another in contravention of subsection (1) above; or
  (b) to be concerned in the supplying of such a drug to another in contravention of that subsection; or
  (c) to be concerned in the making to another in contravention of that subsection of an offer to supply such a drug.

*Restriction of possession of controlled drugs.*

**5.**—(1) Subject to any regulations under section 7 of this Act for the time being in force, it shall not be lawful for a person to have a controlled drug in his possession.

(2) Subject to section 28 of this Act and to subsection (4) below, it is an offence for a person to have a controlled drug in his possession in contravention of subsection (1) above.

(3) Subject to section 28 of this Act, it is an offence for a person to have a controlled drug in his possession, whether lawfully or not, with intent to supply it to another in contravention of section 4(1) of this Act.

(4) In any proceedings for an offence under subsection (2) above in which it is proved that the accused had a controlled drug in his possession, it shall be a defence for him to prove—

(a) that, knowing or suspecting it to be a controlled drug, he took possession of it for the purpose of preventing another from committing or continuing to commit an offence in connection with that drug and that as soon as possible after taking possession of it he took all such steps as were reasonably open to him to destroy the drug or to deliver into the custody of a person lawfully entitled to take custody of it; or

(b) that, knowing or suspecting it to be a controlled drug, he took possession of it for the purpose of delivering it into the custody of a person lawfully entitled to take custody of it and that as soon as possible after taking possession of it he took all such steps as were reasonably open to him to deliver it into the custody of such a person.

(5) [. . .]¹

(6) Nothing in subsection (4) [. . .]¹ above shall prejudice any defence which it is open to a person charged with an offence under this section to raise apart from that subsection.

*Restriction of cultivation of cannabis plant.*

**6.**—(1) Subject to any regulations under section 7 of this Act for the time being in force, it shall not be lawful for a person to cultivate any plant of the genus *Cannabis.*

(2) Subject to section 28 of this Act, it is an offence to cultivate any such plant in contravention of subsection (1) above.

*Authorisation of activities otherwise unlawful under foregoing provisions.*

**7.**—(1) The Secretary of State may by regulations—

(a) except from section 3(1)(a) or (b), 4(1)(a) or (b) or 5(1) of this Act such controlled drugs as may be specified in the regulations; and

(b) make such other provision as he thinks fit for the purpose of making it lawful for persons to do things which under any of the following provisions of this Act, that is to say sections 4(1), 5(1) and 6(1), it would otherwise be unlawful for them to do.

(2) Without prejudice to the generality of paragraph (b) of subsection (1) above, regulations under that subsection authorising the doing of any such thing as is

1 Repealed by Criminal Attempts Act 1981

mentioned in that paragraph may in particular provide for the doing of that thing to be lawful—

(a) if it is done under and in accordance with the terms of a licence or other authority issued by the Secretary of State and in compliance with any conditions attached thereto; or

(b) if it is done in compliance with such conditions as may be prescribed.

(3) Subject to subsection (4) below, the Secretary of State shall so exercise his power to mhake regulations under subsection (1) above as to secure—

(a) that it is not unlawful under section 4(1) of this Act for a doctor, dentist, veterinary practitioner or veterinary surgeon, acting in his capacity as such, to prescribe, administer, manufacture, compound or supply a controlled drug, or for a pharamacist or a person lawfully conducting a retail pharmacy business, acting in either case in his capacity as to such, to manufacture, compound or supply a controlled drug; and

(b) that it is not unlawful under section 5(1) of this Act for a doctor, dentist, veterinary practitioner, veterinary surgeon, pharmacist or person lawfully conducting a retail pharmacy business to have a controlled drug in his possession for the purpose of acting in his capacity as such.

(4) If in the case of any controlled drug the Secretary of State is of the opinion that it is in the public interest—

(a) for production, supply and possession of that drug to be either wholly unlawful or unlawful except for purposes of research or other special purposes; or

(b) for it to be unlawful for practitioners, pharmacists and persons lawfully conducting retail pharmacy businesses to do in relation to that drug any of the things mentioned in subsection (3) above except under a licence or other authority issued by the Secretary of State,

he may by order designate that drug as a drug to which this subsection applies; and while there is in force an order under this subsection designating a controlled drug as one to which this subsection applies, subsection (3) above shall not apply as regards that drug.

(5) Any order under subsection (4) above may be varied or revoked by a subsequent order thereunder.

(6) The power to make orders under subsection (4) above shall be exercisable by statutory instrument, which shall be subject to annulment in pursuance of a resolution of either House of Parliament.

(7) The Secretary of State shall not make any order under subsection (4) above except after consultation with or on the recommendation of the Advisory Council.

(8) References in this section to a person's "doing" things include references to his having things in his possession.

(9) In its application to Northern Ireland this section shall have effect as if for references to the Secretary of State there were substituted references to the Ministry of Home Affairs for Northern Ireland and as if for subsection (6) there were substituted—

"(6) Any order made under subsection (4) above by the Ministry of Home Affairs for Northern Ireland shall be subject to negative resolution within the meaning of section 41(6) of the Interpretation Act (Northern Ireland) 1954 as if it were a statutory instrument within the meaning of that Act."

## Miscellaneous offences involving controlled drugs etc.

*Occupiers etc. of premises to be punishable for permitting certain activities to take place there.*

**8.** A person commits an offence if, being the occupier or concerned in the management of any premises, he knowingly permits or suffers any of the following activities to take place on those premises, that is to say—

   (*a*) producing or attempting to produce a controlled drug in contravention of section 4(1) of this Act;

   (*b*) supplying or attempting to supply a controlled drug to another in contravention of section 4(1) of this Act, or offering to supply a controlled drug to another in contravention of section 4(1);

   (*c*) preparing opium for smoking;

   (*d*) smoking cannabis, cannabis resin or prepared opium.

*Prohibition of certain activities etc. relating to opium.*

**9.** Subject to section 28 of this Act, it is an offence for a person—

   (*a*) to smoke or otherwise use prepared opium; or

   (*b*) to frequent a place used for the purpose of opium smoking; or

   (*c*) to have in his possession—

      (i) any pipes or other utensils made or adapted for use in connection with the smoking of opium, being pipes or utensils which have been used by him or with his knowledge and permission in that connection or which he intends to use or permit others to use in that connection; or

      (ii) any utensils which have been used by him or with his knowledge and permission in connection with the preparation of opium for smoking.

## Powers of Secretary of State for preventing misuse of controlled drugs.

*Power to make regulations for preventing misuse of controlled drugs.*

**10.**—(1) Subject to the provisions of this Act, the Secretary of State may by regulations make such provision as appears to him necessary or expedient for preventing the misuse of controlled drugs.

(2) Without prejudice to the generality of subsection (1) above, regulations under this section may in particular make provision—

   (*a*) for requiring precautions to be taken for the safe custody of controlled drugs;

   (*b*) for imposing requirements as to the documentation of transactions involving controlled drugs, and for requiring copies of documents relating to such transactions to be furnished to the prescribed authority;

   (*c*) for requiring the keeping of records and the furnishing of information with respect to controlled drugs in such circumstances and in such manner as may be prescribed;

   (*d*) for the inspection of any precautions taken or records kept in pursuance of regulations under this section;

(e) as to the packaging and labelling of controlled drugs;

(f) for regulating the transport of controlled drugs and the methods used for destroying or otherwise disposing of such drugs when no longer required;

(g) for regulating the issue of prescriptions containing controlled drugs and the supply of controlled drugs on prescriptions, and for requiring persons issuing or dispensing prescriptions containing such drugs to furnish to the prescribed authority such information relating to those prescriptions as may be prescribed;

(h) for requiring any doctor who attends a person who he considers, or has reasonable grounds to suspect, is addicted (within the meaning of the regulations) to controlled drugs of any description to furnish to the prescribed authority such particulars with respect to that person as may be prescribed;

(i) for prohibiting any doctor from administering, supplying and authorising the administration and supply to persons so addicted, and from prescribing for such persons, such controlled drugs as may be prescribed, except under and in accordance with the terms of a licence issued by the Secretary of State in pursuance of the regulations.

*Power to direct special precautions for safe custody of controlled drugs to be taken at certain premises.*

**11.**—(1) Without prejudice to any requirement imposed by regulations made in pursuance of section 10(2)(a) of this Act, the Secretary of State may by notice in writing served on the occupier of any premises on which controlled drugs are or are proposed to be kept give driections as to the taking of precautions or further precautions for the safe custody of any controlled drugs of a description specified in the notice which are kept on those premises.

(2) It is an offence to contravene any directions given under subsection (1) above.

*Directions prohibiting prescribing, supply etc. of controlled drugs by practitioners etc. convicted of certain offences.*

**12.**—(1) Where a person who is a practitioner or pharmacist has after the coming into operation of this subsection been convicted—

(a) of an offence under this Act or under the Dangerous Drugs Act 1965 or any enactment repealed by that Act; or

(b) of an offence under section 45, 56 or 304 of the Customs and Excise Act 1952 [or under sections 50, 68 or 170 of the Customs and Excise Management Act 1979][2] in connection with a prohibition of or restriction on importation or exportation of a controlled drug having effect by virtue of section 3 of this Act or which had effect by virtue of any provision contained in or repealed by the Dangerous Drugs Act 1965,

the Secretary of State may give a direction under subsection (2) below in respect of that person.

(2) A direction under this subsection in respect of a person shall—

(a) if that person is a practitioner, be a direction prohibiting him from

**2** Inserted by Customs and Excise Management Act 1979

having in his possession, prescribing, administering, manufacturing, compounding and supplying and from authorising the administration and supply of such controlled drugs as may be specified in the direction;

(b) if that person in a pharmacist, be a direction prohibiting him from having in his possession, manufacturing, compounding and supplying and from supervising and controlling the manufacture, compounding and supply of such controlled drugs as may be specified in the direction.

(3) The Secretary of State may at any time give a direction cancelling or suspending any direction given by him under subsection (2) above, or cancelling any direction of his under this subsection by which a direction so given is suspended.

(4) The Secretary of State shall cause a copy of any direction given by him under this section to be served on the person to whom it applies, and shall cause notice of any such direction to be published in the London, Edinburgh and Belfast Gazettes.

(5) A direction under this section shall take effect when a copy of it is served on the person to whom it applies.

(6) It is an offence to contravene a direction given under subsection (2) above.

(7) In section 80 of the Medicines Act 1968 (under which a body corporate carrying on a retail pharmacy business may be disqualified for the purposes of Part IV of that Act and have its premises removed from the register kept under section 75 of the Act, where that body or any member of the board of that body or any officer or any employee of that body is convicted of an offence under any of the relevant Acts as defined in subsection (5)), for the words "and this Act" in subsection (5) there shall be substituted the words "this Act and the Misuse of Drugs Act 1971".

*Directions prohibiting prescribing, supply etc. of controlled drugs by practitioners in other cases.*

**13.**—(1) In the event of a contravention by a doctor of regulations made in pursuance of paragraph (h) or (i) of section 10(2) of this Act, or of the terms of a licence issued under regulations made in pursuance of the said paragraph (i), the Secretary of State may, subject to and in accordance with section 14 of this Act, give a direction in respect of the doctor concerned prohibiting him from prescribing, administering and supplying and from authorising the administration and suppy of such controlled drugs as may be specified in the direction.

(2) If the Secretary of State is of the opinion that a practitioner is or has after the coming into operation of this subsection been prescribing, administering or supplying or authorising the administration or supply of any controlled drugs in an irresponsible manner, the Secretary of State may, subject to and in accordance with section 14 or 15 of this Act, give a direction in respect of the practitioner concerned prohibiting him from prescribing, administering and supplying and from authorising the administration and supply of such controlled drugs as may be specified in the direction.

(3) A contravention such as is mentioned in subsection (1) above does not as such constitute an offence, but it is an offence to contravene a direction given under subsection (1) or (2) above.

*Investigation where grounds for a direction under s. 13 are considered to exist.*

**14.**—(1) If the Secretary of State considers that there are grounds for giving a direction under subsection (1) of section 13 of this Act on account of such contravention by a doctor as is there mentioned, or for giving a direction under subsection (2) of that section on account of such conduct by a practitioner as is mentioned in the said subsection (2), he may refer the case to a tribunal constituted for the purpose in accordance with the following provisions of this Act; and it shall be the duty of the tribunal to consider the case and report on it to the Secretary of State.

(2) In this Act "the respondent", in relation to a reference under this section, means the doctor or other practitioner in respect of whom the reference is made.

(3) Where—

> (a) in the case of a reference relating to the giving of a direction under the said subsection (1), the tribunal finds that there has been no such contravention as aforesaid by the respondent or finds that there has been such a contravention but does not recommend the giving of a direction under that subsection in respect of the respondent; or
>
> (b) in the case of a reference relating to the giving of a direction under the said subsection (2), the tribunal finds that there has been no such conduct as aforesaid by the respondent or finds that there has been such conduct by the respondent but does not recommend the giving of a direction under the said subsection (2) in respect of him,

the Secretary of State shall cause notice to that effect to be served on the respondent.

(4) Where the tribunal finds—

> (a) in the case of a reference relating to the giving of a direction under the said subsection (1), and there has been such a contravention as aforesaid by the respondent; or
>
> (b) in the case of a reference relating to the giving of a direction under the said subsection (2), that there has been such conduct as aforesaid by the respondent,

and considers that a direction under the subsection in question should be given in respect of him, the tribunal shall include in its report a recommendation to that effect indicating the controlled drugs which it considers should be specified in the direction or indication that the direction would specify all controlled drugs.

(5) Where the tribunal makes such a recommendation as aforesaid, the Secretary of State shall cause a notice to be served on the respondent stating whether or not he proposes to give a direction pursuant thereto, and where he does so propose the notice shall—

> (a) set out the terms of the proposed direction; and
>
> (b) inform the respondent that consideration will be given to any representations relating to the case which are made by him in writing to the Secretary of State within the period of twenty-eight days beginning with the date of service of the notice.

(6) If any such representations are received by the Secretary of State within the period aforesaid, he shall refer the case to an advisory body constituted for the purpose in accordance with the following provisions of this Act; and it shall be the duty of the advisory body to consider the case and to advise the Secretary of State as to the exercise of his powers under subsection (7) below.

(7) After the expiration of the said period of twenty-eight days and, in the case of a reference to any advisory body under subsection (6) above, after considering the advice of that body, the Secretary of State may either—

(*a*) give in respect of the respondent a direction under subsection (1) or, as the case may be, subsection (2) of section 13 of this Act specifying all or any of the controlled drugs indicated in the recommendation of the tribunal; or

(*b*) order that the case be referred back to the tribunal, or referred to another tribunal constituted as aforesaid; or

(*c*) order that no further proceedings under this section shall be taken in the case.

(8) Where a case is referred or referred back to a tribunal in pursuance of subsection (7) above, the provisions of subsections (2) to (7) above shall apply as if the case had been referred to the tribunal in pursuance of subsection (1) above, and any finding, recommendation or advice previously made or given in respect of the case in pursuance of those provisions shall be disregarded.

*Temporary directions under s. 13(2).*
**15.**—(1) If the Secretary of State considers that there are grounds for giving a direction under subsection (2) of section 13 of this Act in respect of a practitioner on account of such conduct by him as is mentioned in that subsection and that the circumstances of the case require such a direction to be given with the minimum of delay, he may, subject to the following provisions of this section, give such a direction in respect of him by virtue of this section; and a direction under section 13(2) given by virtue of this section may specify such controlled drugs as the Secretary of State thinks fit.

(2) Where the Secretary of State proposes to give such a direction as aforesaid by virtue of this section, he shall refer the case to a professional panel constituted for the purpose in accordance with the following provisions of this Act; and

(*a*) it shall be the duty of the panel, after affording the respondent an opportunity of appearing before and being heard by the panel, to consider the circumstances of the case, so far as known to it, and to report to the Secretary of State whether the information before the panel appears to it to afford reasonable grounds for thinking that there has been such conduct by the respondent as is mentioned in section 13(2) of this Act; and

(*b*) the Secretary of State shall not by virtue of this section give such a direction as aforesaid in respect of the respondent unless the panel reports that the information before it appears to it to afford reasonable grounds for so thinking.

(3) In this Act "the respondent", in relation to a reference under subsection (2) above, means the practitioner in respect of whom the reference is made.

(4) Where the Secretary of State gives such a direction as aforesaid by virtue of this section he shall, if he has not already done so, forthwith refer the case to a tribunal in accordance with section 14(1) of this Act.

(5) Subject to subsection (6) below, the period of operation of a direction under section 13(2) of this Act given by virtue of this section shall be a period of six weeks beginning with the date on which the direction takes effect.

(6) Where a direction under section 13(2) of this Act has been given in respect of a person by virtue of this section and the case has been referred to a tribunal in accordance with section 14(1), the Secretary of State may from time to time, by notice in writing served on the person to whom the direction applies, extend or

further extend the period of operation of the direction for a further twenty-eight days from the time when that period would otherwise expire, but shall not so extend or further extend that period without the consent of that tribunal, or, if the case has been referred to another tribunal in pursuance of section 14(7) of this Act, of that other tribunal.

(7) A direction under section 13(2) of this Act given in respect of a person by virtue of this section shall (unless previously cancelled under section 16(3) of this Act) cease to have effect on the occurrence of any of the following events, that is to say—

(a) the service on that person of a notice under section 14(3) of this Act relating to his case;

(b) the service on that person of a notice under section 14(5) of this Act relating to his case stating that the Secretary of State does not propose to give a direction under section 13(2) of this Act pursuant to a recommendation of the tribunal that such a direction should be given;

(c) the service on that person of a copy of such a direction given in respect of him in pursuance of section 14(7) of this Act;

(d) the making of an order by the Secretary of State in pursuance of section 14(7) that no further proceedings under section 14 shall be taken in the case;

(e) the expiration of the peroid of operation of the direction under section 13(2) given by virtue of this section.

*Provisions supplementary to ss. 14 and 15.*

**16.**—(1) The provisions of Schedule 3 to this Act shall have effect with respect to the constitution and procedure of any tribunal, advisory body or professional panel appointed for the purposes of section 14 or 15 of this Act, and with respect to the other matters there mentioned.

(2) The Secretary of State shall cause a copy of any order or direction made or given by him in pursuance of section 14(7) of this Act or any direction given by him by virtue of the said section 15 to be served on the person to whom it applies and shall cause notice of any such direction and a copy of any notice served under section 15(6) of this Act, to be published in the London, Edinburgh and Belfast Gazettes.

(3) The Secretary of State may at any time give a direction—

(a) cancelling or suspending any direction given by him in pursuance of section 14(7) of this Act or cancelling any direction of his under this subsection by which a direction so given is suspended; or

(b) cancelling any direction given by him by virtue of section 15 of this Act,

and shall cause a copy of any direction of his under this subsection to be served on the person to whom it applies and notice of it to be published as aforesaid.

(4) A direction given under section 13(1) or (2) of this Act or under subsection (3) above shall take effect when a copy of it is served on the person to whom it applies.

*Power to obtain information from doctors, pharmacists etc. in certain circumstances.*

**17.**—(1) If it appears to the Secretary of State that there exists in any area in Great Britain a social problem caused by the extensive misuse of dangerous or otherwise harmful drugs in that area, he may by notice in writing served on any doctor or pharmacist practising in or in the vicinity of that area, or on any person carrying on a retail pharmacy business within the meaning of the Medicines Act 1968 at any premises situated in or in the vicinity of that area, require him to furnish to the Secretary of State, with respect to any such drugs specified in the notice and as regards any period so specified, such particulars as may be so specified relating to the quantities in which and the number and frequency of the occasions on which those drugs—

(a) in the case of a doctor, were prescribed, administered or supplied by him;

(b) in the case of a pharmacist, were supplied by him; or

(c) in the case of a person carrying on a retail pharmacy business, were supplied in the course of that business at any premises so situated which may be specified in the notice.

(2) A notice under this section may require any such particulars to be furnished in such manner and within such time as may be specified in the notice and, if served on a pharmacist or person carrying on a retail pharmacy business, may require him to furnish the names and addresses of doctors on whose prescriptions any dangerous or otherwise harmful drugs to which the notice relates were supplied, but shall not require any person to furnish any particulars relating to the identity of any person for or to whom any such drug has been prescribed, administered or supplied.

(3) A person commits an offence if without reasonable excuse (proof of which shall lie on him) he fails to comply with any requirement to which he is subject by virtue of subsection (1) above.

(4) A person commits an offence if in purported compliance with a requirement imposed under this section he gives any information which he knows to be false in a material particular or recklessly gives any information which is so false.

(5) In its application to Northern Ireland this section shall have effect as if for the references to Great Britain and the Secretary of State there were substituted respectively references to Northern Ireland and the Ministry of Home Affairs for Northern Ireland.

### Miscellaneous offences and powers

*Miscellaneous offences.*

**18.**—(1) It is an offence for a person to contravene any regulations made under this Act other than regulations made in pursuance of section 10(2)(h) or (i).

(2) It is an offence for a person to contravene a condition or other term of a licence issued under section 3 of this Act or of a licence or other authority issued under regulations made under this Act, not being a licence issued under regulations made in pursuance of section 10(2)(i).

(3) A person commits an offence if, in purported compliance with any obligation to give information to which he is subject under or by virtue of regulations made under this Act, he gives any information which he knows to be false in a material particular or recklessly gives any information which is so false.

(4) A person commits an offence if, for the purpose of obtaining, whether for himself or another, the issue or renewal of a licence or other authority under this Act or under any regulations made under this Act, he—

(a) makes any statement or gives any information which he knows to be false in a material particular or recklessly gives any information which is so false; or

(b) produces or otherwise makes use of any book, record or other document which to his knowledge contains any statement or information which he knows to be false in a material particular.

*Attempts etc. to commit offences.*

**19.** It is an offence for a person [. . .]³ to incite another to commit such an offence.

*Assisting in or inducing commission outside United Kingdom of offence punishable under a corresponding law.*

**20.** A person commits an offence if in the United Kingdom he assists in or induces the commission in any place outside the United Kingdom of an offence punishable under the provisions of a corresponding law in force in that place.

*Offences by corporations.*

**21.** Where any offence under this Act committted by a body corporate is proved to have been committed with the consent or connivance of, or to be attributable to any neglect on the part of, any director, manager, secretary or other similar officer of the body corporate, or any person purporting to act in any such capacity, he as well as the body coporate shall be guilty of that offence and shall be liable to be proceeded against accordingly.

*Further powers to make regulations.*

**22.** The Secretary of State may by regulations make provision—

(a) for excluding in such cases as may be prescribed—

    (i) the application of any provision of this Act which creates an offence; or

    (ii) the application of any of the following provisions of the [Customs and Excise Management Act 1979, that is to say, sections 50(1) to (4), 68(2) and (3) and 170]⁴ in so far as they apply in relation to a prohibition or restriction on importation or exportation having effect by virtue of section 3 of this Act;

(b) for applying any of the provisions of sections 14 to 16 of this Act and Schedule 3 thereto, with such modifications (if any) as may be prescribed—

    (i) in relation to any proposal by the Secretary of State to give a direction under section 12(2) of this Act; or

    (ii) for such purposes of regulations under this Act as may be prescribed;

(c) for the application of any of the provisions of this Act or regulations or orders thereunder to servants or agents of the Crown, subject to such exceptions, adaptations and modifications as may be prescribed.

**Law enforcement and punishment of offences**

*Powers to search and obtain evidence.*

**23.**—(1) A constable or other person authorised in that behalf by a general or special order of the Secretary of State (or in Northern Ireland either of the

---

3   Deleted by Criminal Attempts Act 1981
4   Amended by Customs and Excise Management Act 1979

Secretary of State or the Ministry of Home Affairs for Northern Ireland) shall, for the purposes of the execution of this Act, have power to enter the premises of a person carrying on business as a producer or supplier of any controlled drugs and to demand the production of, and to inspect, any books or documents relating to dealings in any such drugs and to inspect any stocks of any such drugs.

(2) If a constable has reasonable grounds to suspect that any person is in possession of a controlled drug in contravention this Act or of any regulations made thereunder, the constable may—

    (a) search that person, and detain him for the purpose of searching him;

    (b) search any vehicle or vessel in which the constable suspects that the drug may be found, and for that purpose require the person in control of the vehicle or vessel to stop it;

    (c) seize and detain, for the purposes of proceedings under this Act, anything found in the course of the search which appears to the constable to be evidence of an offence under this Act.

In this subsection "vessel" includes a hovercraft within the meaning of the Hovercraft Act 1968; and nothing in this subsection shall prejudice any power of search or any power to seize or detain property which is exercisable by a constable apart from this subsection.

(3) If a justice of the peace (or in Scotland a justice of the peace, a magistrate or a sheriff) is satisfied by information on oath that there is reasonable ground for suspecting—

    (a) that any controlled drugs are, in contravention of this Act or of any regulations made thereunder, in the possession of a person on any premises, or

    (b) that a document directly or indirectly relating to, or connected with, a transaction or dealing which was, or an intended transaction or dealing which would if carried out be, an offence under this Act, or in the case of a transaction or dealing carried out or intended to be carried out in a place outside the United Kingdom, an offence against the provisions of a corresponding law in force in that place, is in the possession of a person on any premises,

he may grant a warrant authorising any constable acting for the police area in which the premises are situated at any time or times within one month from the date of the warrant, to enter, if need be by force, the premises named in the warrant, and to search the premises and any persons found therein and, if there is reasonable ground for suspecting that an offence under this Act has been committed in relation to any controlled drugs found on the premises or in the possession of any such persons, or that a document so found is such a document as is mentioned in paragraph (b) above, to seize and detain those drugs or that document, as the case may be.

(4) A person commits an offence if he—

    (a) intentionally obstructs a person in the exercise of his powers under this section; or

    (b) conceals from a person acting in the exercise of his powers under subsection (1) above any such books, documents, stocks or drugs as are mentioned in that subsection; or

(c) without reasonable excuse (proof of which shall lie on him) fails to produce any such books or documents as are so mentioned where their production is demanded by a person in the exercise of his powers under that subsection.

(5) In its application to Northern Ireland subsection (3) above shall have effect as if the words "acting for the police area in which the premises are situated" were omitted.

**24.** [ . . . ]⁵

*Prosecution and punishment of offences.*
**25.**—(1) Schedule 4 to this Act shall have effect, in accordance with subsection (2) below, with respect to the way in which offences under this Act are punishable on conviction.

(2) In relation to an offence under a provision of this Act specified in the first column of the Schedule (the general nature of the offence being described in the second column)—

(a) the third column shows whether the offence is punishable on summary conviction or on indictment or in either way;

(b) the fourth, fifth and sixth columns show respectively the punishments which may be imposed on a person convicted of the offence in the way specified in relation thereto in the third column (that is to say, summarily or on indictment) according to whether the controlled drug in relation to which the offence was committed was a Class A drug, a Class B drug or a Class C drug; and

(c) the seventh column shows the punishments which may be imposed on a person convicted of the offence in the way specified in relation thereto in the third column (that is to say, summarily or on indictment), whether or not the offence was committed in relation to a controlled drug and, if it was so committed, irrespective of whether the drug was a Class A drug, a Class B drug or a Class C drug;

and in the fourth, fifth, sixth and seventh columns a reference to a period gives the maximum term of imprisonment and a reference to a sum of money the maximum fine.

(3) An offence under section 19 of this Act shall be punishable on summary conviction, on indictment or in either way according to whether, under Schedule 4 to this Act, the substantive offence is punishable on summary conviction, on indictment or in either way; and the punishments which may be imposed on a person convicted of an offence under that section are the same as those which, under that Schedule, may be imposed on a person convicted of the substantive offence.

In this subsection "the substantive offence" means the offence under this Act to which [ . . .]⁶ the incitement [ . . .]⁶ mentioned in section 19 was directed.

(4) Notwithstanding anything in section [127(1) of the Magistrates' Courts Act 1980]⁷ a magistrates' court in England and Wales may try an information for an

5 Repealed by Police and Criminal Evidence Act 1984
6 Deleted by Criminal Attempts Act 1981
7 Amended by Magistrates' Courts Act 1980

offence under this Act if the information was laid at any time within twelve months from the commission of the offence.

(5) Notwithstanding anything in section 23 of the Summary Jurisdiction (Scotland) Act 1954 (limitation of time for proceedings in statutory offences) summary proceedings in Scotland for an offence under this Act may be commenced at any time within twelve months from the time when the offence was committed, and subsection (2) of the said section 23 shall apply for the purposes of this subsection as it applies for the purposes of that section.

(6) Notwithstanding anything in section 34 of the Magistrates' Courts Act (Northern Ireland) 1964, a magistrates' court in Northern Ireland may hear and determine a complaint for an offence under this Act if the complaint was made at any time within twelve months from the commission of the offence.

**26.** [ ... ]⁸

*Forfeiture.*
**27.**—(1) Subject to subsection (2) below, the court by or before which a person is convicted of any offence under this Act may order anything shown to the satisfaction of the court to relate to the offence, to be forfeited and either destroyed or dealt with in such other manner as the court may order.

(2) The court shall not order anything to be forfeited under this section, where a person claiming to be the owner of or otherwise interested in it applies to be heard by the court, unless an opportunity has been given to him to show cause why the order should not be made.

## Miscellaneous and supplementary provisions

*Proof of lack of knowledge etc. to be a defence in proceedings for certain offences.*
**28.**—(1) This section applies to offences under any of the following provisions of this Act, that is to say section 4(2) and (3), section 5(2) and (3), section 6(2) and section 9.

(2) Subject to subsection (3) below, in any proceedings for an offence to which this section applies it shall be a defence for the accused to prove that he neither knew of nor suspected nor had reason to suspect the existence of some fact alleged by the prosecution which it is necessary for the prosecution to prove if he is to be convicted of the offence charged.

(3) Where in any proceedings for an offence to which this section applies it is necessary, if the accused is to be convicted of the offence charged, for the prosecution to prove that some substance or product involved in the alleged offence was the controlled drug which the prosecution alleges it to have been, and it is proved that the substance or product in question was that controlled drug, the accused—

(a) shall not be acquitted of the offence charged by reason only of proving that he neither knew nor suspected nor had reason to suspect that the substance or product in question was the particular controlled drug alleged; but

(b) shall be acquitted thereof—

(i) if he proves that he neither believed nor suspected nor had reason to suspect that the substance or product in question was a controlled drug; or

**8** Repealed by Customs and Excise Management Act 1979

(ii) if he proves that he believed the substance or product in question to be a controlled drug, or a controlled drug of a description, such that, if it had in fact been that controlled drug or a controlled drug of that description, he would not at the material time have been committing any offence to which this section applies.

(4) Nothing in this section shall prejudice any defence which it is open to a person charged with an offence to which this section applies to raise apart from this section.

*Service of documents.*

**29.**—(1) Any notice or other document required or authorised by any provision of this Act to be served on any person may be served on him either by delivering it to him or by leaving it at his proper address or by sending it by post.

(2) Any notice or other document so required or authorised to be served on a body corporate shall be duly served if it is served on the secretary or clerk of that body.

(3) For the purposes of this section, and of section 26 of the Interpretation Act 1889 in its application to this section, the proper address of any person shall, in the case of the secretary or the clerk of a body corporate, be that of the registered or principal office of that body, and in any other case shall be the last address of the person to be served which is known to the Secretary of State.

(4)Where any of the following documents, that is to say—

(a) a notice under section 11(1) or section 15(6) of this Act; or

(b) a copy of a direction given under section 12(2), section 13(1) or (2) or section 16(3) of this Act,

is served by sending it by registered post or by the recorded delivery service, service thereof shall be deemed to have been effected at the time when the letter containing it would be delivered in the ordinary course of post; and so much of section 26 of the Interpretation Act 1889 as relates to the time when service by post is deemed to have been affected shall not apply to such a document if it is served by so sending it.

*Licences and authorities.*

**30.** A licence or other authority issued by the Secretary of State for purposes of this Act or of regulations made under this Act may be, to any degree, general or specific, may be issued on such terms and subject to such conditions (including, in the case of a licence, the payment of a prescribed fee) as the Secretary of State thinks proper, and may be modified or revoked by him at any time.

*General provisions as to regulations.*

**31.**—(1) Regulations made by the Secretary of State under any provision of this Act—

(a) may make different provision in relation to different controlled drugs, different classes of persons, different provisions of this Act or other different cases or circumstances; and

(b) may make the opinion, consent or approval of a prescribed authority or of any person authorised in a prescribed manner material for purposes of any provision of the regulations; and

(c) may contain such supplementary, incidental and transitional provisions as appear expedient to the Secretary of State.

(2) Any power of the Secretary of State to make regulations under this Act shall be exercisable by statutory instrument, which shall be subject to annulment in pursuance of a resolution of either House of Parliament.

(3) The Secretary of State shall not make any regulations under this Act except after consultation with the Advisory Council.

(4) In its application to Northern Ireland this section shall have effect as if for references to the Secretary of State there were substituted references to the Ministry of Home Affairs for Northern Ireland and as if for subsection (2) there were substituted—

"(2) Any regulations made under this Act by the Ministry of Home Affairs for Northern Ireland shall be subject to negative resolution within the meaning of section 41(6) of the Interpretation Act (Northern Ireland) 1954 as if they were a statutory instrument within the meaning of that Act."

*Research.*
**32.** The Secretary of State may conduct or assist in conducting research into any matter relating to the misuse of dangerous or otherwise harmful drugs.

*Amendment of Extradition Act 1870*
**33.** The Extradition Act 1870 shall have effect as if conspiring to commit any offence against any enactment for the time being in force relating to dangerous drugs were included in the list of crimes in Schedule 1 to that Act.

**34.** [. . .][9]

*Financial provisions*
**35.** There shall be defrayed out of moneys provided by Parliament—

(*a*) any expenses incurred by the Secretary of State under or in consequence of the provisions of this Act other than section 32; and

(*b*) any expenses incurred by the Secretary of State with the consent of the Treasury for the purposes of his functions under that section.

*Meaning of "corresponding law" and evidence of certain matters by certificate.*
**36.**—(1) In this Act the expression "corresponding law" means a law stated in a certificate purporting to be issued by or on behalf of the government of a country outside the United Kingdom to be a law providing for the control and regulation in that country of the production, supply, use, export and import of drugs and other substances in accordance with the provisions of the Single Convention on Narcotic Drugs signed at New York on 30th March 1961 or a law providing for the control and regulation in that country of the production, supply, use, export and import of dangerous or otherwise harmful drugs in pursuance of any treaty, convention or other agreement or arrangement to which the government of that country and Her Majesty's Government in the United Kingdom are for the time being parties.

(2) A statement in any such certificate as aforesaid to the effect that any facts constitute an offence against the law mentioned in the certificate shall be evidence, and in Scotland sufficient evidence, of the matters stated.

*Interpretation.*
**37.**—(1) In this Act, except in so far as the context otherwise requires, the

9 Repealed by Domestic Proceedings and Magistrates' Courts Act 1978

following expressions have the meanings hereby assigned to them respectively, that is to say:—

"the Advisory Council" means the Advisory Council on the Misuse of Drugs established under this Act;

["cannabis" (except in the expression "cannabis resin") means any plant of the genus *Cannabis* or any part of any such plant (by whatever name designated) except that it does not include cannabis resin or any of the following products after separation from the rest of the plant, namely—
(*a*) mature stalk of any such plant,
(*b*) fibre produced from mature stalk of any such plant, and
(*c*) seed of any such plant;][10]

"cannabis resin" means the separated resin, whether crude or purified, obtained from any plant of the genus *Cannabis*;

"contravention" includes failure to comply, and "contravene" has a corresponding meaning;

"controlled drug" has the meaning assigned by section 2 of this Act;

"corresponding law" has the meaning assigned by section 36(1) of this Act;

"dentist" means a person registered in the dentists register under the Dentists Act 1957 [or entered in the list of visiting EEC practitioners under Article 6 of the Dental Qualifications (EEC Recognition) Order 1980;][11]

"doctor" means a fully registered person within the meaning of the Medical Acts 1956 to 1969;

"enactment" includes an enactment of the Parliament of Northern Ireland;

"person lawfully conducting a retail pharmacy business" subject to subsection (5) below, means a person lawfully conducting such a business in accordance with section 69 of the Medicines Act 1968;

"pharmacist" has the same meaning as in the Medicines Act 1968;

"practitioner" (except in the expression "veterinary practitioner") means a doctor, dentist, veterinary practitioner or veterinary surgeon;

"prepared opium" means opium prepared for smoking and includes dross and any other residues remaining after opium has been smoked;

"prescribed" means prescribed by regulations made by the Secretary of State under this Act;

"produce", where the reference is to producing a controlled drug, means producing it by manufacture, cultivation or any other method, and "production" has a corresponding meaning;

"supplying" includes distributing;

"veterinary practitioner" means a person registered in the supplementary veterinary register kept under section 8 of the Veterinary Surgeons Act 1966;

"veterinary surgeon" means a person registered in the register of veterinary surgeons kept under section 2 of the Veterinary Surgeons Act 1966.

(2) References in this Act to misusing a drug are references to misusing it by taking it; and the reference in the foregoing provision to the taking of a drug is a reference to the taking of it by a human being by way of any form of self-administration, whether or not involving assistance by another.

10   Substituted by Criminal Law Act 1977
11   Added by S.I. 1980/703

(3) For the purposes of this Act the things which a person has in his possession shall be taken to include any thing subject to his control which is in the custody of another.

(4) Except in so far as the context otherwise requires, any reference in this Act to an enactment shall be construed as a reference to that enactment as amended or extended by or under any other enactment.

(5) So long as sections 8 to 10 of the Pharmacy and Poisons Act 1933 remain in force, this Act in its application to Great Britain shall have effect as if for the definition of "person lawfully conducting a retail pharmacy business" in subsection (1) above there were substituted—

> " 'person lawfully conducting a retail pharmacy business' means an authorised seller of poisons within the meaning of the Pharmacy and Poisons Act 1933;"[. . .]¹²

*Special provisions as to Northern Ireland.*

**38.**—(1) In the application of this Act to Northern Ireland, for any reference to the Secretary of State (except in section 1, 2, 7, 17, 23(1), 31, 35, 39(3) and 40(3) and Schedules 1 and 3) there shall be substituted a reference to the Ministry of Home Affairs for Northern Ireland.

(2) Nothing in this Act shall authorise any department of the Government of Northern Ireland to incur any expenses attributable to the provisions of this Act until provision has been made by the Parliament of Northern Ireland for those expenses to be defrayed out of moneys provided by that Parliament; and no expenditure shall be incurred by the Ministry of Home Affairs for Northern Ireland for the purposes of its funcitons under section 32 of this Act except with the consent of the Ministry of Finance for Northern Ireland.

(3) [. . .]¹³

(4) Without prejudice to section 37(4) of this Act, any reference in this Act to an enactment of the Parliament of Northern Ireland includes a reference to any enactment re-enacting it with or without modifications.

*Savings and transitional provisions, repeals, and power to amend local enactments.*

**39.**—(1) The savings and transitional provisons contained in Schedule 5 to this Act shall have effect.

(2) The enactments mentioned in Schedule 6 to this Act are hereby repealed to the extent specified in the third column of that Schedule.

(3) The Secretary of State may by order made by statutory instrument subject to annulment in pursuance of a resolution of either House of Parliament repeal or amend any provision in any local Act, including an Act confirming a provisional order, or in any instrument in the nature of a local enactment under any Act, where it appears to him that that provision is inconsistent with, or has become unnecessary or requires modification in consequence of, any provision of this Act.

*Short title, extent and commencement.*

**40.**—(1) This Act may be cited as the Misuse of Drugs Act 1971.

(2) This Act extends to Northern Ireland.

(3) This Act shall come into operation on such day as the Secretary of State may by order made by statutory instrument appoint, and different dates may be appointed under this subsection for different purposes.¹⁴

**12** Remainder of clause deleted by S.I. 1976/1213
**13** Repealed by Northern Ireland Constitution Act 1973
**14** The whole Act was in force by 1 July 1973

# SCHEDULE 1
## (Section 1)

CONSTITUTION ETC. OF ADVISORY COUNCIL ON THE MISUSE OF DRUGS

**1.**—(1) The members of the Advisory Council, of whom there shall be not less than twenty, shall be appointed by the Secretary of State after consultation with such organisations as he considers appropriate, and shall include—

  (*a*) in relation to each of the activities specified in sub-paragraph (2) below, at least one person appearing to the Secretary of State to have wide and recent experience of that activity; and

  (*b*) persons appearing to the Secretary of State to have wide and recent experience of social problems connected with the misuse of drugs.

(2) The activities referred to in sub-paragraph (1)(*a*) above are—

  (*a*) the practice of medicine (other than veterinary medicine);
  (*b*) the practice of dentistry;
  (*c*) the practice of veterinary medicine;
  (*d*) the practice of pharmacy;
  (*e*) the pharmaceutical industry;
  (*f*) chemistry other than pharmaceutical chemistry.

(3) The Secretary of State shall appoint one of the members of the Advisory Council to be chairman of the Council.

**2.** The Advisory Council may appoint committees, which may consist in part of persons who are not members of the Council, to consider and report to the Council on any matter referred to them by the Council.

**3.** At meetings of the Advisory Council the quorum shall be seven, and subject to that the Council may determine their own procedure.

**4.** The Secretary of State may pay to the members of the Advisory Council such remuneration (if any) and such travelling and other allowances as may be determined by him with the consent of the Minister for the Civil Service.

**5.** Any expenses incurred by the Advisory Council with the approval of the Secretary of State shall be defrayed by the Secretary of State.

# SCHEDULE 2
## (Section 2)

CONTROLLED DRUGS

### Part 1

CLASS A DRUGS

**1.** The following substances and products, namely:—

(*a*) Acetorphine.             Alphacetylmethadol.
    Alfentanil.[15]           Alphameprodine.
    Allylprodine.             Alphamethadol.

15  Added by S.I. 1984/859

Alphaprodine.
Anileridine.

Benzethidine.
Benzylmorphine (3-benzyl-
    morphine).
Betacetylmethadol.
Betameprodine.
Betamethadol.
Betaprodine.
Bezitramide.
Bufotenine.

Cannabinol, except where con-
    tained in cannabis or cannabis
    resin.
Cannabinol derivatives.[16]
Clonitazene.
Coca leaf.[16]
Cocaine.

Desomorphine.
Dextromoramide.
Diamorphine.
Diampromide.
Diethylthiambutene.
Difenoxin (1-(3-cyano-3,3-
    diphenylpropyl)-4-phenyl-
    piperidine-4-carboxylic acid).[17]
Dihydrocodeinone
    O-carboxymethyloxime.
Dihydromorphine.
Dimenoxadole.
Dimepheptanol.
Dimethylthiambutene.
Dioxaphetyl butyrate.
Diphenoxylate.
Dipipanone.
Drotebanol    (3,4-dimethoxy-17-
    methylmorphinan-6β, 14-diol).[18]

Ecgonine, and any derivative of
    ecogonine which is convertible
    to ecogonine or to cocaine.
Ethylmethylthiambutene.
Eticyclidine.[15]
Etonitazene.
Etorphine.
Etoxeridine.

Fentanyl.

Furethidine.
Hydrocodone.
Hydromorphinol.
Hydromorphone.
Hydroxypethidine.

Isomethadone.

Ketobemidone.

Levomethorphan.
Levomoramide.
Levophenacylmorphan.
Levorphanol.
Lysergamide.
Lysergide and other N-alkyl
    derivatives of lysergamide.

Mescaline.
Metazocine.
Methadone.
Methadyl acetate.
Methyldesorphine.
Methyldihydromorphine
    (6-methyldihydromorphine).
Metopon.
Morpheridine.
Morphine.
Morphine methobromide,
    morphine N-oxide and other
    pentavalent nitrogen morphine
    derivatives.
Myrophine.
[. . .][19]

Nicomorphine (3,6-dinicotinoyl-
    morphine).
Noracymethadol.
Norlevorphanol.
Normethadone.
Normorphine.
Norpipanone.

Opium, whether raw, prepared or
    medicinal.
Oxycodone.
Oxymorphone.

Pethidine.
Phenadoxone.
Phenampromide.
Phenaxocine.

16  See Part IV for definition
17  Added by S.I. 1975/421
18  Added by S.I. 1973/771
19  Deleted by S.I. 1973/771

[Phencyclidine.][20]
Phenomorphan.
Phenoperidine.
Piminodine.
Piritramide.
Poppy-straw and concentrate of poppy-straw
Proheptazine.
Properidine (1-methyl-4-phenyl-piperidine-4-carboxylic acid isopropyl ester).
Psilocin.

Racemethorphan.
Racemoramide.
Racemorphan.
[Rolicyclidine.][21]

[Sufentanil.][22]

[Tenocylidine.][21]

Thebacon.
Thebaine.
[Tilidate.][22]
Trimeperidine.
[4-bromo-2,5-dimethoxy-α-methylphenethylamine.][23]
4-Cyano-2-dimethylamino-4,4-diphenylbutane.
4-Cyano-1-methyl-4-phenylpiperidine
$N,N$-Diethyltryptamine.
$N,N$-Dimethyltryptamine.
2,5-Dimethoxy-α,4-dimethylphenethylamine.
1-Methyl-4-phenylpiperidine-4-carboxylic acid.
2-Methyl-3-morpholino-1,1-diphenypropane carbolic acid.
4-Phenylpiperidine-4-carboxylic acid ethyl ester.

[(b) Any compound (not being a compound for the time being specified in sub-paragraph (a) above) structurally derived from tryptamine or from a ring-hydroxy tryptamine by substitution at the nitrogen atom of the sidechain with one or more alkyl substituents but no other substituent;

(c) any compound (not being methoxyphenamine or a compound for the time being specified in sub-paragraph (a) above) structurally derived from phenethylamine, an $N$-alkylphenthylamine, α-methylphenethyl-amine, an $N$-alkyl-α-methylphenethylamine, α-ethylphenethylamine, or an $N$-alkyl-α-ethylphenethylamine by substitution in the ring to any extent with alkyl, alkoxy, alkylenedioxy or halide substituents, whether or not further substituted in the ring by one or more other univalent substituents.][24]

**2.** Any stereoisomeric form of a substance for the time being specified in paragraph 1 above not being dextromethorphan or dextrophan.

**3.** Any ester or ether of a substance for the time being specified in paragraph 1 or 2 above, [not being a substance for the time being specified in Part II of this Schedule.][25]

**4.** Any salt of a substance for the time being specified in any of paragraphs 1 to 3 above.

**5.** Any preparation or other product containing a substance or product for the time being specified in any of paragraphs 1 to 4 above.

**6.** Any preparation designed for administration by injection which includes a substance or product for the time being specified in any of paragraphs 1 to 3 of Part II of this Schedule.

**20** Added by S.I. 1979/299
**21** Added by S.I. 1984/859
**22** Added by S.I. 1983/765
**23** Added by S.I. 1975/421
**24** Added by S.I. 1977/1243
**25** Added by S.I. 1973/771

PART II

CLASS B DRUGS[26]

1. The following substances and products, namely:—

(a) Acetyldihydrocodeine.
Amphetamine.
Cannabis and cannabis resin.
Codeine.
Dexamphetamine.
Dihydrocodeine.
Ethylmorphine (3-ethylmorphine).
[Mecloqualone.][27]
[Methaqualone.][27]

Methylamphetamine.
Methylphenidate.
[Methylphenobarbitone.][27]
[Nicodilodene, (6-nicotinoyl-dihydrocodeine).][25]
Nicodicodine.
Norcodeine.
Phenmetrazine.
Pholcodine.
[Propiram.][25]

[(b) any 5,5 disubstituted barbituric acid.][27]

2. Any stereoisomeric form of a substance for the time being specified in paragraph 1 of this Part of this Schedule.

3. Any salt of a substance for the time being specified in paragraph 1 or 2 of this Part of the Schedule.

4. Any preparation or other product containing a substance or product for the time being specified in any of paragraphs 1 to 3 of this Part of this Schedule, not being a preparation falling within paragraph 6 of Part I of this Schedule.

PART III

CLASS C DRUGS

1. The following substances namely:—

Benzphetamine.
Chlorphentermine
[Dextropropoxyphene][29]
[Diethylpropion][30]
Mephentermine.

[...][28]
[...][31]
Phendimetrazine.
[...][31]
Pipradrol.
[...][31]

2. Any stereoisomeric form of a substance for the time being specified in paragraph 1 of this Part of this Schedule.

3. Any salt of a substance for the time being specified in paragraph 1 or 2 of this Part of this Schedule.

4. Any preparation or other product containing a substance for the time being specified in any of paragraphs 1 to 3 of this Part of this Schedule.

26 Part II and Part III are amended with effect from 1 April 1986—see Appendix XV
27 Added by S.I. 1984/859
28 Omitted by S.I. 1984/859
29 Added by S.I. 1983/765
30 Added by S.I. 1984/859
31 Omitted by S.I. 1973/771

PART IV

MEANING OF CERTAIN EXPRESSIONS USED IN THIS SCHEDULE

For the purposes of this Schedule the following expressions (which are not among those defined in section 37(1) of this Act) have the meanings hereby assigned to them respectively, that is to say—

"cannabinol derivatives" means the following substances, except where contained in cannabis or cannabis resin, namely tetrahydro derivatives ot cannabinol and 3-alkyl homologues or cannabinol or of its tetrahydro derivatives;

"coca leaf" means the leaf of any plant of the genus *Erythroxylon* from whose leaves cocaine can be extracted either directly or by chemical transformation;

"concentrate of poppy-straw" means the material produced when poppy-straw has entered into a process for the concentration of its alkaloids;

"medicinal opium" means raw opium which has undergone the process necessary to adapt it for medicinal use in accordance with the requirements of the British Pharmacopoeia, whether it is in the form of powder or is granulated or is in any other form, and whether it is or is not mixed with neutral substances;

"opium poppy" means the plant of the species *Papaver somniferum* L;

"poppy straw" means all parts, except the seeds, of the opium poppy, after mowing;

"raw opium" includes powdered or granulated opium but does not include medicinal opium.

SCHEDULE 3

(Section 16.)

TRIBUNALS, ADVISORY BODIES AND PROFESSIONAL PANELS

PART I

TRIBUNALS

*Membership*

**1.**—(1) A tribunal shall consist of five persons of whom—

(*a*) one shall be a barrister, advocate or solicitor of not less than seven years' standing appointed by the Lord Chancellor to be the chairman of the tribunal; and

(*b*) the other four shall be persons appointed by the Secretary of State from among members of the respondent's profession nominated for the purposes of this Schedule by any of the relevant bodies mentioned in sub-paragraph (2) below.

(2) The relevant bodies aforesaid are—

(*a*) where the respondent is a doctor, the General Medical Council, the Royal Colleges of Physicians of London and Edinburgh, the Royal Colleges of Surgeons of England and Edinburgh, the Royal College of Physicians and

Surgeons (Glasgow), the Royal College of Obstetricians and Gynaeco-
logists, the Royal College of General Practitioners, the Royal Medico-
Psychological Association and the British Medical Association;

(b) where the respondent is a dentist, the General Dental Council and the
British Dental Association;

(c) where the respondent is a veterinary practitioner or veterinary surgeon,
the Royal College of Veterinary Surgeons and the British Veterinary
Association.

(3) Sub-paragraph (1) above shall have effect in relation to a tribunal in
Scotland as if for the reference to the Lord Chancellor there were substituted a
reference to the Lord President of the Court of Session.

*Procedure*

**2.** The quorum of tribunal shall be the chairman and two other members of the
tribunal.

**3.** Proceedings before a tribunal shall be held in private unless the respondent
requests otherwise and the tribunal accedes to the request.

**4.**—(1) Subject to paragraph 5 below, the Lord Chancellor may make rules as
to the procedure to be followed, and the rules of evidence to be observed, in
proceedings before tribunals, and in particular—

(a) for securing that notice that the proceedings are to be brought shall be
given to the respondent at such time and in such manner as may be
specified by the rules;

(b) for determining who, in addition to the respondent, shall be a party to the
proceedings;

(c) for securing that any party to the proceedings shall, if he so requires, be
entitled to be heard by the tribunal;

(d) for enabling any party to the proceedings to be represented by counsel or
solicitor.

(2) Sub-paragraph (1) above shall have effect in relation to a tribunal in
Scotland as if for the reference to the Lord Chancellor there were substituted a
reference to the Secretary of State.

(3) The power to make rules under this paragraph shall be exercisable by
statutory instrument, which shall be subject to annulment in pursuance of a
resolution of either House of Parliament.

**5.**—(1) For the purpose of any proceedings before a tribunal in England or
Wales or Northern Ireland the tribunal may administer oaths and any party to
the proceedings may sue out writs of subpoena ad testificandum and duces
tecum, but no person shall be compelled under any such writ to give any
evidence or produce any document which he could not be compelled to give or
produce on the trial of an action.

(2) The provisions of section [36 of the Supreme Court Act 1981][32] or of the
Attendance of Witnesses Act 1854 (which provide special procedures for the issue
of such writs so as to be in force throughout the United Kingdom) shall apply in
relation to any proceedings before a tribunal in England or Wales or, as the case
may be, in Northern Ireland as those provisions apply in relation to causes or

**32** Substituted by Supreme Court Act 1981

matters in the High Court or actions or suits pending in the High Court of Justice in Northern Ireland.

(3) For the purpose of any proceedings before a tribunal in Scotland, the tribunal may administer oaths and the Court of Session shall on the application of any party to the proceedings have the like power as in any action in that court to grant warrant for the citation of witnesses and havers to give evidence or to produce documents before the tribunal.

**6.** Subject to the foregoing provisions of this Schedule, a tribunal may regulate its own procedure.

**7.** The validity of the proceedings of a tribunal shall not be affected by any defect in the appointement of a member of the tribunal or by reason of the fact that a person not entitled to do so took part in the proceedings.

*Financial provisions*

**8.** The Secretary of State may pay to any member of a tribunal fees and travelling and other allowances in respect of his services in accordance with such scales and subject to such conditions as the Secretary of State may determine with the approval of the Treasury.

**9.** The Secretary of State may pay to any person who attends as a witness before the tribunal sums by way of compensation for the loss of his time and travelling and other allowances in accordance with such scales and subject to such conditions as may be determined as aforesaid.

**10.** If a tribunal recommends to the Secretary of State that the whole or part of the expenses properly incurred by the respondent for the purposes of proceedings before the tribunal should be defrayed out of public funds, the Secretary of State may if he thinks fit make to the respondent such payments in respect of those expenses as the Secretary of State considers appropriate.

**11.** Any expenses incurred by a tribunal with the approval of the Secretary of State shall be defrayed by the Secretary of State.

*Supplemental*

**12.** The Secretary of State shall make available to a tribunal such accommodation, the services of such officers and such other facilities as he considers appropriate for the purpose of enabling the tribunal to perform its functions.

## PART II

### ADVISORY BODIES

*Membership*

**13.**—(1) An advisory body shall consist of three persons of whom—

    (*a*) one shall be a person who is of counsel to Her Majesty and is appointed by the Lord Chancellor to be the chairman of the advisory body; and

    (*b*) another shall be a person appointed by the Secretary of State, being a member of the respondent's profession who is an officer of a department of the Government of the United Kingdom; and (*c*) the other shall be a person appointed by the Secretary of State from among the members of the respondent's profession nominated as mentioned in paragraph 1 above.

(2) Sub-paragraph (1) above shall have effect in relation to an advisory body in Scotland as if for the reference to the Lord Chancellor there were substituted a reference to the Lord President of the Court of Session.

*Procedure*
**14.** The respondent shall be entitled to appear before and be heard by the advisory body either in person or by counsel or solicitor.

**15.** Subject to the provisions of this Part of this Schedule, an advisory body may regulate its own procedure.

**16.** Paragraphs 3, 7, 8 and 10 to 12 of this Schedule shall apply in relation to an advisory body as they apply in relation to a tribunal.

## Part III

### Professional Panels

*Membership*
**17.** A professional panel shall consist of a chairman and two other persons appointed by the Secretary of State from among the members of the respondent's profession after consultation with such one or more of the relevant bodies mentioned in paragraph 1(2) above as the Secretary of State considers appropriate.

*Procedure*
**18.** The respondent shall be entitled to appear before, and be heard by, the professional panel either in person or by counsel or solicitor.

**19.** Subject to the provisions of this Part of this Schedule, a professional panel may regulate its own procedure.

*Application of provisions of Part I*
**20.** Paragraphs 3, 7 and 8 of this Schedule shall apply in relation to a professional panel as they apply in relation to a tribunal.

## Part IV

### Application of Parts I to III to Northern Ireland

**21.** In the application of Parts I to III of this Schedule to Northern Ireland the provisions specified in the first column of the following Table shall have effect subject to the modifications specified in relation thereto in the second column of that Table.

## TABLE

| *Provision of this Schedule* | *Modification* |
|---|---|
| Paragraph 1 ... ... | In sub-paragraph (1), for the references to the Lord Chancellor and the Secretary of State there shall be substituted respectively references to the Lord Chief Justice of Northern Ireland, and the Minister of Home Affairs for Northern Ireland. |
| Paragraph 4 ... ... | In sub-paragraph (1), for the reference to the Lord Chancellor there shall be substituted a reference to the Ministry of Home Affairs for Northern Ireland. |
| | For sub-paragraph (3) there shall be substituted— |
| | "(3) Any rules made under this paragraph by the Ministry of Home Affairs for Northern Ireland shall be subject to negative resolution within the meaning of section 41(6) of the Interpretation Act (Northern Ireland) 1954 as if they were a statutory instrument within the meaning of that Act." |
| Paragraphs 8 to 12 ... | For the references to the Secretary of State and the Treasury there shall be substituted respectively references to the Ministry of Home Affairs for Northern Ireland and the Ministry of Finance for Northern Ireland. |
| Paragraph 13 ... ... | In sub-paragraph (1)— |
| | (*a*) for the references to the Lord Chancellor and Secretary of State there shall be substituted respectively references to the Lord Chief Justice of Northern Ireland and the Minister of Home Affairs for Northern Ireland; and |
| | (*b*) for the reference to a department of the Government of the United Kingdom there shall be substituted a reference to a department of the Government of Northern Ireland. |
| Paragraph 16 ... ... | The references to paragraphs 8 and 10 to 12 shall be construed as references to those paragraphs as modified by this Part of this Schedule. |
| Paragraph 17 ... ... | For the reference to the Secretary of State there shall be substituted a reference to the Minister of Home Affairs for Northern Ireland. |
| Paragraph 20 ... ... | The reference to paragraph 8 shall be construed as a reference to that paragraph as modified by this Part of this Schedule. |

## SCHEDULE 4
### (Section 25)

As amended by the Criminal Law Act 1977 s. 27, s. 28 and Sch. 5, the Magistrates Courts Act 1980 s. 32 (2) and (5), the Criminal Justice Act 1982, s. 46 and the Controlled Drugs (Penalties) Act 1985

PROSECUTION AND PUNISHMENT OF OFFENCES

*(The prescribed sum is at present £2,000—S.I. 1984/447)

| Section Creating Offence | General Nature of Offence | Mode of Prosecution | Punishment | | | |
|---|---|---|---|---|---|---|
| | | | Class A drug involved | Class B drug involved | Class C drug involved | General |
| Section 4(2) | Production, or being concerned in the production, of a controlled drug. | (a) Summary | 6 months or the prescribed sum, or both. | 6 months or the prescribed sum, or both. | 3 months or £500, or both. | |
| | | (b) On indictment | Life or a fine, or both. | 14 years or a fine, or both. | 5 years or a fine, or both. | |
| Section 4(3) | Supplying or offering to supply a controlled drug or being concerned in the doing of either activity by another. | (a) Summary | 6 months or the prescribed sum, or both. | 6 months or the prescribed sum, or both. | 3 months or £500, or both. | |
| | | (b) On indictment | Life or a fine, or both. | 14 years or a fine, or both. | 5 years or a fine, or both. | |
| Section 5(2) | Having possession of a controlled drug. | (a) Summary | 6 months or the prescribed sum, or both. | 3 months or £500, or both | 3 months or £200, or both. | |
| | | (b) On indictment | 7 years or a fine, or both. | 5 years or a fine, or both. | 2 years or a fine, or both. | |

MOD–R

| Section Creating Offence | General Nature of Offence | Mode of Prosecution | Punishment | | | |
|---|---|---|---|---|---|---|
| | | | Class A drug involved | Class B drug involved | Class C drug involved | General |
| Section 5(3) | Having possession of a controlled drug with intent to supply it to another. | (a) Summary | 6 months or the prescribed sum or both. | 6 months or the prescribed sum or both. | 3 months or £500, or both. | |
| | | (b) On indictment | Life or a fine, or both. | 14 years or a fine, or both. | 5 years or a fine, or both. | |
| Section 6(2) | Cultivation of cannabis plant. | (a) Summary | — | — | — | 6 months or the prescribed sum or both. |
| | | (b) On indictment | — | — | — | 14 years or a fine, or both. |
| Section 8 | Being the occupier, or concerned in the management, of premises and permitting or suffering certain activities to take place there. | (a) Summary | 6 months or the prescribed sum or both. | 6 months or the prescribed sum or both. | 3 months or £500, both. | |
| | | (b) On indictment | 14 years or a fine, or both. | 14 years or a fine, or both. | 5 years or a fine, or both. | |
| Section 9 | Offences relating to opium | (a) Summary | — | — | — | 6 months or the prescribed sum or both. |
| | | (b) On indictment | — | — | — | 14 years or a fine, or both. |
| Section 11(2) | Contravention of directions relating to safe custody of controlled drugs. | (a) Summary | — | — | — | 6 months or the prescribed sum, or both. |
| | | (b) On indictment | — | — | — | 2 years or a fine, or both. |

| Section Creating Offence | General Nature of Offence | Mode of Prosecution | Punishment | | | |
|---|---|---|---|---|---|---|
| | | | Class A drug involved | Class B drug involved | Class C drug involved | General |
| Section 12(6) | Contravention of direction prohibiting practitioner etc. from possessing, supplying, etc. controlled drugs. | (a) Summary | 6 months or the prescribed sum or both. | 6 months or the prescribed sum or both. | 3 months or £500, or both. | |
| | | (b) On indictment | 14 years or a fine, or both. | 14 years or a fine, or both. | 5 years or a fine, or both. | |
| Section 13(3) | Contravention of direction prohibiting practitioner, etc. from prescribing, supplying, etc. controlled drugs. | (a) Summary | 6 months or the prescribed sum or both. | 6 months or the prescribed sum or both. | 3 months or £500 or both. | |
| | | (b) On indictment | 14 years or a fine, or both. | 14 years or a fine, or both. | 5 years or a fine, or both. | |
| Section 17(3) | Failure to comply with notice requiring information relating to prescribing, supply, etc. of drugs. | Summary | — | — | — | See note 33 |
| Section 17(4) | Giving false information in purported compliance with notice requiring information relating to prescribing, supply, etc. of drugs. | (a) Summary | — | — | — | 6 months or the prescribed sum or both. |
| | | (b) On indictment | — | — | — | 2 years or a fine, or both. |
| Section 18(1) | Contravention of regulations (other than regulations relating to addicts). | (a) Summary | — | — | — | 6 months or the prescribed sum or both. |
| | | (b) On indictment | — | — | — | 2 years or a fine, or both. |

33 By s. 46(1) Criminal Justice Act 1982 the penalty is at Level 3 of the standard scale—at present £400 (S.I. 1984/447)

| Section Creating Offence | General Nature of Offence | Mode of Prosecution | Punishment | | | |
|---|---|---|---|---|---|---|
| | | | Class A drug involved | Class B drug involved | Class C drug involved | General |
| Section 18(2) | Contravention of terms of licence or other authority (other than licence issued under regulations relating to addicts). | (a) Summary | — | — | — | 6 months or the prescribed sum or both. |
| | | (b) On indictment | | | | 2 years or a fine, or both. |
| Section 18(3) | Giving false information in purported compliance with obligation to give information imposed under or by virtue of regulations. | (a) Summary | — | — | — | 6 months or the prescribed sum or both. |
| | | (b) On indictment | | | | 2 years or a fine, or both. |
| Section 18(4) | Giving false information, or producing document, etc. containing false statement, etc., for purposes of obtaining issue or renewal of a licence or other authority. | (a) Summary | — | — | — | 6 months or the prescribed sum or both. |
| | | (b) On indictment | | | | 2 years or a fine, or both. |
| Section 20 | Assisting in or inducing commission outside United Kingdom of an offence punishable under a corresponding law. | (a) Summary | — | — | — | 6 months or the prescribed sum or both. |
| | | (b) On indictment | | | | 14 years or a fine, or both. |
| Section 23(4) | Obstructing exercise of powers of search, etc., or concealing books, drugs, etc. | (a) Summary | — | — | — | 6 months or the prescribed sum or both. |
| | | (b) On indictment | | | | 2 years or a fine, or both. |

SCHEDULE 5

(Section 39.)

SAVINGS AND TRANSITIONAL PROVISIONS

1.—(1) Any addiction regulations which could have been made under this Act shall not be invalidated by any repeal effected by this Act but shall have effect as if made under the provisions of this Act which correspond to the provisions under which the regulations were made; and the validity of any licence issued under any such addiction regulations shall not be affected by any such repeal.

(2) Any order, rule or other instrument or document whatsoever made or issued, any direction given, and any other thing done, under or by virtue of any of the following provisions of the Dangerous Drugs Act 1967, that is to say section 1(2), 2 or 3 or the Schedule, shall be deemed for the purposes of this Act to have been made, issued or done, as the case may be, under the corresponding provision of this Act; and anything begun under any of the said provisions of that Act may be continued under this Act as if begun under this Act.

(3) In this paragraph "addiction regulations" means any regulations made under section 11 of the Dangerous Drugs Act 1965 which include provision for any of the matters for which regulations may be so made by virtue of section 1(1) of the Dangerous Drugs Act 1967.

2. As from the coming into operation of section 3 of this Act any licence granted for the purpose of section 5 of the Drugs (Prevention of Misuse) Act 1964 or sections 2, 3 or 10 of the Dangerous Drugs Act 1965 shall have effect as if granted for the purposes of section 3(2) of this Act.

3.—(1) The Secretary of State may at any time before the coming into operation of section 12 of this Act give a direction under subsection (2) of that section in respect of any practitioner or pharmacist whose general authority under the Dangerous Drugs Regulations is for the time being withdrawn; but a direction given by virtue of this sub-paragraph shall not take effect until section 12 comes into operation, and shall not take effect at all if the general authority of the person concerned is restored before that section comes into operation.

(2) No direction under section 12(2) of this Act shall be given by virtue of sub-paragraph (1) above in respect of a person while the withdrawal of his general authority under the Dangerous Drugs Regulations is suspended; but where, in the case of any practitioner or pharmacist whose general authority has been withdrawn, the withdrawal is suspended at any time when section 12 comes into operation, the Secretary of State may at any time give a direction under section 12(2) in respect of him by virtue of this sub-paragraph unless the Secretary of State has previoulsy caused to be served on him a notice stating that he is no longer liable to have such a direction given in respect of him by virtue of this sub-paragraph.

(3) In this paragraph "the Dangerous Drugs Regulations" means, as regards Great Britain, the Dangerous Drugs (No.2) Regulations 1964 or, as regards Northern Ireland, the Dangerous Drugs Regulations (Northern Ireland) 1965.

4. Subject to paragraphs 1 to 3 above, and without prejudice to the generality of section 31(1)(c) of this Act, regulations made by the Secretary of State under any provision of this Act may include such provision as the Secretary of State thinks fit for effecting the transition from any provision made by or by virtue of

any of the enactments repealed by this Act to any provision made by or by virtue of this Act, and in particular may provide for the continuation in force, with or without modifications, of any licence or other authority issued or having effect as if issued under or by virtue of any of those enactments.

**5.** For purposes of the enforcement of the enactments repealed by this Act as regards anything done or omitted before their repeal, any powers of search, entry, inspection, seizure or detention conferred by those enactments shall continue to be exercisable as if those enactments were still in force.

**6.** The mention of particular matters in this Schedule shall not prejudice the general application of section 38(2) of the Interpretation Act 1889 with regard to the effect of repeals.

## SCHEDULE 6

(Section 39.)

REPEALS

| Chapter | Short Title | Extent of Repeal |
|---------|-------------|------------------|
| 1964 c. 64. | The Drugs (Prevention of Misuse) Act 1964. | The whole Act. |
| 1965 c. 15. | The Dangerous Drugs Act 1965. | The whole Act. |
| 1967 c. 82. | The Dangerous Drugs Act 1967. | The whole Act. |
| 1968 c. 59. | The Hovercraft Act 1968. | Paragraph 6 of the Schedule. |
| 1968 c. 67. | The Medicines Act 1968. | In Schedule 5, paragraphs 14 and 15. |

# The Misuse of Drugs Regulations 1973

(S.I. No. 797)

| | |
|---|---|
| *Made - - - -* | *19th April 1973* |
| *Laid before Parliament* | *7th May 1973* |
| *Coming into Operation* | *1st July 1973* |

## ARRANGEMENT OF REGULATIONS

### Part I : General

1. Citation and commencement.
2. Interpretation.
3. Metric system and imperial system.

### Part II : Exemptions from Certain Provisions of the Misuse of Drugs Act 1971

4. Exceptions for drugs in Schedule 1 and poppy-straw.
5. Licences to produce etc. controlled drugs.
6. General authority to possess.
7. Administration of drugs in Schedules 1, 2 and 3.
8. Production and supply of drugs in Schedules 1 and 2.
9. Production and supply of drugs in Schedule 3.
10. Possession of drugs in Schedules 2 and 3.
11. Exemption for midwives in respect of pethidine.
12. Cultivation under licence of Cannabis plant.
13. Approval of premises for cannabis smoking for research purposes.

### Part III : Requirements as to Documentation and Record Keeping

14. Documents to be obtained by supplier of controlled drugs.
15. Form of prescriptions.
16. Provisions as to supply on prescription.
17. Exemption for certain prescriptions.
18. Marking of bottles and other containers.
19. Keeping of registers.
20. Requirements as to registers.
21. Record-keeping requirements in particular cases.
22. Preservation of registers, books and other documents.
23. Preservation of records relating to drugs in Schedule 1.

**Part IV: Miscellaneous**

24. Destruction of controlled drugs.
25. Transitional provisions.

**Schedules:**

Schedule 1—Controlled drugs excepted from the prohibition on importation, exportation and possession and subject to the requirements of Regulation 23.

Schedule 2—Controlled drugs subject to the requirements of Regulations 14, 15, 16, 18, 19, 20, 21 and 24.

Schedule 3—Controlled drugs subject to the requirements of Regulations 14, 15, 16 and 18.

Schedule 4—Controlled drugs subject to the requirements of Regulations 14, 15, 16, 18, 19, 20 and 24.

Schedule 5—Form of register.

## Part I

### General

*Citation and commencement*

**1.** These Regulations may be cited as the Misuse of Drugs Regulations 1973 and shall come into operation on 1st July 1973.

*Interpretation*

**2.**—(1) In these Regulations, unless the context otherwise requires, the expression—

"the Act" means the Misuse of Drugs Act 1971;

"authorised as a member of a group" means authorised by virtue of being a member of a class as respects which the Secretary of State has granted an authority under and for the purposes of Regulations 8(3), 9(3) or 10(3) which is in force, and "his group authority", in relation to a person who is a member of such a class, means the authority so granted to that class;

["cannabis" has the same meaning as in the Act as amended by section 52 of the Criminal Law Act 1977][1]

"health prescription" means a prescription issued by a doctor or a dentist either under the National Health Service Acts 1946 [to 1973][2], the National Health Service (Scotland) Acts 1947 [to 1973][2], the Health Services Act (Northern Ireland) 1971 or the National Health Service (Isle of Man) Act 1948 (an Act of Tynwald) or upon a form issued by a local authority for use in connection with the health service of that authority;

"installation manager" and "offshore installation" have the same meanings as in the Mineral Workings (Offshore Installations) Act 1971;

1 Inserted by S.I. 1977/1380
2 Amended by S.I. 1974/402

"master" has the same meaning as in the Merchant Shipping Act 1894;

"matron or acting matron" includes any male nurse occupying a similar position;

"the Merchant Shipping Acts" means the Merchant Shipping Acts 1894 to 1971;

"officer of customs and excise" means an officer within the meaning of the Customs and Excise Act 1952;

"prescription" means a prescription issued by a doctor for the medical treatment of a single individual, by a dentist for the dental treatment of a single individual or by a veterinary surgeon or veterinary practitioner for the purposes of animal treatment;

"register" means a bound book and does not include any form of loose leaf register or card index;

"registered pharmacy" has the same meaning as in the Medicines Act 1968;

"retail dealer" means a person lawfully conducting a retail pharmacy business or a pharmacist engaged in supplying drugs to the public at a health centre within the meaning of the Medicines Act 1968;

"sister or acting sister" includes any male nurse occupying a similar position;

"wholesale dealer" means a person who carries on the business of selling drugs to persons who buy to sell again.

(2) In these Regulations any reference to a Regulation or Schedule shall be construed as a reference to a Regulation contained in these Regulations or, as the case may be, to a Schedule thereto; and any reference in a Regulation or Schedule to a paragraph shall be construed as a reference to a paragraph of that Regulation or Schedule.

(3) In these Regulations any reference to any enactment shall be construed as a reference to that enactment as amended, and as including a reference thereto as extended or applied, by or under any other enactment.

(4) Nothing in these Regulations shall be construed as derogating from any power or immunity of the Crown, its servants or agents.

(5) The Interpretation Act 1889 shall apply for the interpretation of these Regulations as it applies for the interpretation of an Act of Parliament.


*Metric system and imperial system*
**3.**—(1) For the purposes of these Regulations—

> (a) a controlled drug shall not be regarded as supplied otherwise than on a prescription or other order by reason only that the prescription or order specifies a quantity of the controlled drug in terms of the imperial system and the quantity supplied is the equivalent of that amount in the metric system;
> (b) where any person may lawfully be in possession of a quantity of a controlled drug determined by or under these Regulations in terms of the imperial system he shall be deemed not to be in possession of a quantity of that controlled drug in excess of the first-mentioned quantity by reason only that he is in possession of a quantity of that drug which is the equivalent of the first-mentioned quantity in the metric system.

(2) For the purposes of this Regulation the quantity of a controlled drug in the metric system which is the equivalent of a particular quantity in the imperial system shall be taken to be the appropriate quantity ascertained in accordance with the provisions of the Weights and Measures (Equivalents for dealing with drugs) Regulations 1970.

## Part II

### Exemptions from Certain Provisions of the Misuse of Drugs Act 1971

*Exceptions for drugs in Schedule 1 and poppy-straw*

**4.**—(1) Sections 3(1) and 5(1) of the Act (which prohibit the importation, exportation and possession of controlled drugs) shall not have effect in relation to the controlled drugs specified in Schedule 1.

(2) Sections 4(1) (which prohibits the production and supply of controlled drugs) and 5(1) of the Act shall not have effect in relation to poppy-straw.

*Licences to produce etc. controlled drugs*

**5.** Where any person is authorised by a licence of the Secretary of State issued under this Regulation and for the time being in force to produce, supply, offer to supply or have in his possession any controlled drug, it shall not by virtue of section 4(1) or 5(1) of the Act be unlawful for that person to produce, supply, offer to supply or have in his possession that drug in accordance with the terms of the licence and in compliance with any conditions attached to the licence.

*General authority to possess*

**6.** Any of the following persons may, notwithstanding the provisions of section 5(1) of the Act, have any controlled drug in his possession, that is to say—

(*a*) a constable when acting in the course of his duty as such;
(*b*) a person engaged in the business of a carrier when acting in the course of that business;
(*c*) a person engaged in the business of the Post Office when acting in the course of that business;
(*d*) an officer of customs and excise when acting in the course of his duty as such;
(*e*) a person engaged in the work of any laboratory to which the drug has been sent for forensic examination when acting in the course of his duty as a person so engaged;
(*f*) a person engaged in conveying the drug to a person authorised by these Regulations to have it in his possession.

*Administration of drugs in Schedules 1, 2 and 3*

**7.**—(1) Any person may administer to another any drug specified in Schedule 1.

(2) A doctor or dentist may administer to a patient any drug specified in Schedule 2 or 3.

(3) Any person other than a doctor or dentist may administer to a patient, in accordance with the directions of a doctor or dentist, any drug specified in Schedule 2 or 3.

*Production and supply of drugs in Schedules 1 and 2*

**8.**—(1) Notwithstanding the provisions of section 4(1)(*a*) of that Act—

(*a*) a practitioner or pharmacist, acting in his capacity as such, may manufacture or compound any drug specified in Schedule 1 or 2;

(*b*) a person lawfully conducting a retail pharmacy business and acting in his capacity as such may, at the registered pharmacy at which he carries on that business, manufacture or compound any drug specified in Schedule 1 or 2.

(2) Notwithstanding the provisions of section 4(1)(*b*) of the Act any of the following persons, that is to say—

(*a*) a practitioner;

(*b*) a pharmacist;

(*c*) a person lawfully conducting a retail pharmacy business;

(*d*) the matron or acting matron of a hospital or nursing home which is wholly or mainly maintained by a public authority out of public funds or by a charity or by voluntary subscriptions;

(*e*) in the case of such a drug supplied to her by a person responsible for the dispensing and supply of medicines at the hospital or nursing home, the sister or acting sister for the time being in charge of a ward, theatre or other department in such a hospital or nursing home as aforesaid;

(*f*) a person who is in charge of a laboratory the recognized activities of which consist in, or include, the conduct of scientific education or research and which is attached to a university, university college or such a hospital as aforesaid or to any other institution approved for the purpose by the Secretary of State;

(*g*) a public analyst appointed under section 89 of the Food and Drugs Act 1955 or section 27 of the Food and Drugs (Scotland) Act 1956;

(*h*) a sampling officer within the meaning of the Food and Drugs Act 1955 or the Food and Drugs (Scotland) Act 1956;

(*i*) a sampling officer within the meaning of Schedule 3 to the Medicines Act 1968;

(*j*) a person employed or engaged in connection with a scheme for testing the quality or amount of the drugs, preparations and appliances supplied under the National Health Service Acts 1946 [to 1973][3] or the National Health Service (Scotland) Acts 1947 [to 1973][3] and the Regulations made thereunder;

(*k*) an inspector appointed by the Pharmaceutical Society of Great Britain under section 25 of the Pharmacy and Poisons Act 1933,

may, when acting in his capacity as such, supply or offer to supply any drug specified in Schedule 1 or 2 to any person who may lawfully have that drug in his possession:

Provided that nothing in this paragraph authorises—

(i) the matron or acting matron of a hospital or nursing home, having a pharmacist responsibe for the dispensing and supply of medicines, to supply or offer to supply any drug;

(ii) sister or acting sister for the time being in charge of a ward, theatre or other department to supply any drug otherwise than for adminis-

3 Amended by S.I. 1974/402

tration to a patient in that ward, theatre or department in accordance with the directions of a doctor or dentist.

(3) Notwithstanding the provisions of section 4(1)(*b*) of the Act, a person who is authorised as a member of a group may, under and in accordance with the terms of his group authority and in compliance with any conditions attached thereto, supply or offer to supply any drug specified in Schedule 1 or 2 to any person who may lawfully have that drug in his possession.

[(4) Notwithstanding the provisions of section 4(1)(*b*) of the Act, a person who is authorised by a written authority issued by the Secretary of State under and for the purposes of this paragraph and for the time being in force may, at the premises specified in that authority and in compliance with any conditions so specified, supply or offer to supply any drug specified in Schedule 1 to any person who may lawfully have that drug in his possession.] [4]

(5) Notwithstanding the provisions of section 4(1)(*b*) of the Act—

(*a*) the owner of a ship, or the master of a ship which does not carry a doctor on board as part of her complement, may supply or offer to supply any drug specified in Schedule 1 or 2—

(i) to any member of the crew;
(ii) to any person who may lawfully supply that drug; or
(iii) to any constable for the purpose of destruction;

(*b*) the installation manager of an offshore installation may supply or offer to supply any drug specified in Schedule 1 or 2—

(i) to any person on that installation, whether present in the course of his employment or not;
(ii) to any person who may lawfully supply that drug; or
(iii) to any constable for the purpose of destruction.

*Production and supply of drugs in Schedule 3*
**9.**—(1) Notwithstanding the provisions of section 4(1)(*a*) of the Act—

(*a*) a practitioner or pharmacist, acting in his capacity as such, may manufacture or compound any drug specified in Schedule 3;
(*b*) a person lawfully conducting a retail pharmacy business and acting in his capacity as such may, at the registered pharmacy at which he carries on that business, manufacture or compound any drug specified in Schedule 3;
[(*c*) a person who is authorised by a written authority issued by the Secretary of State under and for the purposes of this sub-paragraph and for the time being in force may, at the premises specified in that authority and in compliance with any conditions so specified, produce any drug specified in Schedule 3.] [4]

(2) Notwithstanding the provisions of section 4(1)(*b*) of the Act, any of the following persons, that is to say—

(*a*) a practitioner;
(*b*) a pharmacist;
(*c*) a person lawfully conducting a retail pharmacy business;

**4** Substituted by S.I. 1984/1143

(*d*)  the matron or acting matron of a hospital or nursing home;

(*e*)  in the case of such a drug supplied to her by a person responsible for the dispensing and supply of medicines at the hospital or nursing home, the sister or acting sister for the time being in charge of a ward, theatre or other department in a hospital or nursing home;

(*f*)  a person in charge of a laboratory the recognized activities of which consist in, or include, the conduct of scientific education or research;

[(*ff*) in the case of such a drug required for use as a buffering agent in chemical analysis, a person in charge of a laboratory;][5]

(*g*)  a public analyst appointed under section 89 of the Food and Drugs Act 1955 or section 27 of the Food and Drugs (Scotland) Act 1956;

(*h*)  a sampling officer within the meaning of the Food and Drugs Act 1955 or the Food and Drugs (Scotland) Act 1956;

(*i*)  a sampling officer within the meaning of Schedule 3 to the Medicines Act 1968;

(*j*)  a person employed or engaged in connection with a scheme for testing the quality or amount of the drugs, preparations and appliances supplied under the National Health Service Acts 1946 [to 1973][6] or the National Health Service (Scotland) Acts 1947 [to 1973][6] and the Regulations made thereunder;

(*k*)  an inspector appointed by the Pharmaceutical Society of Great Britain under section 25 of the Pharmacy and Poisons Act 1933,

may, when acting in his capacity as such, supply or offer to supply any drug specified in Schedule 3 to any person who may lawfully have that drug in his possession:

Provided that nothing in this paragraph authorises—

(i)  the matron or acting matron of a hospital or nursing home, having a pharmacist responsible for the dispensing and supply of medicines, to supply or offer to supply any drug;

(ii)  a sister or acting sister for the time being in charge of a ward, theatre or other department to supply any drug otherwise than for administration to a patient in that ward, theatre or department in accordance with the directions of a doctor or dentist.

(3) Notwithstanding the provisions of section 4(1)(*b*) of the Act, a person who is authorised as a member of a group may, under and in accordance with the terms of his group authority and in compliance with any conditions attached thereto, supply or offer to supply any drug specified in Schedule 3 to any person who may lawfully have that drug in his possession.

[(4) Notwithstanding the provisions of section 4(1)(*b* of the Act—

(*a*)  a person who is authorised by a written authority issued by the Secretary of State under and for the purposes of this sub-paragraph and for the time being in force may, at the premises specified in that authority and in compliance with any conditions so specified, supply or offer to supply any drug specified in Schedule 3 to any person who may lawfully have that drug in his possession;

5   Inserted by S.I. 1984/1143
6   Amended by S.I. 1974/402

(*b*) a person who is authorised under paragraph (1)(*c*) may supply or offer to supply any drug which he may, by virtue of being so authorised, lawfully produce to any person who may lawfully have that drug in his possession.][7]

(5) Notwithstanding the provisions of section 4(1)(*b*) of the Act—

(*a*) the owner of a ship, or the master of a ship which does not carry a doctor on board as part of her complement, may supply or offer to supply any drug specified in Schedule 3—

(i) to any member of the crew; or
(ii) to any person who may lawfully supply that drug;

(*b*) the installation manager of an offshore installation may supply or offer to supply any drug specified in Schedule 3—

(i) to any person on that installation, whether present in the course of his employment or not; or
(ii) to any person who may lawfully supply that drug.

*Possession of drugs in Schedules 2 and 3*

**10.**—[(1) Notwithstanding the provisions of section 5(1) of the Act—

(*a*) a person specified in one of sub-paragraphs (*a*) to (*k*) of Regulation 8(2) may have in his possession any drug specified in Schedule 2;

(*b*) a person specified in one of sub-paragraphs (*a*) to (*k*) (including sub-paragraph (*ff*)) of Regulation 9(2) may have in his possession any drug specified in Schedule 3,

for the purpose of acting in his capacity as such a person:
Provided that nothing in this paragraph authorises—

(i) a person specified in sub-paragraph (*e*) of Regulation 8(2); or
(ii) a person specified in sub-paragraph (*e*) or (*ff*) of Regulation 9(2),

to have in his possession any drug other than such a drug as is mentioned in the sub-paragraph in question specifying him.][7]

(2) Notwithstanding the provisions of section 5(1) of the Act a person may have in his possession any drug specified in Schedule 2 or 3 for administration for medical, dental or veterinary purposes in accordance with the directions of a practitioner:
Provided that this paragraph shall not have effect in the case of a person to whom the drug has been supplied by or on the prescription of a doctor if—

(*a*) that person was then being supplied with any controlled drug by or on the prescription of another doctor and failed to disclose that fact to the first mentioned doctor before the supply by him or on his prescription; or

(*b*) that or any other person on his behalf made a declaration or statement, which was false in any particular, for the purpose of obtaining the supply or prescription.

(3) Notwithstanding the provisions of section 5(1) of the Act, a person who is authorised as a member of a group may, under and in accordance with the terms

7 Substituted by S.I. 1984/1143

of his group authority and in compliance with any conditions attached thereto, have any drug specified in Schedule 2 or 3 in his possession.

[(4) Notwithstanding the provisions of section 5(1) of the Act—

(*a*) a person who is authorised by a written authority issued by the Secretary of State under and for the purposes of this sub-paragraph and for the time being in force may, at the premises specified in that authority and in compliance with any conditions so specified, have in his possession any drug specified in Schedule 3;

(*b*) a person who is authorised under Regulation 9(1)(*c*) may have in his possession any drug which he may, by virtue of being so authorised, lawfully produce;

(*c*) a person who is authorised under Regulation 9(4)(*a*) may have in his possession any drug which he may, by virtue of being so authorised, lawfully supply or offer to supply.] [7]

(5) Notwithstanding the provisions of section 5(1) of the Act—

(*a*) the owner of a ship, or the master of a ship which does not carry a doctor on board as part of her complement, may have in his possession any drug specified in Schedule 2 or 3 so far as necessary for the purpose of compliance with the Merchant Shipping Acts;

(*b*) the master of a foreign ship which is in a port in Great Britain may have in his possession any drug specified in Schedule 2 or 3 so far as necessary for the equipment of the ship;

(*c*) the installation manager of an offshore installation may have in his possession any drug specified in Schedule 2 or 3 so far as necessary for the purpose of compliance with the Mineral Workings (Offshore Installations) Act 1971.

*Exemption for midwives in respect of pethidine*
**11.**—(1) Notwithstanding the provisions of sections 4(1)(*b*) and 5(1) of the Act, a certified midwife, who has in accordance with the provisions of the Midwives Act 1951, or the Midwives (Scotland) Act 1951, notified to the local supervising authority her intention to practise, may, subject to the provisions of this Regulation—

(*a*) so far as necessary for the practice of her profession or employment as a midwife, have pethidine in her possession;

(*b*) so far as necessary as aforesaid, administer pethidine; and

(*c*) surrender to the appropriate medical officer [ ... ] [8] any stocks of pethidine in her possession which are no longer required by her.

(2) Nothing in paragraph (1) authorises a midwife to have in her possession pethidine which has been obtained otherwise than on a midwife's supply order signed by the appropriate medical officer [ ... ] [8]

(3) In this Regulation, the expression—

"appropriate medical officer" [. . .] [8] means—

**8** Deleted by S.I. 1974/402

[(*a*) a doctor who is for the time being authorised in writing for the purposes of this Regulation by the local supervising authority for the region or area in which the pethidine was, or is to be, obtained][9]

(*b*) [ . . . ][8]

(*c*) for the purposes of paragraph (2), a person appointed under section 17 of the Midwives Act 1951, or, as the case may be, section 18 of the Midwives (Scotland) Act 1951, by that authority to exercise supervision over certified midwives within their area, who is for the time being authorised as aforesaid;

"certified midwife" and "local supervising authority" have the same meanings as in the Midwives Act 1951 or, in Scotland, the Midwives (Scotland) Act 1951;

"midwife's supply order" means an order in writing specifying the name and occupation of the midwife obtaining the pethidine, the purpose for which it is required and the total quantity to be obtained.

## *Cultivation under licence of Cannabis plant*

**12.** Where any person is authorised by a licence of the Secretary of State issued under this Regulation and for the time being in force to cultivate plants of the genus *Cannabis*, it shall not by virtue of section 6 of the Act be unlawful for that person to cultivate any such plant in accordance with the terms of the licence and in compliance with any conditions attached to the licence.

## *Approval of premises for cannabis smoking for research purposes*

**13.** Section 8 of the Act (which makes it an offence for the occupier of premises to permit certain activities there) shall not have effect in relation to the smoking of cannabis or cannabis resin for the purposes of research on any premises for the time being approved for the purpose by the Secretary of State.

## Part III

### Requirements as to Documentation and Record Keeping

## *Documents to be obtained by supplier of controlled drugs*

**14.**—(1) Where a person (hereafter in this paragraph referred to as "the supplier"), not being a practitioner, supplies a controlled drug otherwise than on a prescription, the supplier shall not deliver the drug to a person who—

(*a*) purports to be sent by or on behalf of the person to whom it is supplied (hereafter in this paragraph referred to as "the recipient"); and

(*b*) is not authorised by any provision of these Regulations other than the provisions of Regulation 6(*f*) to have that drug in his possession,

unless that person produces to the supplier a statement in writing signed by the recipient to the effect that he is empowered by the recipient to receive that drug on behalf of the recipient, and the supplier is reasonably satisfied that the document is a genuine document.

(2) Where a person (hereafter in this paragraph referred to as "the supplier") supplies a controlled drug, otherwise than on a prescription or by way of

**9** Substituted by S.I. 1974/402

administration, to any of the persons specified in paragraph (4), the supplier shall not deliver the drug—

(a) until he has obtained a requisition in writing which—

(i) is signed by the person to whom the drug is supplied (hereafter in this paragraph referred to as "the recipient");

(ii) states the name, address and profession or occupation of the recipient;

(iii) specifies the purpose for which the drug supplied is required and the total quantity to be supplied; and

(iv) where appropriate, satisfies the requirements of paragraph (5);

(b) unless he is reasonably satisfied that the signature is that of the person purporting to have signed the requisition and that that person is engaged in the profession or occupation specified in the requisition:

Provided that where the recipient is a practitioner and he represents that he urgently requires a controlled drug for the purpose of his profession, the supplier may, if he is reasonably satisfied that the recipient so requires the drug and is, by reason of some emergency, unable before delivery to furnish to the supplier a requisition in writing duly signed, deliver the drug to the recipient on an undertaking by the recipient to furnish such a requisition within the twenty-four hours next following.

(3) A person who has given such an undertaking as aforesaid shall deliver to the person by whom the controlled drug was supplied a signed requisition in accordance with the undertaking.

(4) The persons referred to in paragraph (2) are—

(a) a practitioner;

(b) the matron or acting matron of a hospital or nursing home;

[(c) a person who is in charge of a laboratory.]¹⁰

(d) the owner of a ship, or the master of a ship which does not carry a doctor on board as part of her complement;

(e) the master of a foreign ship in a port in Great Britain;

(f) the installation manager of an offshore installation.

(5) A requisition furnished for the purposes of paragraph (2) shall—

(a) where furnished by the matron or acting matron of a hospital or nursing home, be signed by a doctor or dentist employed or engaged in that hospital or nursing home;

(b) where furnished by the master of a foreign ship, contain a statement, signed by the [proper officer of the port health authority, or, in Scotland, the medical officer designated under section 21 of the National Health Service (Scotland) Act 1972 by the Health Board]¹¹ within whose jurisdiction the ship is, that the quantity of the drug to be supplied is the quantity necessary for the equipment of the ship.

(6) Where the person responsible for the dispensing and supply of medicines at any hospital or nursing home supplies a controlled drug to the sister or acting sister for the time being in charge of any ward, theatre or other department in that hospital or nursing home (hereafter in this paragraph referred to as "the recipient") he shall—

10 Amended by S.I. 1984/1143
11 Amended by S.I. 1974/402

MOD-S

(a) obtain a requisition in writing, signed by the recipient, which specifies the total quantity of the drug to be supplied; and

(b) mark the requisition in such manner as to show that it has been complied with,

and any requisition obtained for the purpose of this paragraph shall be retained in the dispensary at which the drug was supplied and a copy of the requisition or a note of it shall be retained or kept by the recipient.

(7) Nothing in this Regulation shall have effect in relation to the drugs specified in Schedule 1 or poppy-straw.

*Form of prescriptions*
**15.**—(1) Subject to the provisions of this Regulation, a person shall not issue a prescription containing a controlled drug other than a drug specified in Schedule 1 unless the prescription complies with the following requirements, that is to say, it shall—

(a) be in ink or otherwise so as to be indelible and be signed by the person issuing it with his usual signature and dated by him;

(b) insofar as it specifies the information required by sub-paragraphs (e) and (f) below to be specified, be written by the person issuing it in his own handwriting;

(c) except in the case of a health prescription, specify the address of the person issuing it;

(d) have written thereon, if issued by a dentist, the words "for dental treatment only" and, if issued by a veterinary surgeon or a veterinary practitioner, the words "for animal treatment only";

(e) specify the name and address of the person for whose treatment it is issued or, if it is issued by a veterinary surgeon or veterinary practitioner, of the person to whom the controlled drug prescribed is to be delivered;

(f) specify the dose to be taken and—

    (i) in the case of a prescription containing a controlled drug which is a preparation, the form and, where appropriate, the strength of the preparation, and either the total quantity (in both words and figures) of the preparation or the number (in both words and figures) of dosage units, as appropriate, to be supplied;

    (ii) in any other case, the total quantity (in both words and figures) of the controlled drug to be supplied;

(g) in the case of a prescription for a total quantity intended to be dispensed by instalments, contain a direction specifying the amount of the instalments of the total amount which may be dispensed and the intervals to be observed when dispensing.

(2) Paragraph (1)(b) shall not have effect in relation to a prescription issued by a person approved (whether personally or as a member of a class) for the purposes of this paragraph by the Secretary of State.

[(2A) Paragraph (1)(b) shall not have effect in relation to a prescription containing no controlled drug other than—

(a) phenobarbitone;

(b) phenobarbitone sodium;

(c) a preparation containing a drug specified in sub-paragraph (a) or (b) above; or

(d) a drug specified in Schedule 1.][12]

(3) In the case of a prescription issued for the treatment of a patient in a hospital or nursing home, it shall be a sufficient compliance with paragraph (1)(e) if the prescription is written on the patient's bed card or case sheet.

*Provisions as to supply on prescription*
**16.**—(1) A person shall not supply a controlled drug other than a drug specified in Schedule 1 on a prescription—

(a) unless the prescription complies with the provisions of Regulation 15;

(b) unless the address specified in the prescription as the address of the person issuing it is an address within the United Kingdom;

(c) unless he either is acquainted with the signature of the person by whom it purports to be issued and has no reason to suppose that it is not genuine, or has taken reasonably sufficient steps to satisfy himself that it is genuine;

(d) before the date specified in the prescription;

(e) subject to paragraph (3), later than thirteen weeks after the date specified in the prescription.

(2) Subject to paragraph (3), a person dispensing a prescription containing a controlled drug other than a drug specified in Schedule 1 shall, at the time of dispensing it, mark thereon the date on which it is dispensed and, unless it is a health prescription, shall retain it on the premises on which it was dispensed.

(3) In the case of a prescription containing a controlled drug other than a drug specified in Schedule 1, which contains a direction that specified instalments of the total amount may be dispensed at stated intervals, the person dispensing it shall not supply the drug otherwise than in accordance with that direction and—

(a) paragraph (1) shall have effect as if for the requirement contained in sub-paragraph (e) thereof there were substituted a requirement that the occasion on which the first instalment is dispensed shall not be later than thirteen weeks after the date specified in the prescription;

(b) paragraph (2) shall have effect as if for the words "at the time of dispensing it" there were substituted the words "on each occasion on which an instalment is dispensed".

*Exemption for certain prescriptions*
**17.** Nothing in Regulations 15 and 16 shall have effect in relation to a prescription issued for the purposes of a scheme for testing the quality and amount of the drugs, preparations and appliances supplied under the National Health Service Acts 1946 [to 1973][13] or the National Health Service (Scotland) Acts 1947 [to 1973][13] and the Regulations made thereunder or to any prescriptions issued for the purposes of the Food and Drugs Act 1955 or, in Scotland, the Food and Drugs (Scotland) Act 1956 to a sampling officer within the meaning of those Acts or for the purposes of the Medicines Act 1968 to a sampling officer within the meaning of that Act.

12   Inserted by S.I. 1984/1143
13   Amended by S.I. 1974/402

*Marking of bottles and other containers*

**18.**—(1) Subject to paragraph (2), no person shall supply a controlled drug otherwise than in a bottle, package or other container which is plainly marked—

(a) in the case of a controlled drug other than a preparation, with the amount of the drug contained therein;

(b) in the case of a controlled drug which is a preparation—

  (i) made up into tablets, capsules or other dosage units, with the amount of each component (being a controlled drug) of the preparation in each dosage unit and the number of dosage units in the bottle, package or other container;

  (ii) not made up as aforesaid, with the total amount of the preparation in the bottle, package or other container and the percentage of each of its components which is a controlled drug.

(2) Nothing in this Regulation shall have effect in relation to the drugs specified in Schedule 1 or poppy-straw or in relation to the supply of a controlled drug by or on the prescription of a practitioner.

*Keeping of registers*

**19.**—(1) Subject to paragraph (3) and Regulation 21, every person authorised by or under Regulation 5 or 8 to supply any drug specified in Schedule 2 or 4 shall comply with the following requirements, that is to say—

(a) he shall, in accordance with the provisions of this Regulation and of Regulation 20, keep a register and shall enter therein in chronological sequence in the form specified in Part I or Part II of Schedule 5, as the case may require, particulars of every quantity of a drug specified in Schedule 2 or 4 obtained by him and of every quantity of such a drug supplied (whether by way of administration or otherwise) by him whether to persons within or outside Great Britain;

(b) he shall use a separate register or separate part of the register for entries made in respect of each class of drugs, and each of the drugs specified in paragraphs 1, 3 and 6 of Schedule 2 and paragraphs 1 and 3 of Schedule 4 together with its salts and any preparation or other product containing it or any of its salts shall be treated as a separate class, so however that any stereoisomeric form of a drug or its salts shall be classed with that drug.

(2) Nothing in paragraph (1) shall be taken as preventing the use of a separate section within a register or separate part of a register in respect of different drugs or strengths of drugs comprised within the class of drugs to which that register or separate part relates.

(3) The foregoing provisions of this Regulation shall not have effect in relation to—

(a) a person licensed under Regulation 5 to supply any drug, where the licence so directs; or

(b) the sister or acting sister for the time being in charge of a ward, theatre or other department in a hospital or nursing home.

*Requirements as to registers*

**20.** Any person required to keep a register under Regulation 19 shall comply with the following requirements, that is to say—

(*a*) the class of drugs to which the entries on any page of any such register relate shall be specified at the head of that page;

(*b*) every entry required to be made under Regulation 19 in such a register shall be made on the day on which the drug is obtained or, as the case may be, on which the transaction in respect of the supply of the drug by the person required to make the entry takes place or, if that is not reasonably practicable, on the day next following that day;

(*c*) no cancellation, obliteration or alteration of any such entry shall be made, and a correction of such an entry shall be made only by way of marginal note or footnote which shall specify the date on which the correction is made;

(*d*) every such entry and every correction of such an entry shall be made in ink or otherwise so as to be indelible;

(*e*) such a register shall not be used for any purpose other than the purposes of these Regulations;

(*f*) the person so required to keep such a register shall on demand made by the Secretary of State or by any person authorised in writing by the Secretary of State in that behalf—

(i) furnish such particulars as may be requested in respect of the obtaining or supplying by him of any drug specified in Schedule 2 or 4, or in respect of any stock of such drugs in his possession;

(ii) for the purpose of confirming any such particulars, produce any stock of such drugs in his possession;

(iii) produce the said register and such other books or documents in his possession relating to any dealings in drugs specified in Schedule 2 or 4 as may be requested;

(*g*) a separate register shall be kept in respect of each premises at which the person required to keep the register carries on his business or occupation, but subject to that not more than one register shall be kept at one time in respect of each class of drug in respect of which he is required to keep a separate register, so, however, that a separate register may, with the approval of the Secretary of State, be kept in respect of each department of the business carried on by him;

(*h*) every such register in which entries are currently being made shall be kept at the premises to which it relates.

*Record-keeping requirements in particular cases*

**21.**—(1) Where a drug specified in Schedule 2 is supplied in accordance with Regulation 8(5)(*a*)(i) to a member of the crew of a ship, an entry in the official log book required to be kept under the Merchant Shipping Acts or, in the case of a ship which is not required to carry such an official log book, a report signed by the master of the ship, shall, notwithstanding anything in these Regulations, be a sufficient record of the supply if the entry or report specifies the drug supplied and, in the case of a report, it is delivered as soon as may be to the superintendent of a mercantile marine office established and maintained under the Merchant Shipping Acts.

(2) Where a drug specified in Schedule 2 is supplied in accordance with Regulation 8(5)(*b*)(i) to a person on an offshore installation, an entry in the installation logbook required to be maintained under the Offshore Installations

(Logbooks and Registration of Death) Regulations 1972[14] which specifies the drug supplied shall, notwithstanding anything in these Regulations, be a sufficient record of the supply.

(3) A midwife authorised by Regulation 11(1) to have pethidine in her possession shall—

>   (*a*) on each occasion on which she obtains a supply of pethidine, enter in a book kept by her and used solely for the purposes of this paragraph the date, the name and address of the person from whom the drug was obtained, the amount obtained and the form in which it was obtained; and

>   (*b*) on administering pethidine to a patient, enter in the said book as soon as practicable the name and address of the patient, the amount administered and the form in which it was administered.

*Preservation of registers, books and other documents*

**22.**—(1) All registers and books kept in pursuance of Regulation 19 or 21(3) shall be preserved for a period of two years from the date on which the last entry therein is made.

(2) Every requisition, order or prescription (other than a health prescription) on which a controlled drug is supplied in pursuance of these Regulations shall be preserved for a period of two years from the date on which the last delivery under it was made.

*Preservation of records relating to drugs in Schedule 1*

**23.**—(1) A producer of any drug specified in Schedule 1 and a wholesale dealer in any such drug shall keep every invoice or other like record issued in respect of each quantity of such a drug obtained by him and in respect of each quantity of such a drug supplied by him.

(2) A retail dealer in any drug specified in Schedule 1 shall keep every invoice or other like record issued in respect of each quantity of such a drug obtained by him.

(3) Every document kept in pursuance of this Regulation shall be preserved for a period of two years from the date on which it is issued:

Provided that the keeping of a copy of the document made at any time during the said period of two years shall be treated for the purposes of this paragraph as if it were the keeping of the original document.

## Part IV

### Miscellaneous

*Destruction of controlled drugs*

**24.**—(1) No person who is required by any provision of, or by any term or condition of a licence having effect under, these Regulations to keep records with respect to a drug specified in Schedule 2 or 4 shall destroy such a drug or cause such a drug to be destroyed except in the presence of and in accordance with any directions given by a person authorised (whether personally or as a member or a class) for the purposes of this paragraph by the Secretary of State (hereafter in this Regulation referred to as an "authorised person").

(2) An authorised person may, for the purpose of analysis, take a sample of a drug specified in Schedule 2 or 4 which is to be destroyed.

(3) Where a drug specified in Schedule 2 or 4 is destroyed in pursuance of paragraph (1) by or at the instance of a person who is required by any provision of, or by any term or condition of a licence having effect under, these Regulations to keep a record in respect of the obtaining or supply of that drug, that record shall include particulars of the date of destruction and the quantity destroyed and shall be signed by the authorised person in whose presence the drug is destroyed.

(4) Where the master or owner of a ship or installation manager of an offshore installation has in his possession a drug specified in Schedule 2 which he no longer requires, he shall not destroy the drug or cause it to be destroyed but shall dispose of it to a constable or to a person who may lawfully supply it.

*Transitional provisions*

**25.**—(1) Any licence issued for the purpose of section 6(1) of the Dangerous Drugs Act 1965 (which makes it an offence to cultivate any cannabis plant except under licence) and in force immediately before the repeal of that Act shall continue in force for the same period of time as if that Act had not been repealed and shall have effect as if it had been issued for the purposes of Regulation 12.

(2) Any licence issued for the purposes of any provision of the Dangerous Drugs (No. 2) Regulations 1964[15] and in force immediately before the repeal of the said Act of 1965 shall, insofar as it authorises any person to do anything which could be authorised by a licence issued under Regulation 5, continue in force for the same period of time as if that Act had not been repealed and shall have effect as if it had been issued for the purposes of Regulation 5.

(3) Any authority granted in respect of any class for the purposes of any provision of the said Regulations of 1964 and in force immediately before the repeal of the said Act of 1965 shall, insofar as it authorises any class of persons to do anything which could be authorised by an authority granted for the purposes of Regulation 8(3) or 10(3), continue in force as if that Act had not been repealed and shall have effect as if granted for the purposes of Regulation 8(3) or 10(3) as the case may be.

(4) Any register, record, book, prescription or other document required to be preserved under Regulation 26 of the said Regulations of 1964 shall, notwithstanding the repeal of the said Act of 1965, be preserved for the same period of time as if that Act had not been repealed.

(5) In the case of a prescription issued before the coming into operation of these Regulations, Regulation 16(1) shall have effect as if—

   (a) in the case of a prescription containing a controlled drug specified in the Schedule to the Drugs (Prevention of Misuse) Act 1964 immediately before the repeal of that Act, sub-paragraphs (a) and (b) of that paragraph were ommitted; and

   (b) in any other case, for the said sub-paragraphs (a) and (b) there were substituted the words "unless the prescription complies with the

**15**   S.I. no. 1811

provisions of the Dangerous Drugs (No. 2) Regulations 1964 relating to prescriptions".

(6) In this Regulation, any reference to the repeal of the Dangerous Drugs Act 1965 or the Drugs (Prevention of Misuse) Act 1964 shall be construed as a reference to its repeal by section 39(2) of and Schedule 6 to the Act.

## SCHEDULE 1[16]

### (Regulations 4, 7, 8, 14, 15, 16, 18 and 23)

CONTROLLED DRUGS EXCEPTED FROM THE PROHIBITION ON IMPORTATION, EXPORTATION AND POSSESSION AND SUBJECT TO THE REQUIREMENTS OF REGULATION 23

**1.**—(1) Any preparation of one or more of the substances to which this paragraph applies, not being a preparation designed for administration by injection, when compounded with one or more other active or inert ingredients and containing a total of not more than 100 milligrammes of the substance or substances (calculated as base) per dosage unit or with a total concentration of not more than 2·5 per cent. (calculated as base) in undivided preparations.

(2) The substances to which this paragraph applies are acetyldihydrocodeine, codeine, dihydrocodeine, ethylmorphine, nicocodine, nicodicodine (6-nicotinoyl-dihydrocodeine), norcodeine, pholcodine and their respective salts.

**2.** Any preparation of cocaine containing not more than 0·1 per cent. of cocaine calculated as cocaine base, being a preparation compounded with one or more other active or inert ingredients in such a way that the cocaine cannot be recovered by readily applicable means or in a yield which would constitute a risk to health.

**3.** Any preparation of medicinal opium or of morphine containing (in either case) not more than 0·2 per cent. of morphine calculated as anhydrous morphine base, being a preparation compounded with one or more other active or inert ingredients in such a way that the opium or, as the case may be, the morphine, cannot be recovered by readily applicable means or in a yield which would constitute a risk to health.

**4.** Any preparation of dextropropoxyphene, being a preparation designed for oral administration, containing not more than 135 milligrammes of dextropropoxyphene (calculated as base) per dosage unit or with a total concentration of not more than 2·5 per cent. (calculated as base) in undivided preparations.

**5.** Any preparation of difenoxin (1-(3-cyano-3,3-diphenylpropyl)-4-phenylpiperidine-4-carboxylic acid) containing, per dosage unit, not more than 0·5 milligrammes of difenoxin and a quantity of atropine sulphate equivalent to at least 5 per cent. of the dose of difenoxin.

**16** Substituted by S.I. 1983/788

**6.** Any preparation of diphenoxylate containing, per dosage unit, not more than 2·5 milligrammes of diphenoxylate calculated as base, and a quantity of atropine sulphate equivalent to at least 1 per cent. of the dose of diphenoxylate.

**7.** Any preparation of propiram containing, per dosage unit, not more than 100 milligrammes of propiram calculated as base and compounded with at least the same amount (by weight) of methylcellulose.

**8.** Any powder of ipecacuanha and opium comprising—

10 per cent. opium, in powder,
10 per cent. ipecacuanha root, in powder, well mixed with
80 per cent. of any other powdered ingredient containing no controlled drug.

**9.** Any mixture containing one or more of the preparations specified in paragraphs 1 to 8, being a mixture of which none of the other ingredients is a controlled drug.

## SCHEDULE 2
(Regulations 7, 8, 10, 19, 21 and 24)

CONTROLLED DRUGS SUBJECT TO THE REQUIREMENTS OF REGULATIONS 14, 15, 16, 18, 19, 20, 21 AND 24

**1.** The following substances and products, namely:—

Acetorphine.
[Alfentanil][17].
Allylprodine.
Alphacetylmethadol.
Alphameprodine.
Alphamethadol.
Alphaprodine.
Anileridine.
Benzethidine.
Benzylmorphine (3-benzylmorphine).
Betacetylmethadol.
Betameprodine.
Betamethadol.
Betaprodine.
Bezitramide.
Clonitazene.
Cocaine.
Desomorphine.
Dextromoramide.
Diamorphine.

Diampromide.
Diethylthiambutene.
[Difenoxin (1-(3-cyano-3,3-diphenyl-propyl)-4-phenylpiperidine-4-carboxylic acid)][18].
Dihydrocodeinone *O*-carboxymethyloxime.
Dihydromorphine.
Dimenoxadole.
Dimepheptanol.
Dimethylthiambutene.
Dioxaphetyl butyrate.
Diphenoxylate.
Dipipanone.
Drotebanol (3,4-dimethoxy-17-methyl-morphinan-6$\beta$,14-diol).
Ecgonine, and any derivative of ecgonine which is convertible to ecgonine or to cocaine.
Ethylmethylthiambutene.

17  Added by S.I. 1984/1143
18  Added by S.I. 1975/499

Etonitazene.
Etorphine.
Etoxeridine.
Fentanyl.
Furethidine.
Hydrocodone.
Hydromorphinol.
Hydromorphone.
Hydroxypethidine.
Isomethadone.
Ketobemidone.
Levomethorphan.
Levomoramide.
Levophenacylmorphan.
Levorphanol.
Medicinal opium.
Metazocine.
Methadone.
Methadyl acetate.
Methyldesorphine.
Methyldihydromorphine.
 (6-methyldihydromorphine).
Metopon.
Morpheridine.
Morphine.
Morphine methobromide, morphine *N*-oxide and other pentavalent nitrogen morphine derivatives.
Myrophine.
Nicomorphine.
Noracymethadol.
Norlevorphanol.
Normethadone.

Normorphine.
Norpipanone.
Oxycodone.
Oxymorphone.
Pethidine.
Phenadoxone.
Phenampromide.
Phenazocine.
[Phencyclidine][19].
Phenomorphan.
Phenoperidine.
Piminodine.
Piritramide.
Proheptazine.
Properidine.
Racemethorphan.
Racemoramide.
Racemorphan.
[Sufentanil][20].
Thebacon.
Thebaine.
[Tilidate][20].
Trimeperidine.
4-Cyano-2-dimethylamino-4,
 4-diphenylbutane.
4-Cyano-1-methyl-4-phenylpiperidine.
1-Methyl-4-phenylpiperidine-4-carboxylic acid.
2-Methyl-3-morpholino-1,
 1-diphenylpropanecarboxylic acid.
4-Phenylpiperidine-4-carboxylic acid ethyl ester.

**2.** Any stereoisomeric form of a substance specified in paragraph 1 not being dextromethorphan or dextrorphan.

**3.** Any ester or ether of a substance specified in paragraph 1 or 2, not being a substance specified in paragraph 6.

**4.** Any salt of a substance specified in any of paragraphs 1 to 3.

**5.** Any preparation or other product containing a substance or product specified in any of paragraphs 1 to 4, not being a preparation specified in Schedule 1.

**6.** The following substances and products, namely:—

Acetyldihydrocodeine.
Amphetamine.

Codeine.
Dexamphetamine.

**19** Added by S.I. 1979/326
**20** Added by S.I. 1983/788

[Dextropropoxyphene][21]
Dihydrocodeine.
Ethylmorphine (3-ethylmorphine).
[Mecloqualone][22].
Methaqualone.
Methylamphetamine.
Methylphenidate.

Nicocodine
Nicodicodine.
  (6-nicotinoyldihydrocodeine).
Norcodeine.
Phenmetrazine.
Pholcodine.
Propiram.

**7.** Any stereoisomeric form of a substance specified in paragraph 6.

**8.** Any salt of a substance specified in paragraph 6 or 7.

**9.** Any preparation or other product containing a substance or product specified in any of paragraphs 6 to 8, not being a preparation specified in Schedule 1.

## SCHEDULE 3
(Regulations 7, 9 and 10)

CONTROLLED DRUGS SUBJECT TO THE REQUIREMENTS OF REGULATIONS 14, 15, 16 AND 18

**1.** The following substances, namely:—

(*a*) Benzphetamine.
  Chlorphentermine.
  [Diethylpropion][22]
  Mephentermine.

[Methylphenobarbitone][22]
Phendimetrazine.
Pipradrol.

[(*b*) Any 5,5 disubstituted barbituric acid.][22]

**2.** Any stereoisomeric form of a substance specified in paragraph 1.

**3.** Any salt of a substance specified in paragraph 1 or 2.

**4.** Any preparation or other product containing a substance specified in any of paragraphs 1 to 3, not being a preparation specified in Schedule 1.

## SCHEDULE 4[23]
(Regulations 19 and 24)

CONTROLLED DRUGS SUBJECT TO THE REQUIREMENTS OF REGULATIONS 14, 15, 16, 18, 19, 20 AND 24

**1.** The following substances and products, namely:—

  (*a*) Bufotenine
    Cannabinol

**21**  Added by S.I. 1983/788
**22**  Added by S.I. 1984/1143
**23**  Substituted by S.I. 1977/1380

Cannabinol derivatives
Cannabis and cannabis resin
Coca leaf
Concentrate of poppy-straw
[Eticyclidine] [24]
Lysergamide
Lysergide and other *N*-alkyl derivatives of lysergamide
Mescaline
Psilocin
Raw opium
[Rolicyclidine] [24]
[Tenocyclidine] [24]
4-Bromo-2,5-dimethoxy-α-methylphenethylamine
*N,N*-Diethyltryptamine
*N,N*-Dimethyltryptamine
2,5-Dimethoxy-α,4-dimethylphenethylamine

(*b*) any compound (not being a compound for the time being specified in sub-paragraph (*a*) above) structurally derived from tryptamine or from a ring-hydroxy tryptamine by substitution at the nitrogen atom of the sidechain with one or more alkyl substituents but no other substituent;

(*c*) any compound (not being methoxyphenamine or a compound for the time being specified in sub-paragraph (*a*) above) structurally derived from phenethylamine, an *N*-alkylphenethylamine, α-methylphenethylamine, an *N*-alkyl-α-methylphenethylamine, α-ethylphenethylamine, or an *N*-alkyl-α-ethylphenethylamine by substitution in the ring to any extent with alkyl, alkoxy, alkylenedioxy or halide substituents, whether or not further substituted in the ring by one or more other univalent substituents.

**2.** Any stereoisomeric form of a substance specified in paragraph 1.

**3.** Any ester or ether of a substance specified in paragraph 1 or 2.

**4.** Any salt of a substance specified in any of paragraphs 1 to 3.

**5.** Any preparation or other product containing a substance or product specified in any of paragraphs 1 to 4, not being a preparation specified in Schedule 1.

**24** Added by S.I. 1984/1143

SCHEDULE 5
(Regulation 19)

FORM OF REGISTER

## Part I

*Entries to be made in case of obtaining*

| Date on which supply received | NAME | ADDRESS | Amount obtained | Form in which obtained |
|---|---|---|---|---|
| | Of person or firm from whom obtained | | | |
| | | | | |

## Part II

*Entries to be made in case of supply*

| Date on which the transaction was effected | NAME | ADDRESS | Particulars as to licence or authority of person or firm supplied to be in possession | Amount supplied | Form in which supplied |
|---|---|---|---|---|---|
| | Of person or firm supplied | | | | |
| | | | | | |

APPENDIX V

# The Misuse of Drugs (Safe Custody) Regulations 1973

(S.I. No. 798)

| | |
|---|---|
| *Made -   -   -   -* | *19th April 1973* |
| *Laid before Parliament* | *7th May 1973* |
| *Coming into Operation—* | |
| *Regulations 1, 2, 5 and Schedule 1* | *1st July 1973* |
| *Remainder* | *[1st April 1975]*[1] |

**1.** These Regulations may be cited as the Misuse of Drugs (Safe Custody) Regulations 1973 and (with the exception of Regulations 3 and 4 and Schedule 2 which shall come into operation on [1st April 1975]) shall come into operation on 1st July 1973.

**2.**—(1) In these Regulations, unless the context otherwise requires, the expression—

"the Act" means the Misuse of Drugs Act 1971;

"retail dealer" means a person lawfully conducting a retail pharmacy business or a pharmacist engaged in supplying drugs to the public at a health centre within the meaning of the Medicines Act 1968.

(2) In these Regulations any reference to any enactment shall be construed as a reference to that enactment as amended, and as including a reference thereto as extended or applied, by or under any other enactment.

(3) The Interpretation Act 1889 shall apply for the interpretation of these Regulations as it applies for the interpretation of an Act of Parliament.

**3.**—(1) This Regulation applies to the following premises, that is to say:—

(*a*) any premises occupied by a retail dealer for the purposes of his business;

(*b*) any nursing home within the meaning of Part VI of the Public Health Act 1936 or the Nursing Homes Registration (Scotland) Act 1938;

(*c*) any residential or other establishment provided under or by virtue of section 59 of the Social Work (Scotland) Act 1968;

(*d*) any mental nursing home within the meaning of Part III of the Mental Health Act 1959;

(*e*) any private hospital within the meaning of the Mental Health (Scotland) Act 1960.

(2) Subject to paragraph (4) of this Regulation, the occupier and every person concerned in the management of any premises to which this Regulation applies

1   Amended by S.I. 1974/1449

shall ensure that all controlled drugs (other than those specified in Schedule 1 to these Regulations) on the premises are, so far as circumstances permit, kept in a locked safe, cabinet or room which is so constructed and maintained as to prevent unauthorised access to the drugs.

(3) Subject to Regulation 4 of these Regulations, the relevant requirements of Schedule 2 to these Regulations shall be complied with in relation to every safe, cabinet or room in which controlled drugs are kept in pursuance of paragraph (2) of this Regulation.

(4) It shall not be necessary to comply with the requirements of paragraph (2) of this Regulation in respect of any controlled drug which is for the time being under the direct personal supervision of—

(a) in the case of any premises falling within paragraph (1)(a) of this Regulation, a pharmacist in respect of whom no direction under section 12(2) of the Act is for the time being in force; or

(b) in the case of premises falling within paragraph (1)(b) to (e) of this Regulation, the person in charge of the premises or any member of his staff designated by him for the purpose.

**4.**—(1) Paragraph (3) of Regulation 3 of these Regulations shall not have effect in relation to a safe, cabinet or room situated on any premises occupied for the purposes of his business by a person lawfully conducting a retail pharmacy business (hereafter in this Regulation referred to as "the occupier") if a certificate has been issued in pursuance of paragraph (2) of this Regulation (hereafter in this Regulation referred to as a "certificate") in respect of that safe, cabinet or room and the certificate is for the time being in force.

(2) On receiving written application in that behalf from the occupier, the chief officer of police for the police area in which the premises in question are situated may—

(a) cause the said premises and, in particular, any safe, cabinet or room in which controlled drugs are to be kept, to be inspected; and

(b) if satisfied that, in all the circumstances of the case, the safes, cabinets or rooms in which controlled drugs (other than those specified in Schedule 1 to these Regulations) are to be kept provide an adequate degree of security, issue a certificate in respect of those safes, cabinets or rooms.

(3) Every certificate shall specify—

(a) every safe, cabinet or room to which the certificate relates; and

(b) any conditions necessary to be observed if the safes, cabinets and rooms to which the certificate relates are to provide an adequate degree of security.

(4) Where a certificate is in force in respect of any safe, cabinet or room on any premises, the chief officer of police may cause the premises to be inspected at any reasonable time for the purpose of ascertaining whether any conditions specified in the certificate are being observed and whether as a result of any change of circumstances the safes, cabinets and rooms to which the certificate relates have ceased to provide an adequate degree of security.

(5) A certificate may be cancelled by the chief officer of police if it appears to him that—

(a) there has been a breach of any condition specified ihn the certificate; or

(b) as a result of any change of circumstances, the safes, cabinets and rooms to which the certificate relates no longer provide an adequate degree of security; or

(c) the occupier has refused entry to any police officer acting in pursuance of paragraph (4) of this Regulation.

(6) A certificate shall, unless previously cancelled in pursuance of paragraph (5) of this Regulation, remain in force for a period of one year from the date of issue thereof, but may from time to time be renewed for a further period of one year.

**5.**—(1) Where any controlled drug (other than a drug specified in Schedule 1 to these Regulations) is kept otherwise than in a locked safe, cabinet or room which is so constructed and maintained as to prevent unauthorised access to the drug, any person to whom this Regulation applies having possession of the drug shall ensure that, so far as circumstances permit, it is kept in a locked receptacle which can be opened only by him or by a person authorised by him.

(2) Paragraph (1) of this Regulation applies to any person other than—
- (a) a person to whom the drug has been supplied by or on the prescription of a practitioner for his own treatment or that of another person or an animal; or
- (b) a person engaged in the business of a carrier when acting in the course of that business; or
- (c) a person engaged in the business of the Post Office when acting in the course of that business.

### SCHEDULE 1
(Regulations 3(2), 4(2)(b) and 5.)

#### EXEMPTED DRUGS

**1.** Any controlled drug specified in Schedule 1 to the Misuse of Drugs Regulations 1973.

**2.** Any liquid preparation designed for administration otherwise than by injection which contains any of the following substances and products, that is to say:—
- (a) Amphetamine; dexamphetamine; levamphetamine
- (b) Benzphetamine
- (c) Chlorphentermine
- (d) Mephentermine
- (e) Methaqualone
- (f) Methylamphetamine
- (g) Methylphenidate
- (h) Phendimetrazine
- (i) Phenmetrazine
- (j) Pipradrol
- (k) Any stereoisomeric form of a substance specified in any of paragraphs (b) to (j) above.
- (l) Any salt of a substance specified in any of paragraphs (a) to (k) above.

[**3.** Any of the following substances and products, that is to say:—
- (a) Any 5,5 disubstituted barbituric acid.
- (b) Methylphenobarbitone.

(c) Any stereoisomeric form of a substance specified in paragraph (a) or (b) above.

(d) Any salt of a substance specified in paragraph (a), (b) or (c) above.

(e) Any preparation which contains a substance specified in any of paragraphs (a) to (d) above.][2]

## SCHEDULE 2
### (Regulation 3(3).)

STRUCTURAL REQUIREMENTS IN RELATION TO SAFES, CABINETS AND ROOMS USED FOR KEEPING DRUGS

**1.** In this Schedule, the expression—

"external wall", in relation to any room, means a wall which forms part of the outside of the building in which the room is situated;

"party wall", in relation to any room, means a wall dividing the premises in which the room is situated from other premises under different occupation;

"the Standard of 1963", means the British Standard Specification for Thief Resistant Locks for Hinged Doors B.S. 3621: 1963, as published on 6th May 1963;

"two-leaf door", means a door having two leaves which either close on to each other or on to a central pillar, and the two leaves of any such door shall be treated for the purposes of this Schedule as a single door;

"sheet steel" means mild steel sheet being not lighter than 16 gauge.

*Safes and Cabinets*

**2.**—(1) A safe or cabinet shall be constructed of—

(a) pressed and welded sheet steel; or

(b) pressed and welded steel mesh; or

(c) sheet steel or steel mesh welded upon an angle-iron frame at least 25 millimetres (1 inch) by 25 millimetres (1 inch) section and of at least 5 millimetres ($\frac{3}{16}$ inch) thickness.

(2) The clearance between the door and jamb or, in the case of a two-leaf door, between the two leaves or each leaf and a central pillar shall not be greater than 3 millimetres ($\frac{1}{8}$ inch).

(3) Each door shall be fitted with an effective lock—

(a) having at least 5 differing levers or, in the case of a pin and tumbler mechanism, at least 6 pins;

(b) designed to permit at least 1000 effective key-differs independent of wards or any other fixed obstruction to the movement of the key; and

(c) provided with a dead-bolt which is either of mild steel of at least 19 millimetres ($\frac{3}{4}$ inch) by 8 millimetres ($\frac{5}{16}$ inch) section or incorporates a suitable anti-cutting device and which has a total throw of at least 12 millimetres ($\frac{1}{2}$ inch).

(4) If the length of the vertical closing edge of a door exceeds 914 millimetres (3 feet) and the length of the horizontal edge exceeds 457 millimetres (18 inches) the door shall be fitted with two such locks as are specified in sub-paragraph (3)

**2** Inserted by S.I. 1984/1146

MOD-T

above, one situated at not more than one third of the length of the vertical closing edge from the top and the other at not more than one third from the bottom, but otherwise the lock required by sub-paragraph (3) above shall be situated in the centre of the vertical closing edge.

(5) If a safe or cabinet is fitted with a two-leaf door, either—

(a) the lock or locks required by sub-paragraphs (3) and (4) above shall be fitted with an integrated espagnolette bolt which is of at least 19 millimetres ($\frac{3}{4}$ inch) by 8 millimetres ($\frac{5}{16}$ inch) section and which has a total throw, at both the top and bottom, of at least 12 millimetres ($\frac{1}{2}$ inch); or

(b) the second opening leaf shall be secured at the top and bottom by means of internal bolts of mild steel of at least 6 millimetres ($\frac{1}{4}$ inch) by 6 millimetres ($\frac{1}{4}$ inch) section or 6 millimetres ($\frac{1}{4}$ inch) diameter, each of which has a total throw of at least 12 millimetres ($\frac{1}{2}$ inch), the bolt handles being returnable into a holding recess.

(6) A safe or cabinet shall be rigidly and securely fixed to a wall or floor by means of at least two rag-bolts each passing through an internal anchor plate of mild steel which is of at least 3 millimetres ($\frac{1}{8}$ inch) thickness and which has a surface area of at least 19355 square millimetres (30 square inches).

(7) Nothing shall be displayed outside a safe or cabinet to indicate that drugs are kept inside it.

*Rooms*

**3.**—(1) Each wall shall be securely attached to the floor, ceiling and adjacent walls and shall be constructed of—

(a) bricks laid in cement mortar to at least 229 millimetres (9 inches) thickness or, if the joints are reinforced with metal reinforcing ties, to at least 115 millimetres ($4\frac{1}{2}$ inches) thickness; or

(b) concrete (being solid concrete, reinforced concrete or dense concrete blocks laid in cement mortar) of at least 152 millimetres (6 inches) thickness, the joints being reinforced with metal reinforcing ties where concrete blocks are used; or

(c) steel mesh fixed externally by welding upon angle-iron frames of at least 50 millimetres (2 inches) by 50 millimetres (2 inches) section and 6 millimetres ($\frac{1}{4}$ inch) thickness, having vertical members not more than 610 millimetres (2 feet) apart and horizontal members not more than 1220 millimetres (4 feet) apart; or

(d) sheet steel fixed externally by welding, or bolting with steel bolts of not less than 12 millimetres ($\frac{1}{2}$ inch) diameter and at intervals of not more than 305 millimetres (1 foot), upon either angle-iron frames as specified in (c) above or timber frames of at least 50 millimetres (2 inches) by 100 millimetres (4 inches) section, having vertical and horizontal members spaced as specified in (c) above.

(2) If a party wall or, in the case of a room of which the floor level is less than 2440 millimetres (8 feet) above the external ground level, an external wall is used to form one of the walls of the room, that wall shall be reinforced internally by means of an additional wall which is constructed in accordance with the requirements of sub-paragraph (1) above.

(3) The floor shall be—

(a) constructed of solid concrete or reinforced concrete; or (*b*) covered internally with sheet steel or steel mesh, welded at all joints; or

(*c*) otherwise so constructed that it cannot be readily penetrated from below.

(4) The ceiling shall be constructed of—

(*a*) solid concrete or reinforced concrete as specified in sub-paragraph (1)(*b*) above; or

(*b*) steel mesh fixed externally by welding upon angle-iron frames as specified in sub-paragraph 1(*c*) above, the members of which shall not be more than 610 millimetres (2 feet) apart in one direction or more than 1220 millimetres (4 feet) apart in the other; or

(*c*) sheet steel fixed externally by welding upon angle-iron frames as specified in sub-paragraph (1)(*c*) above, the members being spaced as specified in (*b*) above.

(5) Each door or, in the case of a stable-type door, each half-door shall be constructed of—

(*a*) steel mesh fixed externally by welding upon angle-iron frames as specified in sub-paragraph (1)(*c*) above; or

(*b*) sheet steel fixed externally by welding upon angle-iron frames as specified in sub-paragraph (1)(*c*) above, the members being spaced as specified therein; or

(*c*) sheet steel fixed externally upon a hardwood frame of at least 50 millimetres (2 inches) by 75 millimetres (3 inches) to stiles, rails and braces or muntins by means of coach bolts at intervals of not more than 305 millimetres (1 foot) (the nuts whereof being on the inside of the door) and with non-withdrawable screws between the bolts at intervals not exceeding 100 millimetres (4 inches), the members of the frame being spaced as specified in sub-paragraph (1)(*c*) above; or

(*d*) sheet steel fixed externally upon a solid timber core of at least 50 millimetres (2 inches) thickness.

(6) Each door or, in the case of a stable-type door, each half-door shall be fitted with an effective lock, being a single-sided dead lock having resistance to manipulation and forcing sufficient to comply with the requirements of the Standard of 1963.

(7) If the room is fitted with a two-leaf door, the second opening leaf shall be secured top and bottom by means of—

(*a*) an espagnolette bolt, operated only from within the room, with vertical fastening rods of mild steel of at least 16 millimetres ($\frac{5}{8}$ inch) by 16 millimetres ($\frac{5}{8}$ inch) section or 16 millimetres ($\frac{5}{8}$ inch) diameter; or

(*b*) at least two internal tower bolts of mild steel of at least 16 millimetres ($\frac{5}{8}$ inch) diameter, designed to swivel into a secure holding recess when in the thrown position,

and in either case the bolt shall have a total throw at least 25 millimetres (1 inch) greater than the clearance between the door and the floor or lintel, as the case may be, the lower shooting hole being kept at all times free from obstruction.

(8) The closing frame of each doorway shall be constructed of—

(*a*) an angle-iron frame as specified in sub-paragraph (1)(*c*) above; or

(*b*) hardwood of at least 50 millimetres (2 inches) by 100 millimetres (4 inches) section, covered by sheet steel bolted through the timber at intervals not exceeding 457 millimetres (18 inches) by means of coach bolts (the nuts whereof not being accessible from outside the room); or

(*c*) pressed steel not lighter than 10 gauge welded at all joints.

(9) Each section of the closing frame of each doorway shall be fixed to the

adjoining wall at intervals not exceeding 457 millimetres (18 inches) by means of—

   (a) where the wall is constructed of bricks, bent and tanged straps of wrought-iron, screwed or bolted to the frame and built into the brickwork;

   (b) where the wall is constructed of concrete, rag-bolts; or

   (c) where the wall is constructed of steel mesh or sheet steel, steel bolts or dowels of at least 12 millimetres ($\frac{1}{2}$ inch) diameter or welding to the framework or cladding of the room.

(10) Each glass window shall either be constructed of glass blocks not larger than 190 millimetres ($7\frac{1}{2}$ inches) by 190 millimetres ($7\frac{1}{2}$ inches) and of at least 80 millimetres ($3\frac{1}{8}$ inches) thickness, set in a reinforced concrete frame having a reinforcing bar between every block, or be guarded by a grille consisting of—

   (a) panels of steel mesh fixed on angle-iron frames as specified in subparagraph (1)(c) above and fixed—

      (i) where the surrounding wall or ceiling is constructed of sheet steel on angle-iron frames, by welding to the sheet steel or framework at intervals not exceeding 305 millimetres (1 foot); or

      (ii) where the surrounding wall is constructed of sheet steel on timber frames, by means of steel bolts of at least 12 millimetres ($\frac{1}{2}$ inch) diameter, bolted through the timber at intervals not exceeding 457 millimetres (18 inches); or

      (iii) where the surrounding wall is constructed of bricks, by means of bent and tanged straps of wrought-iron screwed or bolted to the frame and built into the brickwork at intervals not exceeding 457 millimetres (18 inches); or

      (iv) where the surrounding wall or ceiling is constructed of concrete, by means of rag-bolts at intervals not exceeding 457 millimetres (18 inches); or

   (b) vertical bars of solid mild steel of at least 25 millimetres (1 inch) by 25 millimetres (1 inch) square section, having one of their diagonal axes in a plane parallel to that of the window aperture, spaced not more than 127 millimetres (5 inches) apart centre to centre with the outer bars not more than 75 millimetres (3 inches) from the reveals of the window, and running through and welded to flat mild steel horizontal guard-bars which—

      (i) are of at least 62 millimetres ($2\frac{1}{2}$ inches) width and 9 millimetres ($\frac{3}{8}$ inch) thickness;

      (ii) are spaced not more than 762 millimetres ($2\frac{1}{2}$ feet) apart, the upper and lower guard-bars being at a distance not exceeding 100 millimetres (4 inches) from the ends of the vertical bars and not exceeding 75 millimetres (3 inches) from the head and sill of the window;

      (iii) are welded at each end to steel brackets of at least 152 millimetres (6 inches) length, 62 millimetres ($2\frac{1}{2}$ inches) width and 12 millimetres ($\frac{1}{2}$ inch) thickness fixed to the surrounding wall or ceiling, as the case may be, in the manner required by (a) above at a distance of at least 152 millimetres (6 inches) from the reveals of the window;

      (iv) if more than 1830 millimetres (6 feet) in length, have the uppermost and lowermost of them fixed to the head and sill of the window at intervals not exceeding 1830 millimetres (6 feet), by means of angle-iron fixings of at least 50 millimetres (2 inches) by 50 millimetres (2 inches) section and 6 millimetres ($\frac{1}{4}$ inch) thickness welded to the guard-bars and fixed to the surrounding wall or ceiling, as the case may be, in the manner required by (a) above.

(11) Each service-hatch shall be guarded by a grille consisting of—

(i) panels of steel mesh or sheet steel on angle-iron frames as specified in sub-paragraph (1)(c) above; or

(ii) vertical bars of solid mild steel as specified in sub-paragraph (10)(b)(i) and (ii) above,

and the grille shall be secured at all times when the hatch is not in use in such a way as to be secure against removal from outside the room.

(12) Each aperture other than a window or service-hatch shall be guarded by a grille which satisfies the requirements of sub-paragraph (10)(a) or (b) above.

(13) Each shelf in a room shall be so situated as to prevent drugs placed upon it from being extracted from outside through any aperture.

(14) Nothing shall be displayed outside a room to indicate that drugs are kept in the room.

### General

**4.**—(1) [Subject to sub-paragraph (1A) below][3] where sheet steel is used in the construction of a safe, cabinet or room, its edges shall be lapped inwards around the margins of apertures and around the edges of doors and service-hatch covers in such manner as to be inaccessible from the outside; and where sheet steel is fixed on a framework, it shall be so fixed as to prevent removal from outside the safe, cabinet or room of which the framework forms part.

[(1A) Where sheet steel is used in the construction of the door or the leaf of a door of a safe or cabinet, its edges need not be lapped inwards as required by sub-paragraph (1) above if the sheet steel used is not lighter than 10 gauge and the door or leaf of a door fits flush, or is recessed, so that no edge protrudes when the door is closed.][3]

(2) Any steel mesh used in the construction of a safe, cabinet or room shall be—

(a) welded steel mesh not lighter than 10 standard wire gauge having rectangular apertures not exceeding 75 millimetres (3 inches) by 12 millimetres ($\frac{1}{2}$ inch); or

(b) expanded steel not lighter than 12 gauge having diamond apertures not exceeding 44 millimetres ($1\frac{3}{4}$ inches) by 19 millimetres ($\frac{3}{4}$ inch).

(3) Except where otherwise specified in this Schedule, the edges of each panel of sheet steel or steel mesh used in the construction of a safe, cabinet or room shall be arc-welded to a steel frame along their entire length, or, in the absence of a steel frame, continuously arc-welded along the entire length of all joins.

(4) Each hinged door, half-door or leaf of a two-leaf door in a safe, cabinet or room shall be fitted with at least two hinges.

(5) If any part of the hinges of such a door, half-door or leaf of a two-leaf door is on the outside of the door, it shall be fitted—

(a) in the case of a safe or cabinet, with at least two dog-bolts of mild steel of similar gauge and dimensions to the frame of the safe or cabinet or an internal flange or rebate running the entire length of the door and so fitted as to prevent access without unlocking in the event of damage to the hinges;

**3** Inserted by S.I. 1975/294

(*b*) in the case of a room, with at least two dog-bolts of mild steel which—

   (i) are of similar gauge and dimensions to the jamb and either project at least 16 millimetres ($\frac{5}{8}$ inch) into the jamb or are attached to the jamb and project to a similar extent into the frame of the door, where the closing frame of the doorway is constructed of angle-iron; or

   (ii) are of at least 50 millimetres (2 inches) width and 6 millimetres ($\frac{1}{4}$ inch) thickness and either project at least 16 millimetres ($\frac{5}{8}$ inch) into the jamb or are attached to the jamb and project to a similar extent into the edge of the door, where the closing frame of the doorway is constructed of timber or pressed steel.

(6) Each bar, grille or service-hatch cover and each lock, bolt assembly and other means of securing doors and service-hatch covers in a safe, cabinet or room shall be fitted internally.

(7) The bolt of each lock and each other bolt or catch securing the cover of any aperture in a safe, cabinet or room shall be protected against cutting or manipulation from outside.

(8) Each screw, bolt or other fixing device used in the construction of a safe, cabinet or room shall be such as to be incapable of being removed from outside and shall be of a strength at least equal to that of the component part which it fixes.

# The Misuse of Drugs (Notification of and Supply to Addicts) Regulations 1973

(S.I. No. 799)

| | |
|---|---|
| *Made* - - - | *19th April 1973* |
| *Laid before Parliament* | *7th May 1973* |
| *Coming into Operation* | *1st July 1973* |

**1.** These Regulations may be cited as the Misuse of Drugs (Notification of and Supply to Addicts) Regulations 1973 and shall come into operation on 1st July 1973.

**2.**—(1) In these Regulations, the expression—
"drug" means a controlled drug specified in the Schedule to these Regulations;
"hospital"—

(a) as respects England and Wales, has the same meaning as in the National Health Service Act 1946 and includes a nursing home within the meaning of Part VI of the Public Health Act 1936, a mental nursing home within the meaning of Part III of the Mental Health Act 1959 and a special hospital within the meaning of that Act;

(b) as respects Scotland, has the same meaning as in the National Health Service (Scotland) Act 1947 and includes a nursing home within the meaning of the Nursing Homes Registration (Scotland) Act 1938, a private hospital within the meaning of the Mental Health (Scotland) Act 1960 and a state hospital within the meaning of that Act.

(2) For the purposes of these Regulations, a person shall be regarded as being addicted to a drug if, and only if, he has as a result of repeated administration become so dependent upon the drug that he has an overpowering desire for the administration of it to be continued.

(3) In these Regulations any reference to any enactment shall be construed as a reference to that enactment as amended, and as including a reference thereto as extended or applied, by or under any other enactment.

(4) The Interpretation Act 1889 shall apply for the interpretation of these Regulations as it applies for the interpretation of an Act of Parliament.

**3.**—(1) Subject to paragraph (2) of this Regulation, any doctor who attends a person who he considers, or has reasonable grounds to suspect, is addicted to any drug shall, within seven days of the attendance, furnish in writing to the Chief Medical Officer at the Home Office such of the following particulars with respect to that person as are known to the doctor, that is to say, the name, address, sex, date of birth and national health sevice number of that person, the date of the attendance and the name of the drug or drugs concerned.

(2) It shall not be necessary for a doctor who attends a person to comply with the provisions of paragraph (1) of this Regulation in respect of that person if—

(a) the doctor is of the opinion, formed in good faith, that the continued administration of the drug or drugs concerned is required for the purpose of treating organic disease of injury; or

(b) the particulars which, apart from this paragraph, would have been required under those provisions to be furnished have, during the period of twelve months ending with the date of the attendance, been furnished in compliance with those provisions—

  (i) by the doctor; or

  (ii) if the doctor is a partner in or employed by a firm of general practitioners, by a doctor who is a partner in or employed by that firm; or

  (iii) if the attendance is on behalf of another doctor, whether for payment or otherwise, by that doctor; or

  (iv) if the attendance is at a hospital, by a doctor on the staff of that hospital.

**4.**—(1) Subject to paragraph (2) of this Regulation, a doctor shall not administer or supply to a person who he considers, or has reasonable grounds to suspect, is addicted to any drug, or authorise the administration or supply to such a person of, any substance specified in paragraph (3) below, or prescribe for such a person any such substance, except—

(a) for the purpose of treating organic disease of injury; or

(b) under and in accordance with the terms of a licence issued by the Secretary of State in pursuance of these Regulations.

(2) Paragraph (1) of this Regulation shall not apply to the administration or supply by a doctor of a substance specified in paragraph (3) below if the administration or supply is authorised by another doctor under and in accordance with the terms of a licence issued to him in pursuance of these Regulations.

(3) The substances referred to in paragraphs (1) and (2) above are—

(a) cocaine, its salts and any preparation or other product containing cocaine or its salts other than a preparation falling within paragraph 2 of Schedule 1 to the Misuse of Drugs Regulations 1973;[1]

(b) diamorphine, its salts and any preparation or other product containing diamorphine or its salts.

[(c) dipipanone, its salts and any preparation or other product containing dipipanone or its salts.][2]

**5.** These Regulations and, in relation only to the requirements of these Regulations, sections 13(1) and (3), 14, 16, 19 and 25 of and Schedule 4 to the Misuse of Drugs Act 1971 (which relate to their enforcement) shall apply to servants and agents of the Crown.

**6.**—(1) The Dangerous Drugs (Notification of Addicts) Regulations 1968 and the Dangerous Drugs (Supply to Addicts) Regulations 1968 are hereby revoked.

[1]  S.I. no. 797 (see Appendix IV *ante*)
[2]  Added by S.I. 1983/1909

(2) For the purpose of paragraph 2(*b*) of Regulation 3 of these Regulations, any particulars furnished, before the coming into operation of these Regulations, in compliance with the provisions of paragraph (1) of Regulation 1 of the Dangerous Drugs (Notification of Addicts) Regulations 1968 shall be deemed to have been furnished in compliance with paragraph (1) of Regulation 3 of these Regulations.

(3) Notwithstanding anything in paragraph (1) of this Regulation, any licence issued by the Secretary of State in pursuance of the Dangerous Drugs (Supply to Addicts) Regulations 1968 before the coming into operation of these Regulations shall continue in force for the same time as if these Regulations had not been made and shall be deemed to have been issued in pursuance of these Regulations.

## SCHEDULE
### (Regulation 2(1).)

#### CONTROLLED DRUGS TO WHICH THESE REGULATIONS APPLY

1. The following substances and products, namely:—

| | | |
|---|---|---|
| Cocaine | Hydromorphone | Oxycodone |
| Dextromoramide | Levorphanol | Pethidine |
| Diamorphine | Methadone | Phenazocine |
| Dipipanone | Morphine | Piritramide |
| Hydrocodone | Opium | |

2. Any stereoisomeric form of a substance specified in paragraph 1 above, not being dextrorphan.

3. Any ester or ether of a substance specified in paragraph 1 or 2 above not being a substance for the time being specified in Part II of Schedule 2 to the Misuse of Drugs Act 1971.

4. Any salt of a substance specified in any of paragraphs 1 to 3 above.

5. Any preparation or other product containing a substance or product specified in any of paragraphs 1 to 4 above.

# The Misuse of Drugs (Designation) Order 1977

(S.I. No. 1379)

| | |
|---|---|
| *Made* - - - - | *8th August 1977* |
| *Laid before Parliament* | *16th August 1977* |
| *Coming into Operation—* | |
| *Articles 1 and 2* | *8th September 1977* |
| *Remainder* | *20th September 1977* |

**1.**—(1) This Order may be cited as the Misuse of Drugs (Designation) Order 1977, and (with the exception of Articles 3 and 4 and the Schedule which shall come into operation on 20th September 1977) shall come into operation on 8th September 1977.

(2) The Interpretation Act 1889 shall apply for the interpretation of this Order as it applies for the interpretation of an Act of Parliament, and as if any Orders revoked by this Order were Acts of Parliament repealed by an Act of Parliament.

**2.** . . . .

**3.**—(1) The controlled drugs specified in the Schedule hereto are hereby designated as drugs to which section 7(4) of the Misuse of Drugs Act 1971 applies.

(2) In that Schedule, "cannabis" has the same meaning as in the Misuse of Drugs Act 1971 as amended by section 52 of the Criminal Law Act 1977.

**4.** The Misuse of Drugs (Designation) Order 1973 and the Misuse of Drugs (Designation)(Amendment) Order 1975 are hereby revoked.

SCHEDULE
(Article 3.)

CONTROLLED DRUGS TO WHICH SECTION 7(4) OF THE MISUSE OF DRUGS ACT 1971 APPLIES

1.The following substances and products, namely:—

(a) Bufotenine
Cannabinol
Cannabinol derivatives
Cannabis
Cannabis resin
Coca leaf
Concentrate of poppy-straw
[Eticyclidine][1]
Lysergamide
Lysergide and other $N$-alkyl derivatives of lysergamide
Mescaline
Psilocin
Raw opium
[Rolicyclidine][1]
4-Bromo-2,5-dimethoxy-$\alpha$-methylphenethylamine
$N,N$-Diethyltryptamine
$N,N$-Dimethyltryptamine
2,5-Dimethoxy-$\alpha$,4-dimethylphenethylamine

1 Added by S.I. 1984/1144

(b) any compound (not being a compound for the time being specified in sub-paragraph (a) above) structurally derived from tryptamine or from a ring-hydroxy tryptamine by substitution at the nitrogen atom of the sidechain with one or more alkyl substituents but no other substituent;

(c) any compound (not being methoxyphenamine or a compound for the time being specified in sub-paragraph (a) above) structurally derived from phenethylamine, an N-alkylphenethylamine, α-methylphenethylamine, an N-alkyl-α-methylphenethylamine, α-ethylphenethylamine, or an N-alkyl-α-ethylphenethylamine by substitution in the ring to any extent with alkyl, alkoxy, alkylenedioxy or halide substituents, whether or not further substituted in the ring by one or more other univalent substituents.

2. Any stereoisomeric form of a substance specified in paragraph 1 above.

3. Any ester or ether of a substance specified in paragraph 1 or 2 above.

4. Any salt of a substance specified in any of paragraphs 1 to 3 above.

5. Any preparation or other product containing a substance or product specified in any of paragraphs 1 to 4 above.

# The Misuse of Drugs Tribunal (England and Wales) Rules 1974

(S.I. No. 85 (L.1))

| | |
|---|---|
| *Made* - - - | *22nd January 1974* |
| *Laid before Parliament* | *7th February 1974* |
| *Coming into Operation* | *1st March 1974* |

*Citation and commencement*

**1.** These Rules may be cited as the Misuse of Drugs Tribunal (England and Wales) Rules 1974 and shall come into operation on 1st March 1974.

*Interpretation*

**2.**—(1) In these Rules, unless the context otherwise requires—

"the Act" means the Misuse of Drugs Act 1971;

"the chairman" means the person appointed by the Lord Chancellor to be the chairman of the tribunal;

"hearing" means the hearing by the tribunal of a case referred to it under section 14 of this Act;

"the respondent" has the same meaning as in section 14(2) of the Act;

"the secretary" means, in relation to any proceedings, the person whose services are made available by the Secretary of State to act as secretary to the tribunal either generally or in relation to those proceedings;

"the solicitor" means, in relation to any proceedings, the solicitor nominated for the purposes of these Rules by the Secretary of State either generally or in relation to those proceedings;

"the tribunal" means a tribunal in England and Wales constituted under Part I of Schedule 3 to the Act.

(2) In these Rules a form referred to by number means the form so numbered in the Appendix to these Rules, or a form substantially to the like effect, with such variations as the circumstances of the particular case require.

(3) The Interpretation Act 1889 shall apply to the interpretation of these Rules as it applies to the interpretation of an Act of Parliament.

*Terms of reference and parties*

**3.**—(1) As soon as the Secretary of State has referred a case to the tribunal under section 14(1) of the Act, he shall serve on the solicitor and on the respondent a notice in writing specifying the terms of the reference, and the names and addresses of the secretary and of the solicitor.

(2) The solicitor shall thereafter be responsible for the preparation and presentation before the tribunal of the case against the respondent and shall be a party to the proceedings on the reference.

(3) No person other than the solicitor and the respondent shall be a party to the proceedings on the reference.

*Notice of proceedings*

**4.**—(1) Within twenty-eight days after service on him of the notice of the terms of reference the solicitor shall serve on the respondent a notice of proceedings in Form 1, together with a copy of the Act and of these Rules (and of any instrument amending these Rules) and shall send a copy of the notice of proceedings to the tribunal.

(2) The notice of proceedings may be amended—

(a) before the hearing, with the leave of the chairman on an *ex parte* application (which may be disposed of if the chairman thinks fit without a hearing of the application), or

(b) at any time during the hearing, with the leave of the tribunal,

and where the notice of proceedings is amended before the hearing, the solicitor shall forthwith serve notice in writing of the amendment on the respondent and send a copy of the notice to the tribunal.

*Notice of hearing*

**5.** The chairman shall fix a date, time and place at which the proceedings are to be held, and, not less than twenty-eight days before the date so fixed, the secretary shall serve a notice in Form 2 on the solicitor and on the respondent.

*Inspection of documents*

**6.**—(1) The solicitor shall within fourteen days after the issue of the notice of proceedings and the respondent may at any time serve on the other party a list of the documents on which he proposes to rely, and the solicitor and the respondent shall send to the tribunal a copy of any list served under this paragraph.

(2) A list under paragraph (1) shall specify a reasonable period (commencing not earlier than seven days and ending not later than fourteen days after the date of the list) during which, and a reasonable place at which, the other party may inspect and take copies of the documents contained in the list.

(3) A party shall be entitled to inspect and take copies of any document set out in the list of documents served by the other party during the period and at the place specified by such other party in his list of documents or during such period and at such place as the tribunal may direct.

(4) Unless the tribunal otherwise directs, a party shall produce any document set out in his list of documents at the hearing of the case when called upon to do so by the other party.

*Interlocutory applications*

**7.**—(1) An application for directions of an interlocutory nature in connection with the proceedings may be made by the solicitor or the respondent to the chairman.

(2) The application shall be in writing and shall state the matters on which directions are sought and the grounds upon which the application is made.

(3) Notice of the application shall be served on the respondent or on the solicitor, as the case may be, who may send to the chairman and serve on the other party written notice of objection.

(4) Where written notice of objection is sent the chairman shall, before giving any direction on the application, consider such objection and, if he considers it necessary for the proper determination of the application, shall give the parties an opportunity of appearing before him.

(5) The chairman shall serve notice in writing of his decision on the solicitor and on the respondent.

(6) If at any stage the chairman decides that an application involves a question which ought to be decided by the tribunal, he shall fix a date, time and place for a hearing of the application by the tribunal and the secretary shall serve notice thereof on the solicitor and on the respondent not less than fourteen days before the date fixed.

*Right of audience*

**8.** At the hearing and at the hearing of an application under rule 7 the parties shall be entitled to appear and be heard either in person or by counsel or a solicitor.

*Default of appearance*

**9.**—(1) Where, on the date fixed for the hearing, the solicitor does not appear, then, whether or not the respondent appears, the tribunal shall adjourn the proceedings on such terms (if any) as it thinks fit.

(2) Where, on the date fixed for the hearing, the respondent does not appear, it shall be the duty of the solicitor to satisfy the tribunal that the notice of proceedings and the notice of hearing have been served on the respondent in accordance with rule 18 and, if so satisfied, the tribunal may proceed, it it thinks fit, in the absence of the respondent.

(3) Where, on the date fixed for the hearing of any application under rule 7, the solicitor or the respondent does, or both of them do, not appear, the tribunal may make such order as it thinks fit.

*Procedure at hearing*

**10.**—(1) Where the respondent appears at the hearing the following order of proceedings shall, unless the tribunal otherwise directs, be observed, that is to say—

  (a) the solicitor shall read out the allegations in the notice of proceedings;
  (b) the chairman shall ask the respondent whether he admits each such allegation, and if the respondent admits any allegation there shall be recorded a finding that there has been such a contravention or such conduct as is alleged therein;
  (c) in respect of any allegation which is not admitted the chairman may ask the respondent whether he is willing to admit any of the facts stated in the allegation;
  (d) the solicitor may, in relation to any allegation which is not admitted, address the tribunal and adduce evidence in respect of any fact which has not been admitted;
  (e) the respondent may address the tribunal and adduce evidence in relation to any allegation still undisposed of;
  (f) on the application of either party the tribunal may then allow evidence in reply or rebuttal if it considers it to be in the interests of the fair disposal of any such allegation to do so;
  (g) the solicitor may then address the tribunal;
  (h) the respondent may then address the tribunal.

(2) Where the respondent does not appear at the hearing and the tribunal proceeds in his absence, the solicitor may address the tribunal both before and after he has adduced evidence.

*Evidence*
**11.**—(1) Any witness called by a party to the proceedings shall be liable to cross-examination by the other party and, if cross-examined, to re-examination by the party calling him.

(2) The tribunal may accept without proof any matter admitted by a party to the proceedings.

(3) Where any document is put in evidence at the hearing it shall not be necessary to prove its authenticity unless the tribunal otherwise directs.

(4) The tribunal shall not be bound to reject evidence on the ground only that it would be inadmissible in a court of law.

*Findings of tribunal*
**12.** In respect of each allegation, other than one in respect of which a finding has been recorded under rule 10(1)(*b*), the tribunal shall make and record a finding either—
    (*a*) that there has been such a contravention or such conduct as is alleged; or
    (*b*) that there has been no such contravention or conduct.

*Submissions and evidence with reference to recommendation*
**13.** Where there has been recorded any such finding as is mentioned in rule 10(1)(*b*) or 12(*a*) the solicitor and, if he appears, the respondent may address the tribunal and adduce evidence with reference to the recommendation to be made in respect of the respondent.

*Majority decision, etc.*
**14.** In the event of disagreement between the members of the tribunal any decision of the tribunal may be taken by a majority thereof and, if the members are equally divided, the chairman shall have a second and casting vote.

*Report of tribunal*
**15.**—(1) At the conclusion of the hearing the tribunal may adjourn in order to consider its report to the Secretary of State.

(2) The report shall contain a statement—
    (*a*) of the findings of the tribunal;
    (*b*) of the reasons for the findings;
    (*c*) (in the event of a finding under rule 10(1)(*b*) or 12(*a*)—
        (i) of the recommendation of the tribunal, or, as the case may be, of the fact that the tribunal considers that a direction should not be given, and
        (ii) of the reasons for the recommendation, or, as the case may be, for so considering; and
    (*d*) (in the event of a disagreement between the members of the tribunal) of the names of the majority and of the minority, and of the latter's reasons, so far as at variance with those of the majority, on—
        (i) the findings, or, as the case may be,
        (ii) the question whether a recommendation should be made, or
        (iii) the terms of any recommendation.

(3) The chairman shall sign the report on behalf of the tribunal and the secretary shall serve a copy of the report on the solicitor and on the respondent.

(4) Where the hearing has taken place in private the tribunal shall ensure that

the report does not disclose the identity of any person, other than the respondent, about whom an adverse finding of fact has been made, or of any person referred to in the report as being addicted to or having taken controlled drugs of any description.

*Reference back to or to another tribunal*

**16.**—(1) When the Secretary of State has referred a case to the tribunal under section 14(7)(*b*) of the Act he shall serve on the solicitor and on the respondent notice in writing of the terms of the reference under that paragraph, and, subject to paragraph (2) of this rule, the provisions of these Rules shall apply to the proceedings on that reference as they apply to proceedings on a reference under section 14(1) of the Act.

(2) Where the notice of proceedings served under paragraph (1) is the same, or substantially the same, as that on the previous reference under section 14(1) or, as the case may be, under section 14(7)(*b*) of the Act (in this paragraph alike referred to as the "previous reference") an order may be made on an application under rule 7 that the list or lists of documents supplied under rule 6 and any order made under rule 7 or under this paragraph for the purposes of the previous reference shall be deemed to have been supplied or made in the proceedings on the reference (or latest reference) under section 14(7)(*b*) of the Act.

*Application for consent of tribunal under section* 15(6) *of the Act*

**17.**—(1) An application by the Secretary of State for the consent of the tribunal under section 15(6) of the Act to the extension of a direction may be made by sending to the chairman a notice of application in writing, together with a copy of the report of the professional panel, and an application for consent under that subsection to a further extension may be made by sending to him a notice of application in writing.

(2) The Secretary of State shall serve a copy of the notice of application, and, as the case may be, of the report, on the respondent and shall at the same time inform the respondent that he may, within five days of service upon him, send to the chairman written representations relating to the proposed extension or further extension.

(3) On the expiration of the time limit for the sending of representations the chairman shall consider the application and any representations and may give or withhold the consent of the tribunal.

(4) The secretary shall as soon as may be inform the Secretary of State and serve notice on the respondent of the consent or of the withholding of the consent of the tribunal.

*Service of notice*

**18.**—(1) Any notice or document required to be served on the respondent under these Rules shall be deemed to have been duly served if it is sent or given to a solicitor acting on behalf of the respondent or is delivered to the respondent personally or left at his proper address or sent to him there—

    (*a*) in the case of notices under rules 3, 4 and 5, by registered post or by recorded delivery service, or

    (*b*) in any other case, by post.

(2) Any notice or document required to be served on the solicitor may be sent to the address for service specified in the notice of the terms of reference.

(3) Any notice or document to be sent to the tribunal or to the chairman may be sent to the address of the secretary specified in the notice of the terms of reference.

(4) In this rule "proper address" means the address of the respondent for the time being registered in the Register kept by the relevant body within the meaning of paragraph 1 of Schedule 3 to the Act, and where, in the opinion of the person serving the document or notice, a letter addressed to the respondent at that address appears unlikely to reach him, the last-known residential or professional address of the respondent, or any other address at or through which he may be found.

*Extension of time*

**19.** The time appointed by or under these Rules for doing any act or taking any step in connection with any proceedings may be extended by the chairman, whether or not the period has expired, on such terms and conditions, if any, as appear to him just.

*Failure to comply with rules*

**20.** Any failure on the part of any person to comply with the provisions of these Rules shall not render the proceedings, or anything done in pursuance thereof, invalid unless the chairman or the tribunal so directs, but the chairman or the tribunal may give such directions for the purpose of mitigating the consequences of the irregularity as the justice of the case may require.

*Power to regulate procedure*

**21.** Subject to the provisions of the Act and of these Rules the tribunal shall have power to regulate its own procedure, and may adjourn or postpone the proceedings as it thinks fit.

## APPENDIX
### (Rule 4)

### Form 1
### MISUSE OF DRUGS TRIBUNAL
### (England and Wales)

In the matter of ..........................................................[(a doctor)][(a)] [(a practitioner)][(a)].

(a) Delete whichever is inapplicable.

### NOTICE OF PROCEEDINGS

To.....................................................

of ...................................................[*address*]

WHEREAS the Secretary of State considers that there are grounds for giving a direction under section 13[(1)][(a)] [(2)][(a)] of the Misuse of Drugs Act 1971 (hereinafter called "the Act") on account of [an alleged contravention by a doctor][(a)] [alleged conduct by a practitioner][(a)] as is there mentioned.

AND WHEREAS he has referred the case to a tribunal constituted in accordance with the Act and has given notice in writing of the terms of reference to you as the respondent [doctor][a] [practitioner][a] and to me as the person nominated by him to act as solicitor.

NOW I.............................................

of...........................................

...............................................

do hereby give notice that the tribunal is to consider the case on a date to be notified in due course by the tribunal and will inquire in particular into the following [allegation][a] [allegations][a] against you:—

(1) [*If the allegation relates to contravention*] That you did on the day of                          contravene [the provisions of regulation                          of the                          Regulations 19          )][a] [the terms of a licence issued to you [*or as appropriate*] on                          ][a] in that you [*here specify the contravention alleged*].

*Or*

(2) [*if the allegation relates to conduct*] That you are/have been

<table>
<tr><td>(b) Delete any not relied on.</td><td>prescribing[b]<br>administering [b]<br>supplying[b]<br>authorising the administration of [b]<br>authorising the supply of[b]</td><td>}</td><td>controlled drugs in an irresponsible manner</td></tr>
</table>

in that you [*here specify the conduct alleged*]

[*Where there is more than one allegation, the allegations, should be numbered consecutively but each allegation may contain more than one alleged act if appropriate*]

(c) Delete as long as inapplicable.
A copy of the Act and of the Misuse of Drugs Tribunal (England and Wales) Rules 1974 [and of the instrument[s][c] amending those rules][c] are enclosed for your information.

Dated this                          day of                          19     .

*Signed* ...............................................

Solicitor

(Rule 5)

Form 2

MISUSE OF DRUGS TRIBUNAL
(England and Wales)

## NOTICE OF HEARING

In the matter of..................................................................[(a doctor)]<sup>(a)</sup>
[(a practitioner)]<sup>(a)</sup>

(a) Delete
whichever
is inapplic-
able.

    To................................................(the solicitor)

       of................................................

  and to

       ..............................................(the respondent)

       of................................................

TAKE NOTICE that the tribunal will consider the case referred to it
concerning the respondent on      -      the
day of                  at        a.m./p.m. at [*address*].

                Signed................................................
                          Secretary.

# Police and Criminal Evidence Act 1984

(CHAPTER 60)

## ARRANGEMENT OF SECTIONS PRINTED

**Part XI: Miscellaneous and Supplementary**

114. Application of Act to Customs and Excise.
116. Meaning of "serious arrestable offence".
118. General interpretation.

**Schedules:**

Schedule 1—Special procedure.


# Part I

## Powers to Stop and Search

*Power of constable to stop and search persons, vehicles etc.*
**1.**—(1) A constable may exercise any power conferred by this section—
    (*a*) in any place to which at the time when he proposes to exercise the power the public or any section of the public has access, on payment or otherwise, as of right or by virute of express or implied permission; or
    (*b*) in any other place to which people have ready access at the time when he proposes to exercise the power but which is not a dwelling.
  (2) Subject to subsection (3) to (5) below, a constable—
    (*a*) may search—
      (i) any person or vehicle;
      (ii) anything which is in or on a vehicle, for stolen or prohibited articles; and
    (*b*) may detain a person or vehicle for the purpose of such a search.
  (3) This section does not give a constable power to search a person or vehicle or anything in or on a vehicle unless he has reasonable grounds for suspecting that he will find stolen or prohibited articles.
  (4) If a person is in a garden or yard occupied with and used for the purposes of a dwelling or on other land so occupied and used, a constable may not search him in the exercise of the power conferred by this section unless the constable has reasonable grounds for believing—
    (*a*) that he does not reside in the dwelling; and
    (*b*) that he is not in the place in question with the express or implied permission of a person who resides in the dwelling.
  (5) If a vehicle is in a garden or yard occupied with and used for the purposes of a dwelling or on other land so occupied and used, a constable may not search the vehicle or anything in or on it in the exercise of the power conferred by this section unless he has reasonable grounds for believing—
    (*a*) that the person in charge of the vehicle does not reside in the dwelling; and
    (*b*) that the vehicle is not in the place in question with the express or implied permission of a person who resides in the dwelling.
  (6) If in the course of such a search a constable discovers an article which he has reasonable grounds for suspecting to be a stolen or prohibited article, he may seize it.

(7) An article is prohibited for the purposes of this Part of this Act if it is—
  (*a*) an offensive weapon; or
  (*b*) an article—
      (i) made or adapted for use in the course of or in connection with an offence to which this sub-paragraph applies; or
      (ii) intended by the person having it with him for such use by him or by some other person.
(8) The offences to which subsection (7)(*b*)(i) above applies are—
  (*a*) burglary;
  (*b*) theft;
  (*c*) offences under section 12 of thc Theft Act 1968 (taking motor vehicle or other conveyance without authority); and
  (*d*) offences under section 15 of that Act (obtaining property by deception).
(9) In this Part of this Act "offensive weapon" means any article—
  (*a*) made or adapted for use for causing injury to persons; or
  (*b*) intended by the person having it with him for such use by him or by some other person.

*Provisions relating to search under section 1 and other powers.*
  **2.**—(1) A constable who detains a person or vehicle in the exercise—
  (*a*) of the power conferred by section 1 above; or
  (*b*) of any other power—
      (i) to search a person without first arresting him; or
      (ii) to search a vehicle without making an arrest,
need not conduct a search if it appears to him subsequently—
      (i) that no search is required; or
      (ii) that a search is impracticable.
  (2) If a constable contemplates a search, other than a search of an uattended vehicle, in the exercise—
  (*a*) of the power conferred by section 1 above; or
  (*b*) of any other power, except the power conferred by section 6 below and the power conferred by section 27(2) of the Aviation Security Act 1982—
      (i) to search a person without first arresting him; or
      (ii) to search a vehicle without making an arrest,
it shall be his duty, subject to subsection (4) below, to take reasonable steps before he commences the search to bring to the attention of the appropriate person—
      (i) if the constable is not in uniform, documentary evidence that he is a constable; and
      (ii) whether he is in uniform or not, the matters specified in subsection (3) below;
and the constable shall not commence the search until he has performed that duty.
  (3) The matters referred to in subsection (2)(ii) above are—
  (*a*) the constable's name and the name of the police station to which he is attached;
  (*b*) the object of the proposed search;
  (*c*) the constable's grounds for proposing to make it; and
  (*d*) the effect of section 3(7) or (8) below, as may be appropriate.
  (4) A constable need not bring the effect of section 3(7) or (8) below to the attention of the appropriate person if it appears to the constable that it will not be practicable to make the record in section 3(1) below.

(5) In this section "the appropriate person" means—
  (a) if the constable proposes to search a person, that person; and
  (b) if he proposes to search a vehicle, or anything in or on a vehicle, the person in charge of the vehicle.

(6) On completing a search of an unattended vehicle or anything in or on such a vehicle in the exercise of any power as is mentioned in subsection (2) above a constable shall leave a notice—
  (a) stating that he has searched it;
  (b) giving the name of the police station to which he is attached;
  (c) stating that an application for compensation for any damage caused by the search may be made to that police station; and
  (d) stating the effect of section 3(8) below.

(7) The constable shall leave the notice inside the vehicle unless it is not reasonably practicable to do so without damaging the vehicle.

(8) The time for which a person or vehicle may be detained for the purposes of such a search is such time as is reasonably required to permit a search to be carried out either at the place where the person or vehicle was first detained or nearby.

(9) Neither the power conferred by section 1 above nor any other power to detain and search a person without first arresting him or to detain and search a vehicle without making an arrest is to be construed—
  (a) as authorising a constable to require a person to remove any of his clothing in public other than an outer coat, jacket or gloves; or
  (b) as authorising a constable not in uniform to stop a vehicle.

(10) This section and section 1 above apply to vessels, aircraft and hovercraft as they apply to vehicles.

*Duty to make records concerning searches.*
  **3.**—(1) Where a constable has carried out a search in the exercise of any such power as is mentioned in section 2(1) above, other than a search—
  (a) under section 6 below; or
  (b) under section 27(2) of the Aviation Security Act 1982, he shall make a record of it in writing unless it is not practicable to do so.

(2) If—
  (a) a constable is required by subsection (1) above to make a recored of a search; but
  (b) it is not practicable to make the record on the spot,
he shall make it as soon as practicable after the completion of the search.

(3) The record of a search of a person shall include a note of his name, if the constable knows it, but a constable may not detain a person to find out his name.

(4) If a constable does not know the name of a person whom he has searched, the record of the search shall include a note otherwise describing that person.

(5) The record of a search of a vehicle shall include a note describing the vehicle.

(6) The record of a search of a person or a vehicle—
  (a) shall state—
    (i) the object of the search;
    (ii) the grounds for making it;
    (iii) the date and time when it was made;
    (iv) the place where it was made;
    (v) whether anything, and if so what, was found;

(vi) whether any, and if so what, injury to a person or damage to property appears to the constable to have resulted from the search; and

(b) shall identify the constable making it.

(7) if a constable who conducted a search of a person made a record of it, the person who was searched shall be entitled to a copy of the record if he asks for one before the end of the period specified in subsection (9) below.

(8) If—

(a) the owner of a vehicle which has been searched or the person who was in charge of the vehicle at the time when it was searched asks for a copy of the record of the search before the end of the period specified in subsection (9) below; and

(b) the constable who conducted the search made a record of it,

the person who made the request shall be entitled to a copy.

(9) The period mentioned in subsections (7) and (8) above is the period of 12 months beginning with the date on which the search was made.

(10) The requirements imposed by this section with regard to records of searches of vehicles shall apply also to records of searches of vessels, aircraft and hovercraft.

## Part II

### Powers of Entry, Search and Seizure

### Search Warrants

*Power of justice of the peace to authorise entry and search of premises.*

**8.**—(1) If on an application made by a constable a justice of the peace is satisfied that there are reasonable grounds for believing—

(a) that a serious arrestable offence has been committed; and

(b) that there is material on premises specified in the application which is likely to be of substantial value (whether by itself or together with other material) to the investigation of the offence; and

(c) that the material is likely to be relevant evidence; and

(d) that it does not consist of or include items subject to legal privilege, excluded material or special procedure material; and

(e) that any of the conditions specified in subsection (3) below applies,

he may issue a warrant authorising a constable to enter and search the premises.

(2) A constable may seize and retain anything for which a search has been authorised under subsection (1) above.

(3) The condition mentioned in subsection (1)(e) above are—

(a) that is is not practicable to communicate with any person entitled to grant entry to the premises;

(b) that it is practicable to communicate with a person entitled to grant entry to the premises but it is not practicable to communicate with any person entitled to grant access to the evidence;

(c) that entry to the premises will not be granted unless a warrant is produced;

(d) that the purpose of a search may be frustrated or seriously prejudiced unless a constable arriving at the premises can secure immediate entry to them.

(4) In this Act "relevant evidence", in relation to an offence, means anything that would be admissible in evidence at a trial of the offence.

(5) The power to issue a warrant conferred by this section is in addition to any such power otherwise conferred.

*Special provisions as to access.*

**9.**—(1) A constable may obtain access to excluded material or special procedure material for the purposes of a criminal investigation by making an application under Schedule 1 below and in accordance with that Schedule.

(2) Any Act (including a local Act) passed before this Act under which a search of premises for the purposes of a criminal investigation could be authorised by the issue of a warrant to a constable shall cease to have effect so far as it relates to the authorisation of searches—

    (a) for items subject ot legal privilege; or

    (b) for excluded material; or

    (c) for special procedure material consisting of documents or records other than documents.

*Meaning of "items subject to legal privilege".*

**10.**—(1) Subject to subsection (2) below, in this Act "items subject to legal privilege" means—

    (a) communications between a professional legal adviser and his client or any person representing his client made in connection with the giving of legal advice to the client;

    (b) communications between a professional legal adviser and his client or any person representing his client or between such an adviser or his client or any such representative and any other person made in connection with or in contemplation of legal proceedings and for the purposes of such proceedings; and

    (c) items enclosed with or referred to in such communications and made—

        (i) in connection with the giving of legal advice; or

        (ii) in connection with or in contemplation of legal proceedings and for the purposes of such proceedings,

when they are in the possession of a person who is entitled to possession of them.

(2) Items held with the intention of furthering a criminal purpose are not items subject to legal privilege.

*Meaning of "excluded material".*

**11.**—(1) Subject to the following provisions of this section, in this Act "excluded material" means—

    (a) personal records which a person has acquired or created in the course of any trade, business, profession or other occupation or for the purposes of any paid or unpaid office and which he holds in confidence;

    (b) human tissue or tissue fluid which has been taken for the purposes of diagnosis or medical treatment and which a person holds in confidence;

    (c) journalistic material which a person holds in confidence and which consists—

        (i) of documents; or

        (ii) of records other than documents.

(2) A person holds material other than journalistic material in confidence for the purposes of this section if he holds it subject—

(*a*) to an express or implied undertaking to hold it in confidence; or

(*b*) to a restriction on disclosure or an obligation of secrecy contained in any enactment, including an enactment contained in an Act passed after this Act.

(3) A person holds journalistic material in confidence for the purposes of this section if—

(*a*) he holds it subject to such an undertaking, restriction or obligation; and

(*b*) it has been continuously held (by one or more persons) subject to such an undertaking, restiction or obligation since it was first acquired or created for the purposes of journalism.

*Meaning of "personal records".*

**12.** In this Part of this Act "personal records" means documentary and other records concerning an individual (whether living or dead) who can be identified from them and relating—

(*a*) to his physical or mental health;

(*b*) to spiritual counselling or assistance given or to be given to him; or

(*c*) to counselling or assistance given or to be given to him, for the purposes of his personal welfare, by any voluntary organisation or by an individual who—

(i) by reason of his office or occupation has responsibilities for his personal welfare; or

(ii) by reason of an order of a court has responsibilities for his supervision.

*Meaning of "Journalistic material".*

**13.**—(1) Subject to subsection (2) below, in this Act "journalistic material" means material acquired or created for the purposes of journalism.

(2) Material is only journalistic material for the purposes of this Act if it is in the possession of a person who acquired or created it for the purposes of journalism.

(3) A person who receives material from someone who intends that the recipient shall use if for the purposes of journalism is to be taken to have acquired it for those purposes.

*Meaning of "special procedure material".*

**14.**—(1) In this Act "special procedure material" means—

(*a*) material to which subsection (2) below applies; and

(*b*) journalistic material, other than excluded material.

(2) Subject to the following provisions of this section, this subsection applies to material, other than items subject to legal privilege and excluded material, in the possession of a person who—

(*a*) acquired or created it in the course of any trade, business, profession or other occupation or for the purpose of any paid or unpaid office; and

(*b*) holds it subject—

(i) to an express or implied undertaking to hold it in confidence; or

(ii) to a restriction or obligation such as is mentioned in section 11(2)(*b*) above.

(3) Where material is acquired—

(*a*) by an employee from his employer and in the course of his employment; or (*b*) by a company from an assoicated company,

it is only special procedure material if it was special procedure material immediately before the acquisition.

(4) Where material is created by an employee in the course of his employment, it is only special procedure material if it would have been special procedure material had his employer created it.

(5) Where material is created by a company on behalf of an assoicated company, it is only special procedure material if it would have been special procedure material had the associated company created it.

(6) A company is to be treated as another's associated company for the purposes of this section if it would be so treated under section 302 of the Income and Corporation Taxes Act 1970.

*Search warrants—safeguards.*

**15.**—(1) This section and section 16 below have effect in relation to the issue to constables under any enactment, including an enactment contained in an Act passed after this act, of warrants to enter and search premises; and an entry on or search of premises under a warrant is unlawful unless it complies with this section and section 16 below.

(2) Where a constable applies for any such warrant, it shall be his duty—

    (*a*) to state—

        (i) the ground on which he makes the application; and

        (ii) the enactment under which the warrant would be issued;

    (*b*) to specify the premises which it is desired to enter and search; and

    (*c*) to identify, so far as is practicable, the articles or persons to be sought.

(3) An application for such a warrant whall be made ex parte and supported by an information in writing.

(4) The constable shall answer on oath any question that the justice of the peace or judge hearing the application asks him.

(5) A warrant shall authorise an entry on one occasion only.

(6) A warrant—

    (*a*) shall specify—

        (i) the name of the person who applies for it;

        (ii) the date on which it is issued;

        (iii) the enactment under which it is issued; and

        (iv) the premises to be searched; and

    (*b*) shall identify, so far as is practicable, the articles or persons to be sought.

(7) Two copies shall be made of a warrant.

(8) The copies shall be clearly certified as copies.

*Execution of warrants*

**16.**—(1) A warrant to enter and search premises may be executed by any constable.

(2) Such a warrant may authorise persons to accompany any constable who is executing it.

(3) Entry and search under a warrant must be within one month from the date of its issue.

(4) Entry and search under a warrant must be at a reasonable hour unless it appears to the constable executing it that the purpose of a search may be frustrated on an entry at a reasonable hour.

(5) Where the occupier of premises which are to be entered and searched is present at the time when a constable seeks to execute a warrant to enter and search them, the constable—

(*a*) shall identify himself to the occupier and, if not in uniform, shall produce to him documentary evidence that he is a constable;

(*b*) shall produce the warrant to him; and

(*c*) shall supply him with a copy of it.

(6) Where—

(*a*) the occupier of such premises is not present at the time when a constable seeks to execute such a warrant; but

(*b*) some other person who appears to the constable to be in charge of the premises is present,

subsection (5) above shall have effect as if any reference to the occupier were a reference to that other person.

(7) If there is no person present who appears to the constable to be in charge of the premises, he shall leave a copy of the warrant in a prominent place on the premises.

(8) A search under a warrant may only be a search to the extent required for the purpose for which the warrant was issued.

(9) A constable executing a warrant shall make an endorsement on it stating—

(*a*) whether the articles or persons sought were found; and

(*b*) whether any articles were seized, other than articles which were sought.

(10) A warrant which—

(*a*) has been executed; or

(*b*) has not been executed within the time authorised for its execution,

shall be returned—

(i) if it was issued by a justice of the peace, to the clerk to the justices for the petty sessions area for which he acts; and

(ii) if it was issued by a judge, to the appropriate officer of the court from which he issued it.

(11) A warrant which is returned under subsection (10) above shall be retained for 12 months from its return—

(*a*) by the clerk to the justices, if it was returned under paragraph (i) of that subsection; and

(*b*) by the appropriate officer, if it was returned under paragraph (ii).

(12) If during the period for which a warrant is to retained the occupier of the premises to which it relates asks to inspect it, he shall be allowed to do so.

### Entry and search without search warrant

*Entry for purpose of arrest etc.*

17.—(1) Subject to the following provisions of this section, and without prejudice to any other enactment, a constable may enter and search any premises for the purpose—

(*a*) of executing—

(i) a warrant of arrest issued in connection with or arising out of criminal proceedings; or

(ii) a warrant of commitment issued under section 76 of the Magistrates' Courts Act 1980;

(*b*) of arresting a person for an arrestable offence;

(*c*) of arresting a person for an offence under—

(i) section 1 (prohibition of uniforms in connection with political objects), 4 (prohibition of offensive weapons at public meetings and processions) or 5 (prohibition of offensive conduct conducive to breaches of the peace) of the Public Order Act 1936;

(ii) any enactment contained in sections 6 to 8 or 10 of the Criminal Law Act 1977 (offences relating to entering and remaining on property);

(*d*) of recapturing a person who is unlawfully at large and whom he is pursuing; or

(*e*) of saving life or limb or preventing serious damage to property.

(2) Except for the purpose specified in paragraph (*e*) of subsection (1) above, the powers of entry and search conferred by this section—

(*a*) are only exercisable if the constable has reasonable grounds for believing that the person whom he is seeking is on the premises; and

(*b*) are limited, in relation to premises consisting of two or more separate dwellings, to powers to enter and search—

(i) any parts of the premises which the occupiers of any dwelling comprised in the premises use in common and the occupiers of any other such dwelling; and

(ii) any such dwelling in which the constable has reasonable grounds for believing that the person whom he is seeking may be.

(3) The powers of entry and search conferred by this section are only exercisable for the purposes specified in subsection (1) (*c*)(ii) above by a constable in uniform.

(4) The power of search conferred by this section is only a power to search to the extent that is reasonably required for the purpose for which the power of entry is exercised.

(5) Subject to subsection (6) below, all the rules of common law under which a constable has power to enter premises without a warrant are hereby abolished.

(6) Nothing in subsection (5) above affects any power of entry to deal with or prevent a breach of the peace.

*Entry and search after arrest.*

**18.**—(1) Subject to the following provisions of this section, a constable may enter and search any premises occupied or controlled by a person who is under arrest for an arrestable offence, if he has reasonable grounds for suspecting that there is on the premises evidence, other than items subject to legal privilege, that relates—

(*a*) to that offence; or

(*b*) to some other arrestable offence which is connected with or similar to that offence.

(2) A constable may seize and retain anything for which he may search under subsection (1) above.

(3) The power to search conferred by subsection (1) above is only a power to search to the extent that is reasonably required for the purpose of discovering such evidence.

(4) Subject to subsection (5) below, the powers conferred by this section may not be exercised unless an officer of the rank of inspector or above has authorised then in writing.

(5) A constable may conduct a search under subsection (1) above—

(a) before taking the person to a police station; and

(b) without obtaining an authorisation under subsection (4) above,

if the presence of that person at a place other than a police station is necessary for the effective investigation of the offence.

(6) If a constable conducts a search by virtue of subsection (5) above, he shall inform an officer of the rank of inspector or above that he has made the search as soon as practicable after he has made it.

(7) An officer who—

(a) authorises a search; or

(b) is informed of a search under subsection (6) above, shall make a record in writing—

(i) of the grounds for the search; and

(ii) of the nature of the evidence that was sought.

(8) If the person who was in occupation or control of the premises at the time of the search is in police detention at the time the record is to be made, the officer shall make the record as part of his custody record.

### Seizure etc.

*General power of seizure etc.*

**19.**—(1) The powers conferred by subsection (2), (3) and (4) below are exercisable by a constable who is lawfully on any premises.

(2) The constable may seize anything which is on the premises if he has reasonable grounds for believing—

(a) that it has been obtained in consequence of the commission of an offence; and

(b) that it is necessary to seize it in order to prevent it being concealed, lost, damaged, altered or destroyed.

(3) The constable may seize anything which is on the premises if he has reasonable grounds for believing—

(a) that it is evidence in relation to an offence which he is investigating or any other offence; and

(b) that it is necessary to seize it in order to prevent the evidence being concealed, lost, altered or destroyed.

(4) The constable may require any information which is contained in a computer and is accessible from the premises to be produced in a form in which it can be taken away and in which it is visible and legible if he has reasonable grounds for believing—

(a) that—

(i) it is evidence in relation to an offence which he is investigating or any other offence; or

(ii) it has been obtained in consequence of the commission of an offence; and

(b) that it is necessary to do so in order to prevent it being concealed, lost, tampered with or destroyed.

(5) The powers conferred by this section are in addition to any power otherwise conferred.

(6) No power of seizure conferred on a constable under any enactment (including an enactment contained in an Act passed after this Act) is to be taken to authorise the seizure of an item which the constable exercising the power has reasonable grounds for believing to be subject to legal privilege.

*Extension of powers of seizure to computerised information.*

**20.**—(1) Every power of seizure which is conferred by an enactment to which this section applies on a constable who has entered premises in the exercise of a power conferred by an enactment shall be construed as including a power to require any information contained in a computer and accessible from the premises to be produced in a form in which it can be taken away and in which it is visible and legible.

(2) This section applies—

    (*a*) to any enactment contained in an Act passed before this Act;

    (*b*) to sections 8 and 18 above;

    (*c*) to paragraph 13 of Schedule 1 to this Act; and

    (*d*) to any enactment contained in an Act passed after this Act.

*Access and copying.*

**21.**—(1) A constable who seizes anything in the exercise of a power conferred by any enactment, including an enactment contained in an Act passed after this Act, shall, if so requested by a person showing himself—

    (*a*) to be the occupier of premises on which it was seized; or

    (*b*) to have had custody or control of it immediately before the seizure,

provide that person with a record of what he seized.

(2) The officer shall provide the record within a reasonable time from the making of the request for it.

(3) Subject ot subsection (8) below, if a request for permission to be granted access to anything which—

    (*a*) has been seized by a constable; and

    (*b*) is retained by the police for the purpose of investigating an offence,

is made to the officer in charge of the investigation by a person who had custody or control of the thing immediately before it was seized or by someone acting on behalf of such a person, the officer shall allow the person who made the request access to it under the supervision of a constable.

(4) Subject to subsection (8) below, if a request for a photograph or copy of any such thing is made to the officer in charge of the investigation by a person who had custody or control of the thing immediately before it was so seized, or by someone acting on behalf of such a person, the officer shall—

    (*a*) allow the person who made the request access to it under the supervision of a constable for the purpose of photographing or copying it; or

    (*b*) photograph or copy it, or cause it to be photographed or copied.

(5) A constable may also photograph or copy, or have photographed or copied, anything which he has power to seize, without a request being made under subsection (4) above.

(6) Where anything is photographed or copied under subsection (4)(*b*) above, the photograph or copy shall be supplied to the person who made the request.

(7) The photograph or copy shall be so supplied within a reasonable time from the making of the request.

(8) There is no duty under this section to grant access to, or to supply a photograph or copy of, anything if the officer in charge of the investigation for the purposes of which it was seized has reasonable grounds for believing that to do so would prejudice—

    (*a*) that investigation;

    (*b*) the investigation of an offence other than the offence for the purposes of investigating which the thing was seized; or

(c) any criminal proceedings which may be brought as a result of—
  (i) the investigation of which he is in charge; or
  (ii) any such investigation as is mentioned in paragraph (b) above.

*Retention*
  **22.**—(1) Subject to subsection (4) below, anything which has been seized by a constable or taken away by a constable following a requirement made by virtue of section 19 or 20 above may be retained so long as is necessary in all the circumstances.
  (2) Without prejudice to the generality of subsection (1) above—
    (a) anything seized for the purposes of a criminal investigation may be retained, except as provided by subsection (4) below—
      (i) for use as evidence at a trial for an offence; or
      (ii) for forensic examination or for investigation in connection with an offence; and
    (b) anything may be retained in order to establish its lawful owner, where there are reasonable grounds for believing that it has been obtained in consequence of the commission of an offence.
  (3) Nothing seized on the ground that it may be used—
    (a) to cause physical injury to any person;
    (b) to damage property;
    (c) to interfere with evidence; or
    (d) to assist in escape from police detention or lawful custody,
may be retained when the person from whom it was seized is no longer in police detention or the custody of a court or is in the custody of a court but has been released on bail.
  (4) Nothing may be retained for either of the purposes mentioned in subsection (2)(a) above if a photograph or copy would be sufficient for that purpose.
  (5) Nothing in this section affects any power of a court to make an order under section 1 of the Police (Property) Act 1897.

### Supplementary

*Meaning of "premises" etc.*
  **23.** In this Act—
    "premises" includes any place and, in particular, includes—
      (a) any vehicle, vessel, aircraft or hovercraft;
      (b) any offshore installation; and
      (c) any tent or movable structure; and
    "offshore installation" has the meaning given to it by section 1 of the Mineral Workings (Offshore Installations) Act 1971.

### Part III

### Arrest

*Arrest without warrant for arrestable offences.*
  **24.**—(1) The powers of summary arrest conferrred by the following subsections shall apply—

(a) to offences for which the sentence is fixed by law;

(b) to offences for which a person of 21 years of age or over (not previously convicted) may be sentenced to imprisonment for a term of five years (or might be so sentenced but for the restrictions imposed by section 33 of the Magistrates' Courts Act 1980); and

(c) to the offences to which subsection (2) below applies, and in this Act "arrestable offence" means any such offence.

(2) The offences to which this subsection applies are—

(a) offences for which a person may be arrested under the customs and excise Acts, as defined in section 1(1) of the Customs and Excise Management Act 1979;

(b) offences under the Official Secrets Acts 1911 and 1920 that are not arrestable offences by virtue of the term of imprisonment for which a person may be sentenced in repect of them;

(c) offences under section 14 (indecent assault on a woman), 22 (causing prostitution of women) or 23 (procuration of girl under 21) of the Sexual Offences Act 1956;

(d) offences under section 12(1) (taking motor vehicle or other conveyance without authority etc.) or 25(1) (going equipped for stealing, etc.) of the Theft Act 1968; and

(e) offences under section 1 of the Public Bodies Corrupt Practices Act 1889 (corruption in office) or section 1 of the Prevention of Corruption Act 1906 (corrupt transactions with agents).

(3) Without prejudice to section 2 of the Criminal Attempts Act 1981, the powers of summary arrest conferred by the following subsection shall also apply to the offences of—

(a) conspiring to commit any of the offences mentioned in subsection (2) above;

(b) attempting to commit any such offence;

(c) inciting, aiding, abetting, counselling or procuring the commission of any such offence;

and such offences are also arrestable offences for the purposes of this Act.

(4) Any person may arrest without a warrant—

(a) anyone who is in the act of committing an arrestable offence;

(b) anyone whom he has reasonable grounds for suspecting to be committing such an offence.

(5) Where an arrestable offence has been committed, any person may arrest without a warrant—

(a) anyone who is guilty of the offence;

(b) anyone whom he has reasonable grounds for suspecting to be guilty of it.

(6) Where a constable has reasonable grounds for suspecting that an arrestable offence has been committed, he may arrest without a warrant anyone whom he has reasonable grounds for suspecting to be guilty of the offence.

(7) A constable may arrest without a warrant—

(a) anyone who is about to commit an arrestable offence;

(b) anyone whom he has reasonable grounds for suspecting to be about to commit an arrestable offence.

*General arrest conditions.*

**25.**—(1) Where a constable has reasonable grounds for suspecting that any offence which is not an arrestable offence has been committed or attempted, or is being committed or attempted, he may arrest the relevant person if it appears to him that service of a summons is impracticable or inappropriate because any of the general arrest conditions is satisfied.

(2) In this section "the relevant person" means any person whom the constable has reasonable grounds to suspect of having committed or having attempted to commit the offence or of being in the course of committing or attmpting to commit it.

(3) The general arrest conditions are—

(a) that the name of the relevant person is unknown to, and cannot be readily ascertained by, the constable;

(b) that the constable has reasonable grounds for doubting whether a name furnished by the relevant person as his name is his real name;

(c) that—

(i) the relevant person has failed to furnish a satisfactory address for service; or

(ii) the constable has reasonable grounds for doubting whether an address furnished by the relevant person is a satisfactory address for service;

(d) that the constable has reasonable grounds for believing that arrest is necessary to prevent the relevant person—

(i) causing physical injury to himself or any other person;

(ii) suffering physical injury;

(iii) causing loss of or damage to property;

(iv) committing an offence against public decency; or

(v) causing an unlawful obstruction of the highway;

(e) that the constable has reasonable grounds for believing that arrest is necessary to protect a child or other vulnerable person from the relevant person.

(4) For the purposes of subsection (3) above an address is a satisfactory address for service if it appears to the constable—

(a) that the relevant person will be at it for a sufficiently long period for it to be possible to serve him with a summons; or

(b) that some other person specified by the relevant person will accept service of a summons for the relevant person at it.

(5) Nothing in subsection (3)(d) above authorises the arrest of a person under sub-paragraph (iv) of that paragraph except where members of the public going about their normal business cannot reasonably be expected to avoid the person to be arrested.

(6) This section shall not prejudice any power of arrest conferred apart from this section.

26. . . .

*Fingerprinting of certain offenders.*

27.—(1) If a person—

(a) has been convicted of a recordable offence;

(b) has not at any time been in police detention for the offence; and

(c) has not had his fingerprints taken—

(i) in the course of investigation of the offence by the police; or

(ii) since the conviction,

any constable may at any time not later than one month after the date of the conviction require him to attend a police station in order that his fingerprints may be taken.

(2) A requirement under subsection (1) above—

    (*a*) shall give the person a period of at least 7 days within which he must attend; and

    (*b*) may direct him to so attend at a specified time of day or between specified times of day.

(3) Any constable may arrest without warrant a person who has failed to comply with a requirement under subsection (1) above.

(4) The Secretary of State may by regulations make provision for recording in national police records convictions for such offences as are specified in the regulations.

(5) Regulations under this section shall be made by statutory instrument and shall be subject to annulment in pursuance of a resolution of either House of Parliament.

*Information to be given on arrest.*

**28.**—(1) Subject to subsection (5) below, where a person is arrested, otherwise than by being informed that he is under arrest, the arrest is not lawful unless the person arrested is informed that he is under arrest as soon as is practicable after his arrest.

(2) Where a person is arrested by a constable, subsection (1) above applies regardless of whether the fact of the arrest is obvious.

(3) Subject to subsection (5) below, no arrest is lawful unless the person arrested is informed of the ground for the arrest at the time of, or as soon as is practicable after, the arrest.

(4) Where a person is arrested by a constable, subsection (3) above applies regardless of whether the ground for the arrest is obvious.

(5) Nothing in this section is to be taken to require a person to be informed—

    (*a*) that he is under arrest; or

    (*b*) of the ground for the arrest,

if it was not reasonably practicable for him to be so informed by reason of his having escaped from arrest before the information could be given.

*Voluntary attendance at police station etc.*

**29.** Where for the purpose of assisting with an investigation a person attends voluntarily at a police station or at any other place where a constable is present or accompaines a constable to a police station or any such other place without having been arrested—

    (*a*) he shall be entitled to leave at will unless he is placed under arrest;

    (*b*) he shall be informed at once that he is under arrest if a decision is taken by a constable to prevent him from leaving at will.

*Arrest elsewhere than at police station*

**30.**—(1) Subject to the following provisions of this section, where a person—

    (*a*) is arrested by a constable for an offence; or

    (*b*) is taken into custody by a constable after being arrested for an offence by a person other than a constable,

at any place other than a police station, he shall be taken to a police station by a constable as soon as practicable after the arrest.

(2) Subject to subsections (3) and (5) below, the police station to which an arrested person is taken under subsection (1) above shall be a designated police station.

(3) A constable to whom this subsection applies may take an arrested person to any police station unless it appears to the constable that it may be necessary to keep the arrested person in police detention for more than six hours.

(4) Subsection (3) above applies—

(*a*) to a constable who is working in a locality covered by a police station which is not a designated police station; and

(*b*) to a constable belonging to a body of constables maintined by an authority other than a police authority.

(5) Any constable may take an arrested person to any police station if—

(*a*) either of the following conditions is satisfied—

(i) the constable has arrested him without the assistance of any other constable and no other constable is available to assist him;

(ii) the constable has taken him into custody from a person other than a constable without the assistance of any other constable and no other constable is available to assist him; and

(*b*) it appears to the constable that he will be unable to take the arrested person to a designated plice station without the arrested person injuring himself, the constable or some other person.

(6) If the first police station to which an arrested person is taken after his arrest is not a designated police station, he shall be taken to a designated police station not more than six hours after his arrival at the first police station unless he is released previously.

(7) A person arrested by a constable at a place other than a police station shall be released if a constable is satisfied, before the person arrested reaches a police station, that there are no grounds for keeping him under arrest.

(8) A constable who releases a person under subsection (7) above shall record the fact that he has done so.

(9) The constable shall make the record as soon as is practicable after the release.

(10) Nothing in subsection (1) above shall prevent a constable delaying taking a person who has been arrested to a police station if the presence of that person elsewhere is necessary in order to carry out such investigations as it is reasonable to carry out immediately.

(11) Where there is delay in taking a person who has been arrested to a police station after his arrest, the reasons for the delay shall be recorded when he first arrives at a police station.

(12) Nothing in subsection (1) above shall be taken to affect—

(*a*) paragraphs 16(3) or 18(1) of Schedule 2 to the Immigration Act 1971;

(*b*) section 34(1) of the Criminal Justice Act 1972; or

(*c*) paragraph 5 of Schedule 3 to the Prevention of Terrorism (Temporary Provisions) Act 1984 or any provision contained in an order under section 13 of that Act which authorises the detention of persons on board a ship or aircraft.

(13) Nothing in subsection (10) above shall be taken to affect paragraph 18(3) of Schedule 2 to the Immigration Act 1971.

*Arrest for further offence*

**31.** Where—

(*a*) a person—
    (i) has been arrested for an offence; and
    (ii) is at a police station in consequence of that arrest; and
(*b*) it appears to a constable that, if he were released from that arrest, he
would be liable to arrest for some other offence,
he shall be arrested for that other offence.

*Search upon arrest.*

**32.**—(1) A constable may search an arrested person, in any case where the
person to be searched has been arrested at a place other than a police station, if
the constable has reasonable grounds for believing that the arrested person may
present a danger to himself or others.

(2) Subject to subsection (3) to (5) below, a constable shall also have power in
any such case—
    (*a*) to search the arrested person for anything—
      (i) which he might use to assist him to excape from lawful custody; or
      (ii) which might be evidence relating to an offence; and
    (*b*) to enter and search any premises in which he was when arrested or
    immediately before he was arrested for evidence relating to the offence for
    which he has been arrested.

(3) The power to search conferred by subsection (2) above is only a power to
search to the extent that is reasonably required for the purpose of discovering any
such thing or any such evidence.

(4) The powers conferred by this section to search a person are not to be
construed as authorising a constable to require a person to remove any of his
clothing in public other than an outer coat, jacket or gloves.

(5) A constable may not search a person in the exercise of the power conferred
by subsection (2)(*a*) above unless he has reasonable grounds for believing that the
person to be searched may have concealed on him anything for which a search is
permitted under that paragraph.

(6) A constable may not search premises in the exercise of the power conferred
by subsection (2)(*b*) above unless he has reasonable grounds for believing that
there is evidence for which a search is permitted under that paragraph on the
premises.

(7) In so far as the power of search conferred by subsection (2)(*b*) above relates
to premises consisting of two or more separate dwellings, it it limited to a power
to search—
    (*a*) any dwelling in which the arrest took place or in which the person
    arrested was immediately before his arrest; and
    (*b*) any parts of the premises which the occupier of any such dwelling uses in
    common with the occupiers of any other dwellings comprised in the
    premises.

(8) A constable searching a person in the exercise of the power conferred by
subsection (1) above may seize and retain anything he finds, if he has reasonable
grounds for believing that the person searched might use it to cause physical
injury to himself or to any other person.

(9) A constable searching a person in the exercise of the power conferred by
subsection (2)(*a*) above may seize and retain anything he finds, other than an item
subject to legal privilege, if he has reasonable grounds for believing—
    (*a*) that he might use it to assist him to escape from lawful custody; or

(*b*) that it is evidence of an offence or has been obtained in consequence of the commission of an offence.

(10) Nothing in this section shall be taken to affect the power conferred by paragraph 6 of Schedule 3 to the Prevention of Terrorism (Temporary Provisions) Act 1984.

*Execution of warrant not in possession of constable*

**33.** In section 125 of the Magistrates' Courts Act 1980—

(*a*) in subsection (3), for the words "arrest a person charged with an offence" there shall be substituted the words "which this subsection applies";

(*b*) the following subsection shall be added after that subsection—

"(4) The warrants to which subsection 3 above applies are—

(*a*) a warrant to arrest a person in connection with an offence;

(*b*) without prejudice to paragraph (*a*) above, a warrant under section 186(3) of the Army Act 1955, section 186(3) of the Air Force Act 1955, section 105(3) of the Naval Discipline Act 1957 or Schedule 5 to the Reserve Forces Act 1980 (desertion etc.);

(*c*) a warrant under—

(i) section 102 or 104 of the General Rate Act 1967 (insufficiency of distress);

(ii) section 18(4) of the Domestic Proceedings and Magistrates' Courts Act 1978 (protection of parties to marriage and children of family); and

(iii) section 55, 76, 93 or 97 above".

## Part IV

## Detention

### Detention—conditions and duration

*Limitations on police detention*

**34.**—(1) A person arrested for an offence shall not be kept in police detention except in accordance with the provisions of this Part of this Act.

(2) Subject to subsection (3) below, if at any time a custody officer—

(*a*) becomes aware, in relation to any person in police detention, that the grounds for the detention of that person have ceased to apply; and

(*b*) is not aware of any other grounds on which the continued detention of that person could be justified under the provisions of this Part of this Act, it shall be the duty of the custody officer, subject to subsection (4) below, to order his immediate release from custody.

(3) No person in police detention shall be released except on the authority of a custody officer at the police station where his detention was authorised or, if it was authorised at more than one station, a custody officer at the station where it was last authorised.

(4) A person who appears to the custody officer to have been unlawfully at large when he was arrested is not to be released under subsection (2) above.

(5) A person whose release is ordered under subsection (2) above shall be released without bail unless it appears to the custody officer—

(*a*) that there is need for further investigation of any matter in connection with which he was detained at any time during the period of his detention; or

(*b*) that proceedings may be taken against him in respect of any such matter, and, if it so appears, he shall be released on bail.

(6) For the purposes of this Part of this Act a person arrested under section 7(5) of the Road Traffic Act 1972 is arrested for an offence.

*Designated police stations.*

**35.**—(1) The chief officer of police for each police area shall designate the police stations in his area which, subject to section 30(3) and (5) above, are to be the stations in that area to be used for the purpose of detaining arrested persons.

(2) A chief officer's duty under subsection (1) above is to designate police stations appearing to him to provide enough accommodation for that purpose.

(3) Without prejudice to section 12 of the Interpretation Act 1978 (continuity of duties) a chief officer—

(*a*) may designate a station which was not previoulsy designated; and

(*b*) may direct that a designation of station previously made shall cease to operate.

(4) In this Act "designated police station" means a police station for the time being designated under this section.

*Custody officers at police stations.*

**36.**—(1) One or more custody officers shall be appointed for each designated police station.

(2) A custody officer for a designated police station shall be appointed—

(*a*) by the chief officer of police for the area in which the designated police station is situated; or

(*b*) by such other police officer as the chief officer of police for that area may direct.

(3) No officer may be appointed a custody officer unless he is of at least the rank of sergeant.

(4) An officer of any rank may perform the functions of a custody officer at a designated police station if a custody officer is not readily available to perform them.

(5) Subject to the following provisions of this section and to section 39(2) below, none of the functions of a custody officer in relation to a person shall be performed by an officer who at the time when the function falls to be performed is involved in the investigation of an offence for which that person is in the police detention at that time.

(6) Nothing in subsection (5) above is to be taken to prevent a custody officer—

(*a*) performing any function assigned to custody officers—

(i) by this Act; or

(ii) by a code of practice issued under this Act;

(*b*) carrying out the duty imposed on custody officers by section 39 below;

(*c*) doing anything in connection with the identification of a suspect; or

(*d*) doing anything under section 8 of the Road Traffic Act 1972.

(7) Where an arrested person is taken to a police station which is not a designated police station, the functions in relation to him which at a designated police station would be the functions of a custody officer shall be performed—

(*a*) by an officer who is not involved in the investigation of an offence for which he is in the police detention, if such an officer is readily available; and

(*b*) if no such officer is readily available, by the officer who took him to the station of any other officer.

(8) References to a custody officer in the following provisions of this Act include references to an officer other than a custody officer who is performing the functions of a custody officer by virtue of subsection (4) or (7) above.

(9) Where by virtue of subsection (7) above an officer of a force maintained by a police authority who took an arrested person to a police station is to perform the functions of a custody officer in relation to him, the officer shall inform an officer who—

(*a*) is attached to a designated police station; and

(*b*) is of at least the rank of inspector,

that he is to do so.

(10) The duty imposed by subsection (9) above shall be performed as soon as it it practicable to perform it.

*Duties of custody officer before charge.*
   **37.**—(1) Where—

(*a*) a person is arrested for an offence—

   (i) without a warrant; or

   (ii) under a warrant not endorsed for bail, or

(*b*) a person returns to a police station to answer to bail,

the custody officer at each police station where he is detained after his arrest shall determine whether he has before him sufficient evidence to charge that person with the offence for which he was arrested and may detain him at the police station for such period as is necessary to enable him to do so.

(2) If the custody officer determines that he does not have such evidence before him, the person arrested shall be released either on bail or without bail, unless the custody officer has reasonable grounds for believing that his detention without being charged is necessary to secure or preserve evidence relating to an offence for which he is under arrest or to obtain such evidence by questioning him.

(3) If the custody officer has reasonable grounds for so believing, he may authorise the person arrested to be kept in police detention.

(4) Where a custody officer authorises a person who has not been charged to be kept in police detention, he shall, as soon as is practicable, make a written record of the grounds for the detention.

(5) Subject to subsection (6) below, the written record shall be made in the presence of the person arrested who shall at that time be informed by the custody officer of the grounds for his detention.

(6) Subsection (5) above shall not apply where the person arrested is, at the time when the written record is made—

(*a*) incapable of understanding what is said to him;

(*b*) violent or likely to become violent; or

(*c*) in urgent need of medical attention.

(7) Subject to section 41(7) below, if the custody officer determines that he has before him sufficient evidence to charge the person arrested with the offence for which he was arrested, the person arrested—

(*a*) shall be charged; or

(*b*) shall be released without charge, either on bail or without bail.

(8) Where—
    (*a*) a person is released under subsection (7)(*b*) above; and
    (*b*) at the time of his release a decision whether he should be prosecuted for the offence for which he was arrested has not been taken,
it shall be the duty of the custody officer so to inform him.

(9) If the person arrested is not in a fit state to be dealt with under subsection (7) above, he may be kept in police detention until he is.

(10) The duty imposed on the custody officer under subsection (1) above shall be carried out by him as soon as practicable after the person arrested arrives at the police station or, in the case of a person arrested at the police station, as soon as practicable after the arrest.

(11) Where—
    (*a*) an arrested juvenile who was arrested without a warrant is not released under subsection (2) above; and
    (*b*) it appears to the custody officer that a decision falls to be taken in pursuance of section 5(2) of the Children and Young Persons Act 1969 whether to lay an information in respect of an offence alleged to have been committed by the arrested juvenile,
it shall be the duty of the custody officer to inform him that such a decision falls to be taken and to specify the offence.

(12) It shall also be the duty of the custody officer—
    (*a*) to take such steps as are practicable to ascertain the identity of a person responsible for the welfare of the arrested juvenile; and
    (*b*) if—
        (i) he ascertains the identity of any such person; and
        (ii) it is practicable to give that person the information which subsection
           (11) above requires the custody officer to give to the arrested juvenile,
to give that person the information as soon as it is practicable to do so.

(13) For the purposes of subsection (12) above the persons who may be responsible for the welfare of an arrested juvenile are—
    (*a*) his parent or guardian; and
    (*b*) any other person who has for the time being assumed responsibility for his welfare.

(14) If it appears to the custody officer that a supervision order, as defined in section 11 of the Children and Young Persons Act 1969, is in force in respect of the arrested juvenile, the custody officer shall also give the information to the person responsible for the arrested juvenile's supervision, as soon as it is practicable to do so.

(15) In this Part of this Act—
    "arrested juvenile" means a person arrested with or without a warrant who appears to be under the age of 17 and is excluded from this Part of this Act by section 52 below;
    "endorsed for bail" means endorsed with a direction for bail in accordance with section 117(2) of the Magistrates' Courts Act 1980.


*Duties of custody officer after charge.*

**38.**—(1) Where a person arrested for an offence otherwise than under a warrant endorsed for bail is charged with an offence, the custody officer shall order his release from police detention, either on bail or without bail, unless—
    (*a*) if the person arrested is not an arrested juvenile—

(i) his name or address cannot be ascertained or the custody officer has reasonable grounds for doubting whether a name or address furnished by him as his name or address is his real name or address;

(ii) the custody officer has reasonable grounds for believing that the detention of the person arrested is necessary for his own protection or to prevent him from causing physical injury to any other person or from causing loss of or damage to property; or

(iii) the custody officer has reasonable grounds for believing that the person arrested will fail to appear in court to answer to bail or that his detention is necessary to prevent him for interfering with the administration of justice or with the investigation of offences or of a particular offence;

(b) if he is an arrested juvenile—

(i) any of the requirements of paragraph (a) above is satisfied; or

(ii) the custody officer has reasonable grounds for believing that he ought to be detained in his own interests.

(2) If the release of a person arrested is not required by subsection (1) above, the custody officer may authorise him to be kept in police detention.

(3) Where a custody officer authorises a person who has been charged to be kept in police detention, he shall, as soon as practicable, make a written record of the grounds for the detention.

(4) Subject to subsection (5) below, the written record shall be made in the presence of the person charged who shall at that time be informed by the custody officer of the grounds for his detention.

(5) Subsection (4) above shall not apply where the person charged is, at the time when the written record is made—

(a) incapable of understanding what is said to him;

(b) violent or likely to become violent; or

(c) in urgent need of medical attention.

(6) Where a custody officer authorises an arrested juvenile to be kept in police detention under subsection (1) above, the custody officer shall, unless he certifies that it is impracticable to do so, make arrangements for the arrested juvenile to be taken into care of a local authority and detained by the authority; and it shall be lawful to detain him in pursuance of the arrangements.

(7) A certificate made under subsection (6) above in respect of an arrested juvenile shall be produced to the court before which he is first brought thereafter.

(8) In this Part of this Act "local authority" has the same meaning as in the Children and Young Persons Act 1969.

*Responsibilities in relation to persons detained.*

**39.**—(1) Subject to subsections (2) and (4) below, it shall be the duty of the custody officer at a police station to ensure—

(a) that all persons in police detention at that station are treated in accordance with this Act and any code of practice issued under it and relating to the treatment of persons in police detention; and

(b) that all matters relating to such persons which are required by this Act or by such codes of practice to be recorded are recorded in the custody records relating to such persons.

(2) If the custody officer, in accordance with any code of practice issued under this Act, transfers or permits the transfer of a person in police detention—

(*a*) to the custody of a police officer investigating an offence for which that person is in police detention; or

(*b*) to the custody of an officer who has charge of that person outside the police station,

the custody officer shall cease in relation to that person to be subject to the duty imposed on him by subsection (1)(*a*) above; and it shall be the duty of the officer to whom the transfer is made to ensure that he is treated in accordance with the provisions of this Act and of any such codes of practice as are mentioned in subsection (1) above.

(3) If the person detained is subsequently returned to the custody of the custody officer, it shall be the duty of the officer investigating the offence to report to the custody officer as to the manner in which this section and the codes of practice have been complied with while that person was in his custody.

(4) If an arrested juvenile is transferred to the care of a local authority in pursuance of arrangements made under section 38(6) above, the custody officer shall cease in relation to that person to be subject to the duty imposed on him by subsection (1) above.

(5) It shall be the duty of a local authority to make available to an arrested juvenile who is in the authority's care in pursuance of such arrangements such advice and assistance as may be appropriate in the circumstances.

(6) Where—

(*a*) an officer of higher rank than the custody officer gives directions relating to a person in police detention; and

(*b*) the directions are at variance—

(i) with any decision made or action taken by the custody officer in the performance of a duty imposed on him under this Part of this Act; or

(ii) with any decision or action which would but for the directions have been made or taken by him in the performance of such a duty,

the custody officer shall refer the matter at once to an officer of the rank of superintendent or above who is responsible for the police station for which the custody officer is acting as custody officer.


*Review of police detention.*

**40.**—(1) Reviews of the detention of each person in police detention in connection with the investigation of an offence shall be carried out periodically in accordance with the following provisions of this section—

(*a*) in the case of a person who has been arrested and charged, by the custody officer; and

(*b*) in the case of a person who has been arrested but not charged, by an officer of at least the rank of inspector who has not been directly involved in the investigation.

(2) The officer to whom it falls to carry out a review is referred to in his section as a "review officer".

(3) Subject to subsection (4) below—

(*a*) the first review shall be not later than six hours after the detention was first authorised;

(*b*) the second review shall be not later than nine hours after the first;

(*c*) subsequent reviews shall be at intervals of not more than nine hours.

(4) A review may be postponed—

(*a*) if, having regard to all the circumstances prevailing at the latest time for it specified in subsection (3) above, it is not practicable to carry out the review at that time;

    (*b*) without prejudice to the generality of paragraph (*a*) above—

        (i) if at that time the person in detention is being questioned by a police officer and the review officer is satisfied that an interruption of the questioning for the purpose of carrying out the review would prejudice the investigation in connection with which he is being questioned; or

        (ii) if at that time no review officer is readily available.

(5) If a review is postponed under subsection (4) above it shall be carried out as soon as practicable after the latest time specified for it in subsection (3) above.

(6) If a review is carried out after postponement under subsection (4) above, the fact that it was so carried out shall not affect any requirement of this section as to the time as which any subsequent review is to be carried out.

(7) The review officer shall record the reasons for any postponement of a review in the custody record.

(8) Subject to subsection (9) below, where the person whose detention is under review has not been charged before the time of the review, section 37(1) to (6) above shall have effect in relation to him, but with the substitution—

    (*a*) of references to the person whose detention is under review for references to the person arrested; and

    (*b*) of references to the review officer for references to the custody officer.

(9) Where a person has been kept in police detention by virtue of section 37(9) above, section 37(1) to (6) shall not have effect in relation to him but it shall be the duty of the review officer to determine whether he is yet in a fit state.

(10) Where the person whose detention is under review has been charged before the time of the review, section 38(1) to (6) above shall have effect in relation to him, but with the substitution of references to the person whose detention is under review for references to the person arrested.

(11) Where—

    (*a*) an officer of higher rank than the review officer gives directions relating to a person in police detention; and

    (*b*) the directions are at variance—

        (i) with any decision made or action taken by the review officer in the performance of a duty imposed on him under this part of this Act; or

        (ii) with any decision or action which would but for the directions have been made or taken by him in the performance of such a duty,

the review officer shall refer the matter at once to an officer of the rank of superintendent or above who is responsible for the police station for which the review officer is acting as review officer in conncection with the detention.

(12) Before determining whether to authorise a person's continued detention the review officer shall give—

    (*a*) that person (unless he is asleep); or

    (*b*) any solicitor representing him who is available at the time of the review, an opportunity to make representations to him about the detention.

(13) Subject to subsection (14) below, the person whose detention is under review or his solicitor may make representations under subsection (12) above either orally or in writing.

(14) The review officer may refuse to hear oral representations from the person whose detention is under review if he considers that he is unfit to make such representations by reason of his condition or behaviour.

*Limits on period of detention without charge.*

**41.**—(1) Subject to the following provisions of this section and to sections 42 and 43 below, a person shall not be kept in police detention for more than 24 hours without being charged.

(2) The time from which the period of detention of a person is to be calculated (in this Act referred to as "the relevant time")—

    (*a*) in the case of a person to whom this paragraph applies, shall be—

        (i) the time at which that person arrives at the relevant police station; or

        (ii) the time 24 hours after the time of that person's arrest,

whichever is the earlier;

    (*b*) in the case of a person arrested outside England and Wales, shall be—

        (i) the time at which that person arrives at the first police station to which he is taken in the police area in England or Wales in which the offence for which he was arrested is being investigated; or

        (ii) the time 24 hours after the time of that person's entry into England and Wales,

whichever is the earlier;

    (*c*) in the case of a person who—

        (i) attends voluntarily at a police station; or

        (ii) accompanies a constable to a police station without having been arrested,

and is arrested at the police station, the time of his arrest;

    (*d*) in any other case, except where subsection (5) below applies, shall be the time at which the person arrested arrives at the first police station to which he is taken after his arrest.

(3) Subsection (2)(*a*) above applies to a person if—

    (*a*) his arrest is sought in one police area in England and Wales;

    (*b*) he is arrested in another police area; and

    (*c*) he is not questioned in the area in which he is arrested in order to obtain evidence in relation to an offence for which he is arrested;

and in sub-paragraph (i) of that paragraph "the relevant police station" means the first police station to which he is taken in the police area in which his arrest was sought.

(4) Subsection (2) above shall have effect in relation to a person arrested under section 31 above as if every reference in it to his arrest or his being arrested were a reference to his arrest or his being arrested for the offence for which he was originally arrested.

(5) If—

    (*a*) a person is in police detention in a police area in England and Wales ("the first area"); and

    (*b*) his arrest for an offence is sought in some other police area in England and Wales ("the second area"); and

    (*c*) he is taken to the second area for the purposes of investigating that offence, without being questioned in the first area in order to obtain evidence in relation to it,

the relevant time shall be—

        (i) the time 24 hours after he leaves the place where he is detained in the first area; or

        (ii) the time at which he arrives at the first police station to which he is taken in the second area,

whichever is the earlier.

(6) When a person who is in police detention is removed to hospital because he is in need of medical treatment, any time during which he is being questioned in hospital or on the way there or back by a police officer for the purpose of obtaining evidence relating to an offence shall be included in any period which falls to be calculated for the purposes of this Part of this Act, but any other time while he is in hospital or on his way there or back shall not be so included.

(7) Subject to subsection (8) below, a person who at the expiry of 24 hours after the relevant time is in police detention and has not been charged shall be released at that time either on bail or without bail.

(8) Subsection (7) above does not apply to a person whose detention for more than 24 hours after the relevant time has been authorised or is otherwise permitted in accordance with section 42 or 43 below.

(9) A person released under subsection (7) above shall not be re-arrested without a warrant for the offence for which he was previously arrested unless new evidence justifying a further arrest has come to light since his release.

*Authorisation of continued detention*

**42.**—(1) Where a police officer of the rank of superintendent or above who is responsible for the police station at which a person is detained has reasonable grounds for believing that—

   (a) the detention of that person without charge is necessary to secure or preserve evidence relating to an offence for which he is under arrest or to obtain such evidence by questioning him;

   (b) an offence for which he is under arrest is a serious arrestable offence; and

   (c) the investigation is being conducted diligently and expeditiously,

he may authorise the keeping of that person in police detention for a period expiring at or before 36 hours after the relevant time.

(2) Where an officer such as is mentioned in subsection (1) above has authorised the keeping of a person in police detention for a period expiring less than 36 hours after the relevant time, such an officer may authorise the keeping of that person in police detention for a further period expiring not more than 36 hours after that time if the conditions specified in subsection (1) above are still satisfied when he gives the authorisation.

(3) If it is proposed to transfer a person in police detention to another police area, the officer determining whether or not to authorise keeping him in detention under subsection (1) above shall have regard to the distance and the time the journey would take.

(4) No authorisation under subsection (1) above shall be given in respect of any person—

   (a) more than 24 hours after the relevant time; or

   (b) before the second review of his detention under section 40 above has been carried out.

(5) Where an officer authorises the keeping of a person in police detention under subsection (1) above, it shall be his duty—

   (a) to inform that person of the grounds for his continued detention; and

   (b) to record the grounds in that person's custody record.

(6) Before determining whether to authorise the keeping of a person in detention under subsection (1) or (2) above, an officer shall give—

   (a) that person; or

   (b) any solicitor representing him who is available at the time when it falls to the officer to determine whether to give the authorisation,

an opportunity to make representations to him about the detention.

(7) Subject to subsection (8) below, the person in detention or his solicitor may make representations under subsection (6) above either orally or in writing.

(8) The officer to whom it falls to determine whether to give the authorisation may refuse to hear oral representations from the person in detention if he considers that he is unfit to make such representations by reason of his condition or behaviour.

(9) Where—

(a) an officer authorises the keeping of a person in detention under subsection (1) above; and

(b) at the time of the authorisation he has not yet exercised a right conferred on him by section 56 or 58 below,

the officer—

(i) shall inform him of that right;

(ii) shall decide whether he should be permitted to exercise it;

(iii) shall recored the decision in his custody record; and

(iv) if the decision is to refuse to permit the exercise of the right, shall also record the grounds for the decision in that record.

(10) Where an officer has authorised the keeping of a person who has not been charged in detention under subsection (1) or (2) above, he shall be released from detention, either on bail or without bail, not later than 36 hours after the relevant time, unless—

(a) he has been charged with an offence; or

(b) his continued detention is authorised or otherwise permitted in accordance with section 43 below.

(11) A person released under subsection (10) above shall not be re-arrested without a warrant for the offfence for which he was previously arrested unless new evidence justifying a further arrest has come to light since his release.

*Warrants of further detention.*

**43.**—(1) Where, on an application on oath made by a constable and supported by an information, a magistrates' court is satisfied that there are reasonable grounds for believing that the further detention of the person to whom the application relates is justified, it may issue a warrant of further detention authorising the keeping of that person in police detention.

(2) A court may not hear an application for a warrant of further detention unless the person to whom the application relates—

(a) has been furnished with a copy of the information; and

(b) has been brought before the court for the hearing.

(3) The person to whom the application relates shall be entitled to be legally represented at the hearing and, if he is not so represented but wishes to be so represented—

(a) the court shall adjourn the hearing to enable him to obtain representation; and

(b) he may be kept in police detention during the adjournment.

(4) A person's further detention is only justified for the purposes of this section or section 44 below if—

(a) his detention without charge is necessary to secure or preserve evidence relating to an offence for which he is under arrest or to obtain such evidence by questioning him;

(b) an offence for which he is under arrest is a serious arrestable offence; and

(c) the investigation is being conducted diligently and expeditiously.

(5) Subject to subsection (7) below, an application for a warrant of further detention may be made—

(a) at any time before the expiry of 36 hours after the relevant time; or

(b) in a case where—

(i) it is not practicable for the magistrates' court to which the application will be made to sit at the expiry of 36 hours after the relevant time; but

(ii) the court will sit during the 6 hours following the end of that period,

at any time before the expiry of the said 6 hours.

(6) In a case to which subsection (5)(b) above applies—

(a) the person to whom the application relates may be kept in police detention until the application is heard; and

(b) the custody officer shall make a note in that person's custody record—

(i) of the fact that he was kept in police detention for more than 36 hours after the relevant time; and

(ii) of the reason why he was so kept.

(7) If—

(a) an application for a warrant of further detention is made after the expiry of 36 hours after the relevant time; and

(b) it appears to the magistrates' court that it would have been reasonable for the police to make it before the expiry of that period,

the court shall dismiss the application.

(8) Where on an application such as is mentioned in subsection (1) above a magistrates' court is not satisfied that there are reasonable grounds for believing that the further detention of the person to whom the application relates is justified, it shall be its duty—

(a) to refuse the application; or

(b) to adjourn the hearing of it until a time not later than 36 hours after the relevant time.

(9) The person to whom the application relates may be kept in police detention during the adjournment.

(10) A warrant of further detention shall—

(a) state the time at which it is issued;

(b) authorise the keeping in police detention of the person to whom it relates for the period stated in it.

(11) Subject to subsection (12) below, the period stated in a warrant of further detention shall be such period as the magistrates' court thinks fit, having regard to the evidence before it.

(12) The period shall not be longer than 36 hours.

(13) If it is proposed to transfer a person in police detention to a police area other than that in which he is detained when the application for a warrant of further detention is made, the court hearing the application shall have regard to the distance and the time the journey would take.

(14) Any information submitted in support of an application under this section shall state—

(a) the nature of the offence for which the person to whom the application relates has been arrested;

(b) the general nature of the evidence on which that person was arrested;

(c) what inquiries relating to the offence have been made by the police and what further inquiries are proposed by them;

(d) the reasons for believing the continued detention of that person to be necessary for the purposes of such further inquiries.

(15) Where an application under this section is refused, the person to whom the application relates shall forthwith be charged or, subject ot subsection (16) below, released, either on bail or without bail.

(16) A person need not be released under subsection (15) above—
   (a) before the expiry of 24 hours after the relevant time; or
   (b) before the expiry of any longer period for which his continued detention is or has been authorised under section 42 above.

(17) Where an application under this section is refused, no further application shall be made under this section in respect of the person to whom the refusal relates, unless supported by evidence which has come to light since the refusal.

(18) Where a warrant of further detention is issued, the person to whom it relates shall be released from police detention, either on bail or without bail, upon or before the expiry of the warrant unless he is charged.

(19) A person released under subsection (18) above shall not be re-arrested without a warrant for the offence for which he was previously arrested unless new evidence justifying a further arrest has come to light since his release.

*Extension of warrants of further detention.*

**44.**—(1) On application on oath made by a constable and supported by an information a magistrates' court may extend a warrant of further detention issued under section 43 above if it is satisfied that there are reasonable grounds for believing that the further detention of the person to whom the application relates is justified.

(2) Subject to subsection (3) below, the period for which a warrant of further detention may be extended shall be such period as the court thinks fit, having regard to the evidence before it.

(3) The period shall not—·
   (a) be longer than 36 hours; or
   (b) end later than 96 hours after the relevant time.

(4) Where a warrant of further detention has been extended under subsection (1) above, or further extended under this subsection, for a period ending before 96 hours after the relevant time, on an application such as is mentioned in that subsection a magistrates' court may further extend the warrant if it is satisfied as there mentioned; and subsections (2) and (3) above apply to such further extensions as they apply to extensions under subsection (1) above.

(5) A warrant of further detention shall, if extended or further extended under this section, be endorsed with a note of the period of the extension.

(6) Subsections (2), (3) and (14) of section 43 above shall apply to an application made under this section as they apply to an application made under that section.

(7) Where an application under this section is refused, the person to whom the application relates shall forthwith be charged or, subject to subsection (8) below, relaeased, either on bail or without bail.

(8) A person need not be released under subsection (7) above before the expiry of any period for which a warrant of further detention issued in relation to him has been extended or further extended on an earlier application made under this section.

*Detention before charge—supplementary.*

**45.**—(1) In sections 43 and 44 of this Act "magistrates' court" means a court consisting of two or more justices of the peace sitting otherwise than in open court.

(2) Any reference in this Part of this Act to a period of time or a time of day is to be treated as approximate only.

### Detention—miscellaneous

*Detention after charge.*

**46.**—(1) Where a person—

(a) is charged with an offence; and

(b) after being charged—

(i) is kept in police detention; or

(ii) is detained by a local authority in pursuance of arrangements made under section 38(6) above,

he shall be brought before a magistrates' court in accordance with the provisions of this section.

(2) If he is to be brought before a magistrates' court for the petty sessions area in which the police station at which he was charged is situated, he shall be brought before such a court as soon as is practicable and in any event not later than the first sitting after he is charged with the offence.

(3) If no magistrates' court for that area is due to sit either on the day on which he is charged or on the next day, the custody officer for the police station at which he was charged shall inform the clerk to the justices for the area that there is a person in the area to whom subsection (2) applies.

(4) If the person charged is to be brought before a magistrates' court for a petty sessions area other than that in which the police station at which he was charged is situated, he shall be removed to that area as soon as is practicable and brought before such a court as soon as is practicable after his arrival in the area and in any event not later than the first sitting of a magistrates' court for that area after his arrival in the area.

(5) If no magistrates' court for that area is due to sit either on the day on which he arrives in the area or on the next day—

(a) he shall be taken to a police station in the area; and

(b) the custody officer at that station shall inform the clerk to the justices for the area that there is a person in the area to whom subsection (4) applies.

(6) Subject to subsection (8) below, where a clerk to the justices for a petty sessions area has been informed—

(a) under subsection (3) above that there is a person in the area to whom subsection (2) applies; or

(b) under subsection (5) above that there is a person in the area to whom subsection (4) above applies,

the clerk shall arrange for a magistrates' court to sit not later than the day next following the relevant day.

(7) In this section "the relevant day"—

(a) in relation to a person who is to be brought before a magistrates' court for the petty sessions area in which the police station at which he was charged is situated, means the day on which he was charged; and

(b) in relation to a person who is to be brought before a magistrates' court for any other petty sessions area, means the day on which he arrives in the area.

(8) Where the day next following the relevant day is Christmas Day, Good Friday or a Sunday, the duty of the clerk under subsection (6) above is a duty to arrange for a magistrates' court to sit not later than the first day after the relevant day which is not one of those days.

(9) Nothing in this section requires a person who is in hospital to be brought before a court if he is not well enough.

*Bail after arrest*

**47.**—(1) Subject to subsection (2) below, a release on bail of a person under this Part of this Act shall be a release on bail granted in accordance with the Bail Act 1976.

(2) Nothing in the Bail Act 1976 shall prevent the re-arrest without warrant of a person released on bail subject to a duty to attend at a police station if new evidence justifying a further arrest has come to light since his release.

(3) Subject ot subsection (4) below, in this Part of this Act references to "bail" are references to bail subject to a duty—

    (*a*) to appear before a magistrates' court at such time and such place; or

    (*b*) to attend at such police station at such time,

as the custody officer may appoint.

(4) Where a custody officer has granted bail to a person subject to a duty to appear at a police station, the custody officer may give notice in writing to that person that his attendance at the police station is not required.

(5) Where a person arrested for an offence was released on bail subject to a duty to attend at a police station so attends, he may be detained without charge in connection with that offence only if the custody officer at the police station has reasonable grounds for believing that his detention is necessary—

    (*a*) to secure or preserve evidence relating to the offence; or

    (*b*) to obtain such evidence by questioning him.

(6) Where a person is detained under subsection (5) above, any time during which he was in police detention prior to being granted bail shall be included as part of any period which falls to be calculated under this Part of this Act.

(7) Where a person who was released on bail subject to a duty to attend at a police station is re-arrested, the provisions of this Part of this Act shall apply to him as they apply to a person arrested for the first time.

(8) In the Magistrates' Courts Act 1980—

    (*a*) the following section shall be substituted for section 43—

"*Bail on arrest*

    **43.**—(1) Where a person has been granted bail under the Police and Criminal Evidence Act 1984 subject to a duty to appear before a magistrates' court, the court before which he is to appear may appoint a later time as the time at which he is to appear and may enlarge the recognizances of any sureties for him at any time.

    (2) The recognizance of any surety for any person granted bail subject to a duty to attend at a police station may be enforced as if it were conditioned for his appearance before a magistrates' court for the petty sessions area in which the police station named in the recognizance is situated."; and

    (*b*) the following subsection shall be substituted for section 117(3)—

"(3) Where a warrant has been endorsed for bail under subsection (1) above—

    (*a*) where the person arrested is to be released on bail on his entering into a recognizance without sureties, it shall not be necessary to take him to a police station, but if he is so taken, he shall be released from custody on his entering into the recognizance; and

    (*b*) where he is to be released on his entering into a recognizance with sureties, he shall be taken to a police station on his arrest, and the custody officer there shall (subject to his approving any surety tendered in compliance with the endorsement) release him from custody as directed in the endorsement.".

*Remands to police detention.*
**48.** In section 128 of the Magistrates' Courts Act 1980—
    (*a*) in subsection (7) for the words "the custody of a constable" there shall be substituted the words "detention at a police station";
    (*b*) after subsection (7) there shall be inserted the following subsection—
"(8) Where a person is commited to detention at a police station under subsection (7) above—
    (*a*) he shall not be kept in such detention unless there is a need for him to be so detained for the purposes of inquiries into other offences;
    (*b*) if kept in such detention, he shall be brought back before the magistrates' court which committed him as soon as that need ceases;
    (*c*) he shall be treated as a person in police detention to whom the duties under section 39 of the Police and Criminal Evidence Act 1984 (responsibilities in relation to persons detained) relate;
    (*d*) his detention shall be subject to periodic review at the times set out in section 40 of that Act (review of police detention).".

*Records of detention.*
**50.**—(1) Each police force shall keep written records showing on an annual basis—
    (*a*) the number of persons kept in police detention for more than 24 hours and subsequently released without charge;
    (*b*) the number of applications for warrants of further detention and the results of the applications; and
    (*c*) in relation to each warrant of further detention—
      (i) the period of further detention authorised by it;
      (ii) the period which the person named in it spent in police detention on its authority; and
      (iii) whether he was charged or released without charge.
(2) Every annual report—
    (*a*) under section 12 of the Police Act 1964; or
    (*b*) made by the Commissioner of Police of the Metropolis, shall contain information about the matters mentioned in subsection (1) above in respect of the period to which the report relates.

*Children*
**52.** This Part of this Act does not apply to a child (as for the time being defined for the purposes of the Children and Young Persons Act 1969) who is arrested without warrant otherwise than for homicide and to whom section 28(4) and (5) of that Act accordingly apply.

## Part V
### Questioning and Treatment of Persons by Police

*Abolition of certain powers of constables to search persons.*
**53.**—(1) Subject to subsection (2) below, there shall cease to have effect any Act (including a local Act) passed before this Act in so far as it authorises—

(*a*) any search by a constable of a person in police detention at a police station; or

(*b*) an intimate search of a person by a constable;

and any rule of common law which authorises a search such as is mentioned in paragraph (*a*) or (*b*) above is abolished.

(2) Nothing in subsection (1)(*a*) above shall affect paragraph 6(2) of Schedule 3 to the Prevention of Terrorism (Temporary Provisions) Act 1984.

*Searches of detained persons*

**54.**—(1) The custody officer at a police station shall ascertain and record or cause to be recorded everything which a person has with him when he is—

(*a*) brought to the station after being arrested elsewhere or after being committed to custody by an order or sentence of a court; or

(*b*) arrested at the station after—

(i) having attended voluntarily there; or

(ii) having accompanied a constable there without having been arrested.

(2) In the case of an arrested person the record shall be made as part of his custody record.

(3) Subject to subsection (4) below, a custody officer may seize and retain any such thing or cause any such thing to be seized and retained.

(4) Clothes and personal effects may only be seized if the custody officer—

(*a*) believes that the person from whom they are seized may use them—

(i) to cause physical injury to himself or any other person;

(ii) to damage property;

(iii) to interfere with evidence; or

(iv) to assist him to escape; or

(*b*) has reasonable grounds for believing that they may be evidence relating to an offence.

(5) Where anything is seized, the person from whom it is seized shall be told the reason for the seizure unless he is—

(*a*) violent or likely to become violent: or

(*b*) incapable of understanding what is said to him.

(6) Subject to subsection (7) below, a person may be searched if the custody officer considers it necessary to enable him to carry out his duty under subsection (1) above and to the extent that the custody officer considers necessary for that purpose.

(7) An intimate search may not be conducted under this section.

(8) A search under this section shall be carried out by a constable.

(9) The constable carrying out a search shall be of the same sex as the person searched.

*Intimate searches.*

**55.**—(1) Subject to the following provisions of this section, if an officer of at least the rank of superintendent has reasonable grounds for believing—

(*a*) that a person who has been arrested and is in the police detention may have concealed on him anything which—

(i) he could use to cause physical injury to himself or others; and

(ii) he might so use while he is police detention or in the custody of a court; or

(*b*) that such a person—
    (i) may have a Class A drug concealed on him; and
    (ii) was in possession of it with the appropriate criminal intent before his arrest.
he may authorise such a search of that person.

(2) An officer may not authorise an intimate search of person for anything unless he has reasonable grounds for believing that it cannot be found without his being intimately searched.

(3) An officer may give an authorisation under section (1) above orally or in writing but, if he gives it orally, he shall confirm it in writing as soon as is practicable.

(4) An intimate search which is only a drug offence search shall be by way of examiniation by a suitably qualified person.

(5) Except as provided by subsection (4) above, an intimate search shall be by way of examination by a suitably qualified person unless an officer of at least the rank of superintendent considers that this is not practicable.

(6) An intimate search which is not carried out as mentioned in subsection (5) above shall be carried out by a constable.

(7) A constable may not carry out an intimate search of a person of the opposite sex.

(8) No intimate search may be carried out except—
    (*a*) at a police station;
    (*b*) at a hospital;
    (*c*) at a registered medical practitioners's surgery; or
    (*d*) at some other place used for medical purposes.

(9) An intimate search which is only a drug offence search may not be carried out at a police station.

(10) If an intimate search of a person is carried out, the custody record relating to him shall state—
    (*a*) which parts of his body were searched; and
    (*b*) why they were searched.

(11) The information required to be recorded by subsection (10) above shall be recorded as soon as practicable after the completion of the search.

(12) The custody officer at a police station may seize and retain anything which is found on an intimate search of a person, or cause any such thing to be seized and rtained—
    (*a*) if he believes that the person from whom it is seized may use it—
        (i) to cause physical injury to himself or any other person;
        (ii) to damage property;
        (iii) to interfere with evidence; or
        (iv) to assist him to escape; or
    (*b*) if he has reasonable grounds for believing that it may be evidence relating to an offence.

(13) Where anything is seized under this section, the person from whom it is seized shall be told the reason for the seizure unless he is—
    (*a*) violent or likely to become violent; or
    (*b*) incapable of understanding what is said to him.

(14) Every annual report—
    (*a*) under section 12 of the Police Act 1964; or
    (*b*) made by the Commissioner of Police of the Metropolis,
shall contain information about searches under this section which have been

carried out in the area to which the report relates during the period to which it relates.

(15) The information about such searches shall include—

(*a*) the total number of searches;

(*b*) the number of searches conducted by way of examination by a suitably qualified person;

(*c*) the number of searches not so conducted but conducted in the presence of such a person; and

(*d*) the result of the searches carried out.

(16) The information shall also include, as separate items—

(*a*) the total number of drug offence searches; and

(*b*) the result of those searches.

(17) In this section—

"the appropriate criminal intent" means intent to commit an offence under—

(*a*) section 5(3) of the Misuse of Drugs Act 1971 (possession of controlled drug with intent to supply to another); or

(*b*) section 68(2) of the Customs and Excise Management Act 1979 (exportation etc. with intent to evade a prohibition or restriction);

"Class A drug" has the meaning assigned to it by section 2(1)(*b*) of the Misuse of Drugs Act 1971;

"drug offence search" means an intimate search for a Class A drug which an officer has authorised by virtue of subsection (1)(*b*) above; and

"suitably qualified person" means—

(*a*) a registered medical practitioner; or

(*b*) a registered nurse.

*Right to have someone informed when arrested*

**56.**—(1) Where a person has been arrested and is being held in custody in a police station or other premises, he shall be entitled, if he so requests, to have one friend or relative or other person who is known to him or who is likely to take an interest in his welfare told, as soon as is practicable except to the extent that delay is permitted by this section, that he has been arrested and is being detained there.

(2) Delay is only permitted—

(*a*) in the case of a person who is in police detention for a serious arrestable offence; and

(*b*) if an officer of at least the rank of superintendent authorises it.

(3) In any case the person in custody must be permitted to exercise the right conferred by subsection (1) above within 36 hours from the relevant time, as defined in section 41(2) above.

(4) An officer may give an authorisation under subsection (2) above orally or in writing, but, if he gives it orally, he shall confirm it in writing as soon as is practicable.

(5) An officer may only authorise delay where he has reasonable grounds for believing that telling the named person of the arrest—

(*a*) will lead to interference with or harm to evidence connected with a serious arrestable offence or interference with or physical injury to other persons; or

(*b*) will lead to the alerting of other persons suspected of having committed such an offence but not yet arrested for it; or

(*c*) will hinder the recovery of any property obtained as a result of such an offence.

(6) If a delay is authorised—

    (a) the detained person shall be told the reason for it; and

    (b) the reason shall be noted on his custody record.

(7) The duties imposed by subsection (6) above shall be performed as soon as is practicable.

(8) The rights conferred by this section on a person detained at a police station or other premises are exercisable whenever he is transferred from one place to another; and this section applies to each subsequent occasion on which they are exercisable as it applies to the first such occasion.

(9) There may be no further delay in permitting the exercise of the right conferred by subsection (1) above once the reason for authorising delay ceases to subsist.

(10) In the foregoing provisions of this section references to a person who has been arrested include references to a person who has been detained under the terrorism provisions and "arrest" includes detention under those provisions.

(11) In its application to a person who has been arrested or detained under the terrorism provisions—

    (a) subsection (2)(a) above shall have effect as if for the words "for a serious arrestable offence" there were substituted the words "under the terrorism provisions";

    (b) subsection (3) above shall have the effect as if for the words form "within" onwards there were substituted the words "before the end of the period beyond which he may no longer be detained without the authority of the Secretary of State"; and

    (c) subsection (5) above shall have effect as if at the end there were added " or

        (d) will lead to interference with the gathering of information about the commission, preparation or instigation of acts of terrorism; or

        (e) by alerting any person, will make it more difficult—

           (i)  to prevent an act of terrorism; or

           (ii)  to secure the apprehension, prosecution or conviction of any person in connection with the commission, preparation or instigation of an act of terrorism.".

*Additional rights of children and young persons*

**57.** The following subsections shall be substituted for section 34(2) of the Children and Young Persons Act 1933—

"(2) Where a child or young person is in police detention, such steps as are practicable shall be taken to ascertain the identity of a person responsible for his welfare.

(3) If it is practicable to ascertain the identity of a person responsible for the welfare of the child or young person, that person shall be informed, unless it is not practicable to do so—

    (a) that the child or young person has been arrested;

    (b) why he has been arrested; and

    (c) where he is being detained.

(4) Where information falls to be given under subsection (3) above, it shall be given as soon as it practicable to do so.

(5) For the purposes of this section the persons who may be responsible for the welfare of a child or young person are—

    (a) his parent or guardian; or

(*b*) any other person who has for the time being assumed responsibility for his welfare.

(6) If it is practicable to give a person responsible for the welfare of the child or young person the information required by subsection (3) above, that person shall be given it as soon as it is practicable to do so.

(7) If it appears that at the time of his arrest a supervision order, as defined in section 11 of the Children and Young Persons Act 1969, is in force in respect of him, the person responsible for his supervision shall also be informed as described in subsection (3) above as soon as it is reasonably practicable to do so.

(8) The reference to a parent or guardian in subsection (5) above is—

(*a*) in the case of a child or young person in the care of a local authority, a reference to that authority; and

(*b*) in the case of a child or young person in the care of a voluntary organisation in which parental rights and duties with respect to him are vested by virtue of a resolution under section 64(1) of the Child Care Act 1980, a reference to that organisation.

(9) The rights conferred on a child or young person by subsections (2) to (8) above are in addition to his rights under section 56 of the Police and Criminal Evidence Act 1984.

(10) The reference in subsection (2) above to a child or young person who is in police detention incluldes a reference to a child or young person who has been detained under the terrorism provisions; and in subsection (3) above "arrest" includes such detention.

(11) In subsection (10) above "the terrorism provisions" has the meaning assigned to it by section 65 of the Police and Criminal Evidence Act 1984".

*Access to legal advice*

**58.**—(1) A person arrested and held in custody in a police station or other premises shall be entitled, if he so requests, to consult a solicitor privately at any time.

(2) Subject to subsection (3) below, a request under subsection (1) above and the time at which it was made shall be recorded in the custody record.

(3) Such a request need not be recorded in the custody record of a person who makes it at a time while he is at a court after being charged with an offence.

(4) If a person makes such a request, he must be permitted to consult a solicitor as soon as is practicable except to the extent that delay is permitted by this section.

(5) In any case he must be permitted to consult a solicitor within 36 hours from the relevant time, as defined in section 41(2) above.

(6) Delay in compliance with a request is only permitted—

(*a*) in the case of a person who is in police detention for a serious arrestable offence; and

(*b*) if an officer of at least the rank of superintendent authorises it.

(7) An officer may give an authorisation under subsection (6) above orally or in writing but, if he gives it orally, he shall confirm it in writing as soon as is practicable.

(8) An officer may only authorise delay where he has reasonable grounds for believing that the exercise of the right conferred by subsection (1) above at the time when the person detained desires to exercise it—

(*a*) will lead to interference with or harm to evidence connected with a serious arrestable offence or interference with or physical injury to other persons; or (*b*) will lead to the alerting of other persons suspected of having committed such an offence but not yet arrested for it; or

(*c*) will hinder the recovery of any property obtained as a result of such an offence.

(9) If delay is authorised—

(*a*) the detained person shall be told the reason for it; and

(*b*) the reason shall be noted on his custody record.

(10) The duties imposed by subsection (9) above shall be performed as soon as is practicable.

(11) There may be further delay in permitting the exercise of the right conferred in subsection (1) above once the reason for authorising delay ceases to subsist.

(12) The reference in subsection (1) above to a person arrested includes a reference to a person who has been detained under the terrorism provisions.

(13) In the application of this section to a person who has been arrested or detained under the terrorism provisions—

(*a*) subsection (5) above shall have effect as if for the words from "within" onwards there were substituted the words "before the end of the period beyond which he may no longer be detained without the authority of the Secretary of State";

(*b*) subsection (6)(*a*) above shall have effect as if for the words "for a serious arrestable offence" there were substituted the words "under the terrorism provisions"; and

(*c*) subsection (8) above shall have effect as if at the end there were added "or

   (*d*) will lead to interference with the gathering of information about the commission, preparation or instigation of acts of terrorism; or

   (*e*) by alerting any person, will make it more difficult—

       (i)  to prevent an act or terrorism; or

       (ii) to secure the apprehension, prosecution or conviction of any person in connection with the commission, preparation or instigation of an act of terrorism.".

(14) If an officer of appropriate rank has reasonable grounds for believing that, unless he gives a direction under subsection (15) below, the exercise by a person arrested or detained under the terrorism provisions of the right conferred by subsection (1) above will have any of the consequences specified in subsection (8) above (as it has effect by virtue of subsection (13) above), he may give a direction under that subsection.

(15) A direction under this subsection is a direction that a person desiring to exercise the right conferred by subsection (1) above may only consult a solicitor in the sight and hearing of a qualified officer of the uniformed branch of the force of which the officer giving the direction is a member.

(16) An officer is qualified for the purpose of subsection (15) above if—

(*a*) he is of at least the rank of inspector; and

(*b*) in the opinion of the officer giving the direction he has no connection with the case.

(17) An officer is of appropriate rank to give a direction under subsection (15) above if he is of at least the rank of Commander or Assistant Chief Constable.

(18) A direction under subsection (15) above shall cease to have effect once the reason for giving it ceases to subsist.

*Legal aid for persons at police stations*

**59.** In section 1 of the Legal Aid Act 1982 (duty solicitors)—

(*a*) in subsection (1) the following paragraph shall be inserted after paragraph (*a*)—

"(*aa*) for the making, by such committees, of arrangements whereby advice and assistance under section 1 of the principal Act is provided for persons—

(i) such as are mentioned in section 29 of the Police and Criminal Evidence Act 1984; or

(ii) arrested and held in custody who—

(i) exercise the right to consult a solicitor conferred on them by section 58(1) of that Act; or

(ii) are permitted to consult a representative of a solicitor; and";

(*b*) in paragrpah (*b*) after the word "representation" there whall be inserted the words "advice and assistance";

(*c*) the following subsection shall be inserted after that subsection—

"(1A) A scheme under section 15 of the principal Act which relates to advice and representation at magistrates' courts may provide that arrangements made under it may be so framed as to preclude solicitors from providing such advice and representation if they do not also provide advice and assistance in pursuance of arrangements made by virtue of a scheme under that section which relates to the provision of advice and assistance for persons such as are mentioned in section 29 of the Police and Criminal Evidence Act 1984 and for persons arrested and held in custody."; and

(*d*) in subsection (5) for the words "such arrangements as are mentioned in subsection (1) above" there shall be substituted the words "arrangements made under subsection (1) above for the provision of advice and representation at the court".

*Tape-recording of interviews*

**60.**—(1) It shall be the duty of the Secretary of State—

(*a*) to issue a code of practice in connection with the tape-recording of interviews of persons suspected of the commission of criminal offences which are held by police officers at police stations; and

(*b*) to make an order requiring the tape-recording of interviews of persons suspected of the commission of criminal offences, or of such descriptions of criminal offences as may be specified in the order, which are so held, in accordance with the code as it has effect for the time being.

(2) An order under subsection (1) above shall be made by statutory instrument and shall be subject to annulment in pursuance of a resolution of either House of Parliament.

*Fingerprinting*

**61.**—(1) Except as provided by this section no person's fingerprints may be taken without the appropriate consent.

(2) Consent to the taking of a person's fingerprints must be in writing if it is given as a time when he is at a police station.

(3) The fingerprints of a person detained as a police station may be taken without the appropriate consent—

(*a*) if an officer of at least the rank of superintendent authorises them to be taken; or

(*b*) if—
>   (i) he has been charged with a recordable offence or informed that he will be reported for such an offence; and
>   (ii) he has not had his fingerprints taken in the course of the investigation of the offence by the police.

(4) An officer may only give an authorisation under subsection (3)(*a*) above if he has reasonable grounds—
>   (*a*) for suspecting the involvement of the person whose fingerprints are to be taken in a criminal offence; and
>   (*b*) for believing that his fingerpirnts will tend to confirm or disprove his involvement.

(5) An officer may give an authorisation under subsection (3)(*a*) above orally or in writing but, if he gives it orally he shall confirm it in writing as soon as is practicable.

(6) An person's fingerprints may be taken without the appropriate consent if he has been convicted of a recordable offence.

(7) In a case where by virtue of subsection (3) or (6) above a person's fingerprints are taken without the appropriate consent—
>   (*a*) he shall be told the reason before his fingerprints are taken; and
>   (*b*) the reason shall be recorded as soon as is practicable after the fingerprints are taken.

(8) If he is detained at a police station when the fingerprints are taken, the reason for taking them shall be recorded on his custody record.

(9) Nothing in this section—
>   (*a*) affects any power conferred by paragraph 18(2) of Schedule 2 to the Immigration Act 1971; or
>   (*b*) applies to a person arrested or detained under the terrorism provisions.


*Intimate samples*

**62.**—(1) An intimate sample may be taken form a person in police detention only—
>   (*a*) if a police officer of at least the rank of superintendent authorises it to be taken; and
>   (*b*) if the appropriate consent is given.

(2) An officer may only give an authorisation if he has reasonable grounds—
>   (*a*) for suspecting the involvement of the person from whom the sample is to be taken in a serious arrestable offence; and
>   (*b*) for believing that the sample will tend to confirm or disprove his involvement.

(3) An officer may give an authorisation under subsection (1) above orally or in writing but, if he gives it orally, he shall confirm it in writing as soon as is practicable.

(4) The approriate consent must be given in writing.

(5) Where—
>   (*a*) an authorisation has been given; and
>   (*b*) it is proposed that an intimate sample shall be taken in pursuance of the authorisation,

an officer shall inform the person from whom the sample is to be taken—
>   (i) of the giving of the authorisation; and
>   (ii) of the grounds for giving it.

(6) The duty imposed by subsection (5)(ii) above includes a duty to state the nature of the offence in which it is suspected that the person from whom the sample is to be taken has been involved.

(7) If an intimate sample is taken from a person—

(*a*) the authorisation by virtue of which it was taken;

(*b*) the grounds for giving the authorisation; and

(*c*) the fact that the appropriate consent was given,

shall be recorded as soon as is practicable after the sample is taken.

(8) If an intimate sample is taken from a person detained at a police station, the matters required to be recorded by subsection (7) above shall be recorded in his custody record.

(9) An intimate sample, other than a sample of urine or saliva, may only be taken from a person by a registered medical practitioner.

(10) Where the appropriate consent to the taking of an intimate sample from a person was refused without good cause, in any proceedings against that person for an offence—

(*a*) the court, in determining—

(i) whether to commit that person for trial; or

(ii) whether there is a case to answer; and

(*b*) the court or jury, in determining whether that person is guilty of the offence charged,

may draw such inferences from the refusal as appear proper; and the refusal may, on the basis of such inferences, be treated as, or as capable of amounting to, corroboration of any evidence against the person in relation to which the refusal is material.

(11) Nothing in this section affects sections 5 to 12 of the Road Traffic Act 1972.


*Other samples*

**63.**—(1) Except as provided by this section, a non-intimate sample may not be taken from a person without the appropriate consent.

(2) Consent to the taking of a non-intimate sample must be given in writing.

(3) A non-intimate sample may be taken from a person without the appropriate consent if—

(*a*) he is in police detention or is being held in custody by the police on the authority of a court; and

(*b*) an officer of at least the rank of superintendent authorises it to be taken without the appropriate consent.

(4) An officer may only give an authorisation under subsection (3) above if he has reasonable grounds—

(*a*) for suspecting the involvement of the person from whom the sample is to be taken in a serious arrestable offence; and

(*b*) for believing that the sample will tend to confiem or disprove his involvement.

(5) An officer may give an authorisation under subsection (3) above orally or in writing but, if he gives it orally, he shall confirm it in writing as soon as is practicable.

(6) Where—

(*a*) an authorisation has been given; and

(*b*) it is proposed that a non-intimate sample shall be taken in pursuance of the authorisation,

an officer shall inform the person from whom the sample is to be taken—
>    (i) of the giving of the authorisation; and
>    (ii) of the grounds for giving it.

(7) The duty imposed by subsection (6)(ii) above includes a duty to state the nature of the offence in which it is suspected that the person from whom the sample is to be taken has been involved.

(8) If a non-intimate sample is taken from a person by virtue of subsection (3) above—
>    (*a*) the authorisation by virtue of which it was taken; and
>    (*b*) the grounds for giving the authorisation,

shall be recorded as soon as is practicable after the sample is taken.

(9) If a non-intimate sample is taken from a person detained at a police station, the matters required to be recorded by subsection (8) above shall be recorded in his custody record.

*Destruction of fingerprints and samples.*
**64.**—(1) If—
>    (*a*) fingerprints or samples are taken from a person in connection with the investigation of an offence; and
>    (*b*) he is cleared of that offence,

they must be destroyed as soon as is practicable after the conclusion of the proceedings.

(2) If—
>    (*a*) fingerprints or samples are taken from a person in connection with such an investigation; and
>    (*b*) it is decided that he shall not be prosecuted for the offence and he has not admitted it and been dealt with by way of being cautioned by a constable,

they must be destroyed as soon as is practicable after that decision is taken.

(3) If—
>    (*a*) fingerprints or samples are taken from a person in connection with the investigation of an offence; and
>    (*b*) that person is not suspected of having committed the offence.

they must be destroyed as soon as they have fulfilled the purpose for which they were taken.

(4) Proceedings which are discontinued are to be treated as concluded for the purposes of this section.

(5) If fingerprints are destroyed, any copies of them shall also be destroyed.

(6) A person who asks to be allowed to witness the destruction of his fingerprints or copies of them shall have a right to witness it.

(7) Nothing in this section—
>    (*a*) affects any power conferred by paragraph 18(2) of Schedule 2 to the Immigration Act 1971; or
>    (*b*) applies to a person arrested or detained under the terrorism provisions.

*Part V—supplementary.*
**65.** In this Part of this Act—
>    "appropriate consent" means
>>    (*a*) in relation to a person who has attained the age of 17 years, the consent of that person;
>>    (*b*) in relation to a person who has not attained that age but has attained the age of 14 years, the consent of that person and his parent or guardian; and

    (*c*) in relation to a person who has not attained the age of 14 years, the consent of his parent or guardian;

"fingerprints" includes palm prints;

"intimate sample" means sample of blood, semen or any other tissue fluide, urine, saliva or pubic hair, or a swab taken from a person's body orifice;

"non-intimate sample" means—

    (*a*) a sample of hair other than pubic hair;

    (*b*) a sample taken from a nail or from under a nail;

    (*c*) a swab taken from any part of a person's body other than a body orifice;

    (*d*) a footprint or a similar impression of any part of a person's body other than a part of his hand;

"the terrorism provisions" means—

    (*a*) section 12(1) of the Prevention of Terrorism (Temporary Provisions) Act 1984; and

    (*b*) any provision conferring a power of arrest or detention and contained in an order under section 13 of this Act; and

"terrorism" has the meaning assigned to it by section 14(1) of that Act.

## Part VI

### Codes of Practice—General

*Codes of practice*

**66.** The Secretary of State shall issue codes of practice in connection with—

    (*a*) the exercise by police officers of statutory powers—

        (i) to search a person without first arresting him; or

        (ii) to search a vehicle without making an arrest;

    (*b*) the detention, treatment, questioning and identification of persons by police officers;

    (*c*) searches of premises by police officers; and

    (*d*) the seizure of property found by police officers on persons or premises.

*Codes of practice—supplementary*

**67.**—(1) When the Secretary of State proposes to issue a code of practice to which this section applies, he shall prepare and publish a draft of that code, shall consider any representations made to him about the draft and may modify the draft accordingly.

(2) This section applies to a code of practice under section 60 or 66 above.

(3) The Secretary of State shall lay before both Houses of Parliament a draft of any code of practice prepared by him under this section.

(4) When the Secretary of State has laid the draft of a code before Parliament, he may bring the code into operation by order made by statutory instrument.

(5) No order under subsection (4) above shall have effect until approved by a resolution of each House of Parliament.

(6) An order bringing a code of practice into operation may contain such transitional provisions or savings as appear to the Secretay of State to be necessary or expedient in connection with the code of practice thereby brought into operation.

(7) The Secretary of State may from time to time revise the whole or any part of a code of practice to which this section applies and issue that revised code; and the foregoing provisions of this section shall apply (with appropriate modifications) to such a revised code as they apply to the first issue of a code.

(8) A police officer shall be liable to disciplinary proceedings for a failure to comply with any provision of such a code, unless such proceedings are precluded by section 104 below.

(9) Persons other than police officers who are charged with the duty of investigating offences or charging offenders shall in the discharge of that duty have regard to any relevant provision of such a code.

(10) A failure on the part—

(a) of a police officer to comply with any provision of such a code; or

(b) of any person other than a police officer who is charged with the duty of investigating offences or charging offenders to have regard to any relevant provision of such a code in the discharge of that duty,

shall not of itself render him liable to any cirminal or civil proceedings.

(11) In all crimianl and civil proceedings any such code shall be admissible in evidence; and if any provision of such a code appears to the court or tribunal conducting the proceedings to be relevant to any question arising in the proceedings it shall be taken into account in determining that question.

(12) In this section "criminal proceedings" includes—

(a) proceedings in the United Kingdom or elsewhere before a court-martial constituted under the Army Act 1955, the Air Force Act 1955 or the Naval Discipline Act 1957 or a disciplinary court constituted under section 50 of the said Act of 1957;

(b) proceedings before the Courts-Martial Appeal Court; and

(c) proceedings before a Standing Civilian Court.


## Part VIII

### Evidence in Criminal Proceedings—General

### Confessions

*Confessions.*

**76.**—(1) In any proceedings a confession made by an accused person may be given in evidence against him in so far as it is relevant to any matter in issue in the proceedings and is not excluded by the court in pursuance of this section.

(2) If, in any proceedings where the prosecution proposes to give in evidence a confession made by an accused person, it is represented to the court that the confession was or may have been obtained—

(a) by oppression of the person who made it; or

(b) in consequence of anything said or done which was likely, in the circumstances existing at the time, to render unreliable an confession which might be made by him in consequence thereof,

the court shall not allow the confession to be given in evidence against him except in so far as the prosecution proves to the court beyond reasonable doubt that the confession (notwithstanding that it may be true) was not obtained as aforesaid.

(3) In any proceedings where the prosecution proposes to give in evidence a confession made by an accused person, the court may of its own motion require the prosecution, as a condition of allowing it to do so, to prove that the confession was not obtained as mentioned in subsection (2) above.

(4) The fact that a confession is wholly or partly excluded in pursuance of this section shall not affect the admissibility in evidence—

    (*a*) of any facts discovered as a result of the confession; or

    (*b*) where the confession is relevant as showing that the accused speaks, writes or expresses himself in a particular way, of so much of the confession as is necessary to show that he does so.

(5) Evidence that a fact to which this subsection applies was discovered as a result of a statement made by an accused person shall not be admissible unless evidence of how it was discovered is given by him or on his behalf.

(6) Subsection (5) above applies—

    (*a*) to any fact discovered as a result of a confession which is wholly excluded in pursuance of this section; and

    (*b*) to any fact discovered as a result of a confession which is partly so excluded, if the fact is discovered as a result of the excluded part of the confession.

(7) Nothing in Part VII of this Act shall prejudice the admissibility of a confession made by an accused person.

(8) In this section "oppression" includes torture, inhuman or degrading treatment, and the use or threat of violence (whether or not amounting to torture).

*Confessions by mentally handicapped persons*

**77.**—(1) Without prejudice to the general duty of the court at a trial on indictment to direct the jury on any matter on which it appears to the court appropriate to do so, where at such a trial—

    (*a*) the case against the accused depends wholly or substantially on a confession by him; and

    (*b*) the court is satisfied—

        (i) that he is mentally handicapped; and

        (ii) that the confession was not made in the presence of an independent person,

the court shall warn the jury that there is special need for caution before convicting the accused in reliance on the confession, and shall explain that the need arises because of the circumstances mentioned in paragraphs (*a*) and (*b*) above.

(2) In the case where at the summary trial of a person for an offence it appears to the court that a warning under subsection (1) above would be required if the trial were on indictment, the court shall treat the case as one in which there is a special need for caution before convicting the accused on his confession.

(3) In this section—

    "independent person" does not include a police officer or a person employed for, or engaged on, police purposes;

    "mentally handicapped", in relation to a person means that he is in a state of arrested or incomplete development of mind which includes significant impairment of intelligence and social functioning; and

    "police purposes" has the meaning assigned to it by section 64 of the Police Act 1964.

## Miscellaneous

*Exclusion of unfair evidence*
**78.**—(1) In any proceedings the court may refuse to allow evidence on which the prosecution proposes to rely to be given if it appears to the court that, having regard to all the circumstances, including the circumstances in which the evidence was obtained, the admission of the evidence would have such an adverse effect on the fairness of the proceedings that the court ought not to admit it.

(2) Nothing in this section shall prejudice any rule of law requiring a court to exclude evidence.

*Advance notice of expert evidence in Crown Court*
**81.**—(1) Crown Court Rules may make provision for—
   (a) requiring any party to proceedings before the court to disclose to the other party or parties any expert evidence which he proposes to adduce in the proceedings; and
   (b) prohibiting a party who fails to comply in respect of any evidence with any requirement imposed by virtue of paragraph (a) above from adducing that evidence without the leave of the court.

(2) Crown Court Rules made by virtue of this section may specify the kinds of expert evidence to which they apply and may exempt facts or matters of any description specified in the rules.

## Part XI

## Miscellaneous and Supplementary

*Application of Act to Customs and Excise*
**114.**—(1) "Arrested", "arresting", "arrest" and "to arrest" shall respectively be substituted for "detained", "detaining", "detention" and "to detain" wherever in the customs and excise Acts, as defined in section 1(1) of the Customs and Excise Management Act 1979, those words are used in relation to persons.

(2) The Treasury may by order direct—[1]
   (a) that any provision of this Act which relates to investigations of offences conducted by police officers or to persons detained by the police shall apply, subject to such modifications as the order may specify, to investigations conducted by officers of Customs and Excise of offences which relate to assigned matters, as defined in section 1 of the Customs and Excise Management Act 1979, or to persons detained by officers of Customs and Excise; and
   (b) that, in relation to investigations of offences conducted by officers of customes and Excise—
      (i) this Act shall have effect as if the following section were inserted after section 14—

*"Exception for Customs and Excise*
14A. Material in the possession of a person who acquired or created it in the course of any trade, business, profession or other occupation or for the purpose of any paid or unpaid office and which relates to an assigned matter, as defined in

---

1 Such an order has been made by the Police and Criminal Evidence Act 1984 (Application to Customs and Excise) Order 1985 (S.I. no. 1800), effective from 1 January 1986.

section 1 of the Customs and Excise Management Act 1979, is neither excluded material nor special procedure material for the purposes of any enactment such as is mentioned in section 9(2) above."; and

      (ii) section 55 above shall have effect as if it related only to things such as are mentioned in subsection (1)(*a*) of that section.

(3) Nothing in any order under subsection (2) above shall be taken to limit any powers exercisable under section 164 of the Customs and Excise Management Act 1979.

(4) In this section "officers of Customs and Excise" means officers commissioned by the Commissioners of Customs and Excise under section 6(3) of the Customs and Excise Management Act 1979.

(5) An order under this section shall be made by statutory instrument and shall be subject to annulment in pursuance of a resolution of either House of Parliament.

*Meaning of "serious arrestable offence"*

**116.**—(1) This section has effect for determining whether an offence is a serious arrestable offence for the purposes of this Act.

(2) The following arrestable offences are always serious—

      (*a*) an offence (whether at common law or under any enactment) specified in Part 1 of Schedule 5 to this Act; and

      (*b*) an offence under an enactment specified in Part II of that Schedule.

(3) Subject to subsections (4) and (5) below, any other arrestable offence is serious only if its commission—

      (*a*) has led to any of the consequences specified in subsection (6) below; or

      (*b*) is intended or is likely to lead to any of those consequences.

(4) An arrestable offence which consists of making a threat is serious if carrying out the threat would be likely to lead to any of the consequences specified in subsection (6) below.

(5) An offence under section 1, 9 or 10 of the Prevention of Terrorism (Temporary Provisions) Act of 1984 is always a serious arrestable offence for the purposes of section 56 or 58 above, and an attempt or conspiracy to commit any such offence is also always a serious arrestable offence for those purposes.

(6) The consequences mentioned in subsections (3) and (4) above are

      (*a*) serious harm to the security of the State or to public order;

      (*b*) serious interference with the administration of justice or with the investigation of offences or of a particular offence;

      (*c*) the death of any person;

      (*d*) serious injury to any person;

      (*e*) substantial financial gain to any person; and

      (*f*) serious financial loss to any person.

(7) Loss is serious for the purposes of this section if, having regard to all the circumstances, it is serious for the person who suffers it.

(8) In this section "injury" includes any disease and any impairment of a person's physical or mental condition.

*General interpretation.*

**118.**—(1) In this Act—

    "arrestable offence" has the meaning assigned to it by section 24 above;

    "designated police station" has the meaning assigned to it by section 35 above;

"document" has the same meaning as in Part I of the Civil Evidence Act 1968;

"intimate search" means a search which consists of the physical examination of a person's orifices;

"item subject ot legal privilege" has the meaning assigned to it by section 10 above;

"parent or guardian" means—

> (*a*) in the case of a child or young person in the care of a local authority, that authority; and

> (*b*) in the case of a child or young person in the care of a voluntary organisation in which parental rights and duties with respect to him are vested by virtue of a resolution under section 64(1) of the Child Care Act 1980, that organisation;

"premises" has the meaning assigned to it by section 23 above;

"recordable offence" means any offence to which regulations under section 27 above apply;

"vessel" includes any ship, boat, raft or other apparatus constructed or adapted for floating on water.

(2) A person is in police detention for the purposes of this Act if—

> (*a*) he has been taken to a police station after being arrested for an offence; or

> (*b*) he is arrested at a police station after attending voluntarily at the station or accompanying a constable to it,

and is detained there or is detained elsewhere in the charge of a constable, except that a person who is at a court after being charged is not in police detention for those purposes.

**121.**—(1) This Act, except section 120 above, this section and section 122 below, shall come into operation on such day as the Secretary of State may by order made by statutory instrument appoint, and different days may be so appointed for different provisions and for different purposes.[2]

(2) Different days may be appointed under this section for the coming into force of section 60 above in different areas....

## SCHEDULE 1
(Section 9.)

### SPECIAL PROCEDURE

#### Making of orders by circuit judge

1. If on an application made by a constable a circuit judge is satisfied that one or other of the sets of access conditions is fulfilled, he may make an order under paragraph 4 below.

2. The first set of access conditions is fulfilled if—

> (*a*) there are reasonable grounds for believing—

>> (i) that a serious arrestable offence has been committed;

>> (ii) that there is material which consists of special procedure material or includes special procedure material and does not also include excluded material on premises specified in the application;

>> (iii) that the material is likely to be of substantial value (whether by itself

2   All relevant provisions of the Act are expected to have been brought into force by 1 January 1986.

or together with other material) to the investigation in connection with which the application is made; and

   (iv) that the material is likely to be relevant evidence;

  (b) other methods of obtaining the material—

   (i) have been tried without success; or

   (ii) have not been tried because it appeared that they were bound to fail; and

  (c) it is in the public interest, having regard—

   (i) to the benefit likely to accrue to the investigation if the material is obtained; and

   (ii) to the circumstances under which the person in possession of the material holds it, that the material should be produced or that access to it should be given.

3. The second set of access conditions is fulfilled if—

  (a) there are reasonable grounds for believing that there is material which consists of or includes excluded material or special procedure material on premises specified in the application;

  (b) but for section 9(2) above a search of the premises for that material could have been authorised by the issue of a warrant to a constable under an enactment other than this Schedule; and

  (c) the issue of such a warrant would have been appropriate.

4. An order under this paragraph is an order that the person who appears to the circuit judge to be in possession of the material to which the application relates shall—

  (a) produce it to a constable for him to take away; or

  (b) give a constable access to it,

not later than the end of the period of seven days from the date of the order or the end of such longer period as the order may specify.

5. Where the material consists of information contained in a computer—

  (a) an order under paragraph 4(a) above shall have effect as an order to produce the material in a form in which it can be taken away and in which it is visible and legible; and

  (b) an order under paragraph 4(b) above shall have effect as an order to give a constable access to the material in a form in which it is visible and legible.

6. For the purposes of section 21 and 22 above material produced in pursuance of an order under paragraph 4(a) above shall be treated as if it were material seized by a constable.

### Notices of applications for orders

7. An application for an order under paragraph 4 above shall be made inter partes.

8. Notice of an application for such an order may be served on a person either by delivering it to him or by leaving it at his proper address or by sending it by post to him in a registered letter or by the recorded delivery service.

9. Such a notice may be served—

  (a) on a body corporate, by serving it on the body's secretary or clerk or other similar officer; and

  (b) on a partnership, by serving it on one of the partners.

10. For the purposes of this Schedule, and of section 7 of the Interpretation Act 1978 in its application to this Schedule, the proper address of a person, in the case

of secretary or clerk or other similar officer of a body corporate, shall be that of the registered or principal office of that body, in the case of a partner of a firm shall be that of the principal office of the firm, and in any other case shall be the last known address of the person to be served.

11. Where notice of an application for an order under paragraph 4 above has been served on a person, he shall not conceal, destroy, alter or dispose of the material to which the application relates except—

    (*a*) with the leave of a judge; or

    (*b*) with the written permission of a constable, until—

        (i) the application is dismissed or abandoned; or

        (ii) he has complied with an order under paragraph 4 above made on the application.

## Issue of warrants by circuit judge

12. If on an application made by a constable a circuit judge—

    (*a*) is satisfied—

        (i) that either set of access conditions is fulfilled; and

        (ii) that any of the further conditions set out in paragraph 14 below is also fulfilled; or

    (*b*) is satisfied—

        (i) that the second set of access conditions is fulfilled; and

        (ii) that an order under paragraph 4 above relating to the material has not been complied with,

he may issue a warrant authorising a constable to enter and search the premises.

13. A constable may seize and retain anything for which a search has been authorised under paragraph 12 above.

14. The further conditions mentioned in paragraph 12(*a*)(ii) above are—

    (*a*) that it is not practicable to communicate with any person entitled to grant entry to the premises to which the application relates;

    (*b*) that it is practicable to communicate with a person entitled to grant entry to the premises but it is not practicable to communicate with any person entitled to grant access to the material;

    (*c*) that the material contains information which—

        (i) is subject to a restriction or obligation such as is mentioned in section 11(2)(*b*) above; and

        (ii) is likely to be disclosed in breach of it if a warrant is not issued;

    (*d*) that service of notice of an application for an order under paragraph 4 above may seriously prejudice the investigation.

15.—(1) If a person fails to comply with an order under paragraph 4 above, a circuit judge may deal with him as if he had committed a contempt of the Crown Court.

(2) Any enactment relating to contempt of the Crown Court shall have effect in relation to such a failure as if it were such a contempt.

## Costs

16. The costs of any application under this Schedule and of anything done or to be done in pursuance of an order made under it shall be in the discretion of the judge.

# Intoxicating Substances (Supply) Act 1985

(CHAPTER 26)

*Offence of supply of intoxicating substance*

**1.**—(1) It is an offence for a person to supply or offer to supply a substance other than a controlled drug—

    (*a*) to a person under the age of eighteen whom he knows, or has reasonable cause to believe, to be under that age; or

    (*b*) to a person—

        (i) who is acting on behalf of a person under that age; and

        (ii) whom he knows, or has reasonable cause to believe, to be so acting,

if he knows or has reasonable cause to believe that the substance is, or its fumes are, likely to be inhaled by the person under the age of eighteen for the purpose of causing intoxication.

(2) In proceedings against any person for an offence under subsection (1) above it is a defence for him to show that at the time he made the supply or offer he was under the age of eighteen and was acting otherwise than in the course or furtherance of a business.

(3) A person guilty of an offence under this section shall be liable on summary conviction to imprisonment for a term not exceeding six months or to a fine not exceeding level 5 on the standard scale (as defined in section 75 of the Criminal Justice Act 1982),[1] or to both.

(4) In this section "controlled drug" has the same meaning as in the Misuse of Drugs Act 1971.

*Short title, commencement and extent.*

**2.**—(1) This Act may be cited as the Intoxicating Substances (Supply) Act 1985.

(2) This Act shall come into force at the end of the period of two months beginning with the day on which it is passed.[2]

(3) This Act extends to Northern Ireland but not to Scotland.

---

1   At present £2,000
2   It came into force on 13 August 1985

# Single Convention on Narcotic Drugs, 1961

## (AS AMENDED BY THE 1972 PROTOCOL AMENDING THE SINGLE CONVENTION ON NARCOTIC DRUGS, 1961)

### *Resolution III*

#### SOCIAL CONDITIONS AND PROTECTION AGAINST DRUG ADDICTION

*The Conference,*[1]

*Recalling* that the Preamble to the Single Convention on Narcotic Drugs, 1961, states that the Parties to the Convention are "concerned with the health and welfare of mankind" and are "conscious of their duty to prevent and combat" the evil of drug addiction,

*Considering* that the discussions at the Conference have given evidence of the desire to take effective steps to prevent drug addiction,

*Considering* that, while drug addiction leads to personal degradation and social disruption, it happens very often that the deplorable social and economic conditions in which certain individuals and certain groups are living predispose them to drug addiction,

*Recognizing* that social factors have a certain and sometimes preponderant influence on the behaviour of individuals and groups,

*Recommends that the Parties*:

1. Should bear in mind that drug addiction is often the result of an unwholesome social atmosphere in which those who are most exposed to the danger of drug abuse live;

2. Should do everything in their power to combat the spread of the illicit use of drugs;

3. Should develop leisure and other activities conducive to the sound physical and psychological health of young people.

#### PREAMBLE

*The Parties,*

*Concerned* with the health and welfare of mankind,

*Recognizing* that the medical use of narcotic drugs continues to be indispensable for the relief of pain and suffering and that adequate provision must be made to ensure the availability of narcotic drugs for such purposes,

---

1 United Nations Conference to Consider Amendments to the Single Convention on Narcotic Drugs 1961, held at Geneva, 6–24 March 1972

*Recognizing* that addiction to narcotic drugs constitutes a serious evil for the individual and is fraught with social and economic danger to mankind,

*Conscious* of their duty to prevent and combat this evil,

*Considering* that effective measures against abuse of narcotic drugs require co-ordinated and universal action,

*Understanding* that such universal action calls for international co-operation guided by the same principles and aimed at common objectives,

*Acknowledging* the competence of the United Nations in the field of narcotics control and desirous that the international organs concerned should be within the framework of that Organization,

*Desiring* to conclude a generally acceptable international convention replacing existing treaties on narcotic drugs, limiting such drugs to medical and scientific use, and providing for continuous international co-operation and control for the achievement of such aims and objectives,

*Hereby agree* as follows: . . .

## Article 21

### LIMITATION OF MANUFACTURE AND IMPORTATION

1. The total of the quantities of each drug manufactured and imported by any country or territory in any one year shall not exceed the sum of the following:

(*a*) The quantity consumed, within the limit of the relevant estimate, for medical and scientific purposes;

(*b*) The quantity used, within the limit of the relevant estimate, for the manufacture of other drugs, of preparations in Schedule III, and of substances not covered by this Convention;

(*c*) The quantity exported;

(*d*) The quantity added to the stock for the purpose of bringing that stock up to the level specified in the relevant estimate; and

(*e*) The quantity acquired within the limit of the relevant estimate for special purposes.

2. From the sum of the quantities specified in paragraph 1 there shall be deducted any quantity that has been seized and released for licit use, as well as any quantity taken from special stocks for the requirements of the civilian population.

3. If the Board finds that the quantity manufactured and imported in any one year exceeds the sum of the quantities specified in paragraph 1, less any deductions required under paragraph 2 of this article, any excess so established and remaining at the end of the year shall, in the following year, be deducted from the quantity to be manufactured or imported and from the total of the estimates as defined in paragraph 2 of article 19.

4. (*a*) If it appears from the statistical returns on imports or exports (article 20) that the quantity exported to any country or territory exceeds the total of the

estimates for that country or territory, as defined in paragraph 2 of article 19, with the addition of the amounts shown to have been exported, and after deduction of any excess as established in paragraph 3 of this article, the Board may notify this fact to States which, in the opinion of the Board, should be so informed;

(b) On receipt of such a notification, Parties shall not during the year in question authorize any further exports of the drug concerned to that country or territory, except:

(i) In the event of a supplementary estimate being furnished for that country or territory in respect both of any quantity over-imported and of the additional quantity required, or

(ii) In exceptional cases where the export, in the opinion of the Government of the exporting country, is essential for the treatment of the sick.

### Article 21 bis

#### LIMITATION OF PRODUCTION OF OPIUM

1. The production of opium by any country or territory shall be organized and controlled in such manner as to ensure that, as far as possible, the quantity produced in any one year shall not exceed the estimate of opium to be produced as established under paragraph 1 (f) of article 19.

2. If the Board finds on the basis of information at its disposal in accordance with the provisions of this Convention that a Party which has submitted an estimate under paragraph 1 (f) of article 19 has not limited opium produced within its borders to licit purposes in accordance with relevant estimates and that a significant amount of opium produced, whether licitly or illicitly, within the borders of such a Party, has been introduced into the illicit traffic, it may; after studying the explanations of the Party concerned, which shall be submitted to it within one month after notification of the finding in question, decide to deduct all, or a portion, of such an amount from the quantity to be produced and from the total of the estimates as defined in paragraph 2 (b) of article 19 for the next year in which such a deduction can be technically accomplished, taking into account the season of the year and contractual commitments to export opium. This decision shall take effect ninety days after the Party concerned is notified thereof.

3. After notifying the Party concerned of the decision it has taken under paragraph 2 above with regard to a deduction, the Board shall consult with that Party in order to resolve the situation satisfactorily.

4. If the situation is not satisfactorily resolved, the Board may utilize the provisions of article 14 where appropriate.

5. In taking its decision with regard to a deduction under paragraph 2 above, the Board shall take into account not only all relevant circumstances including those giving rise to the illicit traffic problem referred to in paragraph 2 above, but also any relevant new control measures which may have been adopted by the Party.

## Article 22

SPECIAL PROVISION APPLICABLE TO CULTIVATION

1. Whenever the prevailing conditions in the country or a territory of a Party render the prohibition of the cultivation of the opium poppy, the coca bush or the cannabis plant the most suitable measure, in its opinion, for protecting the public health and welfare and preventing the diversion of drugs into the illicit traffic, the Party concerned shall prohibit cultivation.

2. A Party prohibiting cultivation of the opium poppy or the cannabis plant shall take appropriate measures to seize any plants illicitly cultivated and to destroy them, except for small quantities required by the Party for scientific or research purposes.

## Article 23

NATIONAL OPIUM AGENCIES

1. A Party that permits the cultivation of the opium poppy for the production of opium shall establish, if it has not already done so, and maintain, one or more government agencies (hereafter in this article referred to as the Agency) to carry out the functions required under this article.

2. Each such Party shall apply the following provisions to the cultivation of the opium poppy for the production of opium and to opium;

(*a*) The Agency shall designate the areas in which, and the plots of land on which, cultivation of the opium poppy for the purpose of producing opium shall be permitted.

(*b*) Only cultivators licensed by the Agency shall be authorized to engage in such cultivation.

(*c*) Each licence shall specify the extent of the land on which the cultivation is permitted.

(*d*) All cultivators of the opium poppy shall be required to deliver their total crops of opium to the Agency. The Agency shall purchase and take physical possession of such crops as soon as possible, but not later than four months after the end of the harvest.

(*e*) The Agency shall, in respect of opium, have the exclusive right of importing, exporting, wholesale trading and maintaining stocks other than those held by manufacturers of opium alkaloids, medicinal opium or opium preparations. Parties need not extend this exclusive right to medicinal opium and opium preparations.

3. The government functions referred to in paragraph 2 shall be discharged by a single government agency if the constitution of the Party concerned permits it.

## Article 24

LIMITATION ON PRODUCTION OF OPIUM FOR INTERNATIONAL TRADE

1. (*a*) If any Party intends to initiate the production of opium or to increase existing production, it shall take account of the prevailing world need for opium

in accordance with the estimates thereof published by the Board so that the production of opium by such Party does not result in overproduction of opium in the world.

(*b*) A Party shall not permit the production of opium or increase the existing production thereof if in its opinion such production or increased production in its territory may result in illicit traffic of opium.

2. (*a*) Subject to paragraph 1, where a Party which as of 1 January 1961 was not producing opium for export desires to export opium which it produces, in amounts not exceeding five tons annually, it shall notify the Board, furnishing with such notification information regarding:

(i) The controls in force as required by this Convention respecting the opium to be produced and exported, and

(ii) The name of the country or countries to which it expects to export such opium;

and the Board may either approve such notification or may recommend to the Party that it not engage in the production of opium for export.

(*b*) Where a Party other than a Party referred to in paragraph 3 desires to produce opium for export in amounts exceeding five tons annually, it shall notify the Council, furnishing with such notification relevant information including:

(i) The estimated amounts to be produced for export;

(ii) The controls existing or proposed respecting the opium to be produced;

(iii) The name of the country or countries to which it expects to export such opium;

and the Council shall either approve the notification or may recommend to the Party that it not engage in the production of opium for export.

3. Notwithstanding the provisions of subparagraphs (*a*) and (*b*) of paragraph 2, a Party that during ten years immediately prior to 1 January 1961 exported opium which such country produced may continue to export opium which it produces.

4. (*a*) A Party shall not import opium from any country or territory except opium produced in the territory of:

(i) A Party referred to in paragraph 3;

(ii) A Party that has notified the Board as provided in subparagraph (*a*) of paragraph 2; or

(iii) A Party that has received the approval of the Council as provided in subparagraph (*b*) of paragraph 2.

(*b*) Notwithstanding subparagraph (*a*) of this paragraph, a Party may import opium produced by any country which produced and exported opium during the ten years prior to 1 January 1961 if such country has established and maintains a national control organ or agency for the purposes set out in article 23 and has in force an effective means of ensuring that the opium it produces is not diverted into the illicit traffic.

5. The provisions of this article do not prevent a Party:

(*a*) From producing opium sufficient for its own requirements; or

(*b*) From exporting opium seized in the illicit traffic, to another Party in accordance with the requirements of this Convention.

## Article 25
### CONTROL OF POPPY STRAW

1. A Party that permits the cultivation of the opium poppy for purposes other than the production of opium shall take all measures necessary to ensure:

(*a*) That opium is not produced from such opium poppies; and

(*b*) That the manufacture of drugs from poppy straw is adequately controlled.

2. The Parties shall apply to poppy straw the system of import certificates and export authorizations as provided in article 31, paragraphs 4 to 15.

3. The Parties shall furnish statistical information on the import and export of poppy straw as required for drugs under article 20, paragraphs 1 (*d*) and 2 (*b*).

## Article 26
### THE COCA BUSH AND COCA LEAVES

1. If a Party permits the cultivation of the coca bush, it shall apply thereto and to coca leaves the system of controls as provided in article 23 respecting the control of the opium poppy, but as regards paragraph 2 (*d*) of that article, the requirements imposed on the Agency therein referred to shall be only to take physical possession of the crops as soon as possible after the end of the harvest.

2. The Parties shall so far as possible enforce the uprooting of all coca bushes which grow wild. They shall destroy the coca bushes if illegally cultivated.

## Article 27
### ADDITIONAL PROVISIONS RELATING TO COCA LEAVES

1. The Parties may permit the use of coca leaves for the preparation of a flavouring agent, which shall not contain any alkaloids, and, to the extent necessary for such use, may permit the production, import, export, trade in and possession of such leaves.

2. The Parties shall furnish separately estimates (article 19) and statistical information (article 20) in respect of coca leaves for preparation of the flavouring agent, except to the extent that the same coca leaves are used for the extraction of alkaloids and the flavouring agent, and so explained in the estimates and statistical information.

## Article 28
### CONTROL OF CANNABIS

1. If a Party permits the cultivation of the cannabis plant for the production of cannabis or cannabis resin, it shall apply thereto the system of controls as provided in article 23 respecting the control of the opium poppy.

2. This Convention shall not apply to the cultivation of the cannabis plant exclusively for industrial purposes (fibre and seed) or horticultural purposes.

3. The Parties shall adopt such measures as may be necessary to prevent the misuse of, and illicit traffic in, the leaves of the cannabis plant.

## Article 29
### MANUFACTURE

1. The Parties shall require that the manufacture of drugs be under licence except where such manufacture is carried out by a State enterprise or State enterprises.

2. The Parties shall:

(a) Control all persons and enterprises carrying on or engaged in the manufacture of drugs;

(b) Control under licence the establishments and premises in which such manufacture may take place; and

(c) Require that licensed manufacturers of drugs obtain periodical permits specifying the kinds and amounts of drugs which they shall be entitled to manufacture. A periodical permit, however, need not be required for preparations.

3. The Parties shall prevent the accumulation, in the possession of drug manufacturers, of quantities of drugs and poppy straw in excess of those required for the normal conduct of business, having regard to the prevailing market conditions.

## Article 30
### TRADE AND DISTRIBUTION

1. (a) The Parties shall require that the trade in and distribution of drugs be under licence except where such trade or distribution is carried out by a State enterprise or State enterprises.

(b) The Parties shall:

(i) Control all persons and enterprises carrying on or engaged in the trade in or distribution of drugs;

(ii) Control under licence the establishments and premises in which such trade or distribution may take place. The requirement of licensing need not apply to preparations.

(c) The provisions of subparagraphs (a) and (b) relating to licensing need not apply to persons duly authorized to perform and while performing therapeutic or scientific functions.

2. The Parties shall also:

(a) Prevent the accumulation in the possession of traders, distributors, State enterprises or duly authorized persons referred to above, or quantities of drugs and poppy straw in excess of those required for the normal conduct of business, having regard to the prevailing market conditions; and

(b) (i) Require medical prescriptions for the supply or dispensation of drugs to individuals. This requirement need not apply to such drugs as individuals may lawfully obtain, use, dispense or administer in connexion with their duly authorized therapeutic functions; and

(ii) If the Parties deem these measures necessary or desirable, require that prescriptions for drugs in Schedule I should be written on officials forms to be issued in the form of counterfoil books by the competent governmental authorities or by authorized professional associations.

3. It is desirable that Parties require that written or printed offers of drugs, advertisements of every kind or descriptive literature relating to drugs and used for commercial purposes, interior wrappings of packages containing drugs, and labels under which drugs are offered for sale indicate the international non-proprietary name communicated by the World Health Organization.

4. If a Party considers such measures necessary or desirable, it shall require that the inner package containing a drug or wrapping thereof shall bear a clearly visible double red band. The exterior wrapping of the package in which such drug is contained shall not bear a double red band.

5. A Party shall require that the label under which a drug is offered for sale show the exact drug content by weight or percentage. This requirement of label information need not apply to a drug dispensed to an individual on medical prescription.

6. The provisions of paragraphs 2 and 5 need not apply to the retail trade in or retail distribution of drugs in Schedule II.

## Article 31
### SPECIAL PROVISIONS RELATING TO INTERNATIONAL TRADE

1. The Parties shall not knowingly permit the export of drugs to any country or territory except:

(a) In accordance with the laws and regulations of that country or territory; and

(b) Within the limits of the total of the estimates for that country or territory, as defined in paragraph 2 of article 19, with the addition of the amounts intended to be re-exported.

2. The Parties shall exercise in free ports and zones the same supervision and control as in other parts of their territories, provided, however, that they may apply more drastic measures.

3. The Parties shall:

(a) Control under licence the import and export of drugs except where such import or export is carried out by a State enterprise or enterprises;

(b) Control all persons and enterprises carrying on or engaged in such import or export.

4. (a) Every Party permitting the import or export of drugs shall require a separate import or export authorization to be obtained for each such import or export whether it consists of one or more drugs.

(b) Such authorization shall state the name of the drug, the international non-proprietary name if any, the quantity to be imported or exported, and the name and address of the importer and exporter, and shall specify the period within which the importation or exportation must be effected.

(c) The export authorization shall also state the number and date of the import certificate (paragraph 5) and the authority by whom it has been issued.

(d) The import authorization may allow an importation in more than one consignment.

5. Before issuing an export authorization the Parties shall require an import certificate, issued by the competent authorities of the importing country or territory and certifying that the importation of the drug or drugs referred to therein, is approved and such certificate shall be produced by the person or

establishment applying for the export authorization. The Parties shall follow as closely as may be practicable the form of import certificate approved by the Commission.

6. A copy of the export authorization shall accompany each consignment, and the Government issuing the export authorization shall send a copy to the Government of the importing country or territory.

7. (*a*) The Government of the importing country or territory, when the importation has been effected or when the period fixed for the importation has expired, shall return the export authorization, with an endorsement to that effect, to the Government of the exporting country or territory.

(*b*) The endorsement shall specify the amount actually imported.

(*c*) If a lesser quantity than that specified in the export authorization is actually exported, the quantity actually exported shall be stated by the competent authorities on the export authorization and on any official copy thereof.

8. Exports of consignments to a post office box, or to a bank to the account of a Party other than the Party named in the export authorization, shall be prohibited.

9. Exports of consignments to a bonded warehouse are prohibited unless the Government of the importing country certifies on the import certificate, produced by the person or establishment applying for the export authorization, that it has approved the importation for the purpose of being placed in a bonded warehouse. In such case the export authorization shall specify that the consignment is exported for such purpose. Each withdrawal from the bonded warehouse shall require a permit from the authorities having jurisdiction over the warehouse and, in the case of a foreign destination shall be treated as if it were a new export within the meaning of this Convention.

10. Consignments of drugs entering or leaving the territory of a Party not accompanied by an export authorization shall be detained by the competent authorities.

11. A Party shall not permit any drugs consigned to another country to pass through its territory, whether or not the consignment is removed from the conveyance in which it is carried, unless a copy of the export authorization for such consignment is produced to the competent authorities of such Party.

12. The competent authorities of any country or territory through which a consignment of drugs is permitted to pass shall take all due measures to prevent the diversion of the consignment to a destination other than that named in the accompanying copy of the export authorization unless the Government of that country or territory through which the consignment is passing authorizes the diversion. The Government of the country or territory of transit shall treat any requested diversion as if the diversion were an export from the country or territory of transit to the country or territory of new destination. If the diversion is authorized, the provisions of paragraph 7 (*a*) and (*b*) shall also apply between the country or territory of transit and the country or territory which originally exported the consignment.

13. No consignment of drugs while in transit, or whilst being stored in a bonded warehouse, may be subjected to any process which would change the nature of the drugs in question. The packing may not be altered without the permission of the competent authorities.

14. The provisions of paragraphs 11 to 13 relating to the passage of drugs through the territory of a Party do not apply where the consignment in question is transported by aircraft which does not land in the country or territory of

transit. If the aircraft lands in any such country or territory, those provisions shall be applied so far as circumstances require.

15. The provisions of this article are without prejudice to the provisions of any international agreements which limit the control which may be exercised by any of the Parties over drugs in transit.

16. Nothing in this article other than paragraphs 1a) and 2 need apply in the case of preparations in Schedule III.

## Article 32
SPECIAL PROVISIONS CONCERNING THE CARRIAGE OF DRUGS IN FIRST-AID KITS OF SHIPS OR AIRCRAFT ENGAGED IN INTERNATIONAL TRAFFIC

1. The international carriage by ships or aircraft of such limited amounts of drugs as may be needed during their journey or voyage for first-aid purposes or emergency cases shall not be considered to be import, export or passage through a country within the meaning of this Convention.

2. Appropriate safeguards shall be taken by the country of registry to prevent the improper use of the drugs referred to in paragraph 1 or their diversion for illicit purposes. The Commission, in consultation with the appropriate international organizations, shall recommend such safeguards.

3. Drugs carried by ships or aircraft in accordance with paragraph 1 shall be subject to the laws, regulations, permits and licences of the country of registry, without prejudice to any rights of the competent local authorities to carry out checks, inspections and other control measures on board ships or aircraft. The administration of such drugs in the case of emergency shall not be considered a violation of the requirements of article 30, paragraph 2 (*b*).

## Article 33
POSSESSION OF DRUGS

The Parties shall not permit the possession of drugs except under legal authority.

## Article 34
MEASURES OF SUPERVISION AND INSPECTION

The Parties shall require:

(*a*) That all persons who obtain licences as provided in accordance with this Convention, or who have managerial or supervisory positions in a State enterprise established in accordance with this Convention, shall have adequate qualifications for the effective and faithful execution of the provisions of such laws and regulations as are enacted in pursuance thereof; and

(*b*) That government authorities, manufacturers, traders, scientists, scientific institutions and hospitals keep such records as will show the quantities of each drug manufactured and of each individual acquisition and disposal of drugs. Such records shall respectively be preserved for a period of not less than two years. Where counterfoil books (article 30, paragraph 2 (*b*) of official prescriptions are used, such books including the counterfoils shall also be kept for a period of not less than two years.

## Article 35
### ACTION AGAINST THE ILLICIT TRAFFIC

Having due regard to their constitutional, legal and adminstrative systems, the Parties shall:

(a) Make arrangements at the national level for co-ordination of preventive and repressive action against the illicit traffic; to this end they may usefully designate an appropriate agency responsible for such co-ordination;

(b) Assist each other in the campaign against the illicit traffic in narcotic drugs;

(c) Co-operate closely with each other and with the competent international organizations of which they are members with a view to maintaining a co-ordinated campaign against the illicit traffic;

(d) Ensure that international co-operation between the appropriate agencies be conducted in an expeditious manner; and

(e) Ensure that where legal papers are transmitted internationally for the purposes of a prosecution, the transmittal be effected in an expeditious manner to the bodies designated by the Parties; this requirement shall be without prejudice to the right of a Party to require that legal papers be sent to it through the diplomatic channel;

(f) Furnish, if they deem it appropriate, to the Board and the Commission through the Secretary-General, in addition to information required by article 18, information relating to illicit drug activity within their borders, including information on illicit cultivation, production, manufacture and use of, and on illicit trafficking in, drugs; and

(g) Furnish the information referred to in the preceding paragraph as far as possible in such manner and by such dates as the Board may request; if requested by a Party, the Board may offer its advice to it in furnishing the information and in endeavouring to reduce the illicit drug activity within the borders of that Party.

## Article 36
### PENAL PROVISIONS

1. (a) Subject to its constitutional limitations, each Party shall adopt such measures as will ensure that cultivation, production, manufacture, extraction, preparation, possession, offering, offering for sale, distribution, purchase, sale, delivery on any terms whatsoever, brokerage, dispatch, dispatch in transit, transport, importation and exportation of drugs contrary to the provisions of this Convention, and any other action which in the opinion of such Party may be contrary to the provisions of this Convention, and any other action which in the opinion of such Party may be contrary to the provisions of this Convention, shall be punishable offences when committed intentionally, and that serious offences shall be liable to adequate punishment particularly by imprisonment or other penalties of deprivation of liberty.

(b) Notwithstanding the preceding subparagraph, when abusers of drugs have committed such offences, the Parties may provide, either as an alternative to conviction or punishment or in addition to conviction or punishment, that such abusers shall undergo measures of treatment, education, after-care, rehabilitation and social reintegration in conformity with paragraph 1 of article 38.

2. Subject to the constitutional limitations of a Party, its legal system and domestic law,

(*a*) (i) Each of the offences enumerated in paragraph 1, if committed in different countries, shall be considered as a distinct offence;

(ii) Intentional participation in, conspiracy to commit and attempts to commit, any of such offences, and preparatory acts and financial operations in connexion with the offences referred to in this article, shall be punishable offences as provided in paragraph 1;

(iii) Foreign convictions for such offences shall be taken into account for the purpose of establishing recidivism; and

(iv) Serious offences heretofore referred to committed either by nationals or by foreigners shall be prosecuted by the Party in whose territory the offence was committed, or by the Party in whose territory the offender is found if extradition is not acceptable in conformity with the law of the Party to which application is made, and if such offender has not already been prosecuted and judgement given.

(*b*) (i) Each of the offences enumerated in paragraphs 1 and 2 (*a*) (ii) of this article shall be deemed to be included as an extraditable offence in any extradition treaty existing between Parties. Parties undertake to include such offences as extraditable offences in every extradition treaty to be concluded between them.

(ii) If a Party which makes extradition conditional on the existence of a treaty receives a request for extradition from another Party with which it has no extradition treaty, it may at its option consider this Convention as the legal basis for extradition in respect of the offences enumerated in paragraphs 1 and 2 (*a*) (ii) of this article. Extradition shall be subject to the other conditions provided by the law of the requested Party.

(iii) Parties which do not make extradition conditional on the existence of a treaty shall recognize the offences enumerated in paragraphs 1 and 2 (*a*) (ii) of this article as extraditable offences between themselves, subject to the conditions provided by the law of the requested Party.

(iv) Extradition shall be granted in conformity with the law of the Party to which application is made, and, notwithstanding subparagraphs (*b*) (i), (ii) and (iii) of this paragraph, the Party shall have the right to refuse to grant the extradition in cases where the competent authorities consider that the offence is not sufficiently serious.

3. The provisions of this article shall be subject to the provisions of the criminal law of the Party concerned on questions of jurisdiction.

4. Nothing contained in this article shall affect the principle that the offences to which it refers shall be defined, prosecuted and punished in conformity with the domestic law of a Party.

### Article 37
#### SEIZURE AND CONFISCATION

Any drugs, substances and equipment, used in or intended for the commission of any of the offences, referred to in article 36, shall be liable to seizure and confiscation.

## Article 38
### MEASURES AGAINST THE ABUSE OF DRUGS

1. The Parties shall give special attention to and take all practicable measures for the prevention of abuse of drugs and for the early identification, treatment, education, after-care, rehabilitation and social reintegration of the persons involved and shall co-ordinate their efforts to these ends.

2. The Parties shall as far as possible promote the training of personnel in the treatment, after-care, rehabilitation and social reintegration of abusers of drugs.

3. The Parties shall take all practicable measures to assist persons whose work so requires to gain an understanding of the problems of abuse of drugs and of its prevention, and shall also promote such understanding among the general public if there is a risk that abuse of drugs will become widespread.

## Article 38 bis
### AGREEMENTS ON REGIONAL CENTRES

If a Party considers it desirable as part of its action against the illicit traffic in drugs, having due regard to its constitutional, legal and administrative systems, and, if it so desires, with the technical advice of the Board or the specialized agencies, it shall promote the establishment, in consultation with other interested Parties in the region, of agreements which contemplate the development of regional centres for scientific research and education to combat the problems resulting from the illicit use of and traffic in drugs.

## Article 39
### APPLICATION OF STRICTER NATIONAL CONTROL MEASURES THAN THOSE REQUIRED BY THIS CONVENTION

Notwithstanding anything contained in this Convention, a Party shall not be, or be deemed to be, precluded from adopting measures of control more strict or severe than those provided by this Convention and in particular from requiring that Preparations in Schedule III or drugs in Schedule II be subject to all or such of the measures of control applicable to drugs in Schedule I as in its opinion is necessary or desirable for the protection of the public health or welfare.

SCHEDULES[2]

*List of Drugs Included in Schedule 1*

ACETORPHINE (3-*O*-acetyltetrahydro-7α-(1-hydroxy-1-methylbutyl)-6;14-*endo*ethenooripavine)
ACETYLMETHADOL (3-acetoxy-6-dimethylamino-4,4-diphenylheptane)
ALLYLPRODINE (3-allyl-1-methyl-4-phenyl-4-propionoxypiperidine)
ALPHACETYLMETHADOL (alpha-3-acetoxy-6-dimethylamino-4,4-diphenylheptane)
ALPHAMEPRODINE (alpha-3-ethyl-1-methyl-4-phenyl-4-propionoxypiperidine)
ALPHAMETHADOL (alpha-6-dimethylamino-4,4-diphenyl-3-heptanol)

2   Including all amendments up to the end of 1976

ALPHAPRODINE (alpha-1,3-dimethyl-4-phenyl-4-propionoxypiperidine)

ANILERIDINE (1-*para*-aminophenethyl-4-phenylpiperidine-4-carboxylic acid ethyl ester)

BENZETHIDINE (1-(2-benzyloxyethyl)-4-phenylpiperidine-4-carboxylic acid ethyl ester)

BENZYLMORPHINE (3-benzylmorphine)

BETACETYLMETHADOL (beta-3-acetoxy-6-dimethylamino-4,4-diphenylheptane)

BETAMEPRODINE (beta-3-ethyl-1-methyl-4-phenyl-4-propionoxypiperidine)

BETAMETHADOL (beta-6-dimethylamino-4,4-diphenyl-3-heptanol)

BETAPRODINE (beta-1,3-dimethyl-4-phenyl-4-propionoxypiperidine)

BEZITRAMIDE (1-(3-cyano-3,3-diphenylpropyl)-4-(2-oxo-3-propionyl-1-benzimidazolinyl)-piperidine)

CANNABIS and CANNABIS RESIN and EXTRACTS and TINCTURES OF CANNABIS

CLONITAZENE (2-*para*-chlorbenzyl-1-diethylaminoethyl-5-nitrobenzimidazole)

COCA LEAF

COCAINE (methyl ester of benzoylecgonine)

CODOXIME (dihydrocodeinone-6-carboxymethyloxime)

CONCENTRATE OF POPPY STRAW (the material arising when poppy straw has entered into a process for the concentration of its alkaloids when such material is made available in trade)

DESOMORPHINE (dihydrodeoxymorphine)

DEXTROMORAMIDE ((+)-4-[2-methyl-4-oxo-3,3-diphenyl-4-(1-pyrrolidinyl) butyl] morpholine)

DIAMPROMIDE (N-[2-methylphenethylamino propyl] propionanilide)

DIETHYLTHIAMBUTENE (3-diethylamino-1,1-di-(2'-thienyl)-1-butene)

DIFENOXIN (1-(3-cyano-3,3-diphenylpropyl)-4-phenylisonipecotic acid)

DIHYDROMORPHINE

DIMENOXADOL (2-dimethylaminoethyl-1-ethoxy-1,1-diphenylacetate)

DIMEPHEPTANOL (6-dimethylamino-4,4-diphenyl-3-heptanol)

DIMETHYLTHIAMBUTENE (3-dimethylamino-1,1-di-(2'-thienyl)-1-butene)

DIOXAPHETYL BUTYRATE (ethyl-4-morpholino-2,2-diphenylbutyrate)

DIPHENOXYLATE (1-(3-cyano-3,3-diphenylpropyl)-4-phenylpiperidine-4-carboxylic acid ethyl ester)

DIPIPANONE (4,4-diphenyl-6-piperidine-3-heptanone)

DROTEBANOL (3,4-dimethoxy-17-methylmorphinan-6$\beta$,14-diol)

ECGONINE, its esters and derivatives which are convertible to ecgonine and cocaine

ETHYLMETHYLTHIAMBUTENE (3-ethylmethylamino-1,1-di-(2' thienyl)-1-butene)

ETONITAZENE (1-diethylaminoethyl-2-*para*-ethoxybenzyl-5-nitorbenzimidazole)

ETORPHINE (tetrahydro-7$\alpha$-(1-hydroxy-1-methylbutyl)-6,14-*endo*etheno-oripavine)

ETOXERIDINE (1-[2-(2-hydroxyethoxy)-ethyl]-4-phenylpiperidine-4-carboxylic acid ethyl ester)

FENTANYL (1-phenethyl-4-N-propionylanilinopiperidine)

FURETHIDINE (1-(2-tetrahydrofurfuryloxyethyl)-4-phenylpiperidine-4-carboxylic acid ethyl ester)

HEROIN (diacetylmorphine)

HYDROCODONE (dihydrocodeinone)

HYDROMORPHINOL (14-hydroxydihydromorphine)

HYDROMORPHONE (dihydromorphinone)

HYDROXYPETHIDINE (4-*meta*-hydroxyphenyl-1-methylpiperidine-4-carboxylic acid ethyl ester)

ISOMETHADONE (6-dimethylamino-5-methyl-4,4-diphenyl-3-hexanone)
KETOBEMIDONE (4-*meta*-hydroxyphenyl-1-methyl-4-propionylpiperidine)
LEVOMETHORPHAN* ((-)-3-methoxy-N-methylmorphinan)
LEVOMORAMIDE ((-)-4-[2-methyl-4-oxo-3,3-diphenyl-4-(1-pyrrolidinyl) butyl]
    morpholine)
LEVOPHENACYLMORPHAN ((-)-3-hydroxy-N-phenacylmorphinan)
LEVORPHANOL* ((-)-3-hydroxy-N-methylmorphinan)
METAZOCINE (2'-hydroxy-2,5,9-trimethyl-6,7-benzomorphan)
METHADONE (6-dimethylamino-4,4-diphenyl-3-heptanone)
METHADONE INTERMEDIATE (4-cyano-2-dimethylamino-4,4-diphenylbutane)
METHYLDESORPHINE (6-methyl-delta-6-deoxymorphine)
METHYLDIHYDROMORPHINE (6-methyldihydromorphine)
METOPON (5-methyldihydromorphinone)
MORAMIDE INTERMEDIATE (2-methyl-3-morpholino-1,1-diphenylpropane
    carboxylic acid)
MORPHERIDINE (1-(2-morphelinoethyl)-4-phenylpiperidine-4-carboxylic acid ethyl
    ester)
MORPHINE
MORPHINE METHOBROMIDE and other pentavalent nitrogen morphine derivatives
MORPHINE-N-OXIDE
MYROPHINE (myristylbenzylmorphine)
NICOMORPHINE (3,6-dinicotinylmorphine)
NORACYMETHADOL (($\pm$)-alpha-3-acetoxy-6-methylamino-4,4-diphenylheptane)
NORLEVORPHANOL ((-)-3-hydroxymorphinan)
NORMETHADONE (6-dimethylamino-4,4-diphenyl-3-hexanone)
NORMORPHINE (demethylmorphine)
NORPIPANONE (4,4-diphenyl-6-piperidino-3-hexanone)
OPIUM
OXYCODONE (14-hydroxydihydrocodeinone)
OXYMORPHONE (14-hydroxydihydromorphinone)
PETHIDINE (1-methyl-4-phenylpiperidine-4-carboxylic acid ethyl ester)
PETHIDINE INTERMEDIATE A (4-cyano-1-methyl-4-phenylpiperidine)
PETHIDINE INTERMEDIATE B (4-phenylpiperidine-4-carboxylic acid ethyl ester)
PETHIDINE INTERMEDIATE C (1-methyl-4-phenylpiperidine-4-carboxylic acid)
PHENADOXONE (6-morpholino-4,4-diphenyl-3-heptanone)
PHENAMPROMIDE (N-(1-methyl-2-piperidinoethyl) propionanilide)
PHENAZOCINE (2'-hydroxy-5,9-dimethyl-2-phenethyl-6,7-benzomorphan)
PHENOMORPHAN (3-hydroxy-N-phenethylmorphinan)
PHENOPERIDINE    (1-(3-hydroxy-3-phenylpropyl)-4-phenylpiperidine-4-carboxylic
    acid ethyl ester)
PIMINODINE (4-phenyl-1-(3-phenylaminopropyl) piperidine-4-carboxylic acid ethyl
    ester)
PIRITRAMIDE (1-(3-cyano-3,3-diphenylpropyl)-4-(1-piperidino)-piperidine-4-
    carboxylic acid amide)
PROHEPTAZINE (1,3-dimethyl-4-phenyl-4-propionoxyazacycloheptane)
PROPERIDINE (1-methyl-4-phenylpiperidine-4-carboxylic acid isopropyl ester)
RACEMETHORPHAN (($\pm$)-3-methoxy-N-methylmorphinan)
RACEMORAMIDE   (($\pm$)-4-[2-methyl-4-oxo-3,3-diphenyl-4-(1-pyrrolidinyl)   butyl]
    morpholine)
RACEMORPHAN (($\pm$)-3-hydroxy-N-methylmorphinan)
THEBACON (acetyldihydrocodeinone)

THEBAINE
TRIMEPERIDINE (1,2,5-trimethyl-4-phenyl-4-propionoxypiperidine); and
    The isomers, unless specifically excepted, of the drugs in this Schedule whenever the existence of such isomers is possible within the specific chemical designation;
    The esters and ethers, unless appearing in another Schedule, of the drugs in this Schedule whenever the existence of such esters or ethers is possible;
    The salts of the drugs listed in this Schedule, including the salts of esters, ethers and isomers as provided above whenever the existence of such salts is possible.

    *Dextromethorphan ((+)-3-methoxy-N-methylmorphan) and dextrorphan ((+)-3-hydroxy-N-methylmorphinan) are specifically excluded from this Schedule.

## List of Drugs Included in Schedule II

ACETYLDIHYDROCODEINE
CODLINE (3-methylmorphine)
DIHYDROCODEINE
ETHYLMORPHINE (3-ethylmorphine)
NICOCODINE (6-nicotinylcodeine)
NICODICODINE (6-nicotinyldihydrocodeine)
NORCODEINE (N-demethylcodeine)
PHOLCODINE (morpholinylethylmorphine)
PROPIRAM (N-(1-methyl-2-piperidinoethyl)-N-2-pyridylpropionamide); and
    The isomers, unless specifically excepted, of the drugs in this Schedule whenever the existence of such isomers is possible within the specific chemical designation;
    The salts of the drugs listed in this Schedule, including the salts of the isomers as provided above whenever the existence of such salts is possible.

## List of Preparations Included in Schedule III

    1. Preparations of Acetyldihydrocodeine,
                Codeine,
                Dihydrocodeine,
                Ethylmorphine,
                Nicodicodine,
                Norcodeine, and
                Pholcodine
when compounded with one or more other ingredients and containing not more than 100 milligrams of the drug per dosage unit and with a concentration of not more than 2.5 per cent in undivided preparations.
    2. Preparations of propiram containing not more than 100 milligrams of propiram per dosage unit and compounded with at least the same amount of methylcellulose.
    3. Preparations of cocaine containing not more than 0.1 per cent of cocaine calculated as cocaine base and preparations of opium or morphine containing not more than 0.2 per cent of morphine calculated as anhydrous morphine base

and compounded with one or more other ingredients and in such a way that the drug cannot be recovered by readily applicable means or in a yield which would constitute a risk to public health.

4. Preparations of difenoxin containing, per dosage unit, not more than 0.5 milligram of difenoxin and a quantity of atropine sulphate equivalent to at least 5 per cent of the dose of difenoxin.

5. Preparations of diphenoxylate containing, per dosage unit, not more than 2.5 milligrams of diphenoxylate calculated as base and a quantity of atropine sulphate equivalent to at least one per cent of the dose of diphenoxylate.

6. *Pulvis ipecacuanhae et opii compositus*
         10 per cent opium in powder
         10 per cent Ipecacuanha root, in powder
           well mixed with
         80 per cent of any other powdered ingredient containing no drug.

7. Preparations conforming to any of the formulae listed in this Schedule and mixtures of such preparations with any material which contains no drug.

### *List of Drugs Included in Schedule IV*

ACETORPHINE (3-*O*-acetyltetrahydro-7α-(1-hydroxy-1-methylbutyl)-6,14-
    *endo*etheno-oripavine)
CANNABIS and CANNABIS RESIN
DESOMORPHINE (dihydrodeoxymorphine)
ETORPHINE (tetrahydro-7α-(1-hydroxy-1-methylbutyl)-6,14-*endo*etheno-oripavine)
HEROIN (diacetylmorphine)
KETOBEMIDONE (4-*meta*-hydroxyphenyl-1-methyl-4-propionylpiperidine); and
    The salts of the drugs listed in this Schedule whenever the formation of such salts is possible.

# Convention on Psychotropic Substances 1971

*Resolution II*

### RESEARCH ON THE AMPHETAMINE DRUGS

*The Conference,*[1]
*Considering* that the amphetamines are particularly liable to abuse and are objects of illicit traffic,

*Considering* that the therapeutic value of these drugs, though acknowledged, is limited,

1. *Requests* the World Health Assembly to encourage research on less dangerous substances capable of replacing the amphetamine drugs, and to sponsor such research within the limits of the available resources;

2. *Recommends* that governments with the necessary facilities should take similar action.

### PREAMBLE

*The Parties,*
*Being concerned* with the health and welfare of mankind,

*Noting* with concern the public health and soical problems resulting from the abuse of certain psychotropic substances,

*Determined* to prevent and combat abuse of such substances and the illicit traffic to which it gives rise,

*Considering* that rigorous measures are necessary to restrict the use of such substances to legitimate purposes,

*Recognizing* that the use of psychotropic substances for medical and scientific purposes is indispensable and that their availability for such purposes should not be unduly restricted,

*Believing* that effective measures against abuse of such substances require co-ordination and universal action,

*Acknowledging* the competence of the United Nations in the field of control of psychotropic substances and desirous that the international organs concerned should be within the framework of that Organization,

*Recognizing* that an international convention is necessary to achieve these purposes,

*Agree* as follows:

---

1 United Nations Conference for the Adoption of a Protocol on Psychotropic Substances, held at Vienna, 11 January—21 February 1971

## *Article 1*
## USE OF TERMS

Except where otherwise expressly indicated, or where the context otherwise requires, the following terms in this convention have the meanings given below:

(*a*) "Council" means the Economic and Social Council of the United Nations.

(*b*) "Commission" means the Commission on Narcotic Drugs of the Council.

(*c*) "Board" means the International Narcotics Control Board provided for in the Single Convention of Narcotic Drugs, 1961.

(*d*) "Secretary-General" means the Secretary-General of the United Nations.

(*e*) "Psychotropic substance" means any substance, natural or synthetic, or any natural material in Schedule I, II, III or IV.

(*f*) "Preparation" means:

    (i) Any solution or mixture, in whatever physical state, containing one or more psychotropic substances, or

    (ii) One or more psychotropic substances in dosage form.

(*g*) "Schedule I", "Schedule II", "Schedule III" and "Schedule IV" mean the correspondingly numbered lists of psychotropic substances annexed to this Convention, as altered in accordance with article 2.

(*h*) "Export" and "import" mean in their respective connotations the physical transfer of a psychotropic substance from one State to another State.

(*i*) "Manufacture" means all processes by which psychotropic substances may be obtained, and includes refining as well as the transformation of psychotropic substances into other psychotropic substances. The term also includes the making of preparations other than those made on prescription in pharmacies.

(*j*) "Illicit traffic" means manufacture of or trafficking in psychotropic substances contrary to the provisions of this Convention.

(*k*) "Region" means any part of a State which pursuant to article 28 is treated as a separate entity for the purposes of this Convention.

(*l*) "Premises" means buildings or parts of buildings, including the appertaining land.


## *Article 2*
## SCOPE OF CONTROL OF SUBSTANCES

1. If a Party or the World Health Organization has information relating to a substance not yet under international control which in its opinion may require the addition of that substance to any of the Schedules of this Convention, it shall notify the Secretary-General and furnish him with the information in support of that notification. The foregoing procedure shall also apply when a Party or the World Health Organization has information justifying the transfer of a substance from one Schedule to another among those Schedules, or the deletion of a substance from the Schedules.

2. The Secretary-General shall transmit such notification, and any information which he considers relevant, to the Parties, to the Commission and, when the notification is made by a Party, to the World Health Organization.

3. If the information transmitted with such a notification indicates that the substance is suitable for inclusion in Schedule I or Schedule II pursuant to

paragraph 4, the Parties shall examine, in the light of all information available to them, the possibility of the provisional application to the substance of all measures of control applicable to substances in Schedule I or Schedule II, as appropriate.

4. If the World Health Organization finds:

(*a*) That the substance has the capacity to produce

(i) (1) A state of dependence, and

(2) Central nervous system stimulation or depression, resulting in hallucinations or disturbances in motor function or thinking or behaviour or perception or mood, or

(ii) Similar abuse and similar ill effects as a substance in Schedule I, II, III or IV, and

(*b*) That there is sufficient evidence that the substance is being or is likely to be abused so as to constitute a public health and social problem warranting the placing of the substances under international control, the World Health Organization shall communicate to the Commission an assessment of the substance, including the extent or likelihood of abuse, the degree of seriousness of the public health and social problem and the degree of usefulness of the substance in medical therapy, together with recommendations of control measures, if any, that would be appropriate in the light of its assessment.

5. The Commission, taking into account the communication from the World Health Organization, whose assessments shall be determinative as to medical and scientific matters, and bearing in mind the economic social, legal, administrative and other factors it may consider relevant, may add the substance to Schedule I, II, III or IV. The Commission may seek further information from the World Health Organization or from other appropriate sources.

6. If a notification under paragraph 1 relates to a substance already listed in one of the Schedules, the World Health Organization shall communicate to the Commission its new findings, any new assessment of the substance it may make in accordance with paragraph 4 and any new recommendations on control measures it may find appropriate in the light of that assessment. The Commission, taking into account the communciation from the World Health Organization as under paragraph 5 and bearing in mind the factors referred to in that paragraph, may decide to transfer the substance from one Schedule to another or to delete it from the Schedules.

7. Any decision of the Commission taken pursuant to this article shall be communicated by the Secretary-General to all States Members of the United Nations, to non-member States Parties to this Convention, to the World Health Organization and to the Board. Such decision shall become fully effective with respect to each Party 180 days after the date of such communication, except for any Party which, within that period, in respect of a decision adding a substance to a Schedule, has transmitted to the Secretary-General a written notice that, in view of exceptional circumstances, it is not in a position to give effect with respect to that substance to all of the provisions of the Convention applicable to substances in that Schedule. Such notice shall state the reasons for this exceptional action. Notwithstanding its notice, each Party shall apply, as a minimum, the control measures listed below;

(*a*) A Party having given such notice with respect to a previously uncontrolled substance added to Schedule 1 shall take into account, as far as possible, the special control measures enumerated in aticle 7 and, with respect to that substance, shall:

    (i) Require licences for manufacture, trade and distribution as provided in article 8 for substances in Schedule II;

   (ii) Require medical prescriptions for supply of dispensing as provided in article 9 for substances in Schedule II;

  (iii) Comply with the obligations relating to export and import provided in article 12, except in respect to another Party having given such notice for the substance in question;

  (iv) Comply with the obligations provided in article 13 for substances in Schedule II in regard to prohibition of and restrictions on export and import;

   (v) Furnish statistical reports to the Board in accordance with paragraph 4(*a*) of article 16; and

  (vi) Adopt measures in accordance with article 22 for the repression of acts contrary to laws or regulations adopted pursuant to the foregoing obligations.

(*b*) A Party having given such notice with regard to a previously uncontrolled substance added to Schedule II shall, with respect to that substance:

    (i) Require licences for manufacture, trade and distribution in accordance with article 8;

  (ii) Require medical prescriptions for supply or dispensing in accordance with article 9;

  (iii) Comply with the obligaitons relating to export and import provided in article 12, except in respect to another Party having given such notice for the substance in question;

  (iv) Comply with the obligations of article 13 in regard to prohibition of and restriction on export and import;

   (v) Furnish statistical reports to the Board in accordance with paragraphs 4(*a*), (*c*) and (*d*) of article 16; and

  (vi) Adopt measures in accordance with article 22 for the repression of acts contrary to laws or regulations adopted pursuant to the foregoing obligations.

(*c*) A Party having given such notice with regard to a previously uncontrolled substance added to Schedule III shall, with respect to that substance:

    (i) Require licences for manufacture, trade and distribution in accordance with article 8;

  (ii) Require medical prescriptions for supply or dispensing in accordance with article 9;

  (iii) Comply with the obligations relating to export provided in article 12, except in respect to another Party having given such notice for the substance in question;

  (iv) Comply with the obligations of article 13 in regard to prohibition of and restrictions on export and import; and

   (v) Adopt measures in accordance with article 22 for the repression of acts contrary to laws or regulations adopted pursuant to the foregoing obligations.

(*d*) A Party having given such notice with regard to a previously uncontrolled substance added to Schedule IV shall, with respect to that substance:

    (i) Require licences for manufacture, trade and distribution in accordance with article 8;

  (ii) Comply with the obligations of article 13 in regard to prohibition of and restrictions on export and import; and

(iii) Adopt measures in accordance with article 22 for the repression of acts contrary to laws or regulations adopted pursuant to the foregoing obligations.

(*e*) A Party having given such notice with regard to a substance transferred to a Schedule providing stricter controls and obligations shall apply as a minimum all of the provisions of this Convention applicable to the Schedule from which it was transferred.

8. (*a*) The decisions of the Commission taken under this article shall be subject to review by the Council upon the request of any Party filed within 180 days from receipt of notification of the decision. The request for review shall be sent to the Secretary-General together with all relevant information upon which the request for review is based.

(*b*) The Secretary-General shall transmit copies of the request for review and the relevant information to the Commission, to the World Health Organization and to all the Parties, inviting them to submit comments within ninety days. All comments received shall be submitted to the Council for consideration.

(*c*) The Council may confirm, alter or reverse the decision of the Commission. Notification of the Council's decision shall be transmitted to all States Members of the United Nations, to non-member States Parties to this Convention, to the Commission, to the World Health Organization and to the Board.

(*d*) During pendency of the review, the original decision of the Commission shall, subject to paragraph 7, remain in effect.

9. The Parties shall use their best endeavours to apply to substances which do not fall under this Convention, but which may be used in the illicit manufacture of psychotropic substances, such measures of supervision as may be practicable.

## *Article 3*
### SPECIAL PROVISIONS REGARDING THE CONTROL OF PREPARATIONS

1. Except as provided in the following paragraphs of this article, a preparation is subject to the same measures of control as the psychotropic substance which it contains, and, if it contains more than one such substance, to the measures applicable to the most strictly controlled of those substances.

2. If a preparation containing a psychotropic substance other than a substance in Schedule 1 is compounded in such a way that it presents no, or a negligible, risk of abuse and the substance cannot be recovered by readily applicable means in a quantity liable to abuse, so that the preparation does not give rise to a public health and social problem, the preparation may be exempted from certain of the measures of control provided in this Convention in accordance with paragraph 3.

3. If a Party makes a finding under the preceding paragraph regarding a preparation, it may decide to exempt the preparation, in its country or in one of its regions, from any or all of the measures of control provided in this Convention except the requirements of;

(a) article 8 (licences), as it applies to manufacture;

(b) article 11 (records), as it applies to exempt preparations;

(c) article 13 (prohibition of and restrictions on export and import);

(d) article 15 (inspection), as it applies to manufacture;

(e) article 16 (reports to be furnished by the Parties), as it applies to exempt preparations; and

(f) article 22 (penal provisions), to the extent necessary for the repression of acts contrary to laws or regulations adopted pursuant to the foregoing obligations.

A Party shall notify the Secretary-General of any such decision, of the name and composition of the exempt preparation, and of the measures of control from which it is exempted. The Secretary-General shall transmit the notification to the other Parties, to the World Health Organization and to the Board.

4. If a Party or the World Health Organization has information regarding a preparation exempted pursuant to paragraph 3 which in its opinion may require the termination, in whole or in part, of the exemption, it shall notify the Secretary-General and furnish him with the information in support of the notification. The Secretary-General shall transmit such notification, and any information which he considers relevant, to the Parties, to the Commission and, when the notification is made by a Party, to the World Health Organization. The World Health Organization shall communicate to the Commission an assessment of the preparation in relation to the matters specified in paragraph 2, together with a recommendation of the control measures, if any, from which preparation should cease to be exempted. The Commission, taking into account the communication from the World Health Organization, whose assessment shall be determinative as to medical and scientific matters, and bearing in mind the economic, social, legal, administrative and other factors it may consider relevant, may decide to terminate the exemption of the preparation from any or all control measures. Any decision of the Commission taken pursuant to this paragraph shall be communicated by the Secretary-General to all States Members of the United Nations, to non-member States Parties to this convention, to the World Health Organization and to the Board. All Parties shall take measures to terminate the exemption from the control measure or measures in question within 180 days of the date of the Secretary-General's communication.

## Article 4
### OTHER SPECIAL PROVISIONS REGARDING THE SCOPE OF CONTROL

In respect of psychotropic substances other than those in Schedule 1, the Parties may permit:

(a) The carrying by international travellers of small quantities of preparations for personal use; each Party shall be entitled, however, to satisfy itself that these preparations have been lawfully obtained;

(b) The use of such substances in industry for the manufacture of non-psychotropic substances or products, subject to the application of the measures of control required by this Convention until the psychotropic substances come to be in such a condition that they will not in practice be abused or recovered;

(*c*) The use of such substances, subject to the application of the measures of control required by this Convention, for the capture of animals by persons specifically authorized by the competent authorities to use such substances for that purpose.

*Article 5*

## LIMITATION OF USE TO MEDICAL AND SCIENTIFIC PURPOSES

1. Each Party shall limit the use of substances in Schedule 1 as provided in article 7.
2. Each Party shall, except as provided in article 4, limit by such measures as it considers appropriate the manufacture, export, import, distribution and stocks of, trade in, and use and possession of, substances in Schedules II, III and IV to medical and scientific purposes.
3. It is desirable that the Parties do not permit the possession of substances in Schedules II, III and IV except under legal authority.

*Article 6*

## SPECIAL ADMINISTRATION

It is desirable that for the purpose of applying the provisions of this Convention, each Party establish and maintain a special administration, which may with advantage be the same as, or work in close co-operation with, the special administration established pursuant to the provisions of conventions for the control of narcotic drugs.

*Article 7*

## SPECIAL PROVISIONS REGARDING SUBSTANCES IN SCHEDULE I

In respect of substances in Schedule I, the Parties shall:
(*a*) Prohibit all use except for scientific and very limited medical purposes by duly authorized persons, in medical or scientific establishments which are directly under the control of their Governments or specifically approved by them;
(*b*) Require that manufacture, trade, distribution and possession be under a special licence or prior authorization;
(*c*) Provide for close supervision of the activities and acts mentioned in paragraphs (*a*) and (*b*);
(*d*) Restrict the amount supplied to a duly authorized person to the quantity required for his authorized purpose;
(*e*) Require that persons performing medical or scientific functions keep records concerning the acquistion of the substances and the details of their use, such records to be preserved for at least two years after the last use recorded therein; and
(*f*) Prohibit export and import except when both the exporter and importer are the competent authorities or agencies of the exporting and importing country or region, respectively, or other persons or enterprises which are specifically authorized by the competent authorities of their country or region for the

purpose. The requirements of paragraph 1 of article 12 for export and import authorizations for substances in Schedule II shall also apply to substances in Schedule 1

## Article 8
### LICENCES

1. The Parties shall require that the manufacture of, trade (including export and import trade) in, and distribution of substances listed in Schedules II, III and IV be under licence or other similar control measure.

2. The Parties shall:

(*a*) Control all duly authorized persons and enterprises carrying on or engaged in the manufacture of, trade (including export and import trade) in, or distribution of substances referred to in paragraph 1;

(*b*) Control under licence or other similar control measure the establishments and premises in which such manufacture, trade or distribution may take place; and

(*c*) Provide that security measures to be taken with regard to such establishments and premises in order to prevent theft or other diversion of stocks.

3. The provisions of paragraphs 1 and 2 of this article relating to licensing or other similar control measures need not apply to persons duly authorized to perform and while performing therapeutic or scientific function.

4. The Parties shall require that all persons who obtain licences in accordance with this Convention or who are otherwise authorized pursuant to paragraph 1 of this article or sub-paragraph (*b*) of article 7 shall be adequately qualified for the effective and faithful execution of the provisions of such laws and regulations as are enacted in pursuance of this Convention.

## Article 9
### PRESCRIPTIONS

1.The Parties shall require that substances in Schedules II, III and IV be supplied or dispensed for use by individuals pursuant to medical prescription only, except when individuals may lawfully obtain, use, dispense or administer such substances in the duly authorized exercise of therapeutic or scientific functions.

2. The Parties shall take measures to ensure that prescriptions for substances in Schedules II, III and IV are issued in accordance with sound medical practice and subject to such regulation, particularly as to the number of times they may be refilled and the duration of their validity, as will protect the public health and welfare.

3. Notwithstanding paragraph 1, a Party may, if in its opinion local circumstances so require and under such conditions, including record-keeping, as it may prescribe, authorize licensed pharmacists or other licensed retail distributors designated by the authorities responsible for public health in its country or part thereof to supply, at their discretion and without prescription, for

use for medical purposes by individuals in exceptional cases, small quantities, within limits to be defined by the Parties, of substances in Schedules III and IV.

## Article 10
### WARNINGS ON PACKAGES, AND ADVERTISING

1. Each Party shall require, taking into account any relevant regulations or recommendations of the World Health Organization, such directions for use, including cautions and warnings, to be indicated on the labels where practicable and in any case on the accompanying leaflet of retail packages of psychotropic substances, as in its opinion are necessary for the safety of the user.

2. Each Party shall, with due regard to its constitutional provisions, prohibit the advertisement of such substances to the general public.

## Article 11
### RECORDS

1. The Parties shall require that, in respect of substances in Schedule I, manufacturers and all other persons authorized under article 7 to trade in and distribute those substances keep records, as may be determined by each Party, showing details of the quantities manufactured, the quantities held in stock, and for each acquisition and disposal, details of the quantity, date, supplier and recipient.

2. The Parties shall require that, in respect of substances in Schedules II and III, manufacturers, wholesale distributors, exporters and importers keep records, as may be determined by each Party, showing details of the quantities manufactured and, for each acquisition and disposal, details of the quantity, date, supplier and recipient.

3. The Parties shall require that, in respect of substances in Schedule II, retail distributors, institutions for hospitalization and care and scientific institutions keep records, as may be determined by each Party, showing for each acquisition and disposal, details of the quantity, date, supplier and recipient.

4. The Parties shall ensure, through appropriate methods and taking into account the professional and trade practices in their countries that information regarding acquisition and disposal of substances in Schedule III by retail distributors, institutions for hospitalization and care and scientific institutions is readily available.

5. The Parties shall require that, in respect of substances in Schedule IV, manufacturers, exporters and importers keep records, as may be determined by each Party, showing the quantities manufactured, exported and imported.

6. The Parties shall require manufacturers of preparations exempted under paragraph 3 of article 3 to keep records as to the quantity of each psychotropic substance used in the manufacture of an exempt preparation, and as to the nature, total quantity and initial disposal of the exempt preparation manufactured therefrom.

7. The Parties shall ensure that the records and information referred to in this article which are required for purposes of reports under article 16 shall be preserved for at least two years.

*Article 12*

## PROVISIONS RELATING TO INTERNATIONAL TRADE

1.(*a*) Every Party permitting the export or import of substances in Schedule I or II shall require a separate import or export authorization, on a form to be established by the Commission, to be obtained for each such export or import whether it consists of one or more substances.

(*b*) Such authorization shall state the international non-proprietary name, or, lacking such a name, the designation of the substance in the Schedule, the quantity to be exported or imported, the pharmaceutical form, the name and address of the exporter and importer, and the period within which the export or import must be effected. If the substance is exported or imported in the form of a preparation, the name of the preparation, if any, shall additionally be furnished. The export authorization shall also state the number and date of the import authorization and the authority by whom it has been issued.

(*c*) Before issuing an export authorization the Parties shall require an import authorization, issued by the competent authority of the importing country or region and certifying that the importation of the substance or substances referred to therein is approved, and such an authorization shall be produced by the person or establishment applying for the export authorization.

(*d*) A copy of the export authorization shall accompany each consignment, and the Government issuing the export authorization shall send a copy to the Government of the importing country or region.

(*e*) The Government of the importing country or region, when the importation has been effected, shall return the export authorization with an endorsement certifying the amount actually imported, to the Government of the exporting country or region.

2.(*a*) The Parties shall require that for each export of substances in Schedule III exporters shall draw up a declaration in triplicate, on a form to be established by the Commission, containing the following information:

  (i) The name and address of the exporter and importer;

  (ii) The international non-proprietary name, or, failing such a name, the designation of the substance in the Schedule;

  (iii) The quantity and pharmaceutical form in which the substance is exported, and, if in the form of a preparation, the name of the preparation, if any; and

  (iv) the date of despatch.

(*b*) Exporters shall furnish the competent authorities of their country or region with two copies of the declaration. They shall attach the third copy to their consignment.

(*c*) A Party from whose territory a substance in Schedule III has been exported shall, as soon as possible but not later than ninety days after the date of despatch, send to the competent authorities of the importing country or region, by registered mail with return of receipt requested, one copy of the declaration received from the exporter.

(*d*) The Parties may require that, on receipt of the consignment, the importer shall transmit the copy accompanying the consignment, duly endorsed stating the quantities received and the date of receipt, to the competent authorities of his country or region.

3. In respect of substances in Schedules I and II the following additional provisions shall apply:

(*a*) The Parties shall exercise in free ports and zones the same supervision and control as in other parts of their territory, provided however, that they may apply more drastic measures.

(*b*) Exports of consignments to a post office box, or to a bank to the account of a person other than the person named in the export authorization, shall be prohibited.

(*c*) Exports to bonded warehouses of consignments of substances in Schedule I are prohibited. Exports of consignments of substances in Schedule II to a bonded warehouse are prohibited unless the Government of the importing country certifies on the import authorization, produced by the person or establishment applying for the export authorization, that it has approved the importation for the purpose of being placed in a bonded warehouse. In such case the export authorization shall certify that the consignment is exported for such purpose. Each withdrawal from the bonded warehouse shall require a permit from the authorities having jurisdiction over the warehouse and, in the case of a foreign destination, shall be treated as if it were a new export within the meaning of this Convention.

(*d*) Consignments entering or leaving the territory of a Party not accompanied by an export authorization shall be detained by the competent authorities.

(*e*) A party shall not permit any substances consigned to another country to pass through its territory, whether or not the consignment is removed from the the conveyance in which it is carried, unless a copy of the export authorization for consignment is produced to the competent authorities of such Party.

(*f*) The competent authorities of any country or region through which a consignment of substances is permitted to pass shall take all due measures to prevent the diversion of the consignment to a destination other than that named in the accompanying copy of the export authorization, unless the Government of the country or region through which the consignment is passing authorizes the diversion. The Government of the country or region of transit shall treat any requested diversion as if the diversion were an export from the country or region of transit to the country or region of new destination. If the diversion is authorized, the provisions of paragraph 1(*e*) shall also apply between the country or region of transit and the country or region which originally exported the consignment.

(*g*) No consignment of substances, while in transit or while being stored in a bonded warehouse, may be subjected to any process which would change the nature of the substance in question. The packing may not be altered without the permission of the competent authorities..

(*h*) The provisions of sub-paragraphs (*e*) to (*g*) relating to the passage of substances through the territory of a Party do not apply where the consignment in question is transported by aircraft which does not land in the country or region of transit, If the aircraft lands in any such country or region, those provisions shall be applied so far as circumstances require.

(*i*) The provisions of this paragraph are without prejudice to the provisions of any international agreements which limit the control which may be exercised by any of the Parties over such substances in transit.

## Article 13

### PROHIBITION OF AND RESTRICTIONS ON EXPORT AND IMPORT

1. A Party may notify all the other Parties through the Secretary-General that it prohibits the import into its country or into one of its regions of one or more substances in Schedule II, III or IV, specified in its notification. Any such notification shall specify the name of the substance as designated in Schedule II, III or IV.

2. If a Party has been notified of a prohibition pursuant to paragraph 1, it shall take measures to ensure that none of the substances specified in the notification is exported to the country or one of the regions of the notifying Party.

3. Notwithstanding the provisions of the preceding paragraphs, a Party which has given notification pursuant to paragraph 1 may authorize by special import licence in each case the import of specified quantities of the substances in question or preparations containing such substances. The issuing authority of the importing country shall send two copies of the special import licence, indicating the name and address of the importer and the exporter, to the competent authority of the exporting country or region, which may then authorize the exporter to make the shipment. One copy of the special import licence, duly endorsed by the competent authority of the exporting country or region, shall accompany the shipment.

## Article 15

### INSPECTION

The Parties shall maintain a system of inspection of manufacturers, exporters, importers, and wholesale and retail distributors of psychotropic substances and of medical and scientific institutions which use such substances. They shall provide for inspections, which shall be made as frequently as they consider necessary, of the premises and of stocks and records.

## Article 19

### MEASURES BY THE BOARD TO ENSURE THE EXECUTION OF THE PROVISIONS OF THE CONVENTION

1. (*a*) If, on the basis of its examination of information submitted by governments to the Board or of information communicated by United Nations organs, the Board has reason to believe that the aims of this Convention are being seriously endangered by reason of the failure of a country or region to carry out the provisions of this Convention, the Board shall have the right to ask for explanations from the Government of the country or region in question. Subject to the right of the Board to call the attention of the Parties, the Council and the Commission to the matter referred to in sub-paragraph (*c*) below, it shall treat as confidential a request for information or an explanation by a government under this sub-paragraph.

(*b*) After taking action under sub-paragraph (*a*), the Board, if satisfied that it is necessary to do so may call upon the Government concerned to adopt such remedial measures as shall seem under the circumstances to be necessary for the execution of the provisions of this Convention.

(c) If the Board finds that the Government concerned has failed to give satisfactory explanations when called upon to do so under sub-paragraph (a), or has failed to adopt any remedial measures which it has been called upon to take under sub-paragraph (b), it may call the attention of the Parties, the Council and the Commission to the matter.

2. The Board, when calling the attention of the Parties, the Council and the Commission to a matter in accordance with paragraph 1(c), may, if it is satisfied that such a course is necessary, recommend to the Parties that they stop the export, import, or both, of particular psychotropic substances, from or to the country or region concerned, either for a designated period or until the Board shall be satisfied as to the situation in that country or region. The State concerned may bring the matter before the Council.

3. The Board shall have the right to publish a report on any matter dealt with under the provisions of this article, and communicate it to the Council, which shall forward it to all Parties. If the Board publishes in this report a decision taken under this article or any information relating thereto, it shall also publish therein the views of the Government concerned if the latter so requests.

4. If in any case a decision of the Board which is published under this article is not unanimous, the views of the minority shall be stated.

5. Any State shall be invited to be represented at a meeting of the Board at which a question directly interesting it is considered under this article.

6. Decisions of the Board under this article shall be taken by two-thirds majority of the whole number of the Board.

7. The provisions of the above paragraphs shall also apply if the Board has reason to believe that the aims of this Convention are bing seriously endangered as a result of a decision taken by a Party under paragraph 7 of article 2.

## Article 20
### MEASURES AGAINST THE ABUSE OF PSYCHOTROPIC SUBSTANCES

1. The Parties shall take all practicable measures for the prevention of abuse of psychotropic substances and for the early identification, treatment, education, after-care, rehabilitation and social reintegration of the persons involved, and shall co-ordinate their efforts to these ends.

2. The Parties shall as far as possible promote the training of personnel in the treatement, after-care, rehabilitation and social reintegration of abusers of psychotropic substances.

3. The Parties shall assist persons whose work so requires to gain an understanding of the problems of abuse of psychotropic substances and of its prevention, and shall also promote such understanding among the general public if there is a risk that abuse of such substances will become widespread.

## Article 21
### ACTION AGAINST THE ILLICIT TRAFFIC

Having due regard to their constitutional, legal and administrative systems, the Parties shall:

(*a*) Make arrangements at the national level for the co-ordination of preventive and repressive action against the illicit traffic; to this end they may usefully designate an appropriate agency responsible for such co-ordination;

(*b*) Assist each other in the campaign against the illicit traffic in psychotropic substances, and in particular immediately transmit, through the diplomatic channel or the competent authorities designated by the Parties for this purpose, to the other parties directly concerned, a copy of any report addressed to the Secretary-General under article 16 in connexion with the discovery of a case of illicit traffice or a seizure;

(*c*) Co-operate closely with each other and with the competent international organizations of which they are members with a view to maintaining a co-ordinated compaign against the illicit traffic,

(*d*) Ensure that international co-operation between the appropriate agencies be conducted in an expeditious manner; and

(*e*) Ensure that, where legal papers are transmitted internationally for the purpose of judicial proceedings, the transmittal be effected in an expeditious manner to the bodies designated by the Parties; this requirement shall be without prejudice to the right of a Party to require that legal papers be sent to it through the diplomatic channel.

## *Article 22*
## PENAL PROVISIONS

1. (*a*) Subject to its constitutional limitations, each Party shall treat as a punishable offence, when committed intentionally, any action contrary to a law or regulation adopted in pursuance of its obligations under this Convention, and shall ensure that serious offences shall be liable to adequate punishment, particularly by imprisonment or other penalty of deprivation of liberty.

(*b*) Notwithstanding the preceding sub-paragraph, when abusers of psychotropic substances have committed such offences, the Parties may provide either as an alternative to conviction or punishment or in additon to punishment that such abusers undergo measures of treatment, education, after-care, rehabilitation and social reintegration in conformity with paragraph 1 of article 20.

2. Subject to the constitutional limitations of a Party, its legal system and domestic law,

    (*a*) (i) If a series of related actions constituting offences under paragraph 1 has been committed in different countries, each of them shall be treated as a distinct offence;

      (ii) Intentional participation in, conspiracy to commit and attempts to commit, any of such offences, and preparatory acts and financial operations in connexion with the offences referred to in this article, shall be punishable offences as provided in paragraph 1;

     (iii) Foreign convictions for such offences shall be taken into account for the purpose of establishing recidivism; and

    (iv) Serious offences heretofore referred to committed either by nationals or by foreigners shall be prosecuted by the Party in whose territory the offence was committed, or by the Party in whose territory the offender is found if extradition is not acceptable in conformity with the law of the Party to which application is made, and if such offender has not already been prosecuted and judgement given.

(*b*) It is desirable that the offences referred to in paragraph 1 and paragraph 2(*a*)(ii) be included as extradition crimes in any extradition treaty which has been or may hereafter be concluded between any of the Parties, and, as between any of the Parties which do not make extradition conditional on the existence of a treaty or on reciprocity, be recognized as extradition crimes; provided that extradition shall be granted in conformity with the law of the Party to which application is made, and that the Party shall have the right to refuse to effect the arrest or grant the extradition in cases where the competent authorities consider that the offence is not sufficiently serious.

3. Any psychotropic substance or other substance, as well as any equipment, used in or intended for the commission of any of the offences referred to in paragraphs 1 and 2 shall be liable to seizure and confiscation.

4. The provisions of this article shall be subject to the provisions of the domestic law of the Party concerned on questions of jurisdiction.

5. Nothing contained in this article shall affect the principle that the offences to which it refers shall be defined, prosecuted and punished in conformity with the domestic law of a Party.

## Article 23
### APPLICATION OF STRICTER CONTROL MEASURES THAN THOSE REQUIRED BY THIS CONVENTION

A Party may adopt more strict or severe measures of control than those provided by this convention if, in its opinion, such measures are desirable or necessary for the protection of the public health and welfare.

### LISTS OF SUBSTANCES IN THE SCHEDULES

(The names printed in capitals in the left hand column are the International Non-Proprietary Names (INN). With one exception ((+)-LYSERGIDE), other non-proprietary or trivial names are given only where no INN has yet been proposed.)

*List of Substances in Schedule I*

| | INN | Other non-proprietary or trivial names | Chemical Name |
|---|---|---|---|
| 1. | | DET | $N,N$-diethyltryptamine |
| 2. | | DMPH | 3-(1,2-dimethylheptyl)-1-hydroxy-7,8,9,10-tetrahydro-6,6,9-trimethyl-6$H$-dibenzo [$b,d$]pyran |
| 3. | | DMT | $N,N$-dimethyltryptamine |
| 4. | (+)-LYSERGIDE | LSD, LSD-25 | (+)$N,N$-diethyllysergamide (*d*-lysergic acid diethylamide) |
| 5. | | mescaline | 3,4,5-trimethoxyphenethylamine |
| 6. | | parahexyl | 3-hexyl-1-hydroxy-7,8,9,10-tetrahydro-6,6,9-trimethyl-6$H$-dibenzo[$b,d$]pyran |
| 7. | | psilocine, psilotsin | 3-(2-dimethylaminoethyl)-4-hydroxyindole |

|  | INN | *Other non-proprietary or trivial names* | *Chemical Name* |
|---|---|---|---|
| 8. | PSILOCYBINE | | 3-(2-dimethylaminoethyl) indol-4-yl dihydrogen phosphate |
| 9. | | STP, DOM | 2-amino-1-(2,5-dimethoxy-4-methyl)phenylpropane |
| 10. | | tetrahydrocannabinols, all isomers | 1-hydroxy-3-pentyl-6a,7,10 10a-tetrahydro-6,6,9 trimethyl-6-*H*-dibenzo [*b,d*]pyran |

The salts of the substances listed in this Schedule whenever the existence of such salts is possible.[2]

## List of Substances in Schedule II

|  | INN | *Other non-proprietary or trivial names* | *Chemical Name* |
|---|---|---|---|
| 1. | AMPHETAMINE | | $(\pm)$-2-amino-l-phenylpropane |
| 2. | DEXAMPHETAMINE | | $(+)$-2-amino-l-phenylpropane |
| 3. | METHAMPHETAMINE | | $(+)$-2-methylamino-l-phenyl-propane |
| 4. | METHYLPHENIDATE | | 2-phenyl-2-(2-piperidyl)acetic acid, methyl ester |
| 5. | PHENCYCLIDINE | | 1-(1-phenylcyclohexyl)piperi-dine |
| 6. | PHENMETRAZINE | | 3-methyl-2-phenylmorpholine |

The salts of the substances listed in this Schedule whenever the existence of such salts is possible[7]

## List of Substances in Schedule III

|  | INN | *Other non-proprietary or trivial names* | *Chemical Name* |
|---|---|---|---|
| 1. | AMOBARBITAL | | 5-ethyl-5-(3-methylbutyl) barbituric acid |
| 2. | CYCLOBARBITAL | | 5-(1-cyclohexen-1-yl)-5-ethylbarbituric acid |
| 3. | GLUTETHIMIDE | | 2-ethyl-2-phenylglutarimide |
| 4. | PENTOBARBITAL | | 5-ethyl-5-(1-methylbutyl) barbituric acid |
| 5. | SECOBARBITAL | | 5-allyl-5-(1-methylbutyl) barbituric acid |

The salts of the substances listed in this Schedule whenever the existence of such salts is possible.[2]

**2**  Added by the Commission on Narcotic Drugs, 25 February 1977

*List of Substances in Schedule IV*

| INN | Other non-proprietary or trivial names | Chemical Name |
|---|---|---|
| 1. AMFEPRAMONE | | 2-(diethylamino)propiophenone |
| 2. BARBITAL | | 5,5-diethylbarbituric acid |
| 3. | ethchlorvynol | ethyl-2-chlorovinylethinyl-carbinol |
| 4. ETHINAMATE | | 1-ethynylcyclohexanol-carbamate |
| 5. MEPROBAMATE | | 2-methyl-2-propyl-1,3-propanediol dicarbamate |
| 6. METHAQUALONE | | 2-methyl-3-*o*-tolyl-4(3*H*)-quinazolinone |
| 7. METHYL-PHENOBARBITAL | | 5-ethyl-1-methyl-5-phenyl-barbituric acid |
| 8. METHYPRYLON | | 3,3-diethyl-5-methyl-2,4-piperidine-dione |
| 9. PHENOBARBITAL | | 5-ethyl-5-phenylbarbituric acid |
| 10. PIPRADROL | | 1,1-diphenyl-1-(2-piperidyl)-methanol |
| 11. | SPA | (-)-1-dimethylamino-1,2-diphenylethane |

The salts of the substances listed in this Schedule whenever the existence of such salts is possible.[2]

# Naples Convention on Providing Material Assistance to Customs Authorities 1967

## (MADE BETWEEN MEMBER STATES OF THE EUROPEAN ECONOMIC COMMUNITY, 7 SEPTEMBER 1967)

*Article 1*

1. The Contracting States shall, through their customs authorities and in accordance with the conditions set out below, assist each other in ensuring accuracy in the collection of customs duties and other import and export charges and in preventing, investigating and prosecuting contravention of customs laws.

2. If, however, the responsibility for implementing certain provisions of this Convention in a Contracting State rests with an authority other than the customs authority, that authority shall be deemed to be a customs authority for the purposes of this Convention. The Contracting States shall supply each other with all relevant information on this subject.

*Article 2*

For the purposes of this Convention, "customs laws" means provisions laid down by law or regulation concerning the importation, exportation and transit of goods, whether relating to customs duties or any other charges, or to measures of prohibition, restriction or control. The expression "customs duties" applies also to levies introduced in implementation of the Treaty establishing the European Economic Community.

*Article 3*

The customs authorities of the Contracting States shall endeavour to co-ordinate the functions and the working hours of customs offices situated at their common frontiers.

*Article 4*

1. The customs authorities of the Contracting States shall, on request, supply to each other all information which may help to ensure accuracy in the collection of customs duties and other import and export charges and, in particular, information which may help to assess the value of goods for customs purposes and to establish their tariff classification.

2. If the authority so requested does not have the information asked for, it shall initiate inquiries in accordance with the provisions which by law or regulation apply in its country to the collection of customs duties and other import and export charges.

*Article 5*

The customs authorities of the Contracting States shall exchange lists of goods which are known to be the subject of contravention of customs laws on importation, exportation or in transit.

*Article 6*
The customs authorities of each Contracting State shall, on their own initiative or on request, do everything possible to keep a special watch in the area for which they have responsibility over:

    (*a*)    the movements and, in particular, the entry into and exit from their area, of persons suspected of being professional or habitual contraveners of the customs laws of another Contracting State;

    (*b*)    places where abnormal stocks of goods have been assembled, suggesting that they are only intended as supplied for trafficking in contravention of the customs laws of another Contracting State;

    (*c*)    movements of goods notified by another Contracting State as constituting substantial imports into that State in Contravention of its customs laws;

    (*d*)    vehicles, vessels and aircraft suspected of being used in contravening the customs laws of another Contracting State.

*Article 7*
The customs authorities of the Contracting State shall supply to each other, on request, any certificate showing that goods exported from one Contracting State to another have been properly imported into the territory of that State and indicating the nature of the customs control, if any, under which the goods have been placed.

*Article 8*
The customs authorities of each Contracting State shall, on their own initiative or on request, supply to the customs authorities of another Contracting State reports, records of evidence or certified copies of documents giving all available information on transactions, detected or planned, which constitute or appear to constitute a contravention of the customs laws of that State.

*Article 9*
The customs authorities of each Contracting State shall supply to the customs authorities of the other Contracting States all information likely to be of use to them relating to contravention of the customs laws and, in particular, regarding new ways and means employed in committing such contravention and shall supply the other authorities with copies of, or extracts from, reports prepared by their investigation services describing the methods used.

*Article 10*
The customs authorities of the Contracting States shall arrange for their investigation services to be in direct communication with each other so that, through exchange of information, the prevention, investigation and prosecution of contraventions of the customs laws of their respective countries may be facilitated.

*Article 11*
The duly authorised customs officials of a Contracting State may, with the agreement of the customs authorities of another Contracting State and for the purposes of this Convention, obtain from the offices of those authorities any information derived from accounts, registers and other documents kept in those offices for the implementation of customs laws. Those officials shall be permitted to take copies of such accounts, registers and other documents.

*Article 12*
If the courts or the authorities of a Contracting State so request in connection with contraventions of customs laws brought before them, the customs authorities of the other Contracting States may authorise their officials to appear as witnesses or experts before those courts or authorities. Such officials shall, within the limits of their authorisation, give evidence regarding facts established by them in the course of their duties. The request for appearance must clearly indicate in what case and in what capacity the official is to be examined.

*Article 13*
1. If the customs authorities of a Contracting State so request, the customs authorities of the State to whom the request is made shall initiate all official inquiries and in particular the examination of persons sought for contravention of customs laws, and of witnesses or experts. They shall communicate the results of such inquiries to the authorities making the request.
2. These inquiries shall be conducted under the laws and regulations of the State which has been requested to make them.

*Article 14*
Customs officials of a contracting State, authorised to investigate contraventions of customs laws may, with the agreement of the authorised officials of the customs authorities of another Contracting State, be present in the territory of that State when those officials are investigating contraventions which are of concern to the authorities first mentioned.

*Article 15*
The customs authorities of contracting States may, in their records of evidence, reports and testimonies and in proceedings and charges brought before the Courts, use as evidence information obtained and documents consulted in accordance with the provisions of this Convention. The weight to be attached to such information and documents as evidence and the use made thereof in the Courts shall be determined in accordance with national laws.

*Article 16*
When in the circumstances provided for by this Convention customs officials of a Contracting State are present in the territory of another Contracting State, they must at all times be able to furnish proof of their official capacity. They shall, while there, enjoy the protection accorded to customs officials of that other State in accordance with national laws and regulations. They shall be treated in the same way as those officials as regards penal sanctions for offences committed against them or by them.

*Article 17*
The customs authorities of a Contracting State shall, at the request of the customs authorities of another Contracting State, in accordance with the rules in force in the former State notify the parties concerned either direct or through the competent authorities, of all measures and decisions taken by its administrative authorities relating to the application of customs laws.

*Article 18*
The Contracting States shall renounce all claims upon each other for the reimbursement of expenses incurred pursuant to this Convention, except for fees paid to experts.

*Article 19*
1.   The customs authorities of the Contracting States shall not be bound to grant the assistance provided for under this Convention where such assistance is liable to be prejudicial to public policy or to other essential interests of the State whose assistance is requested.
2.   Reasons must be given for any refusal to provide assistance.

*Article 20*
1.   Information, communications and documents obtained shall be used solely for the purposes of this convention. They shall not be communicated to persons other than those required to use them for such purposes unless the authorities supplying them expressly agree and the law governing the authorities which receive them allows such communication.
2.   Requests, information, reports of experts and other communications in the possession of the customs authorities of a Contracting State pursuant to this Convention shall be accorded the same protection as is afforded under the national law of that State to documents and information of like nature.

*Article 21*
The customs authorities of a state may not request assistance of a kind which they are not themselves able to give.

*Article 22*
The assistance provided for under this Convention shall be exchanged directly between the customs authorities of the Contracting States. These authorities shall mutually agree the detailed arrangements for implementation.

*Article 23*
1.   More extensive assistance which certain Contracting States grant or may grant each other under agreements or arrangements shall not be precluded by this Convention.
2.   This convention shall apply only to the European territories of the Contracting States.

*Article 24*
1.   This convention shall be ratified or approved and the instruments of ratification or approval shall be deposited with the Ministry for Foreign Affairs of the Italian Republic which shall advise all Signatory States of the deposit thereof.
2.   For Contracting States which have deposited the instruments of ratification or approval, this Convention shall enter into force on the first day of the third month following the deposit of the second instrument of ratification or approval.
3.   For any State which subsequently ratifies or approves this Convention, it shall enter into force on the first day of the third month following the deposit of its instrument of ratification or approval.

*Article 25*
1. This Convention is concluded for an unlimited period.
2. A Contracting State may denounce this Convention at any time after three years from its entry into force for that State by notifying the Ministry for Foreign Affairs of the Italian Republic which shall notify such denunciation to the other Conging States.
3. Any denunciation shall take effect six months from the day on which its notification is received by the Ministry for Foreign Affairs of the Italian Republic.

**Additional Protocol**

At the time of signature of the Convention between Belgium, the Federal Republic of Germany, France, Italy, Luxembourg and the Netherlands on mutual assistance between their customs authorities, the undersigned Plenipotentiaries have agreed the following declaration which forms an integral part of this Convention.
1. This convention shall not place customs authorities under an obligation to supply information obtained from banks or institutions assimilated thereto.
2. The customs authorities of a Contracting State may refuse to supply information which, in the opinion of that State, would involve violation of an industrial, commercial or professional secret. Reasons must be given for any refusal to provide assistance; if the State seeking information so desires, such refusal shall be orally discussed between the authorities concerned.

# Directory of Services

## 1. SELF HELP GROUPS, ADVISORY SERVICES ETC.—LONDON

This section comprises self-help groups, advisory services, street agencies, day projects and emergency accommodation.

*Narcotics Anonymous*—Help group for drug dependents
  NA Office London, P.O. Box 246, London SW10
  01-351 6794/351 6066

*Families Anonymous*—Help group for families of drug dependents
  88 Caledonian Road, London, N1 9DN
  01-278 8805

*Tranx* (Tranquilliser Recovery and New Existence)
  2 St. John's Road, Harrow, Middlesex. *Telephone*: 01-427 2065
  17 Peel Road, Wealdstone, Harrow, Middx. *Telephone*: 01-427 2065

*Drug Line*—Help group for families of drug dependents
  *Contact*: Margaret McLellan after 6.30 p.m. on 01-291 2341

*The Fulham Connection*—Help group for families of drug dependents
  Bishop Creighton House, 378 Lillie Road, London SW6
  01-736 2007 or 01-381 3124

*Dawn London* (Drugs, alcohol, women, nationally)
  146 Queen Victoria Street, London EC4
  01-236 8125

*Blenheim Project*—Help group for drug dependents
  7 Thorpe Close, London W10 5XL
  01-960 5599

*Hungerford Drug Project*—Help group for those with drug and drug-related problems
  1st Floor, 26 Craven Street, London WC2
  01-930 4688

*Community Drug Project*—Help group for those with drug and drug-related problems
  30 Manor Place, London SE17 3BB
  01-703 0559

*Cadett*—Help and advice group
  22 Lansdown Road, London W11
  01-727 9447

*Release*—National help and advice group
  1 Elgin Avenue, London W9 3PR
  01-289 1123; Emergency service: 01-603 8654

*Parole Release Scheme*—Referral agency for prisoners with drug problems
  30 Sisters Avenue, London SW11
  01-223 2494

*Addiction Telephone Link and Advisory Service (ATLAS)*
  60 Cheyne Path, off Copley Close, Hanwell, London W7
  01-575 0008

*Substance Abuse Unit*—Help group for drug or solvent abusers
  Crossways, Whitehall Road, Uxbridge, Middlesex
  Uxbridge (0895) 57285

*Drug Dependence Unit Community Programme (DDUCP)*
  Clare House, St. George's, Hospital, Blackshaw Road, London SW17
  01-767 8711

## 2. DRUG DEPENDENCY UNITS ETC.—LONDON

This section contains details of drug dependency units and clinics and other hospitals which provide a service for drug users.

*Great Chapel Street Medical Centre*—Walk-in centre for homeless people
  13 Great Chapel Street, London W1 7AL
  01-437 9360

*St. Clement's Hospital DDC (London Hospital)*—Out-patient facilities
  Bow Road, London E3
  01-980 4899 (Dr. John Cookson)

*Charing Cross Hospital DDC*—Out-patient treatment·
  Fulham Palace Road, London W6
  01-385 8834 (Dr. Ashley Robin)

*St. George's Hospital DDC*—In and out-patient treatment
  Blackshaw Road, London SW17
  01-672 1255 Ext. 4098/99 (Dr. Hamid Ghodse)

*St. Giles' Hospital DDC*—In and out-patient facilities
  St. Giles' Road, London SE5
  01-703 0898 (Dr. Judith Morgan)

*St. Mary's Hospital DDC*—Out-patient facilities
  2 Woodfield Road, London W9
  01-286 7371/2 (Dr. S. Das Gupta)

*St. Thomas's Hospital DDC*—In and out-patient facilities
  Lambeth Palace Road, London, SE1.
  01-633 0720 (Dr. Thomas Bewley)   ·

MOD-AA

*Hackney Hospital DDC*—Out-patient facilities
  Homerton High Street, London E9
  01-986 6816 (Dr. J. W. Mack)

*Maudsley Hospital DDC*—Out-patient facilities only
  Denmark Hill, London SE5 8AZ
  01-703 6333 (Dr. Philip Connell)

*Bethlem Royal Hospital*—In-patient unit
  Monks Orchard Road, Beckenham, Kent
  01-777 6611 (Dr. Philip Connell)

*Queen Mary's Hospital DDC*—Out-patient facilities
  Address: Roehampton Lane, London SW15
  Telephone: 01-789 6611 Ext. 309 (Dr Pamela Aylett)

*Banstead Hospital*—G.P. referral only
  Banstead, Sutton, Surrey
  01-624 6611

*St. Luke's Woodside Hospital DDC*—Referrals to Adolescent Unit
  Woodside Avenue, Muswell Hill, London N10
  01-833 6498 (Dr. Philip Boyd)

*St. Bernard's Hospital DDC (Ealing Hospital)*—In and out-patient treatment
  Southall, Middlesex.
  01-843 0736 (Dr. D.W. Marjot)

*Tooting Bec Hospital DDU*—In-patient treatment
  Tooting Bec Road, London SW17 8BL
  01-672 3350 or 01-672 9933 (Dr. H. Ghodse and Dr. T. Bewley)

*University College Hospital DDC*—Out-patient facilities only
  122 Hampstead Road, London NW1 2LT
  01-387 9300 Ext. 452, 453, 455 (Dr. Jean Garner)

*Westminster Hospital DDC*—Out-patient facilities only
  c/o St. Stephen's Hospital, Fulham Road, London SW3
  01-352 8161 Ext 350/351 (Dr. Pamela Aylett)

*Rees House Hospital DDC*—In and out-patient facilities
  214 Morland Road, Croydon, Surrey
  01-654 8100 (Dr. Sathananthan)

*West Middlesex Hospital DDC*—In and out-patient facilities
  Isleworth, Middlesex
  01-560 2121 (Dr. Curry)


## 3. CRISIS INTERVENTION—LONDON

*City Roads (Crisis Intervention)*—Short-term residential facilities
  William Hart House, 358 City Road, London EC1 2PY
  01-837 2772/3

# 4. RESIDENTIAL REHABILITATION HOUSES—LONDON

*Roma*
65-67 Talgarth Road, London W14
01-603 8383

*Elizabeth House*
94 Redcliffe Gardens, London SW10
01-370 1279

*Alwin House*
40 Colville Terrace, London W11
01-229 0311

*Phoenix House*
1 Eliot Bank, Forest Hill, London SE23
01-699 5748/1515

*Crescent House (Richmond Fellowship)*
10 St. Stephen's Crescent, London W2
01-229 3710

*Cranstoun (Oak Lodge)*
136 West Hill, Wandsworth, London SW17
01-788 1648

*Pye Barn Trust*—Men only
16 The Chase, London SW4
01-622 4870

*Parole Release Scheme*
30 Sisters Avenue, London SW11 3SQ
01-223 2494.

*Deliverance International*—Men only
83 Aldersbrooke Road, London E12
01-989 4610.

# 5. SUPPORTIVE ACCOMMODATION—LONDON

*235 Project*
235 Balham High Road, London SW17
01-672 9464.

*Project 85*
85 Trinity Road, London SW17
01-767 7687/672 9464.

## 6. REGIONAL DIRECTORY

**South-East England**

*BUCKINGHAMSHIRE*
*Suffolk House—Uxbridge*—Residential long-term rehabilitation
   Long Bridge, Slough Road, Iver Heath, Bucks
   Uxbridge (0895) 56449/56440

*CAMBRIDGESHIRE*
*Psychiatric Day Centre—Peterborough*—G.P. referrals only. Non-residential
   Peterborough District General Hospital, Thorpe Road, Peterborough.
   Peterborough (0733) 67451

*Addenbrooke's Hospital DDU*—Residential/in-patient facilities. G.P. referrals
   Addenbrooke's Hospital, Hills Road, Cambridge
   Cambridge (0223) 355671

*ESSEX*
*Open Door Service—South Benfleet*—Counselling service for all problems
   Benfleet Methodist Church, High Road, South Benfleet, Essex.
   South Benfleet (03745) 3025/4478

*The Health Services Clinic—South Benfleet*—Advice service for users and families
   The Health Services Clinic, Essex Way, South Benfleet, Essex
   South Benfleet (03745) 2353

*Community Nursing Department—Barking, Havering and Brentwood Area Health
Authority*—Community drug advice
   Office: Warley Hospital, Community Department, Brentwood, Essex.
   Clinic: Oxlow Lane Clinic, Oxlow Lane, Dagenham, Essex.
   01-592 7748

*Still Waters—Basildon*—Christian based "extended family home".
   Nevendon Road, Nevendon, Basildon, Essex SS13 1BY
   South Benfleet (0268) 726357

*Little Bays—Harlow*
   Harlow (0379) 36395

*Ingrebourne Centre—Hornchurch*—G.P. referral only
   Ingrebourne (04024) 43531

*Runwell Hospital*—In and out-patient treatment.
   Runwell Hospital, Wickford, Essex
   Wickford (03744) 5555 Ext. 271

*HERTFORDSHIRE*
*Herts and Beds Standing Conference on Drugs Misuse*—Advice, information and
referral for drug-takers and parents.
   Room 8, Family Centre, 13 Town Square, Stevenage, Herts SG1 1BP
   Stevenage (0438) 315900

*Drugsline—Stevenage*—Support and advisory service
   Room 8, Family Centre, 13 Town Square, Stevenage, Herts SG1 1BP
   Stevenage (0438) 64067

*Bridges—Hatfield—*Advice, information and counselling for young people
9a-9b St. Albans Road East, Hatfield, Herts
Hatfield (07072) 66834 (24-hour answering service)

*Queen Elizabeth II Hospital DDC*
Howlands, Welwyn Garden City, Herts AL7 4HQ
Welwyn Garden City (07073) 28111

*KENT*
*Medway Towns Drug Advice Service*
Medway (0634) 826 700

*Kent and Canterbury Hospital—*Psychiatric out-patient clinic
Canterbury (0227) 66877

*Iden Manor—Staplehurst—*Residential. Women only.
Iden Manor, Staplehurst, Kent.
Staplehurst (0580) 891263

*Springboard Trust—Maidstone—*Residential. Men only
Maidstone (0622) 55626

*NORFOLK*
*The Yare Clinic (DDC)—Norwich—*Out-patient clinic by appointment only
The Yare Clinic DDC, Bowthorpe Road, Norwich NR2 3UD
Norwich (0603) 28377

*St. Martin's Housing Trust—Norwich—* Including detoxification unit
Norwich (0603) 21997

*NORTHAMPTONSHIRE*
*St. Crispin's Hospital—Northampton*
Northampton (0604) 52323

*SURREY*
*Godstone and District Association for the Prevention of Addiction*
Stoneways, 1 High Street, Godstone, Surrey
Godstone (0883) 84842352

*Ashtead and Leatherhead Association for the Prevention of Addiction*
Arcades, 24 Oakfield Road, Ashtead, Surrey KT22 2RG
Ashtead (03722) 73979 (24-hour answering service)

*Surrey Drugs Resource Scheme—Epsom—*Advice and training service
83 East Street, Epsom, Surrey KT17 1DN
Epsom (03727) 29425

*Surrey Drugsline—Epsom—*Telephone advice and information service
Epsom (03727) 29266.

*Brookwood Hospital—Knaphill—*In and out-patient treatment
Brookwood (04867) 4545

*Cranstoun Project—Esher—*Long-term rehabilitation. Self-catering community
5 Ember Lane, Esher, Surrey
01-398 6956

*Kaleidoscope Youth and Community Project—Kingston-upon-Thames*
  40-46 Cromwell Road, Kingston-upon Thames, Surrey
  01-549 2681/7488

*SUSSEX*
*Crawley Association for the Prevention of Addiction*
  30 Punchcopse Road, Three Bridges, Crawley, West Sussex
  Crawley (0293) 22407

*Libra—Goudhurst and Lewes*
  Goudhurst (0580) 211673; Lewes (07916) 77100

*Herbert Hone Clinic—Brighton (DDC)—*In and out-patient treatment
  Drug Dependence Clinic, 11 Buckingham Road, Brighton, Sussex BN1 8LQ
  Brighton (0273) 23395/29604

*St. Christopher's Day Hospital—Horsham*
  Hurst Road, Horsham, West Sussex
  Horsham (0403) 4367

*Abbots Leigh—Haywards Heath—*Christian-based residential community
  Haywards Heath (0444) 454441


**South-West England**

*AVON*
*Bristol Royal Infirmary—*In and out-patient facilities
  Bristol (0272) 22041

*Life for the World Trust—*Residential Christian-based community
  Oldbury House, Oldbury Court Road, Fishponds, Bristol BS16 2JH
  Bristol (0272) 655582

*BERKSHIRE*
*Youth Counselling Service—Reading—*Non-residential advice and counselling
  2–4 Sackville Street, Reading, Berks RG1 1NT
  Reading (0734) 585858.

*Operation Concern (Yeldall Manor)—Hare Hatch—*In-patients, men only
  Hare Hatch, Nr. Twyford, Reading, Berks
  Wargrave (073522) 2287 (open 24 hours)

*DEVON*
*Moorhaven Hospital—Ivybridge*
  Psychiatric Service, Bittaford, Ivybridge, South Devon PL21 0EX
  Plymouth (0752) 892411

*DORSET*
*Drugs Advisory Service—Bournemouth*
  6 Queens Park Road, Bournemouth, Dorset
  Bournemouth (0202) 21990

*St. Anne's Hospital (DDC)—Poole—*G.P. referral only. Detoxification facilities
  Bournemouth (0202) 708881

*Meta House (Formerly the Bournemouth Project)—Bournemouth—*Women only
133 Princess Road, Westbourne, Bournemouth, Dorset BH4 9HG
Bournemouth (0202) 764581

*GLOUCESTERSHIRE*
*Cheltenham General Hospital—*In and out-patient facilities
Sandford Road, Cheltenham, Gloucestershire
Cheltenham (0242) 580 344 or Gloucester (0452) 67033, Ext 235

*HAMPSHIRE*
*Crisis Centre—Andover—*Emergency accommodation and referral service
Andover (0264) 66122

*St. James's Hospital Drug Advice and Treatment Centre—Portsmouth—*In and
out-patient facilities
Locksway Road, Portsmouth, Hants PO4 8LF
Portsmouth (0705) 735211

*Royal South Hampshire Hospital DDC—Southhampton—*In and out-patient
facilities
Southampton (0703) 34288

*Alpha House—Droxford—*Long-term rehabilitation unit
Alpha House, Wickham Road, Droxford, Southampton, Hants SO3 1PD
Droxford (0489) 877478 or 877210

*Coke Hole Trust—Andover—*Christian-based, long-term rehabilitation houses
Referrals can be made to: 70 Junction Road, Andover, Hants
Andover (0264) 61045/61745

*OXFORDSHIRE*
*The Ley Clinic DDC—Oxford—*In and out-patient facilities
Oxford (0865) 778911/45651

*The Ley Community—Yarnton—*Mixed, residential long-term rehabilitation
The Ley Community, Sandy Croft, Sandy Lane, Yarnton, Oxford
Kidlington (08675) 71777

*WILTSHIRE*
*Cyrenians—Swindon—*Residential accommodation for single people
53 County Road, Swindon, Wiltshire
Swindon (0793) 23836


**North-West England**

*CHESHIRE*
*Mersey Regional DDC, West Cheshire Hospital—Chester—*In and out-patients
Chester (0244) 379333

*GREATER MANCHESTER*
*Parents Anonymous—*Support groups for families of drug abusers
7 Park Grove, Worseley, Manchester
Manchester (061) 790 6544

*Lifeline Project—Manchester*—Support and advice day centre
Joddrell Street, Manchester M3 3HE
Manchester (061) 832 6353

*Prestwich Hospital DDU—Manchester*—Residential/in-patient facilities
Prestwich, Manchester
Manchester (061) 773 2236

*LANCASHIRE*
*Winwick Hospital Addiction Unit*—In and out-patient treatment
Warrington (0925) 55211

*Inward House—Lancaster*—Mixed long-term rehabilitation
89 King Street, Lancaster.
Lancaster (0524) 69599

*MERSEYSIDE*
*Parents Against Drug Addiction (PADA)*—Information for addicts and families
Liverpool (051) 677 3849

*Merseyside Drugs Council*—Advice for drug users and their families
Liverpool (051) 709 0074

*Royal Liverpool Hospital DDU*—Men and women. Outpatient treatment.
Assessment for Moston Hospital unit
Liverpool (051) 709 0141

*Sefton General Hospital DDU—Liverpool*—Out-patient treatment
Southdown Road, Liverpool L15 2HE
Liverpool (051) 733 4020

*Arrowe Park Hospital, Birkenhead*—Out-patient detoxification unit
Arrow Park Road, Upton, Birkenhead
Liverpool (051) 678 5111

*St. Helens Hospital, St Helens*—Out-patient, detoxification, counselling
Psychiatric Dept., St. Helens Hospital, Marshalls Cross Rd, St. Helens,
Merseyside WA9 3EA
St. Helens (0744) 26633

*STAFFORDSHIRE*
*St George's Hospital Drug Clinic*—In and out-patients
Personality Disorder Unit, Milford Ward, St George's Hospital, Stafford,
ST1 3AG
Stafford (0785) 3411 Ext 243

*WEST MIDLANDS*
*Drugline Birmingham*—Telephone advice service and counselling
Dale House, New Meeting St., Birmingham 4
Birmingham (021) 632 6363

*All Saints' Hospital DDC—Birmingham*—G.P. referral only. In and out-patients,
no emergencies
Birmingham (021) 523 5151

*Coventry Drug Team*
c/o 36 St Paul's Road, Foleshill, Coventry
Coventry (0203) 662027

*Cyrenians, Coventry*—Men only
62 Grafton St., Coventry
Coventry (0203) 28099

**North-East England**

*CLEVELAND*
*South Tees Health Authority Psychological Service*—Out-patient appointments only
22 Belle Vue Grove, Grove Hill, Middlesbrough, Cleveland
Middlesbrough (0642) 837638

*LEICESTERSHIRE*
*Towers Hospital*—In-patient treatment
Towers Hospital, Humberstone, Leicester LE5 0TD
Leicester (0533) 767184

*NOTTINGHAMSHIRE*
*Mapperley Hospital DDC*—G.P. referral only. In and out-patients. Telephone advice.
Porchester Road, Nottingham NG3 6AA
Nottingham (0602) 608144

*TYNE AND WEAR*
*Alcohol and Drug Advisory Service*—24-hour answer service and advice
(Drop-in centre) 6 Stanhope Road, South Shields, South Tyneside.
South Shields (0632) 569999

*St. Nicholas Hospital Alcohol and Drug Dependency Unit*—In and out-patients
St. Nicholas Hospital, Drug and Alcohol Dependency Unit, Parkwood House,
Gosforth, Newcastle-upon-Tyne, NE3 3XT
Newcastle-upon-Tyne (0632) 850151

*Single Homeless on Tyneside*—Single men and women's accommodation (18 +)
Newcastle-upon-Tyne (0632) 327092

*YORKSHIRE (NORTH)*
*St. Mary's Hospital DDC*—G.P. referrals only. In and out-patients
Dean Road, Scarborough YO12 7SW
Scarborough (0723) 376111

*YORKSHIRE (SOUTH)*
*Drug Line*—Confidential telephone counselling. Interviews by appointment
302 Abbeydale Road, Sheffield 7
Sheffield (0742) 580 033

*Royal Hallamshire Hospital*—Out-patient treatment. G.P. referrals only
Glossop Road, Sheffield. S10 2JF
Sheffield (0742) 26484

*Northern General Hospital—Sheffield*—In and out-patients. G.P. referral only
Sheffield (0742) 382121

*Storth Oaks Phoenix*—Therapeutic (drug free) community
229 Graham Road, Ranmoor, Sheffield S10 3GS
Sheffield (0742) 308230

*YORKSHIRE (WEST)*
*The Bridge*—Advice, counselling and training courses for professionals
Equity Chambers, 40 Piccadilly, Bradford, BD1 3NN
Bradford (0274) 723863

*Waddiloves Hospital DDC—Bradford*—In and out-patients. Detoxification and counselling.
Bradford (0274) 497121

*Stanley Royal Hospital—Wakefield*—In and out-patients. G.P. referral only
Aberford Road, Wakefield, WFI 4DQ
Wakefield (0924) 75217


**Scotland**

*GLASGOW*
*Drugs Information Service*—Telephone advice service (2 pm to 9 pm Mon. to Fri.)
Glasgow (041) 332 0063

*Information and Resource Unit on Addiction*—Range of educational materials
82 West Regent St., Glasgow G2
Glasgow (041) 332 0062

*Scoda Glasgow*—Monitoring trends in problem drug use
266 Clyde St., Glasgow
Glasgow (041) 221 1175

*Families Anonymous*—Self-help group for relatives and friends
Anne Baxter Charing Cross Clinic, 8 Woodside Crescent G3
Glasgow (041) 332 5463

*St. Enoch's Centre*—Day project for users. Counselling
St Enoch's Centre, 13 South Portland St., Glasgow G5
Glasgow (041) 429 5342

*Ecoda*—Advice and counselling for users and families
Easterhouse Campaign on Drug Abuse, c/o 8–12 Arnisdale Rd., Easterhouse
Glasgow G34
Glasgow (041) 773 2255

*Drug Stopping Clinic*—Day project. Self-referral, Mon. to Fri. 1.30—5 pm
Southern General Hospital, Drug Stopping Clinic, Govan Road, Glasgow G51
Glasgow (041) 445 2466

*Denmark St. Day Project*—Information, advice and counselling
Denmark St. Health Centre, Denmark St., Possil, Glasgow G22
Glasgow (041) 336 5311 Ext 228

*Castlemilk Alcohol Advice Centre*—Alcohol and drug users
 c/o Social Work Department, 15 Dougrie Terrace, Castlemilk, Glasgow G45
 Glasgow (041) 634 0331

*Woodilee Hospital Alcohol/Drug Unit*—In and out-patients
 Glasgow (041) 776 2451

*Duke St. Hospital*—Consultant Psychiatrist: Dr Antebi
 Carswell House, 5 Oakley St., Glasgow
 Glasgow (041) 554 6267

*Gartnavel General Hospital*—Consultant Psychiatrist: Dr Macdonald
 Ward 1a, Gartnavel General Hospital, 1053 Gt. Western Rd., Glasgow.
 Glasgow (041) 334 8122

*Leverndale Hospital*—Consultant Psychiatrist: Dr Binns and others
 Leverndale Hospital, 510 Crookston Rd., Glasgow G51
 Glasgow (041) 882 6255

*EDINBURGH*
*Drugs and Narcotics Anonymous (DNA)*—Counselling, prospective day centre
 Simpson House, 52 Queen St., Edinburgh
 Edinburgh (031) 225 6028

*Leith Project*—Telephone advice and drop-in counselling for users
 36 Henderson St., Leith, Edinburgh
 Edinburgh (031) 553 5250

*Shada*—Telephone advice and drop-in centre
 c/o Muirhouse Area Social Work Department, 34 Muirhouse Crescent,
   Muirhouse, Edinburgh
 Edinburgh (031) 332 2314

*Wester Hailes Hot Line*—Telephone advice. Prospective home visits
 The Harbour, Hailsland Road, Wester Hailes, Edinburgh
 Edinburgh (031) 442 2465

*The Gateway Exchange*—Day centre. Counselling, advice, support.
 Abbey Mount, Regent Road, Edinburgh
 Edinburgh (031) 661 0982

*Royal Edinburgh Hospital*—G.P. referral or self-referral. Out-patients.
 Andrew Duncan Clinic, Morningside Terrace, Edinburgh EH10 5HF
 Edinburgh (031) 447 2011

*REST OF SCOTLAND*
*Drugs Training Project*—Research
 Department of Sociology, Stirling University, Stirling
 Stirling (0786) 73171

*Area Unit Addiction, Rehabilitation and Advice Service*—Day Centre, Group and
individual counselling, help and support
 Dalmilling Rd., Ayr
 Ayr (0292) 260122

*Crichton Royal Hospital, Dumfries*—In and out-patients
 Dumfries (0387) 55301

*Dingleton Hospital, Melrose, Roxburghshire*—In and out-patients
  Melrose (089682) 2506

*Royal Dundee Liff Hospital, Liff by Dundee*—In and out-patients
  Dundee (0382) 580441

## Northern Ireland

*Shaftesbury Square Hospital*—Alcohol and drugs, in and out-patients
  116–118 Great Victoria St., Belfast BT2 7BG
  Belfast (0232) 29808

*Northlands Centre, Londonderry*—6-week stay, drug users
  Londonderry (0504) 63011

## Wales

*North Wales Association for the Prevention of Addiciton*—Advice and support for
local drug users
  19 Lombard St., Portmadoc LL49 9AP

*South Wales Association for the Prevention of Addiction*—Therapy and counselling for relatives and families. 24-hour telephone advice
  111 Cowbridge Road East, Cardiff CF1 9AG
  Cardiff (0222) 26113

*West Glamorgan Advisory Council*
  36 Orchard St., Swansea

*University Hospital of Wales—Cardiff*—Tuesday and Friday clinics
  Cardiff (0222) 755944

*Whitchurch Hospital*—Referrals only. In and out-patients. Telephone advice.
  Addiction Treatment Unit, Whitchurch Hospital, Whitchurch, Cardiff
    CF4 7XB
  Cardiff (0222) 62191

*St. Cadoc's Hospital*—In and out-patients
  Caerleon, Gwent
  Newport (0633) 421121

*Llandrindod Wells Hospital, Powys*—Out-patients only
  Hazels Clinic, Llandrindod Wells Hospital, Powys
  Llandrindod Wells (0597) 2951

*Teen Challenge*—Men only (18 +). Drug-free. 12 beds.
  Bryn Road, Penygroes, Llanelli, Dyfed SA14 7PP
  Penygroes (0286) 842718

## 7. NATIONAL ORGANISATIONS

These organisations all offer advice and information to professionals.

*Standing Conference on Drug Abuse (SCODA)*—umbrella organisation for voluntary drugs projects
   1–4 Hatton Place, London ECIN 8ND
   01-430 2341/2

*Institute for Study of Drug Dependence (ISDD)*—information and library
   1–4 Hatton Place, London EC1N 8ND
   01-430 1991

*Addiction Research Unit*
   Institute of Psychiatry, 101 Denmark Hill, London SE5 8AF
   01-703 5411

*Teachers' Advisory Council on Alcohol and Drug Education*
   2 Mount St., Manchester M2 5NG
   Manchester (061) 834 7210

## 8.PRIVATE CLINICS AND HOSPITALS

*LONDON*
*Charter Clinic, Chelsea*—Drug and alcohol, in and out-patients. Telephone advice
   01-351 1272

*Charter Clinic, Hampstead*—As for Charter Clinic, Chelsea
   01-586 8062

*Bowden House, Harrow-on-the-Hill*—Occasional places, in and out-patients
   01-864 0221/2/3

*The Priory, Roehampton*—In and out-patients. Counselling.
   01-876 8261

*PROVINCES*
*St. Andrew's Hospital, Northampton*—In and out-patients, some day places
   Northampton (0604) 21311

*Broadreach, Plymouth*—In and out-patients. Counselling, telephone advice.

*Cheadle Royal Hospital, Cheshire*—In and out-patients. Telephone advice and counselling. Therapeutic community.
   Manchester (061) 428 9511

*The Retreat, York,*—In and out-patients. Occasional places. Telephone advice.
   York (0904) 412551

*Broadway Lodge, Weston-Super-Mare*—Occasional assisted places. In and out-patients. Therapy, telephone advice service.
   Weston-Super-Mare (0934) 812319

# The Misuse of Drugs Act 1971 (Modification) Order 1985

(DRAFT)

Made    -    -    -                                              1985

*Coming into Operation*                              1st April 1986

**1.** This Order may be cited as the Misuse of Drugs Act 1971 (Modification) Order 1985 and shall come into operation on 1st April 1986.

**2.**—(1) Schedule 2 to the Misuse of Drugs Act 1971 (which, as amended specifies the drugs which are subject to control under that Act) shall be amended in accordance with the following provisions of this Article.

(2) In paragraph 1(*a*) of Part II of that Schedule—

(*a*) the word "Dexamphetamine" shall be omitted;

(*b*) after the words "Ethylmorphine (3-ethylmorphine)" there shall be inserted the words "Glutethimide" and 'Lefetamine"; and

(*c*) after the word "Norcodeine" there shall be inserted the word "Pentazocine".

(3) In paragraph 1 of Part III of that Schedule—

(*a*) at the beginning there shall be inserted the word "Alprazolam";

(*b*) after the word "Benzphetamine" there shall be inserted the words "Bromazepam", "Camazepam" and "Chlordiazepoxide";

(*c*) after the word "Chlorphentermine" there shall be inserted the words "Clobazam", "Clonazepam", "Clorazepic acid", "Clotiazepam", "Cloxazolam" and "Delorazepam";

(*d*) after the word "Dextropropoxyphene" there shall be inserted the word "Diazepam";

(*e*) after the word "Diethylpropion" there shall be inserted the words "Estazolam", "Ethchlorvynol", "Ethinamate", "Ethyl loflazepate", "Fludiazepam", "Flunitrazepam", "Flurazepam", "Halazepam", "Haloxazolam", "Ketazolam", "Loprazolam", "Lorazepam", "Lormetazepam", "Mazindol" and "Medazepam";

(*f*) after the word "Mephentermine" there shall be inserted the words "Meprobamate", "Methyprylone", "Nimetazepam", "Nitrazepam", "Nordazepam", "Oxazepam" and "Oxazolam";

(*g*) after the word "Phendimetrazine" there shall be inserted the words "Phentermine" and "Pinazepam"; and

(*h*) after the word "Pipradrol" there shall be inserted the words "Prazepam", "Temazepam", "Tetrazepam" and "Triazolam".

# Index

401

Pergamon
8 5 2 6 3 - 6 6 9 4
2 6 - 6 - 8 6